With Literacy and Justice for All

Rethinking the Social in Language and Education

Third Edition

Language, Culture, and Teaching
Sonia Nieto, Series Editor

Collins	*Community Writing: Researching Social Issues Through Composition*
Nieto	*Language, Culture, and Teaching: Critical Perspectives for a New Century*
Goldstein	*Teaching and Learning in a Multicultural School: Choices, Risks, and Dilemmas*
Vasquez	*Negotiating Critical Literacies With Young Children*
Berlin	*Contextualizing College ESL Classroom Praxis: A Participatory Approach to Effective Instruction*
Harmon/Wilson	*Beyond Grammar: Language, Power, and the Classroom*
Edelsky	*With Literacy and Justice for All: Rethinking the Social in Language and Education, Third Edition*

With Literacy and Justice for All

*Rethinking the Social in Language
and Education*

Third Edition

Carole Edelsky
Arizona State University

LAWRENCE ERLBAUM ASSOCIATES, PUBLISHERS
2006   Mahwah, New Jersey   London

Lawrence Erlbaum Associates, Inc., Publishers
10 Industrial Avenue
Mahwah, New Jersey 07430
www.erlbaum.com

Cover design by Tomai Maridou

CIP information for this volume may be obtained by contacting the Library of Congress

ISBN 0-8058-5507-6 (cloth : alk. paper)
ISBN 0-8058-5508-4 (pbk. : alk. paper)

Edelsky, Carole.
    With Literacy and Justice for All: Rethinking the Social in Language and Education, Third Edition.

Books published by Lawrence Erlbaum Associates are printed on acid-free paper, and their bindings are chosen for strength and durability.

Printed in the United States of America
10 9 8 7 6 5 4 3 2 1

For Noah, Eli, Sophie, and Alex

Contents

Preface   ix

Acknowledgments   xiii

Introduction   1

1   Not Acquiring Spanish as a Second Language:
The Politics of Second Language Acquisition   18

2   Writing in a Bilingual Program: It All Depends   41

3   Contextual Complexities: Written Language
Policies for Bilingual Programs   59

4   The Effect of "Theory" on Several Versions,
Over a Quarter Century, of a Popular Theory:
Plus Ça Change, Plus C'est la Même Chose   79

5   Literacy: Some Purposeful Distinctions   105

6   On Second Thought   134

7   Whole Language: What's New?   155

8   Hookin' 'Em in at the Start of School in a
Whole Language Classroom   179

9   Risky Literacy   196

10   Criticism and Self-Criticism   214

11   Resisting (Professional) Arrest   235

12   Sorely Tested   247

References   271

Author Index   299

Subject Index   307

Preface

The original subheading of this book was, it turns out, more apt than I thought. When I first put many of these essays into the collection called *With Literacy and Justice for All,* "rethinking the social in language and education" referred to both my motivation and also my focus. "The social" as motivation applied to my political stance and project, explicitly acknowledged in the volume, which was to do what I could to help promote an increase in economic and political justice. "The social" as focus of the work meant that as I examined often unexamined assumptions (including my own) underlying theories, policies, and pedagogies in language education, I tried to understand just how—in what ways, at what points, with what ramifications—the social world was implicated in second language learning, literacy learning, whole language practices, professional development of language educators, testing, and academic critiques of whole language.

More than 15 years later, that subtitle is not only still pertinent; it has taken on even greater importance. "The social" again provides my motivation. Economic, political, and social changes at global levels as well as local (e.g., programmatic goings-on in particular schools) have dramatically redefined literacy and language education for students and for teachers—dishearteningly, not in the direction of greater justice. And in this edition, "the social" has not one but two roles to play in the substantive focus of the work. First, it figures more thoroughly and, I hope, more coherently, in my evolving ideas about literacy and language education; and second, it appears as commentary on then-and-now contrasts in the contexts for bilingual education, language policy, language and literacy theory, whole language, testing, and professional development.

STRUCTURE OF THE CHAPTERS AND OF THE VOLUME

Most of the chapters in this edition of *With Literacy and Justice for All* have the same titles as they did 15 years ago. In updating, I wanted to avoid the appearance of having thought back then what I think now, so I did not want to revise by seamlessly substituting old material with new. Besides, I set myself the task—and I want readers to have the experience—of noting contrasts in views across time.[1] Of course, as the pages that follow show, the views expressed in these chapters did not merely "change" over "time." They were forcibly shifted, turned upside down, extended and elaborated, dis-embedded and re-embedded, and differently positioned—all in relation to the social, political, and economic changes discussed herein.

I have used different structural styles to present these changes in my understandings of the social nature of language and literacy education but, regardless of the stylistic method, I have tried to make the distinction clear between the original material and the current additions. (In fact, at the start of each chapter, I note how I have presented the newer and the older material in that chapter.) I chose methods for distinguishing old and new on the basis of my sense of the tightness of fit between contextual changes and the intent of the chapter. For instance, where those changes were less important to the intent, they are more likely to appear as endnotes rather than in the internal structure of the essay. Thus, in chapters 2 and 8 (each based on research in classrooms), the new material appears in footnotes and, only occasionally, in bracketed mentions in the text. A lengthy epilogue in chapter 1, based on the example of one school in Arizona, questions and updates the position originally presented on the connection between second language acquisition and the political position of the language that is supposed to be acquired. A similar device—the long epilogue—is used in chapter 11 that reports the phenomenon of grassroots professional development initiated by teachers for themselves. A prologue augmented by interludes and footnotes distinguishes newer from older writing in chapter 9 on the risks of whole language literacy. Drastically cut summaries of the older material, embedded in lengthy new commentaries, provides the frame for chapter 7 defining whole language and for chapter 3 on written language policies in bilingual education. Two-part essays (discrete summaries of the earlier essays followed by long "sequels" concerning new contradictions, criticisms, and questions) form the structure for chapters 4 and 5, critiquing two theories of language learning. Chapter 10, on criticisms of whole language, borrows from the old and embeds those borrowings in some new arguments. This Preface, chapter 6, on literacy as a case of second language learning; and chapter 12, are start-from-scratch new essays.

The first four chapters focus on the education of minority language children, highlighting areas that need re-examination especially in light of changes in larger social conditions. Together, they argue for the need to

---

[1]These contrasts include choice of terminology; for example, 15 years ago, I wrote *in-service education*, where today I would write *professional development*.

interweave larger and smaller contexts when trying to understand second language learning, writing "development," and written language policies. That is, confining the gaze to inside the classroom fails to show how larger social and political contexts seep right into the classroom, invited or not. Meanwhile, looking only at the big picture hides local particularities that may open up quite new understandings of that big picture. Viewing *then* <u>embedded</u> in *now*—seeing *now* as also a "post" accounting for a *prior,* always a Bahktinian response to a previous conversation—deepens our understandings of the thoroughly social nature of language in the education of minority language students (its theories, its practices, its policies, and its outcomes).

Chapters 5 and 6 focus on theoretical considerations regarding literacy and literacy learning. In each of these chapters, literacy is seen as consisting of socially shaped psychological and linguistic processes, the processes always occurring within and infused with a set of social relations, cultural models, and culturally based activities. Chapters 7 through 10 focus on whole language, a perspective-in-practice that relies on a particular view of literacy that is congruent with the theoretical discussions of literacy presented in the two preceding chapters. Chapter 7 seeks to clarify whole language and to foreground why, despite having been positioned as a "has been" by the corporatist "Reading Wars," it is in even greater need of clarification now. Chapter 8 describes how children are "hooked" into a whole language classroom. Chapter 9 discusses potential conflicts that may result from kinds of literacies promoted in whole language classrooms, and chapter 10 responds to progressive critiques of whole language. The remaining chapters—chapter 11 on teachers controlling their own professional development and chapter 12 on testing—are related to the theoretical discussions of literacy presented earlier in chapters 5 and 6. The teachers whose efforts are reported in chapter 11 tend to view literacy as it is discussed in chapters 5 and 6, and the critique of testing offered in chapter 12 grows out of that same view. The collection, *en toto,* emphasizes recursiveness and questioning within a deliberately political framework.

Acknowledgments

Much of the material in chapter 1, "The Non-Acquisition of Spanish as a Second Language," first appeared in two other publications: (a) "Acquiring a second language when you're not the underdog," by C. Edelsky and S. Hudelson, in R. Scarcella & S. Krashen (Eds.), *Research in second language acquisition*, Rowley, MA: Newbury House, 1980, pp. 36–42; and "Acquisition (?) of Spanish as a second language," by C. Edelsky and S. Hudelson, in F. Barkin, E. Brandt, & J. Ornstein-Galicia (Eds.), *Bilingualism and language contact*, New York: Teachers College Press, 1982, pp. 203–227.

Chapter 2, "Writing in a Bilingual Program: It All Depends," is based on a study reported in full in C. Edelsky (1986), *Writing in a bilingual program: Habia una vez*, Norwood, NJ: Ablex. Copyright © by Greenwood Publishing Group. Portions reproduced with permission of Greenwood Publishing Group, Inc. Westport, CT.

The original version of chapter 3, "Contextual Complexities: Written Language Policies for Bilingual Programs," first appeared as an Occasional Paper (No. 10), by C. Edelsky and S. Hudelson, distributed by the Center for the Study of Writing, University of California, Berkeley, June 1989. Later, it appeared on pp. 75–92 in *ESL in America: Myths and Possibilities*, edited by S. Benesch, published by Boynton/Cook-Heinemann in 1991 (Portsmouth, NH).

Sections of chapter 4, "The Effect of 'Theory' on Several Versions of a Popular THEORY," were first published elsewhere. Some sections appeared in 1983 in "Semilingualism and language deficit" (with S. Hudelson, B. Flores, F. Barkin, B. Altwerger, and K. Jilbert) in *Applied Linguistics, 4*, 1–22 (portions reprinted by permission of Oxford University Press); others in "The Effect of 'Theory' on THEORY—And other phenomena," *Southwest Journal of Linguistics, 7*, 74–86, in 1984. Portions reprinted with permission *Southwest Journal of Linguistics*.

An earlier version of chapter 7, "Whole Language: What's New?," appeared under the same title, by B. Altwerger, C. Edelsky, and B. Flores in *Reading Teacher, 41*, 144–154, 1987. Copyright © 1987 by the International Reading Association. Many of the ideas in the present chapter are discussed at greater length in C. Edelsky, B. Altwerger, and B. Flores (1991), *Whole language: What's the difference?*, Portsmouth, NH: Heinemann. Portions reprinted by permission from *Whole Language: What's the Difference?* Copyright © 1991 by C. Edelsky, B. Altwenger, & B. Flores. Published by Heinemann, a division of Reed Elsevier, Inc. Portsmouth, NH. All rights reserved.

Chapter 8, "Hookin' 'Em in at the Start of School in a Whole Language Classroom," originated as a slightly longer article by that title, coauthored by C. Edelsky, K. Draper, & K. Smith, in *Anthropology and Education Quarterly, 14,* 257–281, 1983. Copyright © 1983 by the American Anthropological Association.

Parts of chapter 9, "Risky Literacy," first appeared in a different form under the title "Risks of whole language literacy: Alienation and connection" in *Language Arts, 66,* 392–406, 1989. The earlier version was written by S. Harman and C. Edelsky. Copyright © 1989 by the National Council of Teachers of English. Portions reprinted with permission.

"Resisting (Professional) Arrest," chapter 11, was first printed in a slightly different form in *Language Arts, 65,* 396–402, 1988. Copyright © 1989 by the National Council of Teachers of English. Portions Reprinted with permission.

One section in chapter 12, "Sorely Tested," appeared in *English Education, 20,* 157–171 as Edelsky, C., & Harman, S. (1988), "One more critique of testing—with two differences." Copyright © 1988 by the National Council of Teachers of English. Portions reprinted with permission.

Introduction

Many of us in language education in the 1970s and 1980s did not notice that the ground was moving beneath our feet. We had our eyes on an up-close horizon as we took great strides in understanding how children learned written language, how teachers might teach literacy in workshop settings, and how multiple languages in the classroom can aid rather than hamper academic development. Only a few of us felt the rumblings along such fault lines as reading and bilingual education and sensed their wider import. Even in the 1990s when a conservative earthquake upended language education in California, many language educators elsewhere barely noticed. If they did, they saw the upheaval as confined to whole language or bilingual education and as leaving the larger contexts essentially unchanged. By now, tectonic shifts in those larger social, political, and economic contexts are hard to ignore. Contrasts between the grounds of the first edition of *With Literacy and Justice for All* and the current situation are dramatic.

HERE COME THE FEDS

A very obvious contrast—even to the casual observer—is the expanded role of the federal government in education. This role is a theme that appears in many of the chapters in this edition. In just these past few years, education—curriculum, instruction, assessment, teacher education, teacher certification, and professional development— went from being primarily—and often proudly—proclaimed as under "local control" to being heavily constrained, directly and indirectly, by federal legislation. As recently as 1995, Republicans had appealed to local control (education is a "quintessentially state and local responsibility"; Will, 2005) in urging the abolishment of the federal Department of Education. Ten years later, federal spending on education is higher than it has ever been, and federal legislation, culminating in the law known as *No Child Left Behind* (NCLB), has extended the federal reach into education to new lengths. High-stakes tests and their sequelae, demanded by the new federal legislation, are probably the most obvious sign of this onslaught—akin to "a plague of locusts that leaves in its wake

1

nervous kids, badgered teachers and a black hole where classroom innovation once existed" (Fox, 1999). It is not only innovation that has been obliterated by specifics of federal mandates; gains in cultural sensitivity have also been rolled back. Federally approved "research-based" reading programs have undone hard-won progress toward gender and ethnic equity in favor of phonics patterns. For example, in *Language Readers,* a phonics program, Greene and Woods (2000) offer a lesson in decoding /ae/ as pronounced in *back* and show a nurse patting a boy patient. But *nurse* does not provide practice with /ae/, so the text offers the retrogressive term *gal* instead (*The gal has a pad*). In another lesson, the text shows a tan-faced man in a sombrero fanning his friend and later sleeping under a tree in the stereotypical posture of Mexicans taking siestas under sombreros (*The pal has a tan hat. The hat can fan Al.... Al can nap. The pal can nap.*)

Contrary to its claims, it is not the crisis identified (more accurately, manufactured; Berliner & Biddle, 1995) by the federal government that is what is behind the increased federal presence in education. Not that there is no crisis for some communities. But the chronic underfunding of schools; inequitable funding formulae; the "savage inequalities" (Kozol, 1991) of school buildings, equipment, and teacher experience and credentialing; and curricular inequalities related to students' language and ethnicity are not what the federal government has tackled. Instead, it has focused on curricular standards and test scores in order, it claims, to eliminate a Black/White and poor/middle-class test score gap. But based on the findings of a RAND Corporation study conducted for the Spencer Foundation, lack of standards and accountability does not seem to be the source of the achievement test score gap. Instead, as the RAND study shows, that gap seems to be related to income and a sense of possibility; the gap has shrunk in times of improvements in social and economic conditions for students and their parents—rising income, occupational status, and racial diversity—and it has grown when income and occupational status drop and racial isolation increases (Berends, Lucas, Sullivan, & Briggs, 2005). In other words, if federal policy were actually intent upon shrinking the test score gap, it would provide social and economic benefits that give people material security and that encourage agency and hope.

With NCLB as the focus of news articles, television programs, and editorials, the near-takeover of K–12 education by the federal government is relatively well known. Less familiar is the fact that teacher education too is falling increasingly under federal control, often under the guise of boosting teacher quality. When only one out of every three English language learners in California is taught by a fully certified teacher with expertise in teaching students with limited English proficiency, and when another one of three English language learners is taught by a teacher who has not completed any teacher education program (Mora, 2001), improving teacher quality certainly seems warranted. But under NCLB, such improvement is not achieved through more professional education; it materializes through a test score. Anyone who teaches subject matter without having majored in that subject must pass a subject matter test. It is the test score of a veteran middle school math teacher with K–8 certification instead of high school subject matter certification and holding a master's degree that trumps that teacher's teaching experience and her advanced licensure (Keller, 2005). Further, an increasing number of state departments of education are usurping academic freedom to control course content and bibliographies in reading methods courses at universities; syllabi in those states must now fit federal (strongly ideological) definitions of "research-based" and "scientifically based" in order for the courses to count toward teacher certification (Altwerger, 2005b).

GALLOPING NEO-LIBERALISM

Although the sales pitch for NCLB (and previous federal literacy legislation, such as the Reading Excellence Act) pointed to a test score gap to justify the federal invasion of education, that discrepancy was never really the issue.[1] Instead, the issue was and continues to be the role education must play in the larger political economy. Here too, at the global level of the world economy and seeping into the most mundane local exchanges, the changes in recent years have been dramatic—not because they reflect an abrupt break with the past but because they represent accelerations and intensifications of what has been underway for decades.

These changes reflect the global circumstances in which education is embedded. These circumstances—known as *neo-liberalism*[2]—make the market an end in itself (an ethic to be used as a guide for all human activity),

---

[1]Invading Iraq to rid it of weapons of mass destruction bears some similarity to invading education to rid it of a test score gap. Of course there are obvious and horrific differences: death, social chaos, physical destruction, and an excuse that was false in one case and true in another, that is, weapons of mass destruction in Iraq did not exist; the test score gap does. The similarity is that in each case, the invasion was actually for some purpose other than how it was "sold." In the case of Iraq, analyses of the real goal(s) vary from controlling oil supplies to establishing imperial status for the United States. In the case of education, the real purpose of the invasion was to benefit corporations (profits, privatizing, producing certain kinds of workers, and spreading market ideology throughout societal domains).

[2]Neo-liberalism is not the polar opposite of neo-conservatism. In fact, current neo-conservatives are the main supporters of the philosophy of neo-liberalism. Despite the similarity in nomenclature, neo-liberalism and the political liberalism of today are not the same. Neo-liberals/neo-conservatives seek liberty for the market. While today's politicians who are designated as liberals are also in support of unregulated markets (note the bilateral support for the North American Free trade Agreement, for instance), ordinary people who call themselves liberals are not likely to approve of deregulation or to want the market to be a metaphor for all of social life and are more likely to be concerned about civil liberties and the liberalization ("humanization") of social programs.

value competition for its own sake, and extend the market and a market ideology to all of social life. (Along with the federal role in education, neo-liberalism is also a thematic undercurrent in many chapters in this volume.) Neo-liberalism aims for an increase in the number, frequency, and rate of transactions so that ultimately every action becomes a market transaction with every human being in competition with every other (Treanor, 2004). It is "capitalism with the gloves off" (McLaren & Farahmandpur, 2002, p. 37)—a world with "everything for sale; with no one and no activity exempt from the pressure of competition, the risk of obsolescence, the specter of ruin" (Scialabba, 2005, p. 37). Its key features are corporate domination of society; infinite concessions to transnational corporations; the use of state force to protect the market; intensified surveillance; cheapened labor (a race to the bottom); commodification and privatization of every sphere of economic, social, cultural, and biological life from education to the human genome (Lipman, 2005); and the control of social life through the pursuit of profits for the few (e.g., through tax cuts, rollbacks of regulations, and dismantling of public education and social welfare programs; McLaren & Farahmandpur, 2002).

On the one hand, neo-liberalism treats the market as if it were a natural phenomenon that, if left alone, maintains a perfect if delicate balance. On the other, its history links the market to Divine Will. By the middle of the 19th century, middle-class evangelicals in the United States reshaped Protestant doctrine to justify growing disparities of wealth (Bigelow, 2005). They saw the free market as a divine instrument, providing moral justification for great wealth and also for excruciating poverty. They found in the ideology of a free market a way to make the business mogul into a heroic figure whose wealth was a sign of righteousness. And, importantly, a way to define the new industrial poor as moral failures; helping them out of poverty would upset divine will and endanger their souls (Bigelow, 2005, p. 35).

Neo-liberalism—venerating the winners and disdaining the losers, supporting policies to benefit the elite few while starving programs to benefit the many—is the ground that grew (and still grows) the federal agenda on education. Because of the nature of neo-liberalism, *federal* is not the most apt descriptor of that agenda. More accurately, it is *corporatist*—a fusion of corporate interests with government authority (M. L. Smith, 2004). As stated in documents of the Business Roundtable, the Alliance for Business, and the Asia-Pacific Economic Corporation, the agenda for education is for giant corporations to profit from it directly through privatization and indirectly through control of its "end products." The Asia-Pacific Economic Corporation document is particularly revealing of neo-liberalist thought. It attacks goals that would provide education for the sake of education or for the good of the civic society and applauds only education that meets the needs of corporations (Ohanian, 2002). It is not a test score gap, then, that accounts for the massive intrusion of the federal government into education but this need to control education to maintain corporate competitiveness in the global market.

One area that must be controlled is the literacy of students—more precisely, of future workers. According to Strauss (2005b), corporate America (in an intensified neo-liberal world) has a new literacy requirement: It needs a labor force with the ability to read, without questioning, for technical information. Inducting young students into school literacy through intensive phonics instruction fits the "narrow type of reading ... that emphasizes the encoding and decoding of the language of software and hardware and various wares in between" (Strauss, 2005b, p. 39). "Reading done freely and volitionally ... for one's own interests ... is to remain the private school curricular privilege of the already privileged" (Strauss, 2005b, p. 38).

Shaping the future workforce is not the only benefit neo-liberals enjoy from taking over public education. A more immediate prize is privatizing schools. Privatizing public schools, along with other public spheres, has been a long-time goal of neo-liberals. In the past decade, there have been "experiments" with vouchers and charter schools. Federal tax legislation signed in 2001 includes tax deductions for tuition to private elementary schools and high schools—a benefit for mostly upper income families whose children already attend these schools (Kessler & Fletcher, 2001). An early version of NCLB included privatizing as the penalty for schools that fail to make adequate yearly progress for 3 successive years. (Congress stripped that requirement from the draft and substituted private tutoring services; Bracey, 2005b.) One motive for the urge to privatize is financial: An estimated $500 billion is spent on public K–12 education in the United States (R. Freeman, 2005). Another is ideological. Neo-liberalism does not want to see public services work. Effective public schools, for instance, repudiate both the faith in and the superiority of "all things private." That superiority, however, is not evident. Voucher schools have lost both money and community support. Three major reports show that charter schools perform more poorly than public schools (A. Wells, 2004) and, when certain school services are turned over to private business, the results are far from beneficial (e.g., privatized food services for the Houston Independent School District ended up costing more for poorer quality food and service; Fleck, 2001).

In the ideal neo-liberal world, every interaction is a transaction, every aspect of life provides an opportunity for profit, and everything becomes a commodity. Educators became familiar with commodification once they began to use scores on standardized tests to signal student identities (*he's a 4.6*), but it is only recently that knowledge and literacy, "once the domain of the humanistic tradition are being redefined within a production imperative" (Brandt, 2005, pp. 307–308) and increasingly linked to competition, surveillance, and regulation. Reading instruction materials—long within the private commercial domain—no longer appeal to the joys of literacy awaiting students taught with the publisher's program. Under neo-liberalism, publishers boast of "co-branding" their modules. As educator Nancy Barth (2005) wrote, reading is now being treated "like Taco Bell and Kentucky Fried Chicken—as a product to be sold."

THE PLAY'S THE THING

Under neo-liberalism, genuine participatory democracy is impossible (McLaren & Farahmandpur, 2002). Instead, conditions of political life under neo-liberalism constitute degenerative politics with policymaking a matter of political spectacle (M. L. Smith, 2004). Several chapters in this volume offer details about recent literacy and language policy as political spectacle. Although the spectacle provides an illusion of democratic participation, voters are merely the audience. What happens on stage (the plot acted out by a cast of villains and heroes) is disconnected from the action backstage. The spectacle presents an illusion of rationality, with "tangible benefits to a few but only symbolic benefits for the many" (M. L. Smith, 2004, p. 12). Federal policies in education in the past decade bear all the marks of political spectacle. And as Smith documents in great detail, policy as spectacle has "create[d] perverse consequences in schools, frustration and perplexity among the public" (p. 5).

A notable element in federal policy-as-spectacle is the extent to which it uses "science" to create the illusion of rationality. For instance, the George W. Bush Administration rejected policy for reducing carbon dioxide emissions from power plants because "the science is still incomplete," refused to reduce acceptable levels of arsenic in drinking water because it was not clear whether that was "the best available science," and walked away from the Kyoto Protocols on global warming because the "state of scientific knowledge was incomplete" (Coles, 2001, p. 3). Consonant with the character of policy as spectacle, actual science is misrepresented or ignored in favor of "junk science" (Kennedy, 2004). During the second Bush Administration, the manipulations of science became so outrageous that over 60 top U.S. scientists, including 20 Nobel laureates and several advisors to past Republican presidents, signed a letter accusing the administration of censoring science for political purposes (Borenstein, 2004).

There are a number of ways that science related to education (as well as other aspects of social life) has become "junky." Reports with the wrong findings can simply be suppressed, as was the Sandia Report on the general performance of American schools (Berliner & Biddle, 1995). Members of committees charged with reviewing research can have ties to corporations poised to profit from the committee's work, as did members of the National

Reading Panel (Garan, 2005). Congressional hearings, presumably to help shape policy, can be skewed so that no one is permitted to testify who would provide an alternative (i.e., "wrong") viewpoint, as were the hearings prior to the Reading Excellence Act (Coles, 2001). Research (e.g., Adams, 1990) and reports of research (e.g., *Report of the National Reading Panel*) can be commissioned so that they produce the answers desired by the governmental entities that commissioned them. Research (e.g., research on *Open Court* and *Language!* among other commercial phonics-focused programs; Coles, 2000, Garan, 2005) can be represented as independent (meeting scientific standards of independence from influence) when, in fact, it is conducted by researchers employed by publishers who profit from the results. In an amazing display of chutzpah, adding insult (and even more injury) to injury, Congress took it upon itself to define *scientific research*. In order to rule out as nonscientific any scholarship on literacy that would not support the corporatist agenda, Congress narrowed the definition of *scientific research* to the testing of hypotheses through experimental design (AERA Analysis, 2000). Research that does not use experimental design (e.g., anthropological, qualitative, descriptive, narrative, linguistic, discourse analytic, etc.) is now not considered scientific. This Congressional action adopts the early 19th-century positivist solution to "the demarcation problem" (to demarcate science from nonscience by limiting the former to beliefs that have so much empirical support that they are considered certain—or positive; Allington, 2002, p. 52). The Congressional definition would be laughable for its naiveté were it not so harmful. Harmful to students subjected to instruction in phonics forever (or so it seems). Harmful to teachers deprived of their right to teach in ways that fit their professional expertise. Harmful to the development of knowledge as research funding is limited not only to experimental design but also to research questions that focus on "what works." Harmful to wider understandings of the nature of science and scientific investigation.[3]

THE MEDIA: DISAPPEARING ACTS

The media figure in discussions in several chapters in this volume because they are complicit in the changing social/political/economic circumstances I have described so far. Given the recent rate of corporate media mergers, it is no wonder. Five conglomerates (Viacom, Disney, AOL TimeWarner,

---

[3]Strauss (2005b) has an excellent (though not all-inclusive) discussion of three broad categories of scientific methodologies—*experimental* for automatic events in the physical universe, *descriptive* for the observation of whole phenomena, and *introspective* for mathematical systems and linguistic structures.

NewsCorp, and NBC/GE) now control 70% of prime time television (Media Reform, 2004). Along with 5 other multinationals, these 10 "rul[e] the cosmos" (Miller, 2002, p. 18) from television, radio, movies, and newspapers to books, bookstores, music, and even Web sites (Solomon, 2002). In 1983, 50 corporations controlled U.S. media. By 2002, that number had shrunk to 6 (Solomon, 2002). Since 1975, two thirds of independent newspaper owners have disappeared (replaced by mega-corporate ownership), as have one third of independent television station owners. Local radio is being obliterated by consolidation. After the 1996 passage of the Telecommunications Act that swept away regulations about radio ownership, Clear Channel was able to buy up 1,200 stations; prior to 1996, all the major owners combined had owned fewer than 65 stations (Media Reform, 2004).

This concentration of ownership reflects the same corporate interests as the Business Roundtable. Indeed, the major media corporations are members of the Business Roundtable and other corporate organizations that are pushing their neo-liberal agenda for education and other public spheres. Theoretically, it shouldn't be like this. The media in a democracy are supposed to constitute an unofficial fourth branch of government—another avenue for checks and balances. In order to "exercise their first amendment function to hold power accountable" (Alterman, 2005, p. 11), their relation to government should be at least somewhat confrontational (Hart & Hollar, 2005). Instead, corporate monopolies—and the tight relations between corporate boardrooms and government officials—ensure that the media serve as an arm of the state (Herman, 2005). Thus, a television "news" story can actually be a prepackaged program complete with government spokespeople acting as reporters, created by a public relations firm contracted by the government and paid for with tax dollars—all made to look like news. The networks are not being hoodwinked; in fact, they help distribute this "info-ganda" to local affiliates that are then "spared the expense" of doing their own reporting (Ivins, 2005). Corporate advertisers have threatened to boycott media that hire progressive alternatives to right wing talk show hosts, and these advertisers have succeeded in getting the anti-corporate personnel fired (Hart & Hollar, 2005). The television network that is supposed to belong to all the public, the Public Broadcasting System (PBS), is aligned with corporate interests. It distributes shows with funding-related conflicts of interest that favor corporate views (e.g., a series on the global economy sponsored in part by Enron, a series on oil sponsored by a company with significant investments in the oil industry). But PBS righteously proclaimed its adherence to "fairness and objectivity" when—invoking its double standard—it refused to distribute a documentary on the World Bank that seemed to have a "bias in favor of poor people" (Fairness and Accuracy in Reporting, 2002a).

If the corporate media act as mouthpieces for government and corporate positions,[4] the government, for its part and with increasing intensity in recent years, exerts considerable control over the media, including media personnel. A White House press pass was denied to bona fide reporter Maureen Dowd of the *New York Times* while a pass was granted to pseudo reporter "Jeff Gannon" (the alias of James Guckert, someone with tax evasion problems who worked as a male sex worker on a gay Internet escort service site), in the knowledge that Gannon/Guckert would pitch only softball questions to the President (Dowd, 2005).[5] The Bush Administration aggressively prevents reporters from doing their job by "withholding routine information, deliberately releasing deceptive information on a regular basis, bribing friendly reporters to report the news in a favorable context ..., and subvert[ing] journalists' ability to report fairly on power and its abuses by attaching the label 'liberal bias' to even the most routine ... information-gathering and reportage" (Alterman, 2005, p. 11). It is not hard to imagine, then, why Reporters without Borders ranked the United States 17th on a worldwide index of press freedom, below Costa Rica and Slovenia (Ivins, 2003).

Despite the neo-liberal push to the contrary, the media are not simply "one more product—a toaster with pictures." Independent media are integral to maintaining the fundamental premise of a democracy: diversity of opinion. Not some trivial diversity of consumer taste but diversity in citizens' opinions about issues of importance to the polity (see http://www. democraticmedia.org/issues/mediaownership). The consolidated corporate media, intimately integrated into corporatist agendas, prevent such diversity—with negative effects for democracy as well as for positive cultural change. They limit what is expressed in both reporting and also in entertainment. For example, when reporting on protests (e.g., against the World Trade Organization or against the war in Iraq)—clear examples where opinions diverge from dominant positions—the corporate media report on comportment (how the police and protestors behaved) rather than on

---

[4]Acting as mouthpieces for corporatist media positions includes creating as well as reporting news. The California Department of Education's Reading Task Force Report, *Every Child a Reader,* urged schools to adopt "systematic, explicit" instruction. The Report did not mention whole language. But across the United States, the media focused their reporting not on the Report but on the corporatist position on whole language (Y. Freeman, Freeman, & Fennacy, 1997).

[5]Of course, it does not require false papers to ensure easy questions from White House reporters. Only 2 of the more than 900 questions posed to White House Press Secretary Scott McClellan in the 3 weeks following the publication in the *London Sunday Times* of the "Downing Street memo," revealing that the White House had fixed the "intelligence and facts" to justify the war in Iraq, concerned that memo (Rich, 2005).

the rationale for the protests. Music, too, is subject to censoring (notably, not of lyrics that are anti-women but that are anti-corporate). Clear Channel, for example, has cut from its playlist songs protesting the war in Iraq (Zavetsky, 2004). (No more *Where have all the flowers gone?* for *this* war!) These barriers to particular "collective aesthetic experiences" made possible only through mass media (Dressman, 2004, p. 42) clearly concern more than entertainment. As Dressman (2004) argued, previous challenges to dominant discourses about bigotry, for instance, came not so much from individual responses to various texts but from "collective conversations" instigated by televised sitcoms like "All in the Family." As the corporate voice emanating from media grows ever louder, the possibility of "controversial" broadcasting, publishing, and reporting recedes to the point of disappearing—and, along with it, the chance for collective conversations that could lead in more progressive directions.

THE NEW McCARTHYISM

Monopolistic media account for some of the narrowing of public discourse about education (and much else) in the past decade, but a new McCarthyism is also to blame.[6] The old McCarthyism was the "most widespread, longest lasting wave of political repression in American history" (Schrecker, 1998, p. x). Under the guise of protecting the United States against Communism, it "hounded an entire generation of radicals and their associates, destroying lives [and] careers" using "the power of the state to turn dissent into disloyalty and, in the process, drastically narrowed the spectrum of acceptable political debate" (Schrecker, 1998, p. x). Named after Wisconsin Sen. Joseph McCarthy, the era actually began prior to McCarthy's entrance into politics and continued after his death. What distinguishes the McCarthy era from other historical periods when fears of some "alien force" (e.g., foreigners or unions) were seen as needing to be rooted out to protect "solid American citizens" is the breadth and intensity of the McCarthy crusade. Historian Ellen Schrecker (1998) gives the credit for breadth and intensity to the federal government. It was the federal government taking on the anti-Communist crusade as its own agenda that is what led to hearings, FBI investigations, prosecutions, and court decisions that not only punished individuals but also damaged democracy throughout the country.

McCarthy was a relatively obscure senator when, on a speaking tour in 1950, he announced that he had in his possession a list (now known to be nonexistent) of 205 Communists in the State Department. The number

---

[6]Much of this section on McCarthyism appeared in Edelsky (2005).

changed to 57 the next day, then 81 ten days later. Other anti-Communist zealots had accused the Truman administration of being "soft on Communism," but no one with McCarthy's credentials had ever used specific numbers (Schrecker, 1998). It was those numbers that attracted the media and helped create the tragic circus that followed.

McCarthyism cost the United States dearly. People lost their jobs, their reputations, their opportunity for being rehired at another job, their neighbors' acceptance, sometimes their lives—for doing what was perfectly legal and constitutionally protected: associating with whomever they chose, attending rallies, writing what they believed, saying what they thought, teaching what they knew. The American political landscape lost the diversity of ideas it had gained just a few years earlier from having been enriched by refugees from Nazi Europe. The range of debate shriveled. As Schrecker (1998) notes, certain terms and topics disappeared from public discourse—for example, *class* and *class struggle, collective action, industrial capitalism* was sanitized to *industrialism,* and *political economy* became simply *the economy.*

By the early 1960s, McCarthyism had receded. McCarthy himself had died of alcoholism in 1957, having publicly discredited himself with his drunken bullying during the Army–McCarthy hearings (McCarthy's attempt to expose Communists in the Pentagon, carried live to the public by the new medium of television). The U.S. Senate censured him in 1954 for his "contemptuous behavior" (Schrecker, 1998). Fair-minded Republicans in the Eisenhower administration began to oppose the heavy-handed squelching of dissent. Some brave employers rehired a few of those who had been fired. News media began reporting an occasional opposing viewpoint. (For example, the recent movie *Good Night and Good Luck* portrayed Edward R. Morrow's efforts to expose McCarthy's tactics on Morrow's television show.) Importantly, the economy was expanding. By the early 1960s, the crusade *qua* crusade had lost its punch. Nevertheless, McCarthyism left a terrible legacy: It showed how few barriers the U.S. Constitution actually offers against using the machinery of government to demonize and then destroy a thus-demonized movement.

Reading education has the dubious distinction of being one of the first sites to experience—after almost four decades—the reappearance of McCarthyism, and California can claim "credit" for providing the first signs of its reincarnation. In the mid-1990s, new California Department of Education regulations and new California statutes prohibited spending monies on programs, consultants, or materials associated with whole language (Y. Freeman et al., 1997). This official activity was used to justify censoring syllabi, creating blacklists, banishing books, requiring oaths of loyalty, and other incursions on civil liberties. Those banned, censored, blacklisted and sworn to loyalty recognized the resemblance to McCarthyism. But it took the further development of the federal government taking phonics on as its own agenda, as well as a national tragedy, to usher in a full-scale new McCarthyism recognized by others outside of education.

To the applause of both Christian fundamentalists and corporate leaders, the federal government made phonics its official agenda. (Christian fundamentalists had long fought for phonics with its aura of tradition and literal-ness; neo-liberals correctly saw phonics as the base for a more appropriate literacy for workers expected to do no more than follow software instructions, more amenable to specific standards, and more testable than "humane" meaning-focused, interpretive, literature-based instruction.) The federal government held hearings with testimony solicited only from phonics advocates. It commissioned research from researchers with ties to commercial phonics programs. It commissioned reports from panels stacked with those steeped in phonics-friendly research. It hired a public relations firm to write and distribute a summary of the *National Reading Panel Report*. It made Reid Lyon, head of the National Institute of Child Health and Development, the agency that had funded much of the phonics-friendly research, the national expert on reading (soon to be deemed reading "czar"). It established a congressional commission to narrow the literacy of a 21st-century workforce. It passed legislation that limited "legal" literacy instruction (for schools getting federal funds) to that which had "scientific" support. In short, what was statewide in California in 1995 had become nationwide by September 10, 2001. And then came the morning of September 11.

The tragedy provided the right wing with a perfect scenario: an alien threat (terrorists) to national security, shared anguish and loss, a press only too anxious to proclaim loyalty and to abandon its obligation to investigate (Solomon, 2001), general ignorance about U.S. policies and actions in the Third World, ever-simmering American authoritarian populism now brought to a boiling point, and an agenda the Right had been pushing for decades. Within months after September 11, the Right was able to push proposals for returning billions in previously paid taxes to major corporations and to seriously erode civil liberties through the U.S.A. Patriot Act. That Act, its passage itself an erosion because it was "smuggled in" by suspending the usual procedures for congressional legislation (Schneider, 2002), allows the Secretary of State to designate any group as a "terrorist organization" (there is no appeal), grants the government new powers to spy on its citizens, and weakens Constitutional checks and balances by giving new powers of detention and surveillance to the executive branch while depriving the judicial branch of oversight to ensure those powers are not being abused.

The secrecy that had already become a hallmark of the Bush Administration intensified after September 11. Federal agencies were urged not to comply with the Freedom of Information Act (Rosen, 2002). Right-inspired harrassment and intimidation for dissenting views increased. Students attending The Ohio State University's June 2002 commencement were warned they would be arrested if they showed any "signs of dissent" when President Bush spoke (Fairness and Accuracy in Reporting, 2002b). The William Bennett-founded Americans for Victory Over Terrorism began its own smear campaign, singling out the editor of *Harpers Magazine* for daring to suggest that the meanings of the word *terrorism* might be "elastic" (Berkowitz, 2002). At a pro-war rally sponsored by a subsidiary of Clear Channel, a tractor was used to smash hundreds of CDs and tapes recorded by the Dixie Chicks after the group's lead singer criticized President Bush (Krugman, 2003). Subpoenas were served on peaceful activists who attended a conference at Drake University, and membership records were subpoenaed for the legal organization that sponsored the conference (Friends Committee on National Legislation, 2004).

As if intimidation were not enough, a non-citizen could now be deported for simply belonging to a group that dissented (guilt by association; D. Cole, 2001). On [then] Attorney General Ashcroft's orders, Arab men were rounded up and questioned. As of December 2001, over 1,200 non-citizens were being held in secret detention as material witnesses with neither their names, charges, or locations revealed and with no access to lawyers ("War, Terrorism," 2001). Those non-citizens suspected of actual connections to terrorism were to be tried, in secrecy, by military tribunals. And a new Justice Department program called *TIPS* (Terrorism Information and Presentation System) was to have been launched in fall 2002, encouraging millions of Americans to spy on their fellow Americans and to feed that information into a centralized database ("Informant Fever," 2002). Public criticism forced the administration to scale back TIPS, but the program did not disappear. By late 2002, it had morphed into something called *Total Information Awareness*, designed to allow the government easy access to oceans of data, integrated through Total Information Awareness, concerning whomever a bureaucrat wished to investigate.

Who passed such laws? No one. With the exception of the U.S.A. Patriot Act for which normal legislative procedures were suspended, none of this was leg-islated. Rather, executive orders, judicial memos, agency edicts, conservative foundations, and private individuals were the authors of this activity. As with the old McCarthyism that was the result of a "concerted campaign" (Schrecker, 1998, p. xiii), these actions too have been orchestrated within an ideological context in which national security trumps all other values and becomes the cover for all excesses. Moreover, they have occurred within a rhetorical context in which the powerful, while stifling dissent, can brazenly present themselves as under assault by "leftist thought police" (Krugman, 2002).

Bearing an obvious resemblance to McCarthyism's anti-Communist cru-sade, the antiterrorist crusade circulates now as a national discourse. It not only colors what is happening in a variety of societal domains (the press, entertainment, visual arts), but it also illuminates the nature of those "insults" suffered by education since the 1990s. Blacklists in California that prevented state funds from being used for professional development that mentioned invented spelling, cueing systems or whole language, and that blackballed consultants whose bibliographies cited Ken or Yetta Goodman, among others; the secrecy surrounding high-stakes tests; a government-imposed "victory" for phonics; and the corporate media-created "Reading Wars" should now be seen retroactively in the light of that tradition of McCarthyism. And the current government-sponsored repressive activity in education must be viewed as a continuation (though intensified) rather than a sudden break with the recent past. Instances of the new McCarthyism in education include irresponsible appeals to patriotism and militarism and accusations of disloyalty, for example, former Assistant U.S. Secretary of Education Chester Finn (2003) calling teachers unions and teacher educators terrorists ("education's version of Iraq's Republican Guards"); Laura Bush's designation of teachers as soldiers of democracy; threats by public officials (e.g., Reid Lyon's statement in a major policy forum that "if there was any piece of legislation that I could pass it would be to blow up colleges of education" [Vermont Society for the Study of Education, 2002]); and "the tight tying of the American flag to government mandated reading instruction at a rally where Secretary Rod Paige occasionally slid from talking about reading into talking about terrorism, with the implication, therefore, that opposing the Bush mandate concerning reading amounted to being an enemy of the state" (Meyer, 2004, p. 102). It includes blatant quashing of dissent: the Assistant Commissioner of Health and Human Services threatening to take legal action against any Head Start program directors or teachers who spoke against Bush's proposed School Readiness Act (Coles, 2003a); less heavy-handed but equally repressive purging of the ed.gov Web site of material that does not mesh with the Bush administration's political philosophy (Davis, 2002); and the passage of the International Studies in Higher Education Act that creates a board to monitor the perspective presented in Middle Eastern studies departments to ensure that it is more aligned with American foreign policy (Goldberg, 2003). Just as FBI investigations of suspected Communists inspired local school boards to fire teachers and prompted neighbors to ostracize neighbors, so the current antiterrorist repression emboldens individuals to act as vigilantes (e.g., a security officer who objected to high school students' artwork that criticized Bush broke into the art classroom in the middle of the night to photograph and "expose" the artwork (McCarthyism Watch, 2003). Such a climate has certainly silenced educators who fear that openly criticizing Reading First or NCLB in district meetings may "jeopardize their job security or impede their school district's ability to obtain federal funds" (Coles, 2004).

HOPE?

The intersection of neo-liberalism with McCarthyesque repression has bludgeoned education. But in these very dark times, there are glimmers of what might be hope. Parents and educators organized in the late 1990s to resist high-stakes testing, and they won some victories, but these were largely trampled by the weight of NCLB mandates. Now, however, some state legislatures and a few media columnists have begun to challenge NCLB and the testing centerpiece to the corporatist education agenda. Not that the challenges have been uncontested. For instance, in 2004, the Utah legislature was entertaining a bill to opt out of NCLB. The federal government threatened retaliation; not only would Utah not receive federal education funds but it would lose a military base (Bracey, 2005a). For the moment, Utah "ducked"—or rather, as Bracey (2005a) said, "had its arm twisted off." But in 2005, Utah is again considering legislation to ignore federal requirements if state monies must pay for them (Davis, 2005). Utah's contention is not only that NCLB is underfunded but that it encroaches on local turf. The states of Vermont, Texas, and Michigan, along with the National Education Association and other education organizations, have joined together to file suit to force the federal government to pay for the requirements NCLB imposes on states. While the focus of the suit is financial (as with Utah), other issues are at stake—in this case, curriculum. The plaintiffs say that the money is needed because they have had to cut funds for art, science, and other programs to pay for NCLB mandates (Rethinking Schools, 2005). As of April 2005, Connecticut, too, was preparing to file a federal lawsuit about NCLB requiring states to spend millions to pay for federal impositions. Along with the other states that are suing for money but that also have substantive complaints that are more difficult to address through the courts, Connecticut has other issues with NCLB, for example, the legality of NCLB, excessive testing, regulations requiring the testing of English Learners and special education students, and its overall inferiority as educational policy (Gillespie, 2005). Another legal challenge comes from Coachella Valley Unified School District in California. It is among the first to focus its legal challenge on more than funding. That small district is challenging NCLB as discriminating against English Learners (Gullingsrud, 2005). The American Civil Liberties Union defended Alfie Kohn in a suit heard in August 2005 against the Massachusetts Board of Education for violating the first amendment to the U.S. Constitution (the board forced organizers of a conference to cancel the appearance of Alfie Kohn, who would have criticized state testing policies; Wheelock, 2005).

Not all resistance involves litigation. Chicago Public Schools (the third largest school district in the United States), along with districts in

California (even high-performing districts), are refusing to outsource tutoring to private firms (one of the avenues for privatization written into NCLB). Several states are trying to change federal regulations for determining adequate yearly progress. They recognize that as the law is written it will soon result in the vast majority of U.S. schools being identified as failing; thus, they are trying to change rigid proficiency levels to growth models (Schemo, 2004a). High school districts are less than enthusiastic about Bush's plan to extend NCLB—in the form of more testing—to high schools. Their resistance stands a fair chance of success since the federal government cannot use the club of Title I funding (reserved for elementary schools) against high schools (Robelen, 2005). Some districts are beginning to turn up their noses at Reading First grants instead of complying with demands to give up existing literacy programs and adopt one commercial series (Manzo, 2005). Anna Quindlen, a former syndicated columnist, has joined other journalists with smaller audiences (e.g., Richard Rothstein) to critique the ground of NCLB: reform through testing and punishing. Using such terms as *forced march, drowning,* and *metastasis,* Quindlen (2005) argued that tests do not fix educational problems any more than weighing people cures obesity. A rally in Oakland, California, to Take Back Our Schools turned away from the walkouts of earlier years (an excuse for students to "ditch") to a teach-in about why Oakland schools should ignore particular mandates of NCLB (Katz, 2005).

The Oakland rally may be part of a more general "crisis of the globalist project." Pauline Lipman (2005) argues that the global neo-liberalism of which NCLB is a part—and which is discussed in an earlier section and referred to both explicitly and implicitly throughout this volume—is meeting with unprecedented resistance across geographic and social boundaries.[7] As the consequences of neo-liberalism have become more brutal in the daily lives of ordinary people around the world,

> a global social movement of farmers, workers, environmentalists, human rights activities, landless people, women, indigenous peoples, and intellectual and cultural workers ... is increasingly defining itself in opposition to capitalism, imperialism, and war.... [Thus] [t]here are now two globalizations—one from above and the other from below. The stakes in this contest are perhaps higher than at any time in human history. (Lipman, 2005, p. 4)

More and more people are challenging the manufactured belief that neo-liberalism and neo-liberal policies are inevitable and natural. In other words, though there is now more danger, there is also more hope. More

---

[7]Two recent examples are the activism that interfered with the World Trade Organization meeting in Seattle and the worldwide protests against invading Iraq that most likely contributed to international refusal to join the U.S. war.

possibility that the corporatist agenda for education will fail. More hope that the entire neo-liberal project can be vanquished from below.

All of these themes, then—the federal intrusion into education, intensifying neo-liberalism, policy-making as political spectacle, the shrinking of independent media, the reappearance of McCarthyesque political repression, and increasing resistance to neo-liberal policies—figure in major ways in the changing social, political, and economic conditions for language and literacy education. They are a significant part of this recent "rethinking" of "the social in language and education."

Chapter 1

Not Acquiring Spanish as a Second Language: The Politics of Second Language Acquisition

This chapter is the original with a few editorial changes. It is followed by a long postscript written in 2005.

Language is political—nothing new in that statement. Yet I must admit that when my colleague Sarah Hudelson and I began the studies I will discuss in this chapter, we both did and did not understand just how political it is.

To begin at the beginning: In studies of "naturalistic" second language acquisition (as opposed to studies of the learning of foreign languages in school, for instance), the political nature of the second language learning situation is largely ignored. Almost always, researchers investigate the "spontaneous" acquisition of a target language that dominates the native language of the learner—English in the United States or the United Kingdom or the local majority language in a community where linguist parents doing fieldwork study their children acquiring the local language. We had been sensitized by Hymes (1970, 1972b) to always consider situational particularities in language use. Certainly, learning a second language would be included in language use. And the relative political positions of native and target languages—and of speakers of those languages—would be an important "situational particularity." Thus, we wondered if second language learning would look different if we investigated a situation in which the usual relationship of more powerful target language/less powerful native language were reversed. Perhaps what had been presented in other research as characteristics of second language acquisition in general were, in fact, only characteristics of the acquisition of a dominant language by minority language speakers. Perhaps the acquisition of a minority language by dominant language speakers entailed different strategies, followed different trajectories, or had different meanings.

We were delighted with our own reasoning, and we carried out a study to investigate this relatively uncharted territory. Unfortunately, we had neglected to consider the larger consequences for second language learning of gross political inequality between two languages. That is, by and large, majority language speakers do not acquire the minority languages in their midst. And that, of course, is what happened (or, rather, didn't happen) in the two bilingual classrooms in which we kept trying to study second language acquisition of a nondominant language. But more interesting than the nonacquisition of Spanish, in this case, is what we came to understand about how the various actors in the classroom played out the larger political conditions of nonacquisition.

HOW WE STARTED

We began with a school-year long study of three Anglo first-graders supposedly acquiring Spanish as a second language in a bilingual classroom near Phoenix, Arizona. Although the goals of that school district did not include explicit attention to mutual second language learning on the part of both Anglos and Chicanos, the teacher expressed that desire. We did limited classroom observations in order to find out who was addressing Spanish to the English speakers, for what purposes, and under what conditions. Every 2 weeks, with one of us posing as a monolingual Spanish speaker, we audiotaped three children, each paired with a bilingual peer, in language testing and play sessions. We left the room for about 10 minutes during those half-hour sessions, leaving the tape recorder on, in order to have samples of completely child–child interaction. Our findings were as follows:

- Spanish was not addressed individually to these children by anyone except us during our biweekly sessions (i.e., neither Spanish-speaking adults nor Spanish-speaking children took the language teacher role).
- When Spanish was used in total-group activities in the classroom and in our taping sessions, the three Anglo children "tuned Spanish out" (i.e., they did not take the language learner role).
- Except for a few color and number words, no Spanish was acquired (Hudelson & Edelsky, 1980).

Despite what seemed to be a clear "message," we hoped we were wrong; we hoped that genuine, mutual second language learning could occur if the conditions were optimal. After all, in that first study, school conditions were *not* optimal. No policy and no person, except for this one teacher, wanted to have the Anglos learn Spanish. And even given this teacher's goal, she used Spanish as the vehicle of instruction for much less of the time than she used English. Of course, such a state of affairs stemmed from a larger "condition"—the relative political position of the two languages. While, on the one hand, we were sensitive to that condition (it was, in fact, what prompted the study in the first place), on the other, we were naïve about it, thinking it could be overridden by local classroom arrangements. Thus, we began a second study the next year, in what we thought would be a more effective setting for problematic second language acquisition, still searching for strategies used by dominant language speakers in the acquisition of a subordinate language. It was finally through this second study that we were able to see non-acquisition as an activity engaged in by many social actors, rather than as an absence or an individual failure.

THE SECOND STUDY

This time we chose a "better" first grade classroom. It was in a district in which one of the explicit goals of the bilingual program was to produce bilinguals among both Spanish and English speaking children. To that end, the district had instituted systematic, "pullout" second language instruction in each language, and it assessed second language proficiency in each language.[1]

In this classroom, an Alternate Days model prevailed, continuing the presentation of content rather than translating it—one day was English Day, the next was Spanish Day. We assumed there would be more Spanish in this Alternate Days allocation than there had been the preceding year.[2] There were 22 children in the class: Ten were bilinguals or monolingual

---

[1]It is not that we looked favorably on such efforts as pulling children out of class and giving them direct instruction in a second language or testing their second language proficiency with questionable test instruments. It is just that these were signs that the District was willing to take seriously the second language learning of *each* language.

[2]It will appear throughout that I am being critical of the bilingual adults involved in these two studies, especially the teachers. On the contrary, I praise them for their motives and their efforts to make bilingual education a two-way street. Especially noteworthy is the extraordinary amount of energy the teacher in the second study must have expended in order to persist in doing what was often followed by signs of incomprehension (just the opposite of what a teacher hopes for!) in the name of a larger principle, to provide the amount of Spanish she did when all around her the push was toward greater English usage, and to maintain her Spanish maintenance desires in the face of contradictory desires from many quarters. These teachers were up against an entire politico-linguistic context—which is the point of this chapter.

Spanish speakers who were bussed in from a barrio. Twelve lived in the neighborhood and were English monolinguals or English dominant children with some limited ability to produce Spanish. Of the neighborhood children, 5 were Anglos; 7 were Latinos.

Again, my colleague Sarah Hudelson (SH) posed as a monolingual Spanish speaker. Contrived though it was, *la Señora Spanish* (as one bilingual child named her) assured the Anglophiles of occasionally getting at least some Spanish directed to them on a one-to-one basis. Moreover, if they wanted to interact with SH, the English-speaking children would have to attempt to understand her and to accommodate to her "monolinguality."

We were classroom volunteers and observers for one-half to a full school day at least three times each month from October through early April. We took special note of code choice, functions of language, and any instances of engagement or withdrawal by Anglophiles in relation to Spanish interactions. We targeted three of the Anglo children (Kathy, Katie, and Nathan) and two Latinos (Vince and Anita) for close observation. Although Vince and Anita were very close to being monolingual in English, the teacher knew that Spanish was used around them at home occasionally. We reasoned (hoped) that occasional exposure to Spanish at home might provide an extra push toward significant second language acquisition for these two children.

As in the previous study, we took each of these five children with a Spanish-speaking peer to a separate room, where we gave them a short comprehension and repetition task (they were asked to show SH the picture of the big boy/little boy, etc., and to repeat sentences such as *es un muchacho grande*/this is a big boy). After SH tested them, she played with them using playdough, puppets, magic slates, and so on, while I observed. Again, during the playtime, we left the children alone for several minutes. The sessions were conducted entirely in Spanish and were audiotape recorded, with one child wearing a lapel microphone.

THE SECOND LANGUAGE LEARNING CONTEXT

Functions of the Use of Spanish and English

Children used "Public Spanish" (the use of Spanish to one or more people in front of an audience) for a wide range of functions—directing, predicting, informing, teasing, threatening, explaining, consoling, and so forth, but only if all present were bilingual. Adults used Public Spanish only for teacher-ish functions: directing, reprimanding, explaining, entertaining (storytelling), keeping order, providing transitions between activities, establishing social contact, and conducting classroom routines (taking attendance, collecting lunch money).

Spanish directed individually to our target children or to other English-dominant children was more rare than Public Spanish and more limited in function. Adults used Spanish to individual English speakers for social routines *(buenos días)*, reprimands, and directions that could also be signaled nonverbally. Though English was used by adults for explaining, joking, warning, or making conversation, Spanish was not. With almost no exceptions, children did not address Spanish to individual English speakers. The rare exceptions were produced by two Mexican immigrants (Elena and Lily) who were monolingual in Spanish at the start of the school year. Once, Elena gave Anita a short direction in Spanish that she followed without pause with an English paraphrase. During a test session, Lily and Kathy provided the only evidence of any explicit argument over code choice.

(1)

Kathy (K):	What's she doing?
Lily (L):	Dice tú [She says you] …
K:	Don't say in Spanish. English.
L:	Que te digo español. [That I tell you Spanish]
K:	English.
L:	No.
K:	Say it in English.
L:	No. [the argument was ended as we resumed testing]

Language "Intrusion" Into the Other Language's "Day"

In an Alternate Days bilingual program, the rule is one language per day. Nevertheless, loudspeaker announcements were made daily in English, and Spanish speakers spoke to each other in Spanish no matter the day—in other words, no day was "language pure." However, the frequency and extent of the other language's intrusion was not symmetrical. Spanish was used very infrequently on English Days. Except for Spanish reading time for Spanish speakers, adults used no Public Spanish on English Day, though they did use Spanish individually to Spanish dominant children only.

The intrusion of English into Spanish Day was another story. English was used publicly to all (not merely to English-dominant children) and for the same functions as Public Spanish. Additionally, it was used for insuring the understanding of the Anglophiles. There was no comparable checking with the Spanish-dominant children on English Day. When adults referred to something on Spanish Day that could not be pointed to or acted out, they switched to English. No matter the day, when nonbilingual outsiders came in to make announcements, adults used English. Even the Spanish-dominant children addressed SH, the "monolingual" researcher, in English.

Children's Perceptions of Second Language Instruction

As part of its two-way bilingual program, the school provided both English as a second language (ESL) and Spanish as a second language (SSL) taught through the audio-lingual method, and an English "booster" program for those who were weakest in English.[3] The children were aware of which children went to which pullout class. They referred to "the kids who come on the bus"; they could name who went to SSL, to ESL, and to Special English; they knew which children could be used as translators; they sometimes commented on which children were potential after-school playmates—for logistical reasons, at least, for the English speakers it was not those who took the bus.

Their perception of the special second language lessons also became part of the context. To the children, the lessons were to be used as games or performances. Kathy occasionally approached SH with cards showing fruit, articles of clothing, and so on, pointed to the cards while repeating *spañol*, and tried to elicit Spanish card naming as a game. The children perceived both SSL and ESL lessons as equally artificial and communicatively useless. Nathan bragged that though he could not speak Spanish, he *had* learned to say *es un (sic) abrelata* (it's a can opener). In one taping session, Kathy told us that what she talked about in the Spanish class was "*es un's*" (/itsa's/—as in *it's a sweater, it's a book*). And Lily, Kathy's taping session partner, responded to SH's question about what they talked about in ESL with *dicen "I'm a fireman." Dicen así.* (They say, *I'm a fireman.* They talk like that.)

Presence of "Monolingual" SH

"Monolingual" SH, persisting in her monolinguality, provided English-speaking children who wanted to interact with her with a *demand* to accommodate. Moreover, since SH was not responsible for directing activities or maintaining order, she could do what the other adults never did: engage children in casual conversation in Spanish. "Shooting the breeze," in turn, enabled SH to use Spanish both publicly and individually in order to get information, make social contact and open a conversation, elicit translations, joke, compliment; that is, to expand the language functions in Spanish. Because she was "monolingual," SH could avoid switching to English when her addressee showed a lack of comprehension. In these language "showdowns,"

---

[3]Special English was provided for children who scored low on the English version of the language proficiency test. Actually, some Spanish surnamed children who appeared to us to be native English speakers also went to Special English. There were no comparable Special Spanish classes for those who scored low on the Spanish version of the test.

it was Spanish speaking SH's language choice that prevailed, an anomaly to be discussed later.

LANGUAGE ACQUISITION (?) IN THIS CONTEXT

Even if they did not become Spanish speakers, the Anglo children did respond to the second language learning context. And their responses are instructive as we think about the roles of all concerned in second language learning. Their responses can be grouped into four categories: (a) display of metalinguistic awareness, (b) taking the learner role, (c) not taking the learner role, and (d) producing Spanish.

Metalinguistic Awareness

Even after only 2 months in first grade, the children appeared to have developed a striking awareness of language as an entity. Sometimes, this awareness was stated neutrally; sometimes with feeling. In class, Kathy and Katie were engaged in a bit of competition.

> (2)
> **Kathy:** I can speak three languages—English and Spanish and Indian.
> **Katie:** Well I can speak four—English and Spanish and Scotland and Jewish!
> **Kathy:** So! I'm gonna learn *Flagstaff!* (a city about 150 miles away)

Some children thought synonyms might really be translations (*"Pony" in English is "horse,"* Anita told us). On several occasions, after we had left the room during a taping session, children echoed Vince's view (*Finally, we can speak English. I hate Spanish*). While school personnel bragged about how well the Anglos were learning Spanish, the children themselves saw it differently (Nathan: *I don't talk Spanish. I just know the colors*).

Taking the Learner Role

In order to acquire a second language naturalistically, one must do two things: (a) make sense out of nonsense and (b) present oneself as a legitimate participant (Fillmore, 1976). Primary aspects of the learner role, then, are to use clues to guess at meanings and to stay in an interaction by taking one's conversational turn. On occasion, the five English speakers we focused on did indeed act as learners; most often, in the taping sessions with SH. There, they would watch faces intently, matching facial expressions with the speaker, with a split-second delay. Frequently, they took their turns nonverbally (nodding their heads or shrugging their shoulders).

More interesting was their verbal turn-taking, which often included uncanny guesses at the speaker's meaning. These guesses seemed to be based on various combinations of verbal and visual clues along with clues from their sociolinguistic knowledge (e.g., knowing that there is a great likelihood that an adult in an interview/testing setting is asking a child a question, that some questions are more likely than others, that topics tend to be maintained across several turns, etc.). For instance, when SH pointed to "Grease," printed on Nathan's t-shirt, and asked, *Nathan ¿qué dice?* (Nathan, what does it say?), Nathan answered *Grease.* Now it could be that he understood that situated *phrase*. Or it could be that what he understood was the *situation.* That is, when adults in school call a beginning reader's name and point at print, they probably want the child to read it. In other words, Nathan could have been "simply" interpreting a gesture in combination with a name cue and his knowledge of likely situational demands.

Many examples of the Anglo children producing appropriate content during their conversational turns make it seem that they had already acquired enough Spanish to understand the *language*-in-context, not only the context. Our contention, however, is that they were, instead, doing what is necessary in order to *begin* to acquire a second language; namely, participate, guess the general gist of an extended exchange, and guess the specific communicative demand of a particular turn. Evidence for our position comes from times children did not respond (e.g., not responding unless someone's name was foregrounded), but especially from times when children took a guess but the guess missed the mark. Because these conversational errors can be accounted for by appealing to the same combinations of clues and knowledge that resulted in appropriate responses, we believe a guessing strategy was at work throughout. For example, the use of a language clue in combination with knowledge of a likely question resulted in the following missed-the-mark responses. (Our inference about the child's thinking is in brackets.)

(3)
(Preceding references have been to Katie's picture of her mother, her father and her sister, Cassie)

SH: ¿Cuántos años tiene? (How old is she?)
Katie: [I recognize *cuántos* as meaning *how many*. The general topic has concerned members of my family. The likely question is how many children are in the family.] Holds up two fingers (Cassie is actually 9 years old).
SH: *Dos. Tiene dos años, dos años.* (Two. She's 2 years old, 2 years)
K: [I understand *dos*. The adult is reiterating my elicited answer that there are two children in my family. I will further elaborate that response.] Me and Cassie.

(4)

(Katie had told us the month before that her father had hurt his back)

SH: *Y Katie, ¿cómo está tu papá?* (And Katie, how is your father?)
K: (no response)
SH: *¿Mejor? ¿Se siente mejor?* (Better? He feels better?)
K: [I recognize *papá*, which must be the new topic. A likely question con-
          cerning my father is: what does he do for a living] Makin' insurance.

Not Taking the Learner Role

The examples above show that the children did occasionally act as second
language learners, guessing and taking their turns. Mostly, this was in interactions with SH, who did not honor the political relationship between the
two languages but who stubbornly persisted in speaking Spanish and in not
understanding English.[4] But there were many more times when the
children either failed to take their turn, failed to guess, or outright refused
to take part or to comprehend. Nonresponse was the response when the
Spanish speaker asked about there/then topics, initiated new topics that
were not accompanied by gestures or supporting context, or subjected the
child to a barrage of successive questions.

There were other instances of non-turn-taking and supposed non-sense-
making that were more emotionally loaded. When an unfamiliar story was
read in Spanish in class without a preceding synopsis in English, the
English-dominant children would quickly escape through misbehavior or by
moving away physically. There were also times when the children played on
their monolinguality in order to defy an adult or to express their frustration.
For example, Nathan had misbehaved; an aide was shepherding him to
another seat, repeating while pointing at the chair *siéntate acá* (sit there). He
glowered *I don't even know what you mean!* Another day, the class was playing
Hokey Pokey in Spanish for the first time, but using the same melody, the
same sequence of body parts being "put in and out and shaken all about"
that the children were familiar with in English. Nathan wailed *I don't understand this.* During our testing sessions, Kathy refused to repeat a phrase,
maintaining she had already done so "privately."

(5)
Kathy: I said it. I said it with myself, like this (moves her lips, goldfish style).
SH: *Es un muchacho chiquito.* (He's a little boy—the test phrase)
Lily: Say, Kathy.
K: I did. Really. (laughs)

---

[4]Fillmore (1978) discusses how even young children come to act "appropriately" in the
United States in English speaker/non-English speaker interactions. The young English speakers hold out longer, making fewer efforts to understand the other; the Spanish speakers eventually submit and switch to English.

Producing Spanish

In class, except for interactions with SH, the only Spanish produced by these five children was color words, number words, *adiós,* and song lyrics. Even to the "monolingual" SH, the English-speaking children's rare Spanish production was mostly single words, uttered in response to an opening gambit from SH.

In the taped sessions, though more Spanish was produced, it was hardly frequent, and there too it usually consisted of single words. Occasionally, the children used a Spanish color or number word to their peers (*I want dos yellow, Lemme have the rojo*). In response to questions from SH, children switched to the Spanish pronunciation *mamá* and *papá* instead of mama or daddy. After SH showed she didn't understand, Anita once converted *this is a hot dog* to the single word *taco.*

When we left the children alone with the tape recorder on, they produced even less Spanish than when we were present. This is not surprising, since our exit removed the peculiar inversion that came with SH's presence, and permitted the "normal" relationship between the two languages to reassert itself. When we were gone, neither Kathy nor Katie produced even one Spanish word. Nathan used a number and a color word once. And Vince said *tortilla, masa* (cornmeal), and *bruja* (witch) once each, and had one exchange with Héctor, his bilingual partner, involving two taboo Spanish words.

The five children, then, used language about language quite frequently. Occasionally, they acted out the second language learner role, though mostly with SH rather than with peers or other bilingual adults. And, less frequently, they produced a few Spanish words when responding to particular people who initiated Spanish with them. As we said at the start, these efforts resulted in no major second language acquisition between October and April.

Changes in the Children's Spanish Performance

When we first met them, these five children already knew some color and number words, a song about the date on the calendar, the names of some letters, and two social routines (*adiós, buenos días*). Six months later, each of the two Latino children had used an additional two- or three-word Spanish formulaic phrase on a couple of occasions. Their performance on the comprehension and repetition tasks had not changed. We can hardly say, then, that being in this bilingual classroom resulted in any significant acquisition of Spanish syntax, morphology, or even lexicon for these two children. More importantly, if the acquisition of syntax, morphology, and lexicon (i.e., a narrowly conceived notion of language acquisition) is dependent on the use of certain discourse strategies (Hatch, 1978), the latter were missing. Neither Vince nor Anita demonstrated any increased inclination to initiate or sustain interactions with Spanish speakers using Spanish.

Of the three Anglos, Nathan showed only one change—he learned the SSL routine about the can opener and used it to show off. Kathy was the only one of the five who (rarely) used Spanish to convey her own intentions over more than one turn, and only with SH (e.g., trying to get SH to play an SSL card-naming game by saying her own name in Spanish, pointing to the cards, and repeating *spañol, spañol*). Katie's performance did improve on the artificial comprehension task we used during part of the taping sessions, but when the input was less predictable her comprehension seemed no better as the months passed. In essence, the three Anglos made no greater or lesser improvement than the Latino children did.

It is important to remember that while these five children were making minimal, if any, progress in Spanish, the Spanish speakers were taking giant steps in English. They produced long English strings, used English to initiate activity and conversation (as opposed to merely responding to others' questions), and attempted to follow extended exchanges and stories with no Spanish translations. English was their increasing choice for use with other Spanish speakers (e.g., once, we heard Andrés and Héctor discussing the Spanish reading group's Spanish worksheet—in English). English was the language they used more and more for their labeling of school-taught concepts (rectangle, circle) despite presentation of these concepts in both languages. It was also the language they used increasingly for social routines, even to "monolingual" SH.

THE SECOND LANGUAGE LEARNING
CONTEXT RECONSIDERED: IN-SCHOOL
REPRODUCTION OF OUT-OF-SCHOOL INEQUALITY

Why didn't the English speakers in the two studies make more gains in learning Spanish? Certainly, there was a problem with quantity (not enough one-to-one interaction in the target language; not enough time— 6 months wasn't long enough, although it *was* long enough for the Spanish speakers to make great strides in English). But the larger problem was political—a condition of language *markedness,* resulting from the relative political position of the target and native languages. It is the phenomenon of markedness that explains why only one language became a target language, only one group assumed the teacher role, and only one group became second language learners.

As Fishman (1976) explained, for particular institutions or domains, a language may be *unmarked;* that is, it is the expected, taken-for-granted language. Any other language is *marked.* A marked language requires some deliberate activity on its behalf before it is used for carrying on the activity of that domain. An unmarked language, on the other hand, is one used "anyway," with no extra effort, the one that is "naturally" the language of that institution or domain. Markedness is a dimension that has its source outside the school. In the United States, in high-status, government-controlled domains such as education, the unmarked language is the dominant language, even in those localities in which non-English speakers are both in the numerical majority and in power in the local government.

Markedness can be artificially upset in a limited way through the establishment of immersion programs. In an immersion program, the marked language becomes an *un*marked language *within that school*. On the other hand, in "regular" bilingual programs, such as the two discussed above, the marked language remains a marked language; even though it is used as one of the languages of instruction, other key activities in the school (including most of the instruction) are carried on primarily through the unmarked language.

Immersion programs are not a second language learning panacea for dominant language monolinguals, however. Other factors[5] besides a program-bound shift in markedness affect whether children learn a nondominant, marked language. As one example, relative lack of parental support for the Spanish immersion program in Culver City, California, appears to have been related to the limited success of the Culver City experiment, in contrast with greater parental support for, and greater success of, some French immersion programs in Canada (Torres, 1988).

Knowing that a language is marked in a particular domain may help predict that it will not be acquired as a second language, but it does not explain just how that nonacquisition occurs. The two studies reported in this chapter, along with comments by Fillmore (1978), offer a beginning sketch of the activities that prevent people from learning a second language.

Since the unmarked language is the normal, expected, taken-for-granted language of the institution, it is also normal, expected, and taken for granted that all students will learn it. Students know this at a very young age. They may initially resist (Itoh & Hatch, 1978; Saville-Troike, 1988), but most eventually succumb, trying to make sense of the babble around them and attempting to get into the action in the other language. There is no mystery to how students learn who the second language learners will be— which language *must* be learned (i.e., which is the unmarked language). It is the language one persists in even when another doesn't understand, the language whose presence no one comments on, the language one gets lunch in, the language the school secretary uses to answer the phone, the

---

[5]In the Postscript I address some additional "other factors."

language of classroom management, the language of most of the trade and textbooks. A small child's personal experience with a reading group that, at first, uses mostly Spanish as the instructional language, does not trick the child into thinking that English is merely an option.

The clues mount up quickly over which language must be learned, and the many "showdowns" over language—like contests over who will blink first—soon begin to turn out the same way. The child who speaks the dominant unmarked language holds out longer, refusing to understand the other; the marked language speaker gives in, pretending to understand or using formulaic utterances to get into the action (Fillmore, 1978). In other words, the speaker of the unmarked language takes on the language teacher role (using a modified version of the unmarked language to the minority language speaker); the marked language speaker takes on the learner role (guessing, pretending, trying out chunks of the new language to accomplish social ends). Once a child becomes the learner, it becomes pragmatically difficult to wiggle out of that asymmetrical relationship; thus, unmarked language speaking teachers stay teachers and marked language speaking learners stay learners (Fillmore, 1978).

And teach and learn they do. A linguistic "underdog" in school, then, is not one more likely to "lose" the second language learning game but rather one destined to "win" it. I do not mean to belittle the severe problems both in and out of school faced by these students. Nevertheless, it is their subordinate status that guarantees considerable second language learning, just as it is privileged linguistic status that prevents comparable acquisition on the part of nonunderdogs.

There is, of course, a subtext to winning the second language learning game. Like learning to read, learning a second language is not an unmitigated, neutral "good." Becoming bilingual, like becoming literate, does not mean the same thing or have the same consequences in all societies or for all people in any given society (see Graff, 1986, for a discussion demystifying the idea of universal meanings of, and benefits from, literacy; see Cummins, 1976, for a discussion distinguishing the sociopolitically determined categories of additive and subtractive bilingualism). For the Spanish speakers in our studies, learning the unmarked language to a high degree of proficiency won them little. They were still considered linguistically inadequate. For the English speakers, however, learning some numbers, colors, and a few songs in the marked language counted as learning Spanish—it was a cause for celebration, evidence of the children's linguistic strengths.

How can such a state of affairs be changed? If markedness originates outside of classrooms in speech communities, then it is outside of classrooms in speech communities where the primary efforts for change must be directed. To offset even slightly the power of the unmarked language, those who plan programs aimed at mutuality in second language acquisition will have to seriously understand the wider society's discriminatory arrangements, including critically analyzing the antecedents and consequences of the political relationship between the target and native languages, and they will have to establish strategies that account for those arrangements.[6]

In our studies, it was SH's status that gave legitimacy to her sociolinguistically peculiar behavior ("facing down" the dominant language speakers, refusing to take on the learner role and implicitly persisting in "teaching" the subordinate language). Had she been someone of lesser status (a child, an aide, perhaps a Latina adult), her rule-breaking might well have been resisted (as it was, it was never even commented on). And had she not been deliberate and determined, she would most likely not have been able to maintain her rule-breaking. But she *did* maintain her violation of politically motivated language norms, and that persistence changed the pragmatic situation in the taping sessions at least. In essence, SH was a one-person immersion program. She gave the usually marked language unmarked status for those taping sessions—evening up the usual asymmetry wherein the Spanish-speaking peer partners were always learners, letting them have a chance to take the teacher role. Even though SH maintained such sociolinguistic contrariness only for short periods of time, it was wearing; she may well have been unable to maintain it on a daily basis.

The two teachers and some of the school personnel who worked with them to further the goal of two-way bilingualism were also opposing the established order. They bucked speech community norms for addressing people in their preferred language, even if they saw little reward for their efforts. These two teachers' efforts, as well as SH's, to undo the effects of markedness in the classroom were undertaken seriously and sincerely, but they were—and had to be—ineffective. Establishing a full-scale immersion program would have provided some relief in the classroom from the inequities of markedness. However, it would not have completely neutralized the impact on second language acquisition of the out-of-school relationship between the two languages, and it would have done nothing to change the out-of-school language situation that gives rise to markedness and all its consequences.

What I am saying, then, is that in the end, bilingual programs cannot compensate for a discriminatory political context. The gross inequality of power between two languages (and two groups of people)—an inequality that ensures that one set of young children will always be language teachers

---

[6]At Valley View, the school featured in the Postscript, there have been consistent, deliberate attempts to address some of those inequitable out-of-school arrangements.

and the other set language learners, that one set will be congratulated for making almost no progress while the other is disparaged for making tremendous (but not "total") progress—is not something that a school program can change. But just because schools cannot undo existing power relations that profoundly affect language learning does not mean they should continue to conduct business as usual, for example, maintaining elitist monolingual language policies and exclusionary canons and privileging only certain discourses. After all, schools—and what goes on within them—are not only mirrors and reproducers of societal arrangements; they can also be sites of resistance. In regard to second language learning such resistance must account for the profoundly political nature of the enterprise.

A LONG POSTSCRIPT, 2004

Valley View K–8 School in the Roosevelt School District in Phoenix mounted (and continues[7] to mount) just such resistance.[8] A neighborhood school for most of its students, it is a "chosen" school for a significant number; about 225 of its 760 students come from outside the school's boundaries. Some of these are children of staff members; some have parents who have heard about Valley View by word of mouth; some have families that have moved out of the area but keep sending their children to Valley View by car, public bus, or bicycle. While other schools, especially those serving low-income populations, experience high rates of student mobility, Valley View's students tend to stay put. Most (90%) Valley View students are Latino; a few (about 7%) are African American; even fewer are Anglo or Native American. About 80% qualify for free or reduced lunch. About 60% of the students are English Language Learners. Three quarters of the students in Valley View's dual language immersion program are English

---

[7]As of June 2005, the resistance at Valley View continues, but who knows what next week or next year will bring. John Wann is seen in his district as a renegade principal. In the 2005 round of high-stakes testing, Valley View's test scores endowed the school with the enviable status of "performing." In other years, however, test scores have not been acceptable. In all years, scores are a source of considerable concern. New regulations or new district maneuvers may well put an end to the exceptional education offered at Valley View. On the other hand, John and the teachers may find yet more new ways around the rules—all in order to keep on resisting through doing what's right.

[8]For this Postscript, I might have used my memories of being a visitor/observer at Valley View since John Wann became its principal in 1990; but, to present a more inside view, I interviewed Valley View teachers and administrators and conducted a focus group with older students. The main questions were: What makes Valley View different from other schools with dual language programs that you know about? What is it about Valley View that gets English speakers to learn Spanish?

language learners; the other quarter is divided evenly between those who enter as Spanish/English bilinguals and those who first enroll as monolingual English speakers. Unlike the students in the studies reported above, at least some of the Anglo, African American, and Latino English speakers in that program learn to understand and speak Spanish.[9]

What propels speakers of the dominant, unmarked language (English) at Valley View toward Spanish, the nondominant, marked language? The mere existence of its dual-language immersion program[10] does not tell the whole tale.

The Principal

That story begins with John Wann, a principal with a vision of an equitable, diverse bilingual world, someone who hires teachers who share his vision, who is a seemingly endless fount of plans for bringing that vision into focus. John is both model and center—a "White guy" who has lived in South Phoenix for 30 years, who does not see his neighbors as "deficient" or "needy" but rather as people with worthy knowledge. While he is clearly the central driving force behind the enormous and largely successful efforts to change the status of Spanish within the school, he rightly insists that his plans and dreams would go nowhere if his vision did not come to be shared by many others in the Valley View community.

Valuing Spanish

At Valley View, speaking Spanish is valued, being bilingual is valued, not speaking English is not stigmatized. Deliberate projects and practices are material signs of the strong intention to raise the status of Spanish. Everything public—a Monday morning rally with the whole school gathered to

---

[9]For the past several years, Spanish-speaking adults at rallies, school board meetings, and other public events have remarked with favor about the Spanish used by Anglo and African American students from Valley View who have addressed these audiences—and responded in question/answer sessions—in Spanish. Latino grandparents of Valley View students have reported their pleasure in having formerly English-speaking grandchildren begin to use Spanish with them. Slightly less anecdotally, a native Spanish-speaking doctoral student, Cristian Aquino, held focus groups in Spanish with Valley View students and alumni (Latinos and African Americans), transcribed the tapes, and attested to the Spanish language proficiency of those young people.

[10]From 1989 to 2003, Valley View offered parents a choice of a bilingual program, an English-based program, and a dual-language immersion program. In the latter, English and Spanish speakers were in the same program, receiving most of their instruction in Spanish in kindergarten, the proportion shifting through the next 8 years until most instruction was in English.

applaud each other's successes, homework, letters to parents, student–parent–teacher conferences, meetings—features both Spanish and English. Without translation. John says, "It puts both languages on the same plane." (Monolingual parents do have "homework partners," bilingual parents who help them on homework assignments with the other language.) An arts integration grant selects artists who can do their art in Spanish. Staff discussions make explicit the need to violate code-switching norms—to persist in speaking Spanish to non-Spanish speakers in order to be Spanish language "teachers"—and to create an on-campus world where Spanish is as "normal" as English. To that end, some of the teachers John has hired are from Latin America and were, at the time of hiring, more proficient in Spanish than English.[11] Indeed, there are Spanish conversations between respected adults and between adults and children, not only in classrooms but also on the sidewalks between school buildings, in the cafeteria, and in the office. Students in the upper grades go on extended "field trips" across the border to a small village in Mexico and also to community agencies in Phoenix in order to study, to provide community service, and also to use Spanish in "authentic" contexts. And there is explicit, frequent affirmation of the need to be bilingual; administrators and faculty, support staff and students all verbalize the importance of knowing both Spanish and English in order to get a good education and a good job. No wonder the entire Valley View community—parents, students, and staff—was alarmed when Proposition 203, to end bilingual education, was put on the ballot in 2000. Students and adults rotated in a 'round-the-clock, week-long vigil in front of the state capitol to demonstrate against the proposition. With bravado, parents and staff vowed to lock arms around the school to prevent the "language police" from entering and "ripping out" its treasured dual-language program.

Despite their efforts, Proposition 203 passed in a landslide. But Valley View continued to provide its dual-language choice—illegally, according to some; legally, according to Valley View. The Arizona Department of Education interpreted the Proposition as permitting bilingual education (or instruction through a language other than English), but only for those who already speak English. Valley View claimed such an interpretation violates rights of equal access, excluding one group of students from a program based solely on those students' native language. Since its dual-language program was open to all students (rather than being targeted for a single population, as bilingual programs are), Valley View maintained that its

---

[11]John didn't anticipate the ensuing struggles between Mexican and Chicana teachers over pedagogy. Those struggles were resolved in typical Valley View fashion: with people on all "sides" engaging with each other over difficult issues over a long period of time while being supported by an outside expert.

dual-language program was exempt from the prohibitions of Proposition 203. By 2003, however, those arguments were rendered moot by federal Reading First funds. Related to the No Child Left Behind legislation, these funds became the "last straw," an escape-proof barrier to using a non-English language for instruction—or so it seemed, until John and the staff came up with the latest plan. The school decided to provide daily Spanish "foreign" language instruction inside the mandated English immersion program for all kindergarten through third-grade students, as well as Saturday Spanish classes, beginning in 2004. John's thinking was that fourth- through eighth-graders, having had 4 years of instruction through English, should be able to pass the English proficiency qualification so they can qualify for the dual-language program. And when children who begin kindergarten in 2004 reach fourth grade, they should be on the road to being able to take part in at least some instruction through Spanish.[12]

A Vision of a Just, Peaceful, Bilingual World

High status for Spanish at Valley View is not the only vision here. In fact, it is just part of a larger vision that is communicated to all who are connected with Valley View, a vision of a world (beginning with a local community) that is bilingual, diverse, equitable, just, and peaceful, and a school that is a healing place, a sanctuary for all within it. Embedded in that vision are key values concerning respect, taking care (of each other, of the school, the animals, the garden), "mattering" (*what* is learned matters, people matter, families and community matter), as well as thinking in terms of "culture" (a culture of literacy, a culture of respect, a culture of caring). This larger vision and these values are reflected in: structure (e.g., multi-age groupings enable teachers to develop stronger connections with families, provide stable learning environments for students, build deeper shared histories with individual students, and provide more opportunities for students to take care of each other), scheduling (ensuring big blocks of uninterrupted time for learning, scheduling "specials" so that groups of teachers can collaborate on planning while students are at music or physical education, building in times for teachers to reflect on issues), and "permeability." Classroom doors are always open to parents. A family literacy program has parents sitting in the kindergartens

---

[12]As a result of Proposition 203, parents of children who already speak English can apply for a waiver to receive their instruction in a language other than English. Parents can also apply for a waiver for children 10 years of age or older—if, in the informed belief of the principal and the educational staff, those children would be better served by an "alternative" program. This feature of the requirements for a waiver allows parents of recent immigrants or students who are still learning English to select dual language in Grades 4 through 8.

and first grades with their children. Parents and grandparents come to school to share their stories. Other school adults (custodians, cafeteria workers, office staff, instructional assistants) teach aspects of various projects and model "caring" for students.

Teachers and Students as Co-learners and Co-relators

It isn't only students who are considered learners; so are the teachers. Faculty meetings are not consumed with school business but rather are devoted to professional development issues (e.g., the environment, second language learning, the meaning of a "culture of literacy"). Each week, teachers attend grade range meetings to plan instruction. Some teachers participate in a book group to read and discuss professional books. Some of the professional development is focused on emotional understanding—expertly guided "focused personal staff development" (through a program called FOCUS) to help teachers and other school adults confront such personal issues as their fears about students and their own desires for control.

Values of respect and caring (for and about) entail particular interpersonal dynamics. A few years ago, students and staff wrote a Compact for Excellence; each year, students renegotiate, revise, and affirm items such as "I will greet three people with 'hello' and a smile." Annual trips (faculty team building and professional development retreats such as a math cadre led by Expeditionary Learning Outward Bound staff in the school's sister pueblo in Sonora Mexico, overnight camping trips for fourth- through sixth-graders, a marine biology camping trip to California for seventh- and eighth-graders, trips to Mexico as part of the school's outreach across the border) help strengthen interpersonal bonds. Traveling to those off-campus locations plays an important part in cementing those bonds. Along with other "we"-focused activities on campus, the trips help to create a school climate permeated with a sense of "caring," "family" and "community."

Taking care of each other extends to each other's learning. Valley View offers a variety of mentoring programs: reading buddies, a Valley View tutoring program, older student aides for younger students, America Reads supporting service learning tutors through Arizona State University, and various after-school and summer tutoring programs sponsored by the League of United Latin American Citizens.

Valley View students "always seem to be preparing for something"—a trip, a festival, a program. For an annual evening Academic Expo, all students display and explain their work to families and community members. Twice a year, a Fine Arts Evening brings the community in for dance and musical performances and visual arts displays. A festival to honor all the cultures represented in the school is another curricular-community event. Each of these gives purpose to the learning of content and provides real and varied audiences.

Conflict Resolution as Working for Truth and Responsibility

The nexus for most of Valley View's values and vision is a program centering around a commitment to peace and education through relationships. It is in this program that respecting diversity (including diverse opinions), promoting equality and justice, caring about each other, "mattering," healing, and the "cultures" (culture of literacy, culture of respect, culture of caring) come together. Cynthia Bernacki, the assistant principal, who keeps the work of communicating-for-the-sake-of-relationships consistently on track, calls this a conflict resolution program based on "truth and responsibility," not punishment. This program requires "wise people" (peer mediators and prevention specialists) and particular formats (referrals, talk-it-outs, writing-your-story, and make-it-works). A peace-building pledge[13] has been written by seventh- and eighth-graders, to "give up put-downs," for instance, and to "speak up about the hurts I have caused." If a student disrupts the learning climate, that student is removed immediately from the setting, but then that student gets a serious, attentive audience as she or he talks about what led up to what happened. A disruption can be handled on the spot by a peer mediator (self-selected students who attend peer mediation training) in a talk-it-out. Disruptions can also be followed by referrals (written memos of complaint). In keeping with the value that all can "come to the table as equal partners," anyone (child or adult) can write a referral about anyone (child or adult). Adults and children use the same form for writing referrals. Referrals are intended to spark support, not to discipline but to deal with issues underlying disruption of learning. Indeed, Cynthia has built a library of self-help books for use by students and teachers to address such issues as fear, anger, power, bullying, grief, and so on. People who get referred write their side of the story, which is then read by a prevention specialist. One or more of a variety of procedures follow, culminating in a make-it-right—a letter (which is not sent until it is in conventional Spanish or English) or community service (working a number of hours for the school community to compensate for the hours of disruption).

Practices that attempt to redistribute power, that promote students and teachers coming "to the table as equal partners," are difficult for adults.

---

[13]The Valley View staff has borrowed and adapted many of the ideas for this program, including the pledge, from a program called Peacebuilders. The work at Valley View, however, goes beyond Peacebuilders.

Teachers at Valley View receive support for this often-disturbing work through the FOCUS retreats, in professional development faculty meetings, and, importantly, in a teacher–principal journal that allows John to help on an individual basis.

Teachers as Professionals

John's contribution to the teacher–principal relationship is also reflected in his efforts to find school time for teachers to talk with each other; to encourage them to take up their professional autonomy (e.g., to try out their ideas without checking with him first); to support them in furthering their education; and to protect them from deprofessionalizing, demoralizing scripted programs. The teachers, for their part, act as the professionals they are, showing enormous dedication, putting in extra hours, extending themselves for individuals students and parents, devising new programs and writing grant proposals to have them funded, and taking part whole-heartedly in creating and leading the atypical activities that make up this school-as-community and school-in-community.

The Curriculum

When first asked, teachers and administrators described these activities— the curriculum—as "literature based, inquiry based, and standards based." They said teachers order whatever Spanish literature they want to use; they develop units of study around students' lives and students' questions; and they use Arizona standards for topics of study (although they give these their own "spin"; e.g., the standards require studying ancient civilizations; Valley View teachers have students interview their parents about possible family connections to Aztecs). After some probing, teachers and administrators began to include as "curriculum" the animals, the garden, the wall, and Expeditionary Learning. The fenced-in barnyard near the front of the school began as a 4-H project several years ago. Now, the goat, geese, turkey, and chickens provide teaching material for science; the kindergarteners and first-graders start their day reading to the animals. (Moreover, the community uses the barnyard—and the picnic tables a few feet away, and therefore the school itself—as a destination; on evenings and weekends, people stroll their babies and toddlers to see the animals.) The wall around the garden (two straw bales high, capped with bricks to match the school buildings) was a year-long project for students and adults. The garden itself, tended by students, is an edible garden (Lappé & Lappé, 2003), the harvest used for cooking (with that activity's rich potential for learning). Through Expeditionary Learning, an arm of the Outward Bound program, expeditions are designed around a theme (e.g., migration—of animals, plants, people). The Expeditionary Learning curriculum provides well-integrated thematic units that include extended fieldwork (the expeditions) and community service. Students keep Expeditionary Learning journals about what they are learning and why.

Back to the Learning of a Marked Language

Given this complex program, what might account for the learning of Spanish by non-Spanish speaking students? Why do Spanish speakers take on the Spanish language teaching role? Why do English-speaking students take on the Spanish language learning role? Here are some possible answers. First, daily life at Valley View (in classrooms, the cafeteria, on the playground, walking to the office, weeding the garden, writing a referral for the Responsible Action Center, attending a Fine Arts Evening, etc.) is deliberately intentional and explicitly value laden. Raising the status of Spanish on campus is a deliberate intention, one all adults express frequently. Teachers know and act on the knowledge that they must provide affirmative action on behalf of Spanish on campus as well as off-campus experiences where only Spanish is spoken, creating genuine pressure upon English speakers to use Spanish. Second, a strong sense of "choice" pervades the dual-language immersion program. Teachers chose to work at Valley View because they share John's vision and values. English-speaking students are in the dual-language program because their parents chose it, in some cases making a considerable effort to transport them across boundary lines. These parents strongly desire that their children learn Spanish. Third, interpersonal dynamics engendered by various aspects of the program create feelings of solidarity (for the teachers, it is "we're all in this together"; for learners, it is "we want to be like them [the bilinguals]"). Fourth, all parties give the gift of time. That means "staying with the program," not looking for immediate results.[14] It also means that undertakings (curricular, relational, linguistic) are planned for the long term, requiring intense engagement by all. Quick fixes have no place at Valley View. Fifth, adults are encouraged to think big—to think in terms of a culture of literacy (in which literacy skills are embedded) or a culture of respect (requiring

---

[14]In the two earlier studies, we did not allot that time, instead monitoring learning within 1 school year. But unlike the Valley View case, we saw very few examples of adults or children acting as Spanish language teachers, a few more where children guessed to interact with SH and thus took their part as Spanish language learners. By contrast, when the kindergarten and first-grade dual-language immersion program teachers were hired at Valley View, they were recent immigrants who were just learning English. The eighth-graders in the focus group facilitated by Cristian Aquino remembered their kindergarten year as a time when they tried to teach English to the teacher as well as trying hard to learn to understand her Spanish.

more than a list of behaviors)—to envision making possible what seems impossible. And to take the time to reflect about what those big ideas mean. Sixth, Valley View adults keep their eyes on the ball; there are frequent explicit reminders (in meetings, in conversations) of the vision of that bilingual, diverse, peaceful world and school. While the vision and the values are constants, the practices for living and teaching that vision and those values are wide open, receptive to experimentation and change. Seventh, these six possible reasons combine to produce "trusting relations" (McDermott, 1977) among the parties, wherein each trusts that the other has its best interests at heart, which encourages students to take the teacher's word about what is worth doing.

As I proposed two decades ago, language markedness remains an issue in learning a marked language. It is because Spanish is the marked language that Valley View must undertake so many different kinds of activities to ensure its presence and its value. But the Valley View case shows that, given extraordinary people and sustained, extraordinary efforts, in a concentrated local arena, markedness can be overcome and the marked language can be learned by those who do not "have to."

Chapter **2**

Writing in a Bilingual Program:
It All Depends

> This chapter is the original, with footnotes that
> comment on changed circumstances.

Alone in his own room, sitting at his desk, coffee cup rings on crumpled papers, involved only with self and text. That has been the popular image of the writer in the act of writing. It is only recently that this supposedly universal image has begun to be understood as one that ignores the social nature of writing—the remembered voices and texts that people the writer's room; the historically and culturally conventionalized meanings attached to different kinds of texts and different ways of producing them; the ways women as writers are excluded from, and contradict, such images (see Brodkey, 1987, for a social practice view of academic writing that critiques this image).

In thinking about writing as a social practice (DeCastell & Luke, 1986; Street, 1984) and the new images of writers such a view would entail, an old question gets a new interpretation. From a social practice perspective, the question "How do people write?" is interpreted as: How are ideological and cultural conditions a part of the writing that is done in a society (Brandt, 1989, p. 43)? Of little interest is the older, cognitivist interpretation of the same question: How do individuals do the minute-by-minute work of writing? As Brandt (1989) says, each interpretation underproblematizes the other perspective; the cognitivist perspective ignores the ways minute-by-minute work is socially constituted; the social view takes for granted a "technical ability to produce texts" (p. 43).

But for young children learning to write, that technical ability and knowledge of socially shared conventions cannot be taken for granted.

41

Even while focusing on text production, however, recent research in young children's writing reveals that just as the prevailing asocial/antisocial image of the adult writer is being challenged, so are similar images featuring children learning to write. Dyson (1989) showed young public school pupils relying on each other as they talked and drew their way into text creations. These children figured out genre conventions, spellings, letter formations—the "technical ability to produce texts"—as they played with, and struggled with, what they wanted to say in particular social contexts. Moreover, as they learned and grew as writers, rather than becoming more isolated and creating increasingly decontextualized texts, their writing became more socially embedded.

So the lone child-writer, unfolding as a flower, is clearly a myth. Yet while children's writing is part of a whole constellation of activities that can be considered literacy-as-social-practice, it is also a phenomenon that includes within-the-child activity such as hypothesizing, predicting, planning, and so on. What is especially intriguing is to try to understand the ways this internal activity gets its shape from social forces. Graves (1983), Calkins (1986), Dyson (1989) and others offer rich descriptions of young writers changing in the midst of social influence "on the spot"—through peers and teachers. There has been little investigation, however, of the social influences on young children's writing when that influence emanates from beyond the classroom walls.[1]

A study of children in a bilingual program permitted a glimpse of the wider reaches of this web of social influences—the local community and school district interwoven with teachers' influences on children's writing activity.[2] Unlike the research of Dyson, Graves, and Calkins, this study did not provide rich descriptions of children in the midst of writing. Like the children's writing, our research design was also influenced by that web. In fact, the director of the program and I feared the imminent demise of

---

[1]Since 1989, when this chapter was first written, there has been considerable study of the out-of-school world finding its way into young children's writing. A small sampling can be seen in Comber and Simpson (2001), Dyson (1993a), and Vasquez (2004).

[2]Because certain conditions of interest to educators generally are often exaggerated in bilingual settings (e.g., political pressures on educational activity), research in bilingual education has much to say to all educators (Edelsky & Jilbert, 1985). Moreover, research in bilingual classrooms can sometimes offer a perspective that can make problematic what is often taken for granted in mainstream language arts education. For instance, bilingual classrooms provide instances of children reading a language before they can speak it, which certainly should cast doubt on taken-for-granted sequences of instruction where all the children come to school speaking the language they will learn to read and write. Unfortunately, because of turf- and status-based parochialism, few articles on bilingual education find their way into journals aimed at an audience of mainstream educators or into the citations of authors who write about mainstream education. The mainstream is missing out.

bilingual education in that school district. Thus, we planned the study as a cross-sectional investigation of changes in written products over one school year, rather than as a several year-long observational investigation of the same children in the act of writing. If it didn't describe richly, however, the study did connect what children produced with teachers' beliefs and activities and with events in the school district.

THE STUDY

The study began in 1980 in Duncan School District, a small district in Arizona that served mostly Hispanic migrant and settled migrant farm workers' children.[3] Since most bilingual programs at that time emphasized reading instruction and paid scant attention to writing, they were not good sites for conducting research on writing. But Duncan's Bilingual Program was a rarity. It defined literacy to include both reading and writing and devoted considerable time to both.[4]

A research team selected 26 children (9 first-graders, 9 second-graders, and 8 third-graders) and collected their regular in-class writing (journal

---

[3]By 2004, what was a semirural area in 1980, home to wealthy retirement communities walled in to ensure separation from the shabby housing of settled migrants who worked the surrounding agricultural fields, had become one of the fastest growing suburbs in Maricopa County. Housing developments now cover the old onion fields. The school district has quadrupled in size; the student population has "Whitened."

[4]As I look back, I can see that much of what children did when they put pencil to paper constituted writing exercises produced for either compliance or evaluation rather than writing produced for some other purpose and under the writer's control. In chapter 5, I take pains to distinguish writing exercises from other kinds of writing. Nevertheless, in this chapter, I will refer to the children's work as *writing*, without qualifying it as writing exercises, in order to locate it among other studies of writing and curricular suggestions about writing—even though those studies and suggestions also are mostly about writing exercises. That is, while a few teachers (e.g., Atwell, 1987; Giaccobbe, 1989) refer to "real" writing versus writing exercises when they describe their own classrooms, and while teachers who understand the theoretical underpinnings of an orientation to education called *whole language* are conscious of trying to eliminate exercises and elicit some other kind of writing instead, most researchers do not make that distinction. Thus, writing researchers present pictures as prompts, ask "subjects" to produce a description, and then equate that writing done simply to comply or be analyzed with writing done for some communicative purpose. Or teachers tell children to think of what they might want to persuade someone of, then to think of someone they might want to persuade, and then to produce a persuasive letter—and they call that artificial activity *writing*. In each case, someone other than the writer is in control of the purpose and consequence of what is produced; the activity amounts to instruction for instruction's sake or is enacted only to produce a product to be evaluated in a classroom or a research study. In other words, print has been produced, but through an exercise in writing. Not making the distinction between exercises and nonexercises in this study allows these children's writing to be compared with other instances of what goes on in school and in research studies that were also labeled *writing* but that were most often a very special kind of writing: writing exercises.

entries, letters, stories, reports, etc.) at four times during the school year. Different researchers analyzed the following aspects of the 524 collected pieces: written code switching; spelling; punctuation; segmentation (*habi-aunavez* [*onceuponatime*], *ab re la ven ta na* [o pen the win dow]); quality of the content; signs of a sense of genre; and structural features such as beginnings, endings, and organizational schemes. Pieces produced by children from other classrooms in the bilingual program were collected to augment the systematic analysis. Serendipitously, the year after the study, a third-grade teacher gave the Program Director some of the work done by four of the second-graders we had followed during the study year. This unplanned-for, 2-year picture of 4 children will figure later as I present connections between District activity and children's writing. In addition to collecting pieces of writing, we interviewed teachers and aides, observed in classrooms, gathered a variety of demographic data, and made use of a language situation survey commissioned by the District.

The data were analyzed in three main ways. First, we derived coding categories (e.g., types of segmentation, our inferred bases for spelling inventions, etc.) from the written pieces. Using these codes, we made various comparisons (e.g., English vs. Spanish writing, assigned vs. unassigned writing, first-grade vs. third-grade writing). Second, we kept dated lists (somewhat like Glaser's, 1978, theoretical memos) of insights and hunches about the writing process, acquisition, influences on the writing, and other issues. Third, we deliberately went on a "myth hunt," searching the data for examples that countered prevailing assumptions about language proficiency, bilingualism, biliteracy, written language learning, and so on.

The main purpose of the study was to plot changes in the written products; that is, to study development. Our concept of development was a general movement (with the possibility of regressions and spirals) toward adult norms. Now there are other conceptions of "development." Vygotsky (1978), for example, saw development as change-in-action of some higher order intellectual process (e.g., developing a new way to solve problems). Increased intellectual power-in-the-act, not adult convention, was his sign of development (K. Jilbert, personal communication, January 26, 1989). However, our fears for the Bilingual Program's future, as well as our wish to document the rarity of writing in bilingual education that was more than fill-in-the-blank, led us to design a study of products. Moreover, we quite deliberately wanted to study what was and still is so common in educational research—change over time with "more expert" as the desired result (e.g., "more expert" is the focus of studies of beginning vs. fluent readers, younger vs. older speakers, even novice vs. expert teachers). The 26 target children were selected because their first writing of the school year seemed to represent a range of quality. We wanted the fullest picture possible of abilities and paths of change. Writing from the three nonstudy classrooms further enlarged this picture. Because our writing data—even the data from the same grade—came from different classrooms taught by teachers with different beliefs giving different assignments in the midst of different resources during a time when District events were creating different configurations of power, we were able to relate many of the changes in products to these contextual differences.

THE CONTEXTS

The Bilingual Program: Rhetoric and Reality

Printed material as well as conversations with Program personnel described the Program as having certain features:

- A whole language approach to literacy (K. Goodman & Goodman, 1981)
- Initial reading instruction in Spanish, with the introduction of English reading only after first language reading was well established (or at the end of second grade)
- An emphasis on writing for a variety of purposes to a variety of audiences

I must re-emphasize how unusual such practices were in 1980—a time when "back to the basics" was the only voice getting a wide hearing—and how doubly unusual this was in bilingual education in the southwestern United States, where programs sometimes lived or died by how well (or how poorly, since funding could be cut off if scores were too high) children scored on tests of "the basics."

While this Bilingual Program in 1980 was clearly honoring at least some of the implications from then-new qualitative studies of writing by Graves and his colleagues and was promoting itself rhetorically as a "whole language," "writing process" program before such labels became educational buzzwords, it did not reach its aims. In each classroom, practice was idiosyncratically out of step with rhetoric, and teachers varied on many dimensions (interactional styles, fluency in Spanish, comfort with leaving textbook-bound teaching, etc.). Still, teachers in each of the three study classrooms did the following:

- Allocate a portion of each day for writing
- Carry on Spanish reading instruction through second grade (though the vehicle for that instruction was both Spanish and English)

- Permit children to choose the language they wrote in and read in during non-reading group time (in the reading group, Spanish dominant children were assigned to read in Spanish)
- Establish a journal writing time
- Accept all topics (none were taboo)
- Accept many unconventional forms (e.g. invented spellings or unconventional segments).

But the teachers did not:

- Establish a need or demand for children to interact with a great variety of published whole texts in either Spanish or English. According to F. Smith (1982b), it is wide reading rather than writing that gives access to what is to be learned for writing.
- Publish selected works. Therefore, there was no real need for children to evaluate their own work, no need for content revisions, no need for editing to achieve a conventional final copy.
- Read aloud extensively to children from children's literature written in Spanish. Hearing written language rendered orally is what gives one a feel for its cadence (F. Smith, 1982a).
- Hold conferences in which peers or adults questioned the writer on the meaning of a text in order to help children anticipate readers' needs in relation to writers' intents.

THE COMMUNITIES: POLITICAL GROUNDS FOR BILINGUAL PROGRAMS

In the same year we were gathering children's writing, opposing forces within the district were gathering momentum. Duncan District's voters comprised three distinct communities: farm workers, ranch owners, and well-to-do retirees. With her membership in multiple overlapping networks, the Bilingual Program Director had managed over the years to develop ties of affection and loyalty with the farm workers' community. Through years of one-to-one lobbying, she had encouraged the Hispanic parents to increase their participation in Bilingual Program activity. By 1980, the farm worker parents were solidly in support of bilingual education. However, they were uninformed about any new curricula, preferring the traditional one they themselves or their older children had failed at or dropped out of.

The ranching and retirement communities did not enter into discussions over curriculum in the Duncan Bilingual Program because they were still arguing about whether there should be a bilingual program at all. And their answer was a resounding "no."[5] They were joined in their opposition by some of the local clergy (one minister warned that bilingual education was the devil's idea) and were rebutted by others (a rural priest praised it).

The divisions over bilingual education had ended, on the surface at least, in the Arizona legislature and the State Department of Education, both of which met just a few miles from Duncan District. Though there were both private opponents and private proponents of even stronger bilingual programs (e.g., programs that would maintain both languages as vehicles of instruction without phasing one out), official policy favored limited transitional bilingual education as a way to get children into an English curriculum as quickly as possible. The state also took a position on curriculum. In this case, their stance was opposite to the direction in which the Bilingual Program Director was moving. Beginning in the mid-1970s, legislative and state agency actions mandating certain materials and kinds of evaluation (of both teachers and students) were pressuring teachers to avoid stepping outside the separate "basic skills" path.

While Duncan District administrators had given everything from grudging acceptance to public support for the idea of bilingual education, and while they showed off writing samples with pride, they often disapproved of teaching that failed to emphasize drills on skills. The Bilingual Program Director, as noted, had a different view of literacy and of education in general. She was designated in charge of the federal monies that funded the Program, which enabled her to hire Program teachers and to determine the Program's in-service education. The key factor allowing the Director to maintain her power within the Program—to make her view "stick" rhetorically and officially—and preventing the principals in the Program schools from forcing the Program to operate according to their own opposing views was the support the Director received from the highest Duncan District administrator, the Superintendent.

A few months before our study began, the Bilingual Program parents (with the help of some retirement community members who wanted to be released from obligations to pay school taxes) organized a petition drive for a special election to redraw District boundaries and exclude the retirement community. During our study year, that election was held and the boundary lines were redrawn, ensuring majority support for continuation of bilingual education. Concurrently, the Arizona legislature and the State Department of Education established a program (in English) to test students' skills to ensure teacher accountability, based on the premise that good teaching requires the instruction of separate skills. The Bilingual

---

[5]The ranch owners and retirees who, in the 1980s, had opposed bilingual education in their own small school district, were solidly behind Proposition 203 twenty years later, to make bilingual education largely illegal in the entire state of Arizona.

Program Director, therefore, spent considerable time reassuring teachers that since she was the one to make personnel decisions about Program teachers, their evaluations and tenure would not be tied to student scores on English language tests. In the meantime, throughout the year, at school building level meetings (to which the Bilingual Program Director was not invited), principals kept contradicting the Director, reiterating the importance of high scores on these tests.

Now, all of this was also taking place at the start of the Reagan years, when right-wing forces would undo past civil rights victories; widen economic disparities; and be increasingly successful in pushing policies for a return to a mythological golden age of harmonious (patriarchal) families, calm (small town, White, Protestant) communities, and respectful and patriotic (obedient, unquestioning) citizens.[6] That larger context must be acknowledged; it certainly had widespread effects over the decade of the 1980s on funding for schools, possibilities for programs, and the very curricular and evaluation emphases that were taking hold in Duncan District. But to connect that larger national climate in the academic year 1980–1981 with writing in this Bilingual Program would require a different analysis and additional data. Therefore, I will simply remind readers of this larger context, but I will set contextual borders in the greater Phoenix area.

CONNECTIONS BETWEEN WRITING AND CONTEXTS

As I said earlier, this study was not designed to show definitive relationships between specific features of texts and classroom, Program, or community contexts. Nor was it designed to reveal exactly how (by what mechanisms) text–context ties were established. Nevertheless, even if we do not understand exactly how it happened, features of children's writing at any one time, analyses of writing over time, and classroom or District-wide goings-on seemed closely connected. Some of these connections were direct and intended; that is, by means of certain policies, purchases, materials, room arrangements, uses of print, assignments, and responses to writing or writers,

---

[6]The wider context has changed again in the United States. The late 1980s were bad for bilingual education. Bilingual programs not only lost financial and "moral" support (Crawford, 1987); they found themselves in a climate in which outrageous proposals for legislating "English only" became reasonable topics for discussion and in which such proposals actually won as referendum items in state elections. With increasing frequency, school programs were offered that should have been characterized as English as a Second Language but were called *bilingual education*. If Duncan District's bilingual program, with its insistence on holding off literacy instruction in English, was unusual in 1980, it may well have been nonexistent a few years later. Indeed, by 2004 in Arizona, except for "dual language" programs that were permitted to serve only those students who already spoke English, bilingual education had been outlawed through ballot Proposition 203.

various people intended to have an impact on a particular aspect of the children's writing. Other connections were indirect. Sometimes a teacher or policymaker would be either unaware of the effect of a particular action or intended to have only the most general effect (e.g. "to make children want to write").

DIRECT INFLUENCES ON CHILDREN'S WRITING

Assignments

Teachers' assignments—shaped by their own beliefs about writing and learning to write, their sense of obligation to state policies, their responses to pressure from principals and counterpressure from the Bilingual Program Director—had a direct impact on the genres children wrote. At the beginning of the year, when Ms. D., the first-grade teacher in our study, thought children could only write their names, she only assigned "signed" drawings, so their own names were all the children wrote officially. When she thought they could write journal entries, they wrote journal entries. By spring, she saw the children as competent writers, and she assigned and received letters, stories, journals, and expository pieces. Third-graders, whose range of assignments remained constant throughout the year, appeared not to "grow" in the genres they tackled.

Material Environment

The planned environment also had its intended effects. In mid-winter, Ms. D "took the lid off" and set up a Writing Center, stocked with many kinds of paper and writing implements, intending for children to want to write more, about a wider range of topics, and with "more feeling." The Writing Center had just that effect (as well as others to be described later). Writing produced at the Center was more often about home and community topics. Moreover, the same child often exhibited a strikingly more poetic style in writing done at the Center. Example 1 is Writing Center writing from late February. Example 2 is a journal entry written by the same child 1 week earlier.

1. Todos los días cae nieve en todas las partes y también caía lluvia en todas las partes. Y un señor se robó y la policía iba. La policía agarría al señor y lo llevó a la cárcel y allí se estuvo todos los días. Era cuando estaba cayendo nieve.[7]

---

[7]Except where spelling is the point being discussed, all examples of children's writing have been rewritten with conventional spelling.

(Every day snow fell everywhere and also rain was falling everywhere. And a man robbed and the police came. The police grabbed the man and took him to jail and there he remained forever. It was when the snow was falling.)

2. Hoy es martes. Hicimos muchos reportes.
(Today is Tuesday. We made a lot of reports.)

In one of the nonstudy second-grade classrooms, the teacher had set up mailboxes and had given the children considerable freedom to write letters to others whenever they wanted to. This resource, Mr. M. told us, was intended to get the children to become more involved with, and to expand, their audiences. Actually, the mailboxes did little to expand audiences since the children preferred writing to, and receiving answers from, their teacher or aide rather than peers, but it did increase the ways in which children related to their audiences in writing. The excerpted letters in Example 3 consist of genuine complaints, apologies, excuses, queries, and threats; rarely was writing from the other classes used for any of these purposes.

3. Querido Mr. M.,

¿Quíenes son las señoras que vinieron y yo he vista a la Sra. que tenía anteojos en la tienda …
(Dear Mr M.,
Who are the women who came and I have seen the woman with glasses at the store …)
Mr M.,
Se me olvidó decirle mi perro tiene 6 dedos y no estoy diciendo mentiras …
(Mr M.,
I forgot to tell you my dog has 6 toes and I'm not telling lies …)
Querido Mr. M.,
¿Porqué no me ha mandado mi carta? Dígame en la carta cuando me va a mandar la carta porque si no me dice yo me voy a enojar con Ud …
(Dear Mr. M.,
Why haven't you sent me my letter? Tell me in the letter when you're going to send the letter because if you don't tell me I'm going to get angry with you …)

Genre

For different reasons, writing by the second-grade children in the study classroom also showed more involvement with the reader than did the writing of first- and third-graders in the study. Ms. C. did not set up mailboxes but, as a way to promote opportunities for writing and as a way to promote the image of the Bilingual Program to administrators whose support was in question, she had children writing frequent letters to administrators—birthday letters, get-well letters, glad-you're-back letters, thank you letters, come-and-see-us-letters, and the like. With so much opportunity for children to address a reader directly and to compare the reader's condition with the writer's (… y yo estaba mala también y me dieron medicina y me alivié … /I was sick too and they gave me medicine and I got better …), it is no wonder that involvement with the reader seemed to be a characteristic of second-grade writing.

Manifest Curriculum

The District had mandated a general curriculum guide as well as a listing and allocation by grade level of language arts skills (e.g. "knows third person singular verb endings," "uses '-er' and '-est' appropriately"). The Bilingual Program Director had convinced the superintendent to exempt Program teachers from having to teach the separate, sequenced list of language arts skills because, she argued, this list was based on English. (As usual, she was able to win such an argument in 1980–1981 by appealing to language bias but not by arguing that the underlying conception of language and literacy was in error.) While the Bilingual Program teachers did not have to teach the list of (English) language arts skills, they did have to—and they wanted to—follow the general curriculum guide. That meant, for example, teaching cursive handwriting in third grade.

Not surprisingly, the manifest curriculum (i.e., that which was explicitly taught) showed up in children's writing, especially in their handwriting and spelling. Third-graders learned to use cursive by midway through the year, though a small percentage of all writing (including that done by first-graders) contained connected script in advance of instruction. Since all the teachers believed that spelling in Spanish was primarily a matter of mapping sound onto letters, they advised children to "sound it out," and they taught phonics lessons about letters that "make the same sound." Thus, children learned that *ll* and *y*, *b* and *v*, *h* and no-*h*, *y* and *i* could be decoded the same way. Their writing reflected that information. Not only did we find *llo* and *io* for *yo* (I), *abia* and *habia* for *había* (there was), *vien* and *bien* for *bien* (well), but when they "sounded it out," the extra glides they produced were also spelled with these equivalents—*maeystra* and *mallestra* for *maestra* (teacher).

Teachers' Idiosyncratic Preferences

Teachers' preferences directly affected what children wrote. Through February, Ms. C. thought long (20+ pages) pieces were a sign of quality. The children gave her what she wanted, leaving empty spaces, making oversized letters, repeating ideas and single words (*bien bien bien bien triste/very very very very sad*). A member of the research team pointed out to Ms. C. that quality was being sacrificed for length. Two months later, in an interview, Ms. C. said she was starting to think that children could do "too much writing." By April, her students no longer produced 20+ page pieces with outsized handwriting, big spaces, and repeated words; their pieces were considerably shorter and contained little or no evidence that the writer was trying to extend the length.

INDIRECT INFLUENCES ON CHILDREN'S WRITING

Assignments, environmental resources, the manifest curriculum, and teachers' values also had unintended effects on particular features of children's writing. So did the political activity within the District. Assignments became more sophisticated toward the end of the year (in the first grade, the progression was from journal entries and signatures at the beginning to stories at the end; in second grade, at the end of the year only, children wrote in "shape books"; for example, all pages cut in the shape of bones for writing a story about magic bones). And the quality of writing at the end of the year was judged better by raters—more insightful, more organized, more creative.

Assignments

The teachers had not intended for their assignments to have an effect on the organizational structure of writing, but they did. Many children organized their pieces according to a chronologic order (first, then). But first- and second-graders also used an organizational principle we called "big shift," in which there was a sudden switch in topic or function. No third grader made use of "big shift," but probably not because they had simply "outgrown" such behavior. The first- and second-grade teachers sometimes gave assignments that can only be described as "motley genres" (e.g., write a letter to the Program Director [letter], tell her about the Creek Indians [report], and invite her to the class party [invitation]). Third grade assignments were not of this type; therefore, third-graders did not have "big shifts" in their writing.

Material Environment; Assigned or Unassigned

The same resource that was intended to, and did, encourage more writing and a greater range of topics also yielded several unintended effects. The teacher placed colored markers at the Writing Center to generate interest.

The markers also generated color-loaded topics with pieces about colorful objects, lettered with the appropriate pen (*rojo* with red, *azul* with blue, etc.). When these first-graders wrote what they wanted to at the Center, unassigned, they used no punctuation at all. On assigned pieces, they invented punctuation, most of it based on units of paper (e.g. a capital to start every page, a period to end each line, etc.) (Edelsky, 1983). But children did not write multiple-page pieces on the large sheets of paper at the Writing Center, so there were no inventions such as a period to end each page. Since the paper was unlined, neither were there line-based punctuation inventions in unassigned first grade writing.

Teacher Control Over Writing

Two nonstudy first-grade teachers offer an interesting contrast. One was most anxious to comply with the Director's wishes that children should write. She once indicated she was certain that children should be taught to read in a structured fashion, but she had no training in teaching children how to write. The other teacher believed children had to be able to "decode" phonetically in order to read and to spell in order to write. Her principal's warnings about the need for high scores on tests of phonics and decoding may well have strengthened these beliefs. Each of these teachers exerted very different kinds of control over writing time. The first teacher exercised minimal control. Since writing was the one "subject" she did not know how to teach, she simply told children it was time to write, and then she kept order during that time. As the year went on, the second teacher controlled what letters, then what words, then what sentences the children would write. By the end of the year, children in the first classroom were writing jokes, stories, notes, song lyrics, and grocery lists. When the children in the second classroom had "free writing time," they produced pieces resembling disconnected phonics worksheets:

4. Es un carro. El niño no iba. La casa de mamá. El carro de papá. Tony iba a su casa. Mamá ama a papá. Es una niña. Es una mamá.
(It's a car. The child didn't go. Mama's house. Papa's car. Tony was going home. Mama loves Papa. It's a girl. It's a mama.)

It is not only that the unintended consequence of the year-long differences in children having control versus being controlled showed up in what genres the children wrote. The genre represented by Example 4 as contrasted with jokes and stories reveals certain notions of "text-ness." Children in the first classroom were learning that texts produced in school can (should?) be coherent; children in the second classroom were learning that they often are not.

Print Environment

The print environment both inside and outside the classroom is a critical resource for learning where writing is used in a particular community, what it is used for, and how it works. Though the teachers may have brought print into classrooms to instruct children in literacy, shopkeepers, parents, and others who brought the great variety of print into this District did not do so to show children how to spell or to teach them which language to use when writing. Even the teachers often used print for something besides instructing. But all the print—whether worksheet exercises meant to instruct or print on cereal boxes meant to increase sales—instructed anyway. In this district, one of the lessons coming from the print environment was that written code-switching rarely appeared. There were even more subtle lessons on code-switching to be derived from contrasts between the Spanish and English print resources. Even though the first and second grades did not offer reading instruction in English, each classroom contained more English than Spanish print. That disparity was repeated outside the classroom. Moreover, of all the printed material in the classrooms, more of the Spanish print was homemade (teacher-made posters, worksheet, labels, children's writing), while English print was overwhelmingly commercially produced. Spanish print, thus, could well have looked informal while English print may have looked authoritative and, to children growing up in a print-saturated popular culture, more "real."

The children in this study switched very frequently between English and Spanish in their speech, and they did so both between sentences and within sentences. However, they rarely code-switched in writing. If they did, it was only within the sentence (which, by the way, is an intriguing bit of counterevidence to those who maintain that poor bilingual children have a language deficit since "they don't know English and they don't know Spanish either"). If they code-switched at all in writing, it was usually in Spanish texts, and it was referentially inspired (e.g., nouns, adjectives, verbs, and address terms). The use of a Spanish word in an English text, however, was four times more rare. If it occurred at all, it was more like a slip of the pen; an article or a conjunction (not a noun or verb packed with referential meaning). It was as if something the children knew in both English and Spanish would "slip out" in Spanish but would quickly be brought into check (… *y es fun, thank you* or *el dinosaur is gonna be* …). Code-switching inside Spanish texts thus seemed more deliberate (or at least more semantically motivated); code-switching inside English texts seemed accidental—something to be avoided. It was as though these children saw written English, the language that had stronger associations with powerful sociocultural domains like the educational establishment, commercial publishing, and the like, as a language that could not so easily be appropriated for their own voices—as a language one had to be careful of, a language that would not be hospitable to a "stranger" in its midst.

Changes in Administration

The most drastic indirect influence from the goings-on in the District became noticeable a year after the study was over. As I said earlier, during our study year (1980–1981), as a result of a special election instigated by the Bilingual Program parents, new District boundary lines had been drawn. The new majority elected a new school board whose members showed only lukewarm confidence in the superintendent. Even though he had been a strong supporter of the Bilingual Program, the superintendent's ties with the retirement community were not so easily forgiven. As he lost favor, so did those associated with him (crucially, the Bilingual Program Director). During the next school year, it became increasingly clear that his contract would not be renewed. In that 1981–1982 school year, then, with an apparently lame duck superintendent, principals were able to overrule the Bilingual Program Director in hiring teachers for the Bilingual Program and in deciding on the substance of in-service education for Bilingual Program teachers. They were also coming closer to winning their demand that the Bilingual Program should teach lists of separate English language arts skills and should evaluate teachers on the basis of children's scores on standardized tests in English. The Bilingual Program Director could no longer protect the teachers or ensure that the Program would keep moving, albeit at a snail's pace, in a holistic direction.[8]

During that school year, a third-grade teacher saved children's writing and gave it to the Bilingual Program Director. In the batch was the output produced by four of the children who had been part of the study when they were in second grade. It is most instructive to look at the writing of those four children over 2 years while keeping in mind the events in the District. There were some changes in spelling and punctuation conventions and a switch to cursive handwriting, but little change in content. Almost all of the pieces seemed to be perfunctory compliances with assignments, offering "acceptable" responses to the teacher's topics. There was no evidence of the use of writing in new genres for new purposes or new audiences or with new rhetorical means. Where were the touted benefits of writing as a way of learning, the benefits that were to come from using written language to

---

[8]In 1982, the superintendent was replaced. In 1983, the Bilingual Program Director's contract was not renewed. The new Program Director had been a high school foreign language teacher; one of her first acts was to order phonics and grammar workbooks for all Bilingual Program classrooms. The days of writing in the Bilingual Program were over.

explore new ideas and find the limits of (or make new connections between) old ideas? Were the children actually using writing for such purposes?

It should come as no surprise, given the turn of events in the District office, that the answer is no. During their third-grade year, more time was spent on basal readers, more importance attached to spelling and punctuation through direct instruction with worksheets and in evaluation of their narrative output and less importance to making sense or having an impact on a reader. No wonder the children seemed to have turned their attention so completely to matters of form.

To be fair, I must reiterate that this 1981–1982 school year does not stand in complete contrast to the preceding year. It is not that all the teachers in 1980–1981 were helping children write for their own purposes or that they were causing them to reflect on and revise their writing. In that study year, too, the children were often merely complying superficially with an assignment. The difference is that in that year, ambivalence was in the air. Both protected and goaded by the Program Director, the teachers were trying to get beyond exercises—and that showed in the children's experimentation with genres, spelling, handwriting, and rhetorical devices. A year later, to accommodate shifting political (and therefore curricular and evaluational) winds, the teachers were embracing exercises—a stance reflected as much in what was missing from children's writing as in what was there.

ANOTHER LOOK AT WRITING DEVELOPMENT

We went into this study assuming that change would certainly occur over time and that these changes would be evidence of development. Though we expected the changes to vary with external conditions, we still imagined that development was somehow a property or activity of the child. Yet the many examples we saw of the way teachers, administrators, and legislators influenced the children's writing put that image into question. People with positivist leanings and those wedded to looking at development from the standpoint of the lone individual would say there was nothing wrong with thinking of development in this way, that the problem was our research design. A different study, one in which conditions are controlled so that variables like assignments, resources, and the like would be held constant, would make "development" unproblematic by sorting out the impact of assignments, teachers' beliefs, and so on, from the developmental activity the child would have been engaged in without such contextual influences.

Such a solution is no solution, however. In the first place, it would be impossible to control everything involved—from subtleties of teachers' beliefs to children's perceptions of the task and definitions of the situation to children's motives and purposes (according to activity theorists like Leont'ev [Minick, 1985], if motives change, the activity changes). More importantly, in the second place, stripping away (and thereby controlling for) context not only does violence to writing; it distorts human activity in general. As Bateson (1972) said of language, we erroneously think of utterances (or other human endeavor) in a context, as though the talk or the activity were a dependent variable and the context were the independent variable. But the talk or activity is actually part of an ecological system (the context), not just what remains after the background is removed; nor is the background what is left after the talk or behavior is cut away. Writing always happens in messy, nonreproducible contexts. If we want to study it, we have to study that messy, context-dependent practice, not some neatened-up substitute.

The evidence presented here shows something of writing's context dependence and, therefore, of the context dependence of writing development. However, I do not want to imply that writing and writers do not change, that these children did not "develop" at all, that they simply responded to different demands, made use of different resources, were receptive to different pressures and preferences. Such a message misleads on two accounts:

1. It makes the children look like mere passive responders.
2. It renders invisible their more progressive changes in writing.

First, children were not only surrounded by multiple literacy practices; they were themselves agents in those practices. And their "practicings" concerned both the social uses of writing as well as writing as a tool (a system that works to do other work). In fact, it is in regard to writing as a tool—how it works, what its parts are like, and how they fit with different social uses—that we have the most obvious evidence that something highly active was going on within the child.

Children must have been actively creating new hypotheses to invent stable unconventional spellings, punctuation patterns, and segments. By extension, it is likely they were also hypothesizing about minute details of all that goes into creating a text in a context within a context within a context within a context. That is, no matter what close-in or far-off (and then brought close in) conditions influenced the children's writing, children had to be actively construing those conditions (or their consequences) in order to include them within the hypotheses they made. Given the vast number of possible hypotheses, the narrow range that was actually displayed (along with the fact that we could make sense of them and infer their logic) shows that children must have been not only actively creating as individuals, but creating based on a socially constituted model.

While these socially constrained hypotheses changed depending on assignments, resources, teachers' values, principals' demands, state agency edicts, and District politics, many of those changes showed progress. That is, over time or under particular conditions, the children's writing did become more like adult writing. For example, while at first children segmented unconventionally by chunking together major syntactic units (whole sentences, entire noun phrases, entire verb phrases) or by separating into syllables, later on they wrote in single words and only chunked more minor units (e.g., prepositional phrases). Earlier hypotheses about spelling seemed to be based on phonetic features and manner and place of articulation and some unknown features. Later hypotheses were more "literate" (i.e., based on phonics generalizations and knowledge of orthographic conventions such as the silent *e* in English). The earliest invented punctuation marked units of paper (e.g., periods to end each line, capitals to begin each page). Later inventions were related to units of text (e.g., a capital to start and a period to end an entire story). Later-in-the-year writing, the writing of older children, and unassigned writing was also evaluated by raters as having higher quality content.[9]

I am not saying, then, that there was no development (though I have no evidence or explanation to offer on just how that development occurred). There were indeed these general trends in the direction of adult norms. Yet to understand even this common and elementary conception of development focusing on mere residues of past development (as Vygotsky criticizes), it is necessary to think of the person in a new way. We cannot simply envision a meaning-making, hypothesizing, predicting, planning, strategizing being; we have to envision a person who never hypothesizes, predicts, plans outside of contexts. Even if we drop the idea of "development" altogether and think instead only of changes in children's writing, the same requirement would pertain. The various interwoven socio-politico-historical contexts children live through are the contexts that show them what writing is, the contexts through which they write, the contexts they change (in).

---

[9]In an important sense, however, the general trends are misleading. Each child followed a unique path toward adult-like writing. One became more conventional steadily in all aspects; one seemed to make no improvement but then took leaps in both content and form; another improved at first and then regressed. Yet another adopted more conventions in content but not form; for another, it was the reverse. One of the second-graders, whose writing we had also obtained from his third-grade teacher, abandoned his highly unconventional way of segmenting and also the totally conventional spellings he had used for 2 years in favor of not only unconventional but also less literate spellings (he reverted to phonetic-based rather than phonics-based inventions, but only for two sounds: /s/ and /y/). As D. Taylor (1989) argued, there may be predictable global patterns, but local individual patterns are unpredictable.

Chapter **3**

Contextual Complexities: Written Language Policies for Bilingual Programs

> This chapter begins with a new prologue and is followed by the original chapter. The original version of this chapter was coauthored with Sarah Hudelson.

PROLOGUE

Maybe we were naïve. Or maybe we didn't understand the reach of our own central point in the original version of this chapter (Edelsky & Hudelson, 1989); that is, that contexts are complexly layered and intricately variable— from place to place and also from time to time. In either case, our advice to teachers, researchers, and scholars of language education who we thought would influence policymakers (at least we were not so naïve as to believe we were writing for policymakers themselves) was crafted with several assumptions that have not withstood the passage of time. Maybe they were also questionable back then, but certainly by now it is clear that they are sadly out of touch with events and also with recent analyses. For one thing, we assumed the continued official existence of bilingual education and, therefore, the existence of Directors of Bilingual Education in school districts throughout the United States. For another, we believed written language policies were based on research and reasoned argument. Third, we assumed that our audience (scholar–teachers) could influence policymakers. We were wrong to take bilingual education's existence for granted. And we were wrong to see research and knowledge about written language as the grounds for literacy education policy. I'll come back to the third assumption shortly.

A major new analysis of educational policy by Mary Lee Smith (2004) not only undermines our second assumption about the rationality of language policy but also helps us understand how our first assumption—taking for granted the existence of bilingual education—could be shattered. Smith used Murray Edelman's (1985, 1988) theoretical metaphor of *policy as political spectacle* as a lens for looking at several educational policies. Edelman had proposed that in eras dominated by a degenerate form of politics, policymaking becomes a political spectacle. During such times, a small group "contends over real goods behind the scenes," constructing policies that make policymakers look like they are "doing something" and creating symbols to gain the public's approval. Meanwhile, the public acts as spectators, reacting to these symbols but excluded from the behind-the-scenes, material exchanges (M. L. Smith, 2004, p. viii). Smith brilliantly documents how policies regarding high-stakes testing, school choice, desegregation, reading, and school reform (the No Child Left Behind [NCLB] legislation) were created through the elements of political spectacle: symbolic language, political actors cast as allies or enemies in a storyline or plot, political stages and props, democratic participation as a sham, the illusion of rationality, disconnections between means and ends, and disconnections between onstage and backstage actions (Wright, 2005b).

Written language education and bilingual education—the dual focus of this chapter—have had the misfortune to be spotlighted in several such theatrics. Federal reading policy—the Reading Excellence Act that became Reading First and was folded into the NCLB legislation—bears all the markings of political spectacle (M. L. Smith, 2004). It has plot (the Reading Wars), tension (threats of illiteracy and failing schools), and symbolic language ("science," "research," "phonics first"). It has intrigue and largely hidden strategies (e.g., conflicting "scientific" reports created with the help of hidden conflicts of interest).[1] And it has a public willing to act

---

[1]The lengthy Report of the National Reading Panel stating "there were insufficient data to draw any conclusions about the effects of phonics instruction with normally developing readers above first grade" (Garan, 2001, p. 506, citing the Report) was accompanied by a Summary. The Summary, which contradicted the full Report ("systematic phonics instruction produces significant benefits for students in kindergarten through sixth grade"; Garan, 2001, p. 506, citing the Summary) was what was disseminated widely and what was used as the justification for policy. The Summary was written by the National Institutes of Child Health and Development and Widmeyer Communications, a public relations firm. Both the National Institutes of Child Health and Development and Widmeyer had ties to a major educational publisher (McGraw-Hill) and to the Business Roundtable (M. L. Smith, 2004). McGraw-Hill and the Business Roundtable benefit from research showing that phonics "wins." This victory for phonics, in its overstated form in the Summary and also in the more restrained version in the larger Report has been hotly contested—from the accuracy of its meta-analysis (Camilli, Vargas, & Yurecko, 2003) to its definition of reading (Coles, 2003b; Garan, 2002) to the categories it used and its working procedures (Yatvin, 2002) to the original research studies it relied on (Coles, 2003b) to the political commissioning of the panel and the use of its conclusions (Allington, 2002; K. Goodman, Goodman, Shannon, & Rapaport, 2004).

as cheerleading spectators, manipulated by media owned by corporations that belong to the same Business Roundtable that has been mounting an increasingly successful campaign to undermine public education (Altwerger & Strauss, 2002).

Bilingual education stars in a similar policy drama, except that, for the last 30 years (after the 1974 Supreme Court's ruling in *Lau v. Nichols*) it has played at state venues rather than on the national stage. There are the concocted actors (a bilingual establishment, mad-as-hell voters, a gridlocked tax-supported system, narrow special interest groups, a few professionals making fortunes off the backs of children; Crawford, 2000b). There are plots (a boycott [orchestrated, it turns out, by an opponent of bilingual education] by immigrant parents in California who claimed their children were being prevented from learning English because of bilingual education, a similar story in Arizona about bilingual education violating immigrant children's right to learn English [Wright, 2005b]) and culturally available storylines that lend themselves to media "reportage by template" (e.g., "stubborn bureaucrats defend narrow self-interest" and "well-intentioned social program fails to work as promised"; Crawford, 2000b, p. 34). There is a disconnection between what happens onstage (the altruistic selling of the proposal) and what happens backstage (both the staging and the deals).[2] There are charged symbols (English for the Children, "the right to learn English") as well as a symbolic crisis (immigrant students not learning English, as evidenced by the annual rate of 97% of Limited English Proficient students failing to be reclassified as proficient English speakers; like all language panics, this one is not in fact about language but rather is about race; Hill, 2000).[3] There is the illusion of rationality by means of

---

[2]On center stage was a seemingly altruistic ballot initiative to provide English for "English-deprived" immigrant children in California, Arizona, Massachusetts, and Colorado by requiring a year of Structured English Immersion (SEI) instead of any form of bilingual education. Backstage was a California multimillionaire, Ron Unz, with aspirations to political office, who, in an unsuccessful prior campaign vowed to roll back gains from the 1960s in social programs and civil rights, and in the campaigns for these ballot propositions enlisted local Hispanic English Only proponents to create the illusion of grassroots efforts. Also backstage was a candidate for an elected state education position in Arizona who gave high level appointments to a few who campaigned for the ballot proposition as well as the candidate (Crawford, 2000b; Wright, 2005b). The "altruism" of what was onstage was not sufficiently dimmed by the shenanigans backstage; only Colorado rejected the ballot proposition.

[3]Prior to these ballot propositions, only 30% of ELLs received any form of bilingual education. Thus, the fact that each year 97% failed to achieve the status of proficient English speaker should be blamed on English-only instruction, just what was called for by the ballot initiatives. More adequate evidence about English language learning from studies of language shift show that Anglicization is proceeding more quickly among new immigrants to the United States than old, with the shift to English taking only two generations instead of the older pattern of three (Crawford, 2000a). Moreover, as Hill (2000) proposed, when discourse about technical matters regarding language (e.g., teaching techniques, language of instruction,

statistics, research evidence, and a provision adding seeming flexibility to the propositions.[4] This illusion is intensified by conventions of political reporting wherein unsupported charges by the Unz campaign and the comments of "vested interests" (i.e., researchers and professionals) are given equal credence in the media (although not equal space or time) in the spirit of "let the best sound bite win" (Crawford, 2000b, p. 35). And there is the public—spectators again—being treated to theatrical displays such as the State of Education Address staged by Arizona Superintendent Tom Horne, upholder of Proposition 203; this particular display was enhanced with patriotic, militaristic symbols (e.g., a full military style presentation of the colors, the Pledge of Allegiance led by a local high school Reserve Officers Training Corps group, singing of the national anthem, and a performance of "Proud to be an American" by fourth-graders' Wright, 2005b).[5]

In the aftermath of these propositions, bilingual education has been drastically—and officially—curtailed in Arizona, California, and Massachusetts; in other states, bilingual education has both the pressures

---

dialect diversity) intensifies and quickly spreads across the United States, and when that discourse disdains professional information but falls back on common sense (imagine, by contrast, discussions of global warming that bypass information from climatologists in favor of anecdotes and folk wisdom), the ensuing panic about language is actually a cover for anxiety about race. The hysteria over the "problems" of Ebonics (but not nonstandard varieties of English spoken by Whites) and of ELLs who are largely brown-skinned Latinos is a glaring example of how language panics are enlisted to racialize people and then provide the focus of policies that deny resources to those so racialized.

[4]Statistics on test scores of ELLs provide the aura of science—except that the rise in scores for ELLs attributed to the passage of Proposition 227 in California was matched by a rise in scores for non-ELLs; the gap between ELLs and non-ELLs remained constant. The rise was most likely related to a co-occurring dramatic decrease in class size rather than any effect of Proposition 227 (Wright, 2005a). A "fact" supported by "science" and by common sense was put forth about young children learning second languages quickly—except that a large body of research shows that children who do not become literate in their first language have more trouble with literacy in their second language (August & Hakuta, 1997). A study was offered as proof of the ineffectiveness of bilingual education—except that this one study had design flaws that even the author acknowledged, while well-designed studies show that bilingual education is more effective than English as a second language or structured English immersion at increasing English language test scores of academic achievement (Mahoney, Thompson, & MacSwan, 2004). The propositions were presented as permitting flexibility through waivers—except that each subsequent proposition increasingly tightened the "loophole" of waivers (Wright, 2005a).

[5]One of many similar theatrics staged for federal reading policy took place in Albuquerque, New Mexico at a rally for Reading First, replete with the Pledge of Allegiance, patriotic songs, and a military band. In his remarks at the rally, Secretary of Education Rod Paige equated support of Reading First with loyalty to the United States and fighting terrorism (Meyer, 2004). Ah, the power of a literacy policy!

from NCLB weakening it at the moment as well as the threat from Unz still (in 2005) looming on the horizon. Clearly, our assumptions about the continuous (and growing, even if troubled) existence of bilingual education were wrong, as was our belief in reason and research as the basis for written language policy in bilingual settings. But these were not separate errors. Policymaking as political spectacle and its breeding ground of degenerate politics (a time when democratic processes become a sham [Edelman, 1988] and when less effective public participation leads to less commitment to democracy, and vice versa, in an antidemocratic dynamic that picks up momentum over time [Bowles & Gintis, 1986]) are implicated in the ballot assaults on bilingual education. Degenerate politics and policy-as-spectacle also help explain policy regarding reading education.

This chapter, however, emphasizes literacy—both reading and writing. Now the distinction between reading and writing may be blurred for literacy professionals, but for policy makers the two are separate—and, fortunately for writing, unequal. It is reading that receives most of the attention by the public and by policymakers; it is reading that is invested with more symbolic and moral meaning (e.g., literacy campaigns are about reading, not writing; media messages tying criminality and illiteracy refer to reading, not writing); it is reading that earns huge corporate profits from instructional materials and assessment instruments. Nevertheless, even though writing enjoys relatively more freedom from oversight and control by policymakers, high-stakes tests may indirectly subject writing, too, to policy mandates that bypass professional knowledge.[6] Even in the rare cases when a policy about writing instruction is based on solid theoretical grounds (e.g., the Teachers College Reading and Writing Project's program, written by Lucy Calkins and her colleagues, and mandated for about 400 New York City public schools), the fact of imposition by a mandate may well change the character of what is mandated.

Recent policies concerning written language, language of instruction, and high-stakes testing (and others not as pertinent to the focus of this chapter) are wrong-headed and need to be changed (see Amrein & Berliner, 2002a; Coles, 2003a; Crawford, 2000a; Gonzales, 2000; M. L. Smith, 2004). So does the degenerate political situation that breeds such policies. To make these changes, popular struggle will be required. And that is where our third assumption enters the picture. In presenting the policy

---

[6]High-stakes tests, put in place through policymaking as political spectacle (M. L. Smith, 2004), have been criticized on many grounds by professional research and measurement organizations (Amrein & Berliner, 2002b; Mahoney et al., 2004; M. L. Smith, 2004). And there is considerable evidence that forcing ELLs to become literate in their second rather than first language imposes additional difficulties on the learners (August & Hakuta, 1997).

advice below, Hudelson and I assumed that our audience—teacher-scholars—could directly influence policy makers (through reasoned argument, for instance). We were wrong; political spectacle makes such direct influence highly unlikely. But teacher-scholar activists can influence the shape and direction of popular struggles against the latest rash of damaging language policies, and those struggles can in turn influence policymakers and other politicians. In that spirit, I offer suggestions on two aspects of such struggles: some brief comments about tactics and the original chapter that concerns the demands.

If teacher-scholars are to influence the tactics of popular struggles, they should consider frames, threats, and contexts. Lakoff (2002, 2004) argues that progressives believe "the truth will set us free—that if we just tell people the facts, they'll reach the right conclusion" (Lakoff, 2004, p. 17). Instead, people tend to fit facts to frames—their own huge, largely unconscious metaphors that guide seemingly unrelated decisions. Facts that do not fit an existing frame either do not "register" or get reformulated (and therefore twisted) to fit the frame already held. Lakoff urges progressives to reframe; for example, from *tax relief* wherein taxes are a metaphorical burden to *public investment* with its evocation of a future benefit. Albert (2001) offers a different perspective on tactics, arguing that in any popular struggle, numbers are what matter. What makes an elite give in to the demands of those engaged in mild civil disobedience is the threat of greater disobedience. The greater the numbers of people involved in the struggle, the more likely that a threat is conveyed and that the elite will concede. It is also important to be aware of the tactical importance of contexts. The effectiveness of a tactic may depend not on the tactic but on the group using it or events surrounding its use.[7]

As for demands, the original suggestion that policies should be broad and that they should promote both equity and local autonomy still seem right. And so does the information we provided about language variation, language attitudes, and language situations. Our intent, then, was to complicate the understandings of activists as they work on behalf of literacy education for language minority students. That intent remains—except that "work" in the context of this chapter now means "shape the struggle" rather than "convince the policymakers."

---

[7]The "No on 227" campaign took the advice of media consultants and, as a tactic, refused to challenge English for the Children's charges against bilingual education or to answer questions about its effectiveness (Crawford, 2000a). In that particular context—in the hands of an underdog with little control over the media, and undertaken late in the campaign—the tactic of "do not defend" made bilingual education appear indefensible.

THE CHAPTER

Imagine this situation. You are interviewing for the position of Director of Bilingual/Second Language Education[8] in an urban school district of almost 100,000 students. Until 20 years ago, the District's student population was 85% White and 15% Black, with a few Mexican American migrant children. Since that time, immigration has resulted in an influx of students from a variety of ethnic and language backgrounds. The largest population of non-English speakers, about 10,000 in number, is Hispanic. The earliest Hispanic immigrants were Cubans, followed by Venezuelans and Colombians, but now most of the Spanish speakers entering the District come from war-torn Central America. Most of the first waves of Spanish- speaking immigrant children came from well-educated middle-class families. Many of the more recent immigrants have not been to school or have had their schooling interrupted by war.

The next most populous group of immigrants (about 1,000 students) are of Haitian origin. Their home language is Haitian Creole. The majority of the Haitian students enrolled in this District have not been to school in their own country. The few who did go to school in Haiti were in schools conducted in French, a language the children did not use in their homes. Only after the Duvaliers were overthrown in 1986 did Haiti award Haitian Creole official language status along with French. And only since 1982 has Haitian Creole been permitted to be a medium of instruction.

Another smaller group of immigrants are southeast Asian refugees from Vietnam, Thailand, and Laos. The educational backgrounds (as well as the languages) of these 500 students vary. Most of the more recent arrivals have spent considerable time in refugee camps waiting to come to this country. In these camps, schooling focused on teaching English.

There is also a group of about 100 Russian speakers in the schools, since this is one of the official ports of entry for Russian Jewish immigrants. In addition, there are small numbers of students from more than 80 other language groups, including Afghani, Arabic, Chinese, French, and Portuguese.

Student populations vary tremendously from school to school. Some schools are almost 100% Hispanic or African American and Haitian. Others are almost exclusively White non-Hispanic with a few non-English

---

[8]This position no longer exists in all states because of events described in the Prologue to this chapter. Instead, the position is now usually called *Director of English Language Acquisition,* or *English Language Development,* or some other title that foregrounds English and renders invisible possibilities for multilingualism.

speakers from different native language backgrounds. And there is every possible combination between those two extremes.

One of the questions posed during your hypothetical interview is the following: Given the situation just described, what kind of a design would you propose for bilingual and/or second language instruction in the school district? More specifically, what would you propose in terms of the language or languages used for non-English-speaking students' writing and reading instruction?

From our perspective, the "ideal" or theoretically preferred answer would be: Students' native languages should be used in written language instruction, and students should have an opportunity to develop first as readers and writers in their home languages and then gradually add on English literacy. We base our answer on: (1) the theoretical and political stance articulated by UNESCO (1953) for initial literacy in the vernacular followed by second language literacy and (2) research evidence that has demonstrated that quality bilingual education programs benefit children in both their academic and English language achievement (Edelsky, 1986; General Accounting Office, 1987; Hakuta, 1986; Hudelson, 1987; Rosier & Holm, 1979; Troike, 1981).

But while there may be a theoretically "correct" answer, the educational and noneducational realities that individual communities face—the conditions permitting (or not)—make it impossible to offer one policy regarding written language instruction that would be appropriate for all educational scenes. Therefore, instead of offering a single policy, we will present a general position.

OUR POSITION

For teaching and learning written language, teachers and students must have autonomy and must be able to account for local conditions.[9] Therefore, upper-level governmental policies should be broad, nonspecific, and linked to appropriate equity-oriented general goals. Local program policies should be developed locally to consider (but not always acquiesce

---

[9]On occasion, we have been asked to specify what we think would be appropriate policies or programs for some of the situational characteristics we describe. To be true to our call for autonomy for local administrators, teachers, and students, we believe we must refrain from specifying policies or programs. To do so would reify our suggestions while implying that one could mechanistically relate Condition A, Condition C, and Condition F to Policy 1; Conditions B, D, and E to Policy 2, and so on. Worse, it would contradict our major point; that is, the complexity of each situation, which can be known only by insiders and sensitive, long-time outside observers, requires tailor-made locally specified policies about written language education, not policies generated in the abstract by outsiders to fit generic combinations of features.

to) the details of the local situation while still leaving responsibility for major decisions to individual teachers. We take this position for three interlocking reasons: (1) learning written language in school (whether or not in a bilingual program) always happens in multiple co-occurring contexts; (2) each of these contexts has profound effects on writing inside the classroom; and (3) the contexts are complex in ways that may not be immediately obvious.

CONTEXTUAL VARIATION *PRECLUDES* UNIFORM POLICIES

The Languages Involved

Writing and reading occur in classrooms, within schools, within communities, within school districts, and within larger geographic and political regions that exist at certain historical times, peopled by those with varying interests and beliefs. Although larger contexts influence smaller ones, and vice versa, and although the smaller contexts are tied together at least through membership in the same governmental entity (e.g., the United States in 1987), these smaller contexts present a dizzying variety of details.

In the United States, the "other" school language (the marked language; Fishman, 1976) may not be a student's home language (e.g., the student may speak nonstandard Puerto Rican Spanish and be placed in a Standard Mexican Spanish bilingual program in Chicago). If the non-English school language is the student's home language, it is not simply an uncomplicated "other." Students may come to school speaking a standardized dialect of a world language (e.g. Standard Mexico City Spanish), a nonstandardized dialect of a world language (e.g. a nonstandard lower-class dialect of Mexican Spanish), a standardized dialect of a regional written language (e.g. Standard Vietnamese), a nonstandard dialect of a regional language with a long written tradition (e.g. certain dialects of Chinese), or a regional language without a long written tradition (e.g., Hopi or Haitian Creole). Furthermore, there are many possibilities for what varieties of English are used in the students' communities.

Teachers' Bilinguality and Biliteracy

Teachers' language profiles may also be complicated. Teachers may have been educated as professionals in the students' home language and then received some additional professional education in the second language. Thus, they may be more literate in the home language than in English, as well as more familiar with oral school registers in the home language (e.g., Cuban teachers in Miami). Or teachers may share the students' home language but have no school experience with it, having been educated only in their second language. These teachers would be considerably more literate in their second language than in their first (e.g. some Latino teachers in the southwestern United States, many Haitian teachers educated in French in Haiti). Or teachers may have attended lower grades in the students' home language and then received higher levels of schooling and all professional education in the second language (e.g., teachers who immigrated to the United States in their teens).

Language Use in the Community

Moreover, outside the classroom, the community is not one that simply "uses Language X plus English" or "just" Language Y. In each community, there will be differences in the settings and uses of English and the other languages. There may be clear boundaries for the use of one language or the other, with business and government requiring English, and home and religion the other language. Or each language might be able to be used in all settings but variation within the setting (who is speaking, who is listening, who is listening in, what purposes the language is being used for, the formality or informality of the particular moment) demands a shift from one language to the other (Grosjean, 1982).

Pressure From the "Larger" Context

As noted in chapter 2, other larger contexts contribute their own entanglements to how written language occurs in particular classrooms. What complicates here is not the variety but the potential for tremendous and often deleterious impact. More global contexts (e.g., the climate of opinion in states and regions, the national temper of the times, prevailing values), with their embedded discourses and ideologies, become concrete through policies, mandates, statutes, recommendations, and court decisions. (Some examples are discussed in the Prologue to this chapter.)

Testing, for instance, is a central influence in every public classroom in the United States (and in almost all private school classrooms too). The general public's faith in tests as valid indicators of learning and in testing as the best way of holding teachers and schools accountable,[10] reliance on test data in recent national reports on education, increased numbers of required tests for increased numbers of children, and the growing practice of publishing test scores in local newspapers are sources of intense pressure. Widespread acceptance of the supposed value and benefits of mass testing makes the language of the tests (usually English) the "real" language of the classroom; the tasks demanded by the tests the "real" tasks,

---

[10]Chapter 12 reviews some of the arguments against putting such faith in tests and testing.

and the way test language is conceptualized (as consisting of small separable, relatively easily measurable components) the "real" way to think about language. In effect, a discourse of testing reconstitutes the "real"-ities for teachers and students.

Mandated tests are tied to a push for a standard curriculum (with its added benefit of greater control over teachers)—a district-established sequence for district-specified objectives.[11] Like standardized tests, atomized objectives and scope and sequence charts emphasize low-level conventions. Such an emphasis stands in the way of learning to use written language effectively and appropriately for one's own purposes (R. Brown, 1987).

Still another factor pressing on bilingual programs and all that goes on within them, writing included, is the political climate for bilingual education. Relative to the later 1970s in the United States at least, that climate has deteriorated. Federal guidelines for ensuring children's access to education through a language they can understand are being ignored; high-ranking federal officials publicly state their opposition to bilingual education; support grows for proposals calling for making English the "official language" and for curbing any activity (including bilingual education) that would "endanger" the position of English;[12] bilingual education is being required to prove its effectiveness via test scores to an extent beyond that demanded of other educational interventions (Crawford, 1987).

These are just a few of the factors that complicate decisions about written language instruction in bilingual programs. Some of these factors have similar effects across all bilingual programs (e.g., pressure from testing). Others vary widely from program to program (e.g., particular home language, or extent and type of teachers' experiences with each of the school languages). This variation is what is behind our premise that highly specified blanket policies are bound to conflict with particular conditions at local sites.

CONSIDERATIONS FOR GENERAL POLICIES

If we are urging policymakers to refrain from being bulls in the subtle china shops of individual community language situations, we are not asking them to be idle. Nor are we promoting extreme decentralization ("home rule," as it is known in the United States). It is imperative to establish broad state and national policies regarding language rights and educational

---

[11]That push has become an even worse reality in the years since this chapter was originally published. State-wide (not merely district-wide) standards assessed through a state-wide test with high stakes attached—an agenda item of the Business Round Table (Altwerger & Strauss, 2002)—are now a feature of K–12 education in well over half the states.

[12]The success of just such proposals is discussed in the Prologue to this chapter.

access for discriminated-against (not just numerical) minorities. Policymakers *must* make *general* policies. And they must make them according to a principle of equity. That means that even while they refrain from highly specifying the policies they make about bilingual programs (in order to allow for the diversity within many publics), they must see bilingual education in the light of equity issues. After all, the "temper of the times" and "current political climates" are never monoliths connected automatically to one line of action. They have minor keys and single clarion notes; they shift and change. While policymakers cannot ignore prevailing mentalities, they need not slavishly follow them either. They can listen to many voices and then *lead* in establishing *general* policy. They do not have to acquiesce to each aspect of the local situation, incorporating, for example, racist language attitudes into curriculum policies simply because such attitudes exist in the community. To prevent a potentially regressive "tyranny of the local" (Wexler, 1987), they can create broad policies that promote equity while still taking care to permit local autonomy.

One way to accomplish such a feat is to establish broadly outlined goals (rather than highly specified policies) that respond to deep, consensual wishes. Now the various publics' wishes—consensual at some level, though conflicting at others—will almost certainly show evidence of the hegemony of dominant class interests. But hegemony is full of contradictions (R. Williams, 1989). And so these common, often "colonized" social desires (A. Luke, personal communication, May 16, 1990) also frequently contain widely shared progressive kernels (e.g., desires for fairness, satisfying work, etc.). It is those kernels that policymakers must use as the basis for enlightened policy. (And if policymakers themselves have oppressive agendas, then contesting parties will have to be the ones to appeal to those kernels in their struggles for change.)

One such kernel of overwhelming consensus in the United States concerns literacy; people want all children to be able to read and write. (There is much less agreement on the importance of being able to read particular texts or write particular genres in particular languages, or on who should read and write what.) It is up to policymakers to take this kernel, at the level at which there is general agreement, and put it into a general goal (e.g., we aim to develop literate people) and then to *lead* by first refusing to derail that goal by subdividing it into subgoals and, further, by then interpreting that goal progressively. Progressive interpretation would extend literacy to mean the ability to read and write critically,[13] to be able to evaluate texts for

---

[13]In 2005, I no longer equate *progressive* and *critical*. To me, *critical* implies critique as a *sine qua non*, a deliberate questioning of how the text supports and/or interrupts systemic privilege. *Progressive* implies a direction (Willinsky, 2001), progress toward greater democracy. While a *progressive* stance inherently criticizes the status quo and envisions improvement, it does not necessarily criticize from within a *critical* frame of systems of dominance.

their support of democratic values. Of course a literacy goal interpreted in this way would have to be protected; it would have to remain general. It could not be subdivided into multiple trivial subgoals that can never add up to the ideal and that actually prevent the achievement of what was wanted in the first place.

ISSUES TO BE CONSIDERED WHEN DEVELOPING LOCAL POLICIES

While decision makers at high governmental levels should be making general policy that seeks to promote equity, they should also permit those on the local scene to develop congruent local policies. Being closer to classroom scenes, the local decision makers would be more able to see details in local language situations. But they must also know what to look at.

What, then, must be considered in local policies regarding literacy in bilingual settings? We see four general questions that must be asked, all of them implicating to some extent people's attitudes toward language in general and written language in particular:

1. What is the nature of written language acquisition?
2. What language resources are available?
3. How are written products treated in each language?
4. What is the value and what are the consequences of being able to write in each language?

Nature of Written Language Acquisition

In formulating policies about literacy education, the basic question is: What is the best current understanding of how written language is acquired? And how do the details of the local language situation relate to what is known about written language acquisition?

Like oral language, written language is acquired through actual use.[14] Some of that use occurs during interaction with others who, while reading or writing themselves, demonstrate what written language is for and how it works (Harste, Woodward, & Burke, 1984; F. Smith, 1981b). In these interactions, meaning and purpose are central—making sense of and with print

---

[14]Chapter 6 offers a lengthy discussion based on an alternative comparison—not learning to read and write as analogous to learning to talk, but learning to read and write as analogous to learning a second language. Despite my newer understandings, I still believe learning a language through using it remains a key feature of language learning—first, second, or written.

for getting information, for reminding someone, for warning, for getting attention, for keeping track, for killing time, and so on. On other occasions, the learner is alone but still using a social tool; that is, the written language being used and learned is shaped by a culture, governed by conventions shared by other members of the society, subject to social and historical constraints on how and for what it can be used. As with oral language, what is being learned in written language are the systems of rules/conventions/constraints for exercising freedom-within-cultural- bounds, for making one's own meanings for culturally possible purposes in particular situations. That is, both conventionality and autonomy are critical aspects of oral and written language acquisition. The best "teaching" of oral (Edelsky, 1978; B. Wells, 1981) and written (Calkins, 1986; Graves, 1983; Hudelson, 1986; F. Smith, 1973, 1981b) language seems to require responding to what the reader/writer is trying to do. (This means responding not to the child's completion of a worksheet but to a child's sincere effort to warn, wonder, inquire, scold, forgive, direct, etc.) In order for a learner to have such purposes in school, and in order for a teacher to be free to respond to these, both learner and teacher need autonomy to devise their own curricula, to become genuinely engaged. Local decision makers must work hard to encourage the existence of situations in which language can be acquired through real use and eliminate policies that prevent such situations from occurring.

Language Resources

Making decisions about literacy instruction requires consideration of local language resources, local attitudes toward those resources, and local ways of organizing those resources (Hymes, 1980a). Bilingual educators would argue that children's main language resource—their home language—is the language that should be used for initial literacy development; after all, it is easier to create and interpret texts in a language one already knows rather than a language one is just learning.

But learning to read and write also involves language resources beyond one's oral language. Take the availability of published texts. In some Native American communities, the native language has never been written down. Therefore, bilingual programs in those communities will not have authentic native language texts for use by learners. A variation of this situation occurs in communities where writing systems are just being developed or standardized. In these cases, there will be relatively few printed materials. Sometimes, the creation of texts is slowed down by debates about which of several orthographies to use. For example, some Haitian Creole material in this country is not widely accepted because there is disagreement about which Haitian Creole orthography is definitive.

Even when written texts in the native language exist, the community may question the use of the home language and literature in the school. If the home language is accorded low status, its use in the school domain may be seen as inappropriate. In Haiti, for instance, French has a history of high status and prestige; Creole has been the lowly language of the poor and uneducated. To this day, many Haitians, having internalized the negative attitudes toward Creole, refuse to acknowledge that they speak Creole. These same individuals oppose the use of Creole for literacy instruction in school.

Sometimes, the issue is not status but the broader issue of the acceptability of vernacular literacy *per se*. In the Navajo Nation, for example, Navajo traditionally has been the oral language of the home, community, and tribal activities, but English is the expected written language. Although Navajo literacy was introduced in the early 1900s, it has been slow to take hold; in fact, it is often associated with governmental, religious and educational efforts to assimilate Navajos into mainstream American culture. Teaching children to write and read in Navajo has thus been viewed by many as the first step toward cultural assimilation and often engenders conflict over classroom use of readily available written Navajo texts (Spolsky & Irvine, 1982). In other Native American communities, community members disagree as to whether native stories should be written down and included in the curriculum. Like the Navajos, some elders believe such a move would contribute to assimilation; others believe the stories would enhance their children's chances of school success.

Even where the languages in bilingual programs are languages with written traditions, it is often difficult to get the quantity and variety of reading materials that are available in English (K. Goodman, Goodman, & Flores, 1979). Few other countries in the world have a children's literature industry comparable to that of the United States. There are problems in importing books from other countries, and the books tend to be more expensive than those purchased from U.S. publishers. Even for Spanish–English bilingual programs, where some high-quality children's books originally written in Spanish have been identified (Schon, 1978), availability is limited. The lack of authentic texts is even more pronounced in less common languages, such as Vietnamese and Lao. And then the issue of dialect creates additional problems, as Chicano Spanish speakers complain that they want material written in Chicano or at least Mexican Spanish rather than Cuban or Puerto Rican or Castilian Spanish.

Another complicating factor is the quality of material available in home languages. Learners need "real" texts (not books written merely to give reading/writing lessons) that will demonstrate "book language" (e.g., styles of written narratives, the syntax of written directions, lexical choices for written exposition, etc.). Many of the non-English language texts do not meet the criteria of variety, natural language, and authenticity. Rather, they resemble American basal reading texts in their approach to literacy (see Goodman, Shannon, Freeman, & Murphy, 1988, for an extensive critique of basal readers). In some cases, local bilingual programs have even translated or adapted the mechanistic approaches used in English basal readers. In Dade County, Florida, for example, *The Miami Linguistic Readers,* a series of phonics materials written originally for learners of English as a second language, was adapted for Spanish as part of the Spanish Curriculum Development Component. Later, the same principles of teaching reading through sound-letter correspondences and syllable patterns were used in the creation of beginning reading materials in Haitian Creole.[15]

A human language resource of critical importance for teaching and learning writing is the teacher. We know that in many mainstream classrooms, teachers do not view themselves as writers and do almost no writing either for themselves or with their students. But to develop literacy in others, teachers must see themselves as readers and writers. Indeed, a key assumption of in-service education efforts by the National Writing Project is that, in order to become effective writing teachers, teachers must themselves become writers. In many bilingual programs, as we have mentioned earlier, teachers have been educated in their second language, and most of the reading and writing that they do occurs in that language. There is a strong possibility, therefore, that bilingual education teachers do not view themselves as writers in their home language, nor (like mainstream teachers) do they see themselves as writers in English. Denigrating the variety of the home language they speak and lamenting their lack of written language ability, these teachers are not likely to be able to nurture children's development as writers.

Children learning to write need access to others who write. Teachers who write themselves can serve this role. So can writers of the native language in the local community. But the case of Navajo shows that the availability of adult speakers of a language in a community does not guarantee readers and writers. As mentioned earlier, English is the language most

---

[15]Whether or not published materials written in languages other than English can make their way to bilingual programs in the English-speaking world, and whether other-than-English texts will follow the format and content of highly profitable English language materials like basal readers is not simply a coincidental given in a particular educational setting. Decisions made by former salesmen turned editors and corporate managers in an industry organized for profit figure heavily in producing these conditions (Apple, 1989). So do the politics of establishing selective literary traditions that privilege certain genres and voices and exclude others (Kimberley, 1989; Wald, 1989).

often used for writing by Navajos. If children do not see adults using written Navajo in their lives, they are likely to regard writing in Navajo as a mere exercise. In fact, no matter the language, if children do not see adults using writing for a wide range of purposes, they are unlikely to incorporate "writer" into their own identities.[16] As we look at various communities as possible sources for demonstrations of written language, we must ask questions: Who in the community knows how to write? In what languages do people write? What kinds of writing do people do? For what purposes do people write? How can schools both use and extend community resources so that children will become writers?

Treatment of Written Products

Considerable research shows that children learn to write by seeing demonstrations of authentic written language, by writing for real and varied purposes, by sharing what they have written with varied audiences, by using the reactions of others as they revise some of what they create. As writers construct meaning, they experiment with forms, generating and testing hypotheses about how written language works and using what they know at that time about written language. Any product a writer produces, therefore, is really a reflection of the ongoing process and context of creating text. Further, the written products provide evidence of children making use of what they know about written language and the resources they have to work out their ideas as they respond to the contexts of composition.

But not all teachers agree with this. Many teachers believe that children learn to write by practicing a set of discrete and isolated skills until these have been "mastered." Only then should they work out ideas in connected text. Our experience has been that many bilingual teachers share the latter view, regardless of whether children are learning to write in their home language or their second language (Edelsky, 1986; Hudelson, 1985). This view may reflect conventional wisdom or professional education (e.g., many Spanish-speaking teachers educated in Cuba or Mexico have been taught to teach writing by teaching letter sounds and syllables; many Haitian teachers have learned to direct children to memorize words and

---

[16]In 1989, we might have used Atwell's comments about children needing to learn that "people like us" take on writing (or don't) as part of their identities. In 2005, I would be more likely to refer to situated learning in communities of practice (Lave & Wenger, 1991) and Discourses (Gee, 1999), because these theoretical constructs have been developed at length with considerable specificity. But going along with what is expected for "people like us" still gets at the heart of the matter.

take dictation; the writing approach in many U.S. bilingual programs emphasizes exercises with small segments of language). In any case, evidence mounts that teachers' beliefs about how writing and reading are learned have a direct effect on how they teach (DeFord, 1985; DeFord & Harste, 1982), including how they react to student products and student errors.

As one example, here is a short piece written by a first-grade Spanish-speaking child enrolled in a bilingual program that emphasized children's written expression:

Cuando llo se lla grande boyaser una maestra y boy garar mucho dinero para comprarles as misinos niños les boya comprar ropa y jugetes.

Standard Adult Spanish: *Cuando yo sea grande voy a ser una maestra. Y voy a ganar mucho dinero para comprarles a mis niños. Les voy a comprar ropa y juguetes.*

English translation: When I am grown up I am going to be a teacher. And I am going to earn a lot of money to buy (things) for my children. I am going to buy them clothes and toys.

From one perspective, this piece could be viewed as a demonstration of creative problem solving, risk-taking, and using what one knows about the written system of Spanish to express an idea. The child's invented spellings, unconventional segmentation, cross-outs, and lack of punctuation might be analyzed in terms of working hypotheses about how written Spanish is organized (Edelsky, 1986; Hudelson, 1981–1982). But from a different perspective, the piece could be viewed as riddled with mistakes—as a demonstration of the writer's lack of knowledge of sound–letter correspondences, inability to spell words correctly, laziness about punctuation, and forgetfulness about leaving spaces between words. The piece may be used to judge what the child does not know about standard adult forms of the language, instead of what the child knows. Teachers who believe that products such as the one just presented show children's inability to write may discourage further experimentation; may fail to promote early and sustained writing experiences; and may, in spite of good intentions, actually prevent a child from learning to write effectively.

If educators and/or community members believe that writing stories is a waste of time, this kind of writing will probably not happen much in classrooms. If educators and/or community members believe that to display less than perfect writing (in terms of standard forms) is to encourage sloppy work or provide a bad model for the others, little work may be displayed, and the same children's work will always (not) be displayed. Questions need to be asked in order to find out what the local beliefs and actions are, and efforts must be made to educate teachers and community members about beliefs that interfere with children's development as written language users.

Value and Consequences of Writing Ability

Bilingual programs of any stripe claim that first language writing is important. No matter how it is seen—as an entry to the world of literacy, as a bridge to writing in a new language, as a lifelong ability to be nurtured throughout school, as the ability to perform spelling and punctuation exercises, or as the working out of ideas—first language writing has a place in U.S. bilingual programs. However, having a place does not mean having a place that really counts. Does the first language appear in writing on signs? Tests? Forms? Bulletin boards? Is it limited to use on notes to parents who would not otherwise understand? All the various ways print is used in the school affect what is learned about print, including which language has what level of importance.

The same questions must be asked regarding first language writing outside of school. Being able to write and read in English clearly matters (note the recent mass media campaigns regarding illiteracy). But what about being able to write in Spanish or Hopi or Chinese? How does first language writing function in the students' community? It is necessary to find out who writes in what languages (their social status, age, gender, societal roles) and for what purposes (whether these are private or public) in order to understand, even in part, how students and their families and their communities will view the inclusion of first language writing in the curriculum.

To educators, being able to write is presumed to be empowering. It is necessary (though not sufficient) for access to certain societal resources (e.g., jobs requiring writing) and services initiated or legalized through writing. As a tool for thinking, it offers additional, perhaps unique, opportunities for reasoning, reflection, and interacting with oneself. It expands ways of interacting with others, including increasing the possibility of having a public voice. In a society where tested literacy "levels" help to uphold a myth of meritocracy, we learn to consider an inability to read and write as shameful—disempowering in the extreme.

But whether writing has such benefits or not, learning to write can change the *status quo* for the community as well as the child. In opening up new social roles for the writer (and possibilities for new relationships), learning to write in either language brings social change in its wake (Hymes, 1972a). For example, communities of newly arrived immigrants may not yet have established any stable pattern to their written language use in the new community. If the native language included literacy, it has been disrupted through immigration since print resources (newspapers, signs, books, etc.) and written language networks have changed (Weinstein-Shr, 1993). As the children learn to write English, what impact does that have on the older immigrants? Does it change the children's relation to family members or elders in interaction with the larger mainstream society?

If the children learn to write in the home language but first language writing in the native country was limited by gender or social class, what happens to social roles as writing ability "spreads?" Or do the children refuse to learn to write in the first language rather than violate native norms about who should write that language?

In contrast with communities of new arrivals, communities of either indigenous people or established immigrants are more likely to have stable patterns of written language use. The question, then, is whether learning to write in both the first and second language would produce a challenge to the community's language situation. If it does, it is important to identify who wants the change and who does not. In anticipating whether there will be arguments over first language writing in school, it is equally important to learn whether first language writing will be a red herring. That is, what other community battles (e.g., battles over traditional vs. "modern" ways, over separation and nationhood vs. annexation) may underlie disagreements over whether, which, how much, and who learns to write in the first language?

CONCLUSION

The picture for written language learning in bilingual programs is indeed complicated. What happens in any given classroom will be influenced by a host of locally varying factors related to many larger contexts. Thus, there can be no uniform, highly specified written language policies or programs that will be effective everywhere. Nor can there be one automatic local policy response to a given local detail. In fact, there are so many possibilities, each with so many possible attendant pitfalls, that a reasonable question to ask is: Why would anyone even try to develop a local policy or program that would require accommodating so many contingencies and that would be fraught with so much opportunity for creating havoc in the speech community? The answer is vision. To engage in such a precarious endeavor, local planners have to be able to see beauty in the idea that goals can remain general and that plans can be built on equity. To weave their way through such a complex contextual tapestry, they have to be able to envision a chance to create a plan that challenges the usual relations of domination and subordination—relations that not only affect education, literacy, and bilingual programs but also, as R. Williams (1989) says, that saturate the whole process of living.

Chapter 4

The Effect of "Theory" on Several Versions, Over a Quarter Century, of a Popular Theory: Plus Ça Change, Plus C'est la Même Chose

This chapter begins with the original chapter with a few editorial changes. In this original chapter, there is an insert written in 2005. A long postscript was written in 2005.

Both "theory" and THEORY are systems of beliefs that organize expectations and perceptions and influence decisions and behavior. People's "theories," however, are usually unexamined taken-for-granted foundations for more explicit beliefs and overt actions, while THEORY is a system of explicit coherent beliefs formalized according to the conventions of some scientific community. As part of a general trend to attend to meanings and not just behaviors, researchers have become interested in people's "theories"— teachers' and students' "theories" about what reading is (Harste & Burke, 1977), and teachers' "theories" about teaching (Clandinin & Connelly, 1987; Nespor, 1987).[1] Teachers and students, however, are not the only ones who have tacit beliefs that are implicated in their work. Researchers too have taken-for-granted beliefs that affect what they do professionally (e.g., how they see phenomena, what they identify as interesting problems, which

---

[1]Young bilingual students' "theories" about language and bilingualism should now be added to the list (Moll, 2004).

methodologies they choose, what models they develop). Thus, before their research has ever begun (Bogdan & Biklen, 1982), their "theories" permeate their research findings—and ultimately find their way into their THEORIES. One such "theory"-influenced THEORY is that developed by Jim Cummins to explain the relationships between second language proficiency and success in school. Like a match thrown on dry brush, this THEORY has caught on and swept across a discipline and, like that same match, it is both useful and dangerous. Because it was adopted so quickly and so widely (i.e., its constructs are now part of conventional wisdom in bilingual education in North America; its arguments set the parameters for conversation about the education of children who do not speak the majority language), it is important to look closely at the "theory" that pervades this THEORY.

Initially, Cummins's THEORY was proposed to account for various inconsistencies: (1) home-school language switches have been detrimental to "submersion" but not "immersion" students (Lambert & Tucker, 1972; U.S. Commission on Civil Rights, 1975), (2) bilingualism has provided a cognitive advantage to some but not others (Peal & Lambert, 1962), and (3) older immigrant children have been more successful in school than younger ones (Toukomaa & Skutnabb-Kangas, 1977). Later versions aim, additionally, to elucidate the changing nature of language proficiency in relation to school achievement.

All versions of the THEORY are appealing, well argued, unquestionably well intentioned—and wrong. They are wrong in basic premises (i.e., in "theory") about reading, writing, and pragmatics; wrong about what should constitute markers of educational achievement; and wrong in relying primarily on test data for support. Wrong or not, from its earliest presentations until now, Cummins's formal THEORY, with its intent of improving the educational fortunes of poor, minority language children,[2] continues to offer a convenient and helpful argument for why minority students' first language should be their language of instruction and, therefore, a useful argument (as long as the details are not scrutinized) in bilingual education's fight for survival. Nevertheless, *in the long run,* progressive intentions notwithstanding, Cummins's underlying "theory" is likely to make his THEORY dangerous to the very children who are supposed to be its beneficiaries.

---

[2]Clearly, cultural differences within the population called "poor minority language children" make the category a questionable one. Heath (1982) shows how two groups, each non-mainstream and non-middle class, organize literacy events in different ways and how these match or counter schools' organization of literacy events. However, since Cummins (1979) used this designation in an early major presentation of his THEORY, I use it here.

THE THEORY IN BRIEF

Hypotheses and Constructs

At first (e.g., Cummins, 1978, 1979), the THEORY proposed a distinction between "surface competence" and "cognitive competence" in language (later to become the constructs BICS [*basic interpersonal communicative skill*] and CALP [*cognitive academic language proficiency*]); borrowed one old construct *(semilingualism)*; and used all three in discussing two hypotheses (the *developmental interdependence hypothesis* and the *threshold hypothesis*). Later versions (Cummins, 1981, 1984) kept the idea of *semilingualism* but renamed it *limited bilingualism,* added another pair of acronyms (CUP [*common underlying proficiency*] and SUP [*separate underlying proficiency*]), and introduced two continua: *context-reduced* versus *context-embedded situations for language use* and *cognitively demanding* versus *cognitively undemanding language tasks*. A still later version (2000) abandons the term *semilingualism* but not the phenomenon, and shifts its focus to pedagogies.

The *threshold hypothesis* stated that there is a threshold level of linguistic competence that must be attained in each language in order for bilinguals to avoid cognitive deficits and benefit cognitively from their bilingualism (Cummins, 1979, p. 229). The *developmental interdependence hypothesis* claimed that "the level of L2 competence which a bilingual child attains is partially a function of the type of competence the child has developed in L1 at the time when intensive exposure to L2 begins" (Cummins, 1979, p. 233). *BICS* refers to "surface competence"—oral fluency and sociolinguistic competence (Cummins, 1979). *CALP,* the higher level, concerns those aspects of language proficiency "related to the development of literacy skills," namely, "vocabulary-concept knowledge, meta-linguistic insights, and knowing how to process decontextualized language" (Cummins, 1979, p. 242). CALP is required for success in school and takes longer to develop. *Semilingualism* is the language (dis)ability of a bilingual child who may have "surface" fluency in each language (i.e., high BICS) but who knows neither well enough to handle "abstract cognitive/language tasks" (Cummins, 1979, p. 231; i.e., low CALP).

The additional acronyms in the versions from the 1980s—CUP and SUP—are competing notions. If first and second language proficiencies are based on CUP, skills in one language could transfer to the other (bolstering the developmental interdependence hypothesis), so that children who learned to read in their first language would not have to learn to read all over again in the second. If, instead, underlying proficiencies are separate (SUP), reading skills would have to be relearned in the second language.

To further develop the older dichotomous CALP and BICS, newer versions of the THEORY proposed two intersecting continua. *Context embedded to context-reduced communication* refers to the amount of contextual support available in different communicative situations. The other continuum, *cognitively demanding to cognitively undemanding language tasks,* addresses "developmental aspects of communicative proficiency in terms of the degree of active cognitive involvement in the task" (Cummins, 1984, p. 13).

MY CRITIQUE FROM THE 1980S AND 1990S

Disputed "Theory"

The fundamental problem with the various versions of Cummins's THEORY is that it is based on an erroneous, psychologically derived "theory" of the nature of literacy—a conception of reading and writing as consisting of separate skills involving discrete components of language.[3]

Harste and Burke (1977) described three implicit "theories" or orientations people might have toward literacy:

1. A *decoding orientation* (Reading is a two-step process: first, turning symbols into sound; then turning sounds into meaning. Pronunciation of print is the primary datum for assessment.)
2. A *skills orientation* (Reading and writing are composed of individual "skills" in decoding, vocabulary, grammar, and composition; the word is primary. Tests of separate skills are the appropriate means of assessment.)
3. A *whole language* (or *sociopsycholinguistic*) orientation (When reading or writing, a person uses interdependent and inseparable cueing systems—orthographic, syntactic, semantic, and pragmatic—to predict and construct meaning. Appropriate assessment requires observing the entire [whole] context-bound, purpose-driven language-using activity within a particular situation.)

It is not possible to hold a "theory" that reading consists of separable skills and, simultaneously, a "theory" that explicitly rejects discrete skills of reading.

Despite occasional use of "whole language" terminology (e.g., "inferring," "predicting," "large chunks of discourse," even "miscues") and approval of a sociopsycholinguistic model of reading (Cummins, 1986, p. 28), Cummins has an underlying skills orientation. He writes of reading as consisting of

---

[3]I now understand the fundamental problem to be a broader one, concerning not only Cummins's "theory" of literacy but also his "theory" about language in general, including language competence, language proficiency, and discourse. That discussion appears in the Postscript to this chapter.

meaning-making separate from decoding ("as development progresses, word meaning and reasoning-in-reading [e.g., inferring and predicting text meaning] rather than word decoding skills account for the variance between good and poor readers" [Cummins, 1981, p. 15]). He cites approvingly school reading programs that emphasize a basal technology (which is premised on separable skills of word attack, comprehension, decoding, etc.) and programs that evaluate their work through tests of separate skills (Cummins, 1986). To support his THEORY, he relies on school achievement data that come almost entirely from studies using tests of supposedly separate reading skills. When he discusses his THEORY to relate language proficiency to school success, it is that skills "theory" of reading and writing that permits him to accept prevailing instructional and assessment practices as givens. However, when Cummins simply refers to (rather than presents) his THEORY of language proficiency and instead devotes his attention to school and what should be happening there, he uses a discourse of empowerment, and he puts forward a set of suggestions that implicitly contradict his "theory" of reading as consisting of separate skills (Cummins, 1986).

Is it the case, then, that Cummins really does not hold this "theory"? After all, empowering minority students does in fact require a conception of reading that highlights meaning-making and culturally based knowledge and, therefore, something other than a "skills" conception of academic tasks, academic skills, and academic success. Moreover, Cummins uses the right rhetoric. He talks of students setting their own goals and generating their own knowledge, and he mentions congruent educational practice (e.g., he refers to the writings of Donald Graves and to the Bullock Report). Nevertheless, his separate skills "theory" slips out, and he contradicts his own message. For example, for empirical support, he relies heavily on test score data that can only provide evidence of how well students perform on skill exercises. He applauds and describes at length school programs driven by skills-based basal programs. It is hard to believe, then, that when he uses Graves's, Lindfors's, and Giaccobbe's terminology (e.g., "generating one's own knowledge," "setting one's own goals"), he means the same things they do. It is more likely that this is another case of something I will discuss shortly: Cummins's tendency to take trivial activity (e.g., a psychometrically defined skill or a surface behavior) and cloak it in important sounding, even trendy, terminology.

In the various presentations of the THEORY itself, Cummins's "theory" about literacy leads to other errors, such as locating deficiencies within the learner (even if he blames external factors for the existence of those in-the-head deficiencies). That "theory" also explains why his THEORY gained popularity so fast and was so prevalent in policy debates. Separate skills—as to what language is, what curriculum should be about, what should be assessed—are the organizing idea in the "theory" that pervades education in North America. Cummins's contribution is to argue that the language of skills instruction need not be English. His THEORY about language proficiency changes nothing but the language of instruction. It not only leaves intact beliefs in a skills "theory" of reading and writing; it actually strengthens those beliefs and, along with them, the legitimacy of a congruent goal for education: the attainment of higher scores on skills-based tests.

Disputed Data

Almost all the evidence Cummins uses comes from research that operationalizes, that lets one thing stand for another.[4] Although the substitutions may seem reasonable, they often turn out to distort the phenomenon of interest (see Mehan & Wood, 1975, and Blumer, 1969, for a discussion of problems in operationalizing). Once something (e.g., reading) is operationalized as something else (e.g., responses to test items), one is prevented in the research from counting reading a book and talking about it as a case of reading even though such activity surely represents the phenomenon of reading at least as well as test responses.

Rarely does Cummins specify how the original research he cites operationalized "reading," "English skill," "academic skill," "native-like levels in both languages," "cognitive retardation," "French achievement," "deeper levels of cognitive competence," or "higher levels of cognitive skills." Lack of specification leads one to believe that what was studied was some common-sense notion of reading or, for instance, some important instance of remembering. But in fact, that is not the case. "Cognitive aspects of language" (Cummins, 1979, p. 231) turned out to be merely the ability to match synonyms. "Cognitive advantage in bilingualism" meant the ability to find ambiguities in isolated printed sentences (Cummins, 1979, p. 232). And "native-like competence" in a language was a score on a vocabulary test (Cummins, 1979, p. 231).

The quintessential example of operationalization is standardized tests, the source of much of the evidence for the THEORY. Thus, the notions of CALP/BICS and semilingualism are granted legitimacy by data from tests such as the Peabody Picture Vocabulary Test, the Inter-American Test of Reading, Inter-American Prueba de Lectura, Metropolitan Achievement

---

[4]Strauss (2005b, p. 41) pointed out that operationalizations are at the root of why, in science, researchers concern themselves with validity, why they are forced to talk about it, and why the scientific meaning of the term *valid* has negative connotations. In colloquial usage, a valid point of view is something positive; it rests on some reality. But an experiment can never be fully valid because "the phenomenon of interest is not the object of study in the experiment." The validity of the experiment reflects not only "how much a certain variable reflects the phenomenon of interest but also how much it does not."

Test, Illinois Test of Psycholinguistic Ability, Wepman Auditory Discrimination Test, Canadian Test of Basic Skills, and so on. Even in the newer versions of the THEORY, though the model implies that what is cognitively demanding in a context-reduced setting could be any language task, the supporting research appeals to "reading skills," "grade level in reading," and "finding ambiguities in sentences"—that is, to language tests.

Language and literacy test data, however, are misleading. They can be affected by a variety of nonliteracy/language phenomena (e.g., the color of the test booklet; Orasanu, McDermott, Boykin, & The Laboratory for Human Cognition, 1977). They pretend to be responses to a standardized task, but different test takers interpret the "same" task differently and thus are actually engaged in different tasks (Labov, 1970; G. Wells, 1977). Moreover, when the tests are norm referenced, that statistical procedure forces half the scores to fall below the norm. Programs that raise scores for large numbers of children up the ante for subsequent test-takers, since new norms have to be established to ensure that half the scores are again below average. And with token exceptions, it is easy to predict which half will be overloaded with poor and minority language children.

PROBLEMS WITH THE CONSTRUCTS THEMSELVES

CALP and BICS

In disputing the validity of the constructs (CALP vs. BICS; semilingualism), I am not claiming that all children are equally talented in how they use language. Nor do I believe that an ability to use *any* language variety enables one to do *everything* humanly possible with that language. Members of any speech community have nonidentical repertoires (Graff, 1986; Hymes, 1980b). However, the relationship between, on the one hand, the quality, functioning, and distribution of repertoires and on the other hand, other social resources cannot be determined by performance in one (testing) context that is subject to extensive criticism on multiple grounds.

Cummins's dichotomy of language proficiencies, while an improvement over a unitary proficiency, does not account for the complexity of these repertoires. It oversimplifies and it blames the victim. CALP is presented as the highest level of not only language development but also cognitive development. Thus, the message (intentional or not) is that since poor minority language students consistently score lower on tests of "academic language ability" (e.g., standardized reading, vocabulary, and verbal intelligence tests; Samuda,1975), their cognitive ability too is distributed differentially according to native language, social class, or ethnicity.

I believe it is more accurate to call "cognitive academic language proficiency" by a different name: test-wiseness. It is then more understandable that middle-class mainstream populations score higher; they are coached from infancy (Heath, 1982). Test-wiseness also explains why older child immigrants who have gone to school in their home country would do better in school than younger ones. The older children have learned to cope in their first language with the "highly abstract school curriculum" that Cummins respects but that could also be seen as nonsense (F. Smith, 1986). Their greater success comes not from more advanced first language proficiency but from having been "schooled" (literally) in nonsense through something that makes sense—their first language. They do not have to learn about school nonsense through another type of nonsense, the strange sounds of a second language. In fact, minus references to nonsense, this is what Cummins refers to when he proposes a common underlying proficiency (CUP) that can be instantiated (with help and experience) in any of the languages a person knows. But *proficiency* is not intransitive; it is always enacted with something. Based on the research Cummins cites, the "something" in this THEORY is test-like literacy exercises.

Though there have been occasional disclaimers (which few of his colleagues took seriously [see Rivera, 1984]), BICS and CALP have been presented as being essentially separate and unequally valuable in school. BICS is supposedly social; CALP is cognitive. BICS, therefore, should not entail the knowledge and abilities included in CALP—linguistic manipulation, cognitive strategies, logic, conceptual knowledge, metalinguistic awareness, and so on. Even scant familiarity with the child language literature should reveal the absurdity here. BICS is also not supposed to lead to success in school. But research cited by Cummins himself (Wells, 1979; Wells & Raban, n.d.) to support the BICS/CALP distinction showed that while assessments of spontaneous language use did not correlate highly with later reading test scores, high correlations were indeed found between test scores and conversations in which the child and an "enabling adult" negotiated meaning. One can only wonder why Cummins did not consider such conversations evidence of BICS. Or why he ignored the wealth of information on the social and interactive knowledge (presumably closer to BICS) required for participating in mundane reading lessons or for taking tests (closer to CALP; Baker & Freebody, 1989; Jennings & Jennings 1974; Moll, 1981), or the extent to which children's writing (including everything from the content of their stories to their spellings)—a CALP-like activity—is fine tuned to their social histories and current interactions with peers (Dyson, 1989). All these occur through BICS. Positing separate language proficiencies is not only an error regarding language but also a barrier to imagining bridges between home and school.

Semilingualism

Bilingual students' limited ability to work with meaningless, nonfunctional print on tests or in lessons are explained in the THEORY by appealing to *semilingualism*, less than native competence in each language (Cummins,

1979, p. 230). The label dates back at least to the early 1960s (Hansegard, 1962, cited in Skuttnab-Kangas & Toukomaa, 1976). Then and now, *semilingualism* is a confused grab bag of prescriptive and descriptive components, including the size of vocabulary; correctness (based on standardized usage), ability to neologize; and mastery of cognitive, emotional, and volitional functions of language. The same tasks and abilities that constitute CALP are also the markers of semilingualism (Cummins, 1979, pp. 230–231). Thus, poor test performance means low CALP—which may also mean "semilingual." Having less than native-like abilities in a second language is understandable, but semilingualism also means being less than native-like in one's native language. One obvious question is: When such a large population is considered to have less than native proficiency in their native language, who are the natives whose language and cognitive abilities *are* native-like? How can so many be semilingual in anything other than the trivial sense of not being able to perform well on tests?

Unfortunately, regardless of its triviality, the term *semilingualism* fits all too well into popular stereotypes about children who "don't know English and don't know Spanish either" and "therefore" do poorly in school. That schools' (and researchers') faulty "theories" of literacy underpinning their pedagogical practices, and not children's language proficiency, might be the culprit is not considered.

Context-Embedded/Reduced and Cognitively Demanding/Undemanding

The addition of the two continua (context embedded to reduced, cognitively undemanding to demanding) increases the subtlety of the THEORY, but it doesn't change the basic tie to a skills "theory" of literacy. How much reduction, for example, can a context tolerate? From the research Cummins cites, it appears that "context" can be reduced to the point where whole subsystems of written language (e.g., syntax or semantics) are eliminated, as they are in many tests, literacy workbook exercises, and experiments. Given the high ranking he accords to an ability to do such exercises, Cummins seems to be saying that separate skills (e.g., decoding, finding synonyms, etc.) are more important, more elegant, more worthy—more something—than reading for one's own communicative purposes (a more context-embedded activity).

Cummins also implies that better, more advanced readers or listeners do not rely on nonlinguistic context. But in fact, the opposite is the case; the more proficient the reader, the more nonlinguistic context (e.g., prior information, discourse expectations) and the less written information that person uses (F. Smith, 1982a). Even young children's writing develops through becoming more rather than less context embedded (Dyson, 1987). In other words, in naturally occurring "context-reduced" situations the proficient reader *re-embeds*. Moreover, those naturally occurring "context-reduced" situations outside of school are actually more context embedded than the context-reduced situations of "highly abstract school curriculum" (see Enright, 1986, pp. 151–155 for a critique of the idea of decontextualized language use.)[5]

One sign of the inadequacy of Cummins's THEORY is that he has to go almost entirely outside of it, appealing to reasons that sound remarkably like Ervin-Tripp's (1970) still-pertinent analysis, to explain why immersion students succeed through schooling in their second language while submersion (poor minority language) students do not or why an empowering education is optimum for minority language students. He tacitly indicates (Cummins, 1981) that the relative political positions of the two languages is what ensures that immersion students' first language is not swamped (in school or out) by their second language. He explains immersion (vs. submersion) students' success by different levels of prestige for the respective first languages, differences in security of identity, and differences in level of support for first language development (Cummins, 1981, 1986). (This is not exactly the same class-based, power-based, status-based explanation I offer in chapter 1, but it is certainly more socially and politically inclined than would be an appeal to his own hypotheses about thresholds, linguistic interdependence, semilingualism, or two kinds of language proficiency.)

OTHER RECURRENT PROBLEMS

This section, with subsections on shifts and confusions, is a 2005 addition even though it refers to Cummins's earlier work. A review of shifts and confusions in Cummins's later work appears in the section called "Postscript 2005."

Shifts

Across the years, Cummins has shifted labels, most often without explaining the shifts. Prior to the 1980s, he was referring to *competence*. By 1981, competence had shifted to *proficiency*. The idea was the same; the label had changed—but without explanation. *Semilingualism* was the designation prior to 1981. In more recent versions up through the early 1990s, that same idea is termed *limited bilingualism*.[6]

---

[5]Gee's (1990) critique is taken up in the Postscript.

[6]It is not until much later (e.g., 1994) that Cummins offers a sociopolitical rationale for this substitution, acknowledging but not crediting his critics' complaints about the pejorative nature of *semilingualism*. In disputing the term, however, his critics disputed the phenomenon, too. In 1994, Cummins relinquished only the term.

He has also shifted (or contradicted) claims—positing language (and cognitive) deficits, yet also denying them. For instance, in 1978 (p. 402), he described semilingual children as those with "poor command of [their] first language" who are then "inadequate in their L2," and he wrote about "linguistically unstimulating home-language environment[s]" (p. 398). In 1979, he implicated code-switching as a factor in semilingualism ("Because the languages are not separated, each acts as a crutch for the other with the result that the children may fail to develop full proficiency in either language"; p. 238), and he argued for the need for students to reach certain thresholds in each language in order to avoid "cognitive deficits" (p. 229). In the same article, these deficit statements are then denied ("semilingualism does not in any sense imply that minority children's language is itself deficient" [Cummins, 1979, p. 231]) because that concept is not "strictly linguistic." Rather (to make matters worse), it is cognitive too. And it comes into play only in relation to education—as represented by test-like curricula and assessment measures. There is also a shift from discussions in the 1970s that implicitly accepted traditional curricula as givens—as establishing the tasks for which CALP was necessary—to proposals in the mid-1980s for a kind of education that would empower minority students. Such shifts and contradictions permit room for disputed interpretations and for blaming readers rather than acknowledging changes in his thinking.

Confusions

Some of these shifts and contradictions may stem from confusion about both linguistics and pedagogy. In the 1970s, when Chomskyan linguistics was "hot" in language education, Chomsky's distinction between *competence* and *performance* was used to make a variety of arguments on behalf of students, communities, and pedagogies (e.g., all students have language strengths, students create tacit hypotheses about abstract rules). In those years, Cummins consistently used the term *competence*. In fact, he used it so consistently, without synonyms, that it is reasonable to assume that he meant for his work to benefit from an association with that Chomskyan term. But Cummins did not mean what Chomsky meant (i.e., a tacit, deep, knowledge of syntactic abstractions). Instead, he referred to "'surface' linguistic competence" (Cummins, 1978, p. 397) and to "competence in a language" as meaning the "use of the cognitive functions of the language" (Cummins, 1978, p. 398). By 1981, he was consistently using *proficiency* in its place, possibly because he had been challenged on his use of *competence*—a use that bore little resemblance to notions of competence as used by Chomsky.

In discussing semilingualism and his threshold and interdependence hypotheses, Cummins refers to *native languages* and to some people not knowing their native languages as well as others do. Now, to a linguist or sociolinguist, *native language* is shorthand for the language variety/ies someone learns from birth within a particular speech community; it does not refer to something like a language (e.g., English) in general or to a standard dialect of a language. Thus, native speakers of English (or any other language) are actually native speakers of only the variety of English of the household they were born into; they are not native speakers of the varieties of English used by speech communities they were not born into. However, in claiming that some students lack proficiency in their native language, Cummins appears to be comparing native language knowledge of people from a lower status speech community (e.g., the Finnish of lower-class Finnish migrants to Sweden) with that of people from a higher status community (e.g., the Finnish of middle-class Finns in Finland; Cummins, 1979).

In the 1980s, Cummins began advocating "context-embedded" settings for language instruction (Cummins, 1981), and he developed strong principles for an empowering pedagogy, including instruction that "promotes intrinsic motivation" and that helps students "generate their own knowledge" (Cummins, 1986). Moreover, as a contrast with that empowering pedagogy, he critiqued the transmission model of education for focusing on surface features of language, workbook exercises, achievement of short-term instructional objectives, and for "contraven[ing] central principles of language and literacy acquisition" (Cummins, 1986, p. 28). Yet his main source of data (scores on tests of separate literacy skills) focuses on just those surface features of language and hardly promotes intrinsic motivation or generation of one's own knowledge. Moreover, his actual exemplars of practice in his writings in the 1980s include programs that depended heavily on workbook-like exercises and the achievement of short-term instructional objectives—not at all congruent with the "principles" that show meaningful, purposeful language use as central to language and literacy acquisition (K. Goodman, 1984). For example, he applauds the use of drama and student collaboration in interpreting texts (Cummins, 1986, p. 25) but fails to note that the dramatizing and collaborating in the classroom examples he cites was in the service of finding the right answers to questions in basal readers that present comprehension as a discrete skill. Or he mistakes the surface form for the complex process when he points to the work of Donald Graves on children's writing. Contrary to Cummins's claims, it is not having students write and publish their own books that is what makes Graves's work so valuable for "knowledge generation." If it were, then schools around North America that have taken up just those surface pedagogical features (book writing and book publishing) would be seeing the kind of growth in writing and thinking that Graves described. Instead, what is knowledge-generating about Graves's pedagogy is (1) students seriously revising content and (2) sincerely conferring with other authors because (3) they believe that what they write matters. In foregrounding the surface (the books and the publishing centers), Cummins (along with the schools that install publishing centers without learning how to change the focus of curriculum to students' meaning and how to change student beliefs about the value of those meanings) misses the main point.

BACK TO THE ORIGINAL VERSION: A DIFFERENT VIEW

I believe that what Cummins calls *skill with academic language* is really *skill in instructional nonsense* (SIN, if another acronym is needed). By contrast, I am arguing for developing *power literacy*, reading and writing that serves individual and group interests. In power literacy, what children read and write are not analytical parts stripped of pragmatic cues (parts such as paragraph, sentence, word, letter). Rather, children read and write functional wholes (stories for entertainment; recipes written for cooking—and the cooking gets done; letters written for permission for something that is really desired; editorials read for critique as part of projects that will be used to persuade out-of-school audiences; investigative reports written to inform—and the informing does occur). That is, the *goals of power literacy are at the same time the means for learning it and the evidence for assessing it.*[7]

Classrooms where this conception of literacy and congruent pedagogy prevail are in the minority. Still, they exist (see Calkins, 1986; Dyson, 1989; and Kamler, 1980, for descriptions of their various inner workings). These are not just classrooms where creative teachers make instructional nonsense culturally congruent or where they spice up a traditional transmission-based curriculum with assorted authentic props. Nor do these teachers confuse comprehension with comprehension exercises in commercial reading programs (Harste, 1989). What the teachers do instead requires perceptiveness and courage but no unusual materials. They write letters to children, they discuss literature with them, they support children as they investigate their own questions about and critique the world around them, and they highlight the parts of language (e.g., spelling patterns, punctuation, handwriting) for explicit instruction in relation to individual needs, keeping the instruction embedded as much as possible in students' projects.

Data

To learn about the development of power literacy, it is necessary to collect data on both products and processes of readers and writers actually reading and writing. A body of naturalistic research (Atwell, 1987; Calkins, 1983; Dyson, 1989; K. Goodman & Goodman, 1978; Harste, Woodward, & Burke, 1984) shows the benefits of such an approach. In contrast with the

---

[7]The No Child Left Behind legislation of 2002, with its push for standardized test-driven instruction, makes *power literacy* impossible on any broad scale.

data on which Cummins's THEORY relies, which conceives of reading as a composite of separate skills that can be performed outside the act of reading or writing for real (i.e., for a communicative purpose), research using rigorous observation of literacy "on-the-hoof" does not conceive of reading (or writing) as a composite of separate skills. Nor does it see reading (or writing) as performing tasks that hypothetically represent reading (or writing) but that actually represent the requirements of a particular instructional tradition (e.g., phonics, word attack skills). Instead, the research I am advocating here is based on a view of reading and writing as simultaneously linguistic, cognitive, and social phenomena.

Hypotheses

To counter Cummins's hypotheses regarding the relationship of language and school achievement, I offer the following:

- It is difficult to acquire skill with instructional nonsense in any language, but it is easier to learn it in one's first language.
- It is difficult to acquire skill with instructional nonsense through literacy exercises alone; that is, regardless of language of instruction, if children's experience with literacy is primarily through texts written for instruction, they will have difficulty becoming skilled in instructional nonsense.
- It is difficult to become literate through instructional nonsense. Corollary: Test scores of children who have been fed a restricted diet of reading exercises will result in some "false positives"—children who develop skill with some exercises but who have meager abilities with genuine texts-in-the-world.
- Interpersonal oral communicative activity plays a significant role in learning to use written language.
- It is easy to learn to read and write in school when the school emphasizes reading and writing, not reading and writing exercises.
- When students have learned to *read* and *write,* they can more easily learn instructional nonsense if that is necessary for some narrow instrumental purpose. Corollary: Test scores may reflect "false negatives"—test performances that underrepresent how well students can read and write for their own purposes.

Accounting for Group Differences

If the above hypotheses are correct, why is it that middle-class mainstream children (who are also exposed to schooldays full of exercises *in* rather than the exercise *of* reading and writing) acquire skill with instructional nonsense (i.e., score higher on tests) while poor minority language children do not? And why do middle-class children *seem* to become truly literate as a result of a diet of worksheets? Three possible explanations follow.

1. Mainstream middle-class children are primed at home for playing the prevailing school reading-exercise game. With better priming, they are more likely to be successful with early lessons on pseudo-reading and, therefore, more likely to pursue actual reading on their own. *It is this out-of-school, self-directed reading rather than in-school exercises, that promotes reading. And it is already knowing how to read that is what allows students to increase their skill with instructional nonsense (e.g., with exercises meant to teach reading).*

2. Middle-class mainstream children and teachers do not expend energy in relational battles over language. All parties share norms for how to talk during reading time, sharing time, and so on (Collins & Michaels, 1986). One reason immersion program children succeed in school is that while they use linguistic features of a foreign variety to "do lessons," they are already tuned in (from priming at home) to the interactional norms for "doing school."

3. Middle-class mainstream children and teachers are more likely to have "trusting relations" with each other—working agreements wherein each party can make sense of the other's interactional work and where the children can trust that the teacher's "coercion" is in their best interests (McDermott, 1977). When such a happy state of affairs exists, even nonsense can be seen as worthy of attention.

CONCLUSION

Because Cummins's THEORY is such a good fit with prevailing "theories" in education, it has been readily accepted; and because it has advocated education through the first language, it has produced short-term benefits for bilingual education. But in the long run, a THEORY that locates failure in children's heads (in their language deficits, their cognitive deficits, their underdeveloped CALP), a THEORY based on inadequate "theories" of literacy will not benefit those children. Instead of notions of language proficiency that support harmful conceptions of children and of academic activity, what is needed in bilingual education is a THEORY of the relationship of language and an empowering education. That THEORY must begin with a "theory" that rejects separate skills notions of oral and written language and honors what people actually do as they talk, read, and write.

POSTSCRIPT 2005

There have been several important critiques of Cummins's work in the past
decade. MacSwan (2000) argues that semilingualism is "indistinguishable
from classical prescriptivism" (p. 3) and that the Threshold Hypothesis that
incorporates this notion is morally and theoretically flawed. MacSwan provides empirical evidence from sociolinguistic studies of language shift and
linguistic analyses of bilingual children's test performance to make his case.

Wiley (1996, in press) locates Cummins's work within a long tradition
now known as *The Great Divide*, wherein a chasm is presumed to exist between
societies/cultures. At first the divide was between "savage" and "civilized"
societies; then it was a more enlightened distinction between "primitive"
and "civilized;" then "oral" and "literate;" now "conversational" and "academic." Wiley notes that although Cummins has repositioned his terms (e.g.,
additive and *subtractive bilingualism* and *semilingualism*) from their origins in
an autonomous view of literacy and moved them into the discourse of
social practices (Cook-Gumperz, 1986), he has retained elements of The
Great Divide. Wiley also indicates dangers in Cummins's persistence in
using terminology such as *semilingualism* and in his promotion of that phenomenon. His critique includes a discussion of Cummins's tendency through
the years to redefine and reformulate in response to criticisms without
crediting either the critics or the criticisms.

MacSwan and Rolstad (2003) critique the class-biased nature of *semilingualism*. They also criticize the sociolinguistic naiveté of, on the one hand,
using responses to oral proficiency tests that fail to account for interactive
norms and that actually test meta-language (e.g., a child's knowledge of what
"complete sentence" means) but on the other hand, calling these measures
of "language ability." MacSwan and Rolstad propose an alternative acronym,
SLIC (Second Language Instructional Competence). SLIC does not apply, as
CALP does, to native language development, does not potentially denigrate
a child's cognitive abilities, does not give special status to the language of
school, and yet allows for stressing the need for a child to "continue to
receive interesting, challenging instruction that she can understand during
the time needed to achieve second language instructional competence"
(MacSwan & Rolstad, 2003, p. 338).

The extension below of my own earlier critique focuses on Cummins's
presentations regarding both language proficiency and also pedagogy.

Changes to the THEORY

While Cummins's THEORY has undergone relatively minor modifications in
the last quarter century, his focus has changed dramatically. And although a
skills "theory" of literacy remains as an undercurrent of his THEORY, I now
believe the more important problematic underpinnings are broader than his

view of literacy; that is, they include confusions regarding scholarship on language as well as on what constitutes a critical stance.

In 21st-century versions of the THEORY (Cummins, 2000, 2003), as MacSwan (2000), Wiley (1996, in press), and MacSwan and Rolstad (2003) note, Cummins still positions language proficiency as an intervening variable in academic success, with CALP as the higher level of proficiency—the proficiency that is tied to achievement and that allows students to make sense of presumably cognitively demanding, decontextualized language and language tasks. However, Cummins now relaxes the sequence, saying that in some cases CALP might develop prior to BICS.[8] He also expands the notion of CALP, acknowledging that it is not a unitary phenomenon because academic settings and tasks are not unitary.

By 1981, without comment, he had replaced *semilingualism* with *limited bilingualism;* in 2000, he rejected *limited bilingualism* and the synonymous *limited proficiency in two languages* because they were each "ill-defined" (Cummins, 2000, p. 105). The current replacement is *below-grade-level verbal academic performance in both languages* (Cummins, 2000, p. 58) varying with *less access to academic registers in both languages* (Cummins, 2000, p. 105). In the newer descriptor (i.e., "less access" instead of "limited proficiency") as well as in explicit argumentation, Cummins foregrounds what he says was present in his THEORY all along (and what his critics argue is absent): a sociopolitical perspective.

Strikingly, Cummins has changed focus, from THEORY about language proficiency to what he claims are educational implications of his THEORY. However, he provides few connections between any specific aspect of his THEORY and any particular presumed implication for education—for example, what detail of his THEORY would imply a curriculum that is hopeful and visionary? In advocating for language minority students, it is reasonable to propose changes to the basic character of the pedagogies these students encounter and to look beyond the nature of students' language to a more comprehensive understanding of a variety of sociocultural phenomena that should impinge on pedagogy (Garcia & Curry-Rodriguez, 2000). But if that broader view is prompted by a THEORY about language proficiency, then it is necessary to identify how the pedagogical recommendations grow out of particular features of the THEORY.

When Cummins first began writing at length about education (Cummins, 1984, 1986), his implicit claim was that his THEORY implied an education that *empowers* minority students—an education that incorporates their

---

[8]MacSwan and Rolstad (2003, p. 331) contend that permitting CALP to develop in advance of BICS severely weakens the usefulness of the entire distinction. That is, if CALP can be acquired faster than BICS, what remains as an argument for not exiting students quickly from bilingual education?

language and culture into the school program, encourages minority community participation, promotes intrinsic motivation with a *reciprocal interaction* pedagogy through which students use language actively to generate their own knowledge, and has professionals acting as advocates for minority students rather than "legitimizing the location of the 'problem' in the students" (Cummins, 1986, p. 21). More recently (Cummins, 2000), the favored pedagogy is *transformative;* that is, it has qualities described by B. Bigelow, Christensen, Karp, Miner, and Peterson (1994; also see Edelsky, 1994b, 1999). Those qualities are: grounded in students' lives; critical; multicultural, antiracist, pro-justice; participatory; hopeful; activist; academically rigorous; and culturally sensitive.

More Shifting: Slip-Slidin' Around

As with prior changes in his THEORY and his discussions, as Wiley (in press) noted, more recent shifts simply appear, without being explicitly addressed. The exception is Cummins's renunciation of the terms *semilingualism, limited bilingualism,* and *limited proficiency in two languages.* He explicitly notes their pejorative connotations and their potential for suggesting linguistic deficits "despite denials to the contrary" (Cummins, 2000, p. 104). While he renounces the terminology, he does not correspondingly retract his earlier statements; for example, those about some bilinguals having less than normal or native-like competence (Cummins, 1978, p. 399), or low-socioeconomic status students having more restricted linguistic orientations than middle-class students (Cummins, 1978, p. 400) or experiencing a "linguistically unstimulating home-language environment" (Cummins, 1978, p. 398), or about code-switching acting as an impediment to developing "full proficiency" in either language (Cummins, 1979, p. 238). These statements, not only the construct itself, would certainly lead to interpreting (not misinterpreting) *semilingualism, limited bilingualism,* and the other substitute terms as being part of a deficit theory.[9]

Other shifts remain unaccounted for. Cummins moves *language proficiency*—a phenomenon central to the THEORY—out of psychology and now aligns it with systemic linguistics (by invoking *registers*) and with sociolinguistics (by using *language proficiency* interchangeably with *language functions*) and with discourse analysis (by using *Discourses* with a capital *D* and *discourse domains*). Just as *competence* disappeared after 1979, to be replaced by *proficiency* in 1981 with no accounting for the switch, so do *register, function,* and even *Discourse* appear in 2000 as synonyms for *proficiency,*

---

[9]A deficit theory, according to MacSwan and Rolstad (2003) citing R. Valencia (1997), attributes school failure to students' internal deficiencies—deficits in language, intellect, moral behavior—which can be transmitted by genetics, culture, class, or familial socialization.

without comment as to why what was being talked about as *language proficiency* in earlier work should now be considered something else (or why distinct constructs, such as *register, function,* and *Discourse,* should be used interchangeably).

Equally striking are the unacknowledged shifts in his discussions of education. The "empowering education" proposed in the 1980s has been replaced by transformative pedagogy. Does transformative pedagogy provide empowering education PLUS? If so, why not simply point out the character of what is added? Why propose an entirely new set of features? Or does it, perhaps, abandon *reciprocal interaction* (from Cummins, 1986) in favor of some particular feature of transformative pedagogy? If so, which one? And why? Cummins has argued that over the years, his later discussions build on earlier ones (e.g., he maintains, contrary to his critics' arguments, that sociopolitical ideas that he foregrounds in later discussions were already present in the THEORY he presented in earlier iterations). But "building on" usually entails explicating connections between earlier and later versions. Those explications are missing.

More Confusion

Language

The shift from *competence* to *proficiency* and the more recent slide that allows *register, function, language proficiency,* and *secondary discourse* to be used as synonyms for CALP reveal serious confusions about the theoretical and empirical study of language. If the language world in school is simplistically divided into two proficiencies (BICS and CALP), and if a *register,* a *language function,* and a *secondary discourse* (Cummins erroneously uses the lowercase *d*) are equivalent to the "typical" CALP, then for typical academic tasks and activities (Cummins, 2000, p. 67), only one register, only one function of language, only one discourse is required. Such a conclusion is contradicted by scholars who study variety in language—from Hymes (1970) to Halliday (Lemke, 1990) to Gee (1999). Moreover, *language function, register, discourses,* and *Discourses* (primary and secondary) each have different meanings and different theoretical roots. The idea of language having varying *functions* stems from early work in sociolinguistics (e.g., Cazden, John, & Hymes, 1972; Wells, 1977). *Register* is Halliday's construct for relating text and context within a view of language as a social semiotic (Lemke, 1990). *Discourses* and how they encompass small "d" discourses belong to the tradition of discourse analysis. Big "D" Discourses are "forms of life," "identity kits," not a way of talking. It is these, not small "d" discourses (ways of talking) that Gee (1990, 1999) calls *primary* or *secondary.* A register may entail language used for a variety of functions. A person's secondary Discourse (a community [of practice] that shares a rich stew of beliefs, values, attitudes, and behaviors, including language behavior) may require the use of many registers. While *register, language function,* and *Discourse* all highlight language as a social phenomenon, they are not interchangeable with each other or with CALP. Nor does invoking these constructs allow CALP, posited originally as a psychological phenomenon (proficiency), to—presto-chango—become a social phenomenon (J. MacSwan, personal communication, November 20, 2004).

The kernel of truth in Cummins's THEORY is that language proficiency is not a monolithic phenomenon. His conversational/academic distinction seems to be a step forward, an improvement over talking about a single language proficiency—but actually, it sidesteps a serious look at variety in favor of a hierarchy.[10] His more recent acknowledgment that academic contexts and tasks are multiple is in fact an improvement, but he then undercuts that beneficial move by continuing to posit one general typical CALP, the proficiency required for "typical academic tasks and activities" (Cummins, 2000, p. 67). But a CALP/BICS distinction—with or without an appeal to cognition and context, with or without an acknowledgment of multiple contexts—in no way captures the complexity or even the character of the phenomena. For one thing, a person does not know "a language," whether first or subsequent. What people learn are *social languages* (Gee, 1990, 1999)—ways of talking that signal kinds of people (social identities) doing kinds of things (activities)—all of which entail, at the least, beliefs, values, priorities, and ways of thinking embedded in those ways of talking. It is true that immigrant students who have been successful in school in their home country are more likely to learn the social languages required for schooling in the second language than indigenous minority language students who have no family history of success in school. But what explains this is not language proficiency; rather, it is a complicated combination of identities, memberships, and Discourses. What can help students learn these social languages is a pedagogy that aims for the untestable. (For a depiction of some aspects of that pedagogy, see chap. 7, this volume; Edelsky & Smith, in press; as well as Cummins's [2000] description of International High School at La Guardia Community College—a description he then undermines, as I argue below.)

Accompanying the confusion about *register, language function,* and *Discourse* is confusion about issues in linguistics. For example, in refuting his critics, Cummins (2000) refers to "an extreme Chomskyan perspective that identifies 'language proficiency' as Universal Grammar" (p. 92), indicating that MacSwan (1999, 2000) appears to hold just such a position. Neither MacSwan nor any other Chomskyan identifies language proficiency

---

[10]I appreciate Kellie Rolstad's e-mailed comments on this point.

(with or without the scare quotes)—or even Chomsky's notion of language-specific competence (the term Cummins first used but without Chomsky's meaning)—as Universal Grammar. Universal Grammar is theorized by Chomskyans as the "innate ideas" that are presumably part of the human genetic inheritance. Claiming that Chomskyans equate these "ideas" with psychometrically oriented language proficiency reveals considerable confusion about linguistic scholarship on language.

At the same time as he advocates respect for students' languages, Cummins appears to harbor what MacSwan and Rolstad (2003) and Petrovic and Olmstead (2001) identify as *prescriptivism;* that is, his position is that it is poor and minority students who do not know academic registers who "fail to realize the full range of options in their two languages" (Cummins, 2000, p. 104). But he does not accuse middle-class students of failing to realize that "full range" if they don't know gangsta' rap or other decidedly nonacademic varieties (MacSwan, 2004). In other words, *full range* really means just one part of the range: the academic part. Moreover, the notion of a single person knowing or even having access to the "full range of options" denies decades of work on speech communities and communities of practice. The issue is not whether students have access to a theoretically impossible "full range of options" but to particular options for particular contexts.

Cummins also appears to be ignorant of Gee's argument that language in use cannot be context reduced or decontextualized. Instead, Cummins maintains the validity of his context-embedded/reduced continuum and the reality of a point on that continuum at which communication relies "exclusively on linguistic cues" to meaning and on knowledge of the language itself (Cummins, 2000, p. 92). By contrast, Gee (1999) argued at length that no such exclusively linguistic cues exist. Rather, "linguistic cues" are always interpretable through social cues—socially situated meanings, social languages, and social conversations. A sentence such as "Lung cancer death rates are clearly associated with an increase in smoking" is interpreted as having only 1 of its 112 possibly meanings. That single interpretation is not a result of readers knowing the linguistic cues (which could just as well allow them to interpret "death rates" as "the speed of dying" instead of "the incidence of deaths"). It results instead from readers knowing the contextual cues—the social conversations in which this example of a social language (a specific kind of academic language) has been embedded (Gee, 1999, pp. 30–34).

Other instances where Cummins misconstrues theoretical terminology or key ideas concern scholarship on literacy. For example, Wiley's (1996, in press) critique relies on Street's (1984, 1999) distinction between *autonomous* and *ideological* orientations to literacy. Autonomous orientations toward literacy are those that attribute universal consequences to literacy—for example, cognitive or economic consequences. Graff's (1987) historical research showed that widespread literacy has no universal consequences for an economy, and Scribner and Cole's (1981) cognitive anthropological work revealed no universal cognitive consequences for individuals. Nevertheless, the autonomous orientation lives on. Wiley (1996) argues that Cummins's claims on behalf of the educational and economic consequences of literacy (e.g., "mastery of these formal language skills is directly linked to future educational and economic opportunities" [Cummins, 2000, p. 104]) and his assumptions of its cognitive implications (built into CALP) is in the tradition of an autonomous orientation to literacy.

In his rebuttal, Cummins (2000) misunderstands *autonomous* and *ideological* perspectives on literacy. Instead of giving Street (1984) credit for the enormous theoretical contribution of describing these two orientations to literacy, Cummins blames Wiley for creating a dichotomy. Cummins (2000) argues (p. 94) that an autonomous/ideological distinction reflects Wiley's "rigid either–or perspective" and asks plaintively why an "approach to inquiry" cannot be some of both. But Street's two orientations (cited by, not originated by, Wiley) are not about approaches to inquiry; they are about *beliefs* about what literacy is—an abstract in-the-head phenomenon with inherent acontextual consequences (the autonomous perspective) or a social phenomenon with socially determined consequences (the ideological perspective).

Just as Cummins confuses this distinction between two major perspectives on literacy with approaches to research, so does he confuse the idea of *tacit* "theory" with *explicit* advocacy. A major point in my earlier critiques (Edelsky, with Hudelson, et al., 1983; chap. 4 in the two previous editions of this book) has been that what drives Cummins's use of particular research to justify his THEORY and also his applause for certain examples of pedagogy is his *tacit* unexamined belief that literacy consists of separable skills (decoding skills, word attack skills, comprehension skills). He may well "have never advocated or endorsed any theory of reading as consisting of separate skills" (Cummins, 2000, p. 91)—by which, presumably, he means advocating an explicit THEORY (which is the point of my THEORY/ "theory" distinction). But he certainly "advocates" or "endorses" implicitly by using research on separate skills (e.g., reading vocabulary, matching synonyms, phonological awareness, and letter recognition) to support his arguments. He adds to that implicit endorsement by holding up as exemplary specific instructional programs (e.g., Cummins, 1986, p. 25; 2000, pp. 265–266) that rely on basal readers, which, by definition, are based on a view of literacy as consisting of separable skills.

Pedagogy. Cummins's proposals for pedagogy have much to recommend them. He argues that empowering pedagogy (1986) and transformative pedagogy (2000) highlight the importance of accounting for intergroup power relations, community participation, incorporating students' culture and language into curriculum, holistic principles in curriculum, authenticity in assessment, students generating their own knowledge, students' identities, and (in the case of transformative pedagogy) transforming society in the direction of social justice. Unfortunately, some of the explanations and examples provided for these pedagogical notions are off target and contradictory. This muddying of important concepts or applying of lofty labels to business-as-usual instructional programs encourages wider confusion. For example, he correctly describes the New London Group's (1996) ideas about literacy education that would account for multiple literacies; that is, building on vernacular literacies and expanding "traditional definitions of literacy beyond the text-based reading and writing of western schooling" (Cummins, 2000, p. 271). But nowhere does he indicate that such a project is incompatible with a focus on CALP, the typical "academic register" that is the epitome of exactly what he urges going beyond: "the text-based reading and writing of western schooling."

Cummins (2000, pp. 158–161) applauds authentic performance assessment, including portfolio assessment—assessment built on a critique of assessing stand-in behaviors or operationalizations. At the same time, he recommends combining portfolio assessment with just such stand-in assessments (he chooses as an example the Texas high-stakes test, Texas Assessment of Academic Skills, i.e., TAAS). He seems unaware of testing experts' widespread criticism of TAAS (e.g., Haney, 2001)—a test whose only history is as a high-stakes test and which, therefore, carries the meanings of high-stakes tests into all conversations of which it is a part—and the ways it *prevents* the broader, integrated, culturally tied curriculum he proposes (see chap. 12, this volume). Instead, he takes pains to allocate what percentage of an overall evaluation could be based on portfolios and what percentage should be based on a TAAS score, depending on students' "length of residence and stage of English academic development" (Cummins, 2000, p. 161). Younger, less advanced students would be evaluated primarily through portfolios, while more advanced students would be evaluated primarily through TAAS. The implication is that assessments of rich language use and opportunities for in-depth literacy are for less advanced students— for those with less developed CALP. Tests heavily dependent on standard language conventions and superficial literacy exercises are apparently appropriate measures of more developed academic English or CALP. Since assessment is known to shape curriculum, despite his calls for student-generated knowledge and integrated curriculum, Cummins seems to be contradictorily advocating TAAS-like curricula. And since both assessment and curriculum reflect conceptions of "theories" of what is to be learned, it appears that CALP—still—amounts to test-wiseness.

Cummins's (2000) calls for an education that encourages students to question the status quo, to find hidden assumptions in texts, and to read books about "issues that really matter" (p. 264) are undermined not only by his appeal to standardized tests such as TAAS but also by his preference for vocabulary tests, both of which necessarily narrow the curriculum. For example, he suggests a fourth-grade science unit on sounds (2000, p. 163), with predetermined concepts and vocabulary to be assessed through a computerized reading vocabulary test. Indeed, one reason he praises vocabulary tests is that they lend themselves to the creation of item banks of words representing concepts that can be categorized according to the "time of year that concept should be covered" (2000, p. 142). Along with supporters of high-stakes tests who see no problem with teaching to their favored test, Cummins too accepts and indeed urges teaching to the vocabulary test because the lexicon would reflect the "totality of the curriculum" (2000, p. 164). So much for his call for a transformative pedagogy with curricula built around asking critical questions, developing a vision of a more just world, deepening values of multiculturalism, or acting in pursuit of social justice (2000, p. 262)!

Cummins's descriptions of the extraordinary International High School at La Guardia Community College in New York—the interdisciplinary curriculum (e.g., units of study such as "origins, growth, and structure" that integrate chemistry, math, linguistics and art), assessment through portfolios and exhibitions, first languages and English used according to students' choice, written productions with out-of-school audiences, ongoing language planning by the faculty—is embedded in a discussion that accepts the movement for standards-driven education. It is as though he does not understand that the flexibility that he himself notes is what makes possible the innovations at the alternative International High would be precluded by the state-wide or even merely district-wide standards he also, and in contradiction, favors.

Discussions of transformative pedagogy are equally internally contradictory. For example, there is the mismatch between how he describes transformative (or critical) pedagogy/literacy in the abstract and his specific suggestions. On the one hand, he (correctly) says transformative pedagogies help students go beneath surface meanings to understand root causes and ideologies (Cummins, 2000, p. 260). On the other hand, he suggests a sequence of phonemic awareness for lower grades and the intersection of language and power for upper grades (Cummins, 2000, p. 259). By contrast, critical literacy educators (e.g., A. Luke & Freebody, 1997; Vasquez, 2004; Comber & O'Brien, 1993) argue against such a sequence, maintaining the need to weave critical issues into literacy instruction from the very beginning.

Cummins (2000, pp. 260–262) presents Ira Shor's depiction of critical literacy and Bob Peterson's list of components of critical/transformative pedagogy, each of which feature the need to grapple with political issues—root causes, ideologies, systems of privilege and how they work. A transformative pedagogy, as discussed by both Shor and Peterson, would help students investigate community language practices (as Cummins notes), asking questions about who benefits and how things got to be the way they are. With minority language students who are said to have little access to "academic registers," such studies should surely include examining the lower status accorded to peer conversation (a reflection of BICS) as compared to the higher status given to textbook language (a reflection of CALP). Such studies should include looking at the language attitudes folded into the relative statuses of BICS and CALP and the activities (e.g., experimental research, theorizing, standardized testing) that legitimize the distinction so it seems to be "natural" rather than constructed. But for Cummins, transformative pedagogy is a road to gaining CALP, not critiquing it.[11]

Perhaps the most perplexing anomaly is his juxtaposition of transformative pedagogy with Success for All. Although in a footnote he acknowledges that this packaged program, requiring the teacher to follow a verbatim script, is rooted in a transmission pedagogy and that its research evidence is "hotly debated," he nevertheless includes it in a discussion that relates research on school effectiveness with characteristics of transformative pedagogy. The strong implication—since, on the one hand, it is discussed several times in a chapter on transformative pedagogy and, on the other, there is no disavowal—is that, if qualities of a transformative pedagogy can be shown to be effective, then a program such as Success for All that shares some of those qualities is an example of transformative pedagogy. The same must be said of Cummins's offer of Oyster Bilingual School as an example of a school with a transformative orientation. Using language authentically and focusing on meaning, affirming identities, and writing in two languages—as is done at Oyster—are important on many grounds, but they do not constitute a transformative pedagogy.

On Not Being Critical

Cummins is uncritical in two senses. First—related to "critical thinking"—he does not discriminate among conflicting premises of various programs and practices. Thus, he presents a mishmash of pedagogies, some based on a transmission model, some with a transformative orientation, some progressive, some based on a separate skills "theory" of reading, some based on a holistic view of reading; some are compatible with the principles that

---

[11]Critiquing the relative statuses of BICS and CALP might help students *want* to become members of a particular academic community of practice or Discourse (Gee, 1999) that takes critique as a central activity. As new members (or even as *wannabes*), they would be immersed for periods of time in the values + beliefs + discourses of that Discourse and would begin to take up the practices of that community. Thus, if CALP were treated as an object of critical study—distanced rather than taken as given—it could well figure in students acquiring an academic social language.

he discusses, and some are not. Such a mishmash obscures and subverts the meanings of the principles he proposes.

Cummins is also uncritical in a second sense—that related to a critical or transformative pedagogy. That is, he fails to do what a transformative pedagogy entails: question what is taken for granted. He accepts the "autonomous" position (Street, 1984; Wiley, in press) that literacy has positive economic consequences without questioning under what economic and political conditions such consequences might occur. He agrees with the corporate-driven rhetoric about a shift to a knowledge-based economy and an ensuing need for knowledge workers without questioning the extent to which new jobs are indeed knowledge jobs in contrast to the extent to which they are low-paying service jobs (i.e., McJobs) (A. Smith, 2004) and without noting the increasing overseas outsourcing of knowledge jobs. He mentions that critically oriented research and pedagogy are ideological but, by omission in that context, he appears to accept mainstream assumptions that test-score- based research and test-oriented pedagogy are nonideological. He challenges coercive power relations in educational contexts but does not question how packaged pedagogies (e.g., Success for All) and standardized assessment-driven curricula promote such coercive relations. He discusses some dilemmas of assessing English language learning students within standards-based reform. But he is uncritical about the standards movement itself, failing to look beneath the surface to see the ways standards and their high-stakes test companions are implicated in a political agenda to undermine and ultimately privatize public education (Altwerger & Strauss, 2002; K. Goodman, Goodman, Shannon, & Rapoport, 2004).

TO SUM UP

A THEORY that explains the intricate relationship among language, pedagogy, and school achievement of minority students is *still* needed. It would be a THEORY explicitly grounded in "theories" that are examined rather than unacknowledged, a THEORY that does not undermine itself by trying to curry support by citing contradictory THEORIES and policies or practices based on contradictory "theories," a THEORY guided by "theories" that take seriously the sociopolitical nature of language and literacy and the ideological nature of both "theories" and THEORIES.

Chapter **5**

Literacy: Some Purposeful Distinctions

This chapter has three parts: an introduction written in 2005 establishing a basis for the topic, a condensation of the original chapter with a bit of updating of the background for the earlier proposals, and a section on some current ideas on the topic.

PART 1: WHY, DESPITE RECENT SCHOLARSHIP ON LITERACY, DO I PERSIST IN DISCUSSING DISTINCTIONS ONLY IN RELATION TO PRINT LITERACY?

What began as a trickle of interest over 40 years ago in reading nonprint texts (e.g., Hall, 1966, on reading spatial relations and gestures; Fiske & Hartley, 1979, on reading television) has, in the past decade, become a river. And a muddy one at that. It wasn't always so. For most scholars in the 1970s and before (though not for Hall, Fiske, Hartley, and a few others), when literacy was the topic it meant reading and writing print—and in generally White, middle-class ways. The last quarter of the 20th century changed that for literacy scholars. Studies of cultural variation in how people value print, what they believe it is for, who does what with it, and which written language is treated and how by multiliterate people (Heath, 1983; Scollon & Scollon, 1981; Scribner & Cole, 1981) shattered myths (prevailing even in the academy) about the existence of a single literacy. Certainly, there were holdouts; for example, those who followed the Havelock-Goody-Watt-Ong line of work relied on a notion of an essentialized literacy that divided cultures into oral and literate (Street, 1984). The Great Divide between primitive and civilized, recognized by then for its racism, was no longer acceptable, but the gap between oral (and concrete thought) and literate (and abstract thought) took its place (Gee, 1990). By and large, however, work describing cultural variation in literacy practices encouraged scholars to abandon the idea of a single literacy in favor of multiple literacies—a cornucopia of culturally and historically based practices related to the use of print.

Meanwhile, work in semiotics, semiology, and cultural studies (Fiske & Hartley, 1979; Kress & Trew, 1978) pushed academics to apply the terms *literacy* and *reading* to other media. At the same time, the explosion of new technologies helped the general public make its own extensions. At first, popular use of *literacy* was applied to electronic technology (computer literacy, media literacy, graphics literacy), later to other fields (e.g., mathematical literacy, musical literacy), then to such areas as financial literacy. Some of the extensions (not all of them recent) were clearly metaphorical (*she reads situations well; it's written all over his face*); some not as clearly so (we read maps but we do not write them; rather, we draw maps). Some were not metaphorical at all; for example, *reading* music is a matter of knowing how to use a formal system of graphic symbols to make music(al meaning); musical *literacy*, on the other hand, which entails going well beyond knowing a formal system of symbols to include knowing about composers, styles, and the like, seems more metaphorical. The latter part of the 20th century's "linguistic" turn in various academic fields to the text and its associates (literacy, reading, and writing), contributed to the easy acceptance of such metaphors. *Multiple literacies,* then, came to refer not only to culturally varied practices with print but also with non-print entities. At least it became such a thing to scholars—and sometimes (e.g., when talking about computer literacy, finances, etc.) to the general public.

Is there any way, then, to "pin down" literacy? Spencer (1986) argued that literacy has to be seen in relation to what a society counts as knowing (p. 443). Since there were suddenly so many different technological means and ways of knowing, the "old literacy" involving only two-dimensional print was inadequate; a "new literacy" now demanded going beyond print to the reading of images and three-dimensional objects (Kress & van Leeuwen, 1996). Thus, there were now serious justifications for bringing the broadest range of activities under the umbrella of the term *literacy.*

One problem with such a broad view, however, is that it leaves a lexical void. Institutional requirements and common understandings create a continuing need to distinguish reading and writing print from interpreting and producing other entities. As Halliday (1990) argued, if the term *literacy* is extended to "spoken discourse, gestures, numbers, and the like, another term will be needed for what we called literacy before" (p. 3).[1]

This problem aside, it is still important to reflect on Spencer's (1986) call to think of literacy in relation to what a society counts as knowing. Her advice acknowledges the sociopolitical significance of knowledge and skills. At the same time, it requires clarifying which society is the one that does the counting, and for what purpose, and also what counts as counting. Many academics (myself included) currently interested in literacy would like to see gatekeeping institutions such as schools expand their views of literacy to include not only a wider range of practices with print but also to include images and three-dimensional objects—to catch up, at least somewhat, to the gap discussed by O'Brien and Bauer (2005) between scholarship (New Literacy Studies) and the needs perceived by schools (Institutions of Old Learning). However, the general public and its political representatives (with their corporate "handlers") look in the opposite direction. While the public and the politicians may refer to computer literacy and financial literacy in casual contexts, they hold to a narrow tradition for gatekeeping purposes. Enlarge the canon? A fury ensues. Use advertising campaigns to promote the dangers of illiteracy? Those ads do not feature the musically illiterate. *Why Johnny Can't Read* is not a treatise on computer literacy. The public consensus is that, in important ways, literacy means reading and writing *print*—a feat made possible, in the public's view, through in-the-head knowing.

If the public and the politicians are the ones who do the counting, "what counts as counting," especially under the regime of the federal legislation called No Child Left Behind, is scores on standardized reading tests. Those tests are infused with values anchored in traditional romanticism. As Gee (1992a) wrote, traditional romanticism, as a value-laden view, might be

---

[1]A somewhat more arcane problem in merging the "old literacy" of print with the "new literacy" of images and objects is that it misleads, promoting a view of the old literacy as homogeneous. It was anything but. Densely printed pages coexisted with image–print combinations; 16th-century title pages with different sizes of printing to create a pleasing design "without regard to the relative importance of the words" were read as advertisements are read today—as whole semiotic objects (Kress & van Leeuwen, 1996). The word, too, has had multiple meanings. Over the centuries, *literacy* has meant polite learning through reading (the 14th century); has been equated with the term *literature* (16th century); has meant well-read and well-educated; and has had as its opposite the now-obsolete *illiterature,* meaning poorly read and poorly educated (rather than unable to read at all). It wasn't until the 19th century that literacy lost its denotative ties with education and meant simply "general and necessary skill with print" (R. Williams, 1983). Then and now, however, the connotations of literacy often include its earlier class history of connections with being well read and well educated.

"dead among the avant-garde, but it is alive and well at the gates to status and power" (p. 67).

What counts as counting in school—those test scores—do more than gate-keep. They seep into identities (self-created and attributed). People with educational histories that include low reading test scores often maintain they cannot read even if, on a daily basis, they read forms at work and the TV guide and newspapers at home. They may have reading material at home and a full schedule of evening literacy activities (e.g., homework), but if low literacy test scores run in their family, they are considered and often consider themselves to be illiterate. Print literacy as an individual in-the-head possession may be a misguided view, but it is pervasive and it has major consequences in the lives of individuals. Moreover, unlike computer or television or image literacy, quantity is a serious issue when it comes to print literacy. The quantity of in-the-head print literacy is associated with: (1) an industry (for producing tests, test preparation materials, research results, remedial coaches), (2) a political agenda aimed at privatizing public schools (see Introduction and chap. 7), and (3) a moral position (a low quantity of print literacy, linked through advertising campaigns with poverty and prison, is seen as immoral).

Given popular beliefs, current legislation that enforces those beliefs, and congruent curricular emphases, it is unlikely that academics' desires for schools to expand what counts as literacy will be instituted in the near future. More likely, print literacy—along with a narrow range of texts and practices—will continue to be powerfully implicated in "what this society counts as (educated) knowing." It is that literacy—shot through with gate-keeping power in schools, research, and the popular consciousness—that I continue to believe is worth problematizing and (theoretically) fiddling around with.

PART 2: THEN LET'S START FIDDLING

- Language Arts, Room 201: Read "And off they flew." Answer questions 1–5, p. 60.
- Social Studies, Room 167: Write a report on slavery. Be sure you pay attention to the six traits of good writing: ideas, organization, voice, word choice, sentence "flow," and conventions.

Typical school reading and writing assignments. Both ask students to do exercises.

- This study compares the quality of children's writing as dependent on genre. Children will be shown photos of three people and asked to write (1) a fictional story with those people as characters and (2) a brief biographical sketch of each person in the photos.

A typical example from research on writing. The data gathered will consist of exercises.

- Read the paragraphs on the next pages. Then answer the following questions. Do not turn the page until the examiner tells you to begin.
- If you could have any pet in the world, what would it be? In the space below, write a paragraph stating your choice and giving reasons for your choice. You will have 15 minutes to write, including whatever time you take to plan your response.

Typical means of evaluating reading and writing. Again, both will evaluate how well students do exercises.

What does it matter if we intend to teach, research, and evaluate reading and writing but, instead, we teach, research, and evaluate reading and writing exercises? Can't we learn about how people read the advice column in the newspaper at home from how they read test passages in a classroom or a research laboratory? After all, presumably reading and writing exercises (teaching them, researching them, evaluating them) are somehow connected (revealing, predicting, or transferring) to "regular" reading and writing. The problem is that this connection remains more presumed than proven. What is more, the presumption may be just wrong enough that it contributes heavily to educational failure and to general misinformation about reading and writing—and, ironically, even about reading and writing exercises.

BACKGROUND FOR THE PROPOSALS

The proposals set forth here each attempt to establish theoretical bases for distinguishing two main classes of literacy experiences; reading or writing as an exercise as contrasted with reading and writing that does not feel like an exercise. (From here on, for stylistic ease, I will let the single term *reading* stand for both reading and writing except where writing is highlighted.) It is the contrast between reading and rereading a passage on a reading test in order to answer questions about it and reading and rereading a similar passage for one's own enjoyment, the contrast between writing disconnected sentences to practice spelling words and writing a letter to a friend. Many scholars have appealed to that contrast: Atwell (1987) writing about her early teaching of writing, deCastell and Luke (1986) critiquing so-called stories in basal readers, Edelsky and Smith (1984), Gee (1989c), K. Goodman (1986), Gladwin (1985) writing about arithmetic problem-solving, Graves (1979), Krashen (1988), Raimes (1983) in relation to the talk in English as a second language classrooms, F. Smith

(1986), Torbe (1988), and Wilde (1988) have all contrasted exercises or school contrivances with "the real thing." Their distinction was based on features of what was read or written (was the language "natural" or "artificial?"), why it was read or written (was the purpose communicative?) and for whom it was read or written (was the teacher the only "true" audience?)

Others explained the difference by associating it with different domains or sources of authority. Black and Martin (1982) and Moss and Stansell (1983) distinguished "school reading" and "home reading." Florio and Clark (1982) contrasted "authorized" versus "unauthorized" writing. Hudson (1988) and Shuck (2005) referred to ownership as a distinguishing feature. In a sad turn of affairs, many of the children studied by Hudson refrained from calling the unauthorized, furtive notes they passed to each other *writing*, reserving that designation for school assignments. Erickson (1984) distinguished school reading from other reading through a more extensive analysis of pertinent social relations, a direction I took on myself in the mid-1990s and have continued to follow. Clearly, then, the major distinction I am making is not unique. But the proposals I offer below differ from other work in focus and comprehensiveness; along the way, they unify and sometimes reorder what various scholars have discussed.

My purpose in this enterprise has been and continues to be admittedly normative and frankly political. That is, fiddling with this distinction between exercises and nonexercises[2] follows from a "meta-narrative" about what I think literacy should be for (A. Luke, 1991) and what education should be about. (These are not just vague "shoulds," but, as demonstrated in many of the chapters in this volume, specific, detailed visions of educational practice.) That meta-narrative is ultimately about improving children's educational chances by improving literacy instruction, evaluation, and research. It advocates a literate Subject in Freire's (1970) sense who reads and writes, at times at least, for critical citizenship (Edelsky, 1999). Thus, it constitutes a political agenda, one aimed at undermining hierarchies and enhancing political and economic equity. That is, I am not trying to simply understand or describe literacy practices and their relations with the social order; I am trying to do what I can to transform them. In Erickson's (1979) words, I am trying to "make this canoe better."

And the canoe certainly continues to need improvement. In the 1991 edition of this book, I wrote, "Curriculum content is fragmented (F. Smith,

---

[2]Although I once talked about this contrast as one between exercises and "the real thing" (Edelsky & Draper, 1989; Edelsky & Smith, 1984), I no longer believe one is more "real" (or more authentic). Thus, in this introduction to my various proposals, I use a term that holds no matter which decade's proposal I am talking about. Even though the negation *nonexercise* is cumbersome and difficult to process, it more accurately captures the type of literacy experiences that contrast with what I am calling *exercises*.

1986); little time is spent reading and writing (Anderson et al., 1985); decisions affecting a student's entire educational career are based on responses to tests of questionable validity" (p. 78). But those of us who made such a critique then had no way of knowing that those were actually "the good old days" in literacy education. By 2005, under pressure from federal and state legislation, teachers were using scripted reading programs; curriculum in urban schools especially had devolved largely to "test prep"; and a student's opportunities were decided not on the basis of tests (plural) but on the basis of a single test, assembled quickly to meet federal and state mandates. At least some of these tests have been critiqued roundly for shoddy test construction (M. L. Smith, 2004).

Underlying this state of affairs is a theory about literacy prevalent in both folk wisdom and professional knowledge. This conception of literacy has at its center the idea that reading is a complex mechanical process consisting of separable skills (e.g. decoding, word attack, comprehending) internal to the reader and that teaching, testing, or researching even one of these separate skills is part of, or sometimes the same as, teaching, testing, or researching reading.[3] Closely related is a belief in transfer; that is, practicing separable reading skills transfers to reading because the skill or skills are already a subset of reading. Moreover, enveloping this entire conception is an assumption of "naturalness"—how could it possibly be any other way?

One of the major recent efforts to change conceptions of literacy does not rebut particulars of this theory; instead, it changes the ground altogether. It switches the focus from psychological goings-on to social ones. This social theory conceives of literacy as literacies and argues that, rather than being one abstract psychological process, literacies are historically and culturally defined social practices. According to social practice scholars (e.g. Bloome, 1987; deCastell & Luke, 1986; Graff, 1987; Scribner & Cole, 1981; Street, 1984; Szwed, 1981), literacy is what it *is* by virtue of how it is *used* in social life.

Like all scientific endeavor, these theoretical propositions too seem "purposeful," either motivated by or serving a political agenda. Graff's (1987) research on the context-dependent consequences of literacy

---

[3]This folk theory, the cultural common sense that decoding and comprehending are separate and sequential skills (decode first, comprehend afterward) has recently been granted scientific status by means of research using functional magnetic resonance imaging (fMRI) (Shaywitz et al., 1996). Not only is this a case of available technology driving theory—an upside-down approach to science—but the limits of the technology are such that these studies of (presumably) reading *must* actually be confined to studies of responses to letter-like shapes, actual letter clusters, or nonsense syllables. Functional MRI cannot be performed on reading phrases or sentences, let alone longer texts. See Strauss (2005b) for a long and lucid explanation of why fMRI studies can not legitimize this folk theory of reading or its accompanying view that reading begins with decoding which, in turn, depends on phonics.

throughout history delegitimizes both the myth that literacy always brings with it social and individual gains and the myth that illiteracy causes ills as varied as poverty and alcoholism. Street (1984) exposed racist undersides to academic and popular variations on The Great Divide (the presumed gap between civilized and primitive cultures, literate and preliterate societies, and written and oral traditions). Several researchers in the literacy-as-social-practice tradition aimed to improve literacy education by broadening existing school definitions of literacy (Heath, 1983; Szwed, 1981). All used the terms *literacy* and *reading* (or *writing*) interchangeably. In fact, Graff (1987, p. 3) made the equation explicit by defining *literacy* as "basic or primary levels of reading and writing."

Thinking of literacy as any social practice involving print and offering rich descriptions or fresh historical analyses of particular social practices, these researchers provide legitimacy for a general shift toward more inclusiveness in educational practice. But their equations could just as well provide a new theoretical rationale for the status quo. After all, if reading is literacy, and literacy (and therefore reading) is anything one does with print, why not continue to see any use of print in school or in research as a legitimate instance of reading? Why do any more than add to existing school literacy practices? Why eliminate any? It is a short step, after all, from seeing literacy as a social practice to seeing it as *only* a social practice. And, in fact, because the literacy-as-social-practice view has discredited interior processes as "psychological," this work discourages a serious consideration of the profoundly social nature of interior processes and, reciprocally, the extent to which underlying processes are involved in social practice. The proposals below are different in that they rely on both social practices and interior processes (to different extents, depending on the decade) to help transform teaching, researching, and evaluating reading.

BEGINNING—AND CONTINUING—ASSUMPTIONS

The basic theoretical premise that initially prompted my thinking about reading exercises as distinct from nonexercises is that written language is language.[4] Taking that premise seriously suggests two major implications. First, if written language is language, then it has the characteristics of language; and second, if written language is language it is learned like language. Thus, like oral language, written language is a system of abstract

---

[4]Scholars such as Gee (2004b), MacSwan (2000) and others disagree. They maintain that language is "hard-wired" into the human species, which accounts for the fact that language (speech) is universal among human societies. But writing, they argue, has arrived too recently on the evolutionary scene for it to have been "hard-wired" inside the human brain; thus, writing is not universal, and it is not language. I respond to these arguments in chapter 6.

conventions for making meanings in a context (Halliday, 1985). Like oral language, the "default" function of written language is informational (Gee, 1989b). Written language, like oral, is socially shared and socially organized. Neither can exist without context (language always appears at some place at some time, for some reason; Hymes, 1970). Both are reflexive, occurring through contexts and themselves creating the contexts in which they occur. Each is necessarily ambiguous (always requiring interpretation, always open to multiple uses and multiple meanings). Each is also predictable (offering cues for meaning) and redundant (offering more than one set of cues).

Like oral language, written language is learned primarily through actual use, not through exercises for later use.[5] An important question, then, is: What is *use?* Drawing on the research and theories of K. Goodman (1969, 1984), Harste, Burke, and Woodward (1982); Halliday (1978); Hymes (1972b); and F. Smith (1982b), I believe language use is purpose-driven sense-making within embedded contexts in which particular relationships obtain to people and to texts (spoken or written). The language user constructs meanings from systems of cues (phonological—or graphic and orthographic in the case of written language—syntactic, semantic, and pragmatic). Because each of these language cuing systems (e.g., the syntactic system) is conventionalized and interacts with the other systems that are also conventionalized (e.g., the semantic system), and since conventions necessarily mean social conventions, the meanings constructed through these cues—no matter what else they are—are always social constructions.

The social conventions are conventions, not guarantees. They entail choice and interpretation. They anticipate violation; there are norms for repairing and norms for violating the norms for repair, and so on. This implies that language use also includes a huge potential for individual— but still interpretable, and therefore socially derived—variation (Becker, 1988). Most often, when people use language, they have considerable (if shared) control over how they use it, what they use it for, if they use it, when they stop using it, and so on. In other words, while all language use is socially constrained, it is usually not coerced.

Whenever language is used, it is used in events—events that capture and create relationships among people and between people and objects (material and otherwise), events that also reflect worldviews (perspectives, values, and beliefs, etc.). What is learned when people learn language includes all

---

[5]For this chapter, "learned like language" relies heavily on the concept of "use." I maintain the adequacy of that concept for thinking about language learning, although I now believe that second language learning and literacy learning share certain features that are not shared in the same ways by first language learning. I explore those differences in chapter 6.

those relationships and worldviews that were part of the events enacted largely through language use. The language used within those events is usually used for some purpose other than instruction in or evaluation of the language use itself—for informing, persuading, joking, warning, teasing, explaining, cajoling, and so forth. Though language is learned *through* using it, it is not usually used consciously and deliberately *for* learning it. And though language might be used to create impressions and thus enters into evaluations, appraisals, and categorizations people are constantly making as they conduct their daily lives, it is evaluation of the person (her ideas, her status, her origins) that occurs through evaluation of her language use, not evaluation of her language solely for the sake of evaluating the language. What "use" offers is demonstrations and engagement—demonstrations of how language works and what it's for and an opportunity to engage with or participate with others. What learning through use requires is sensitivity to the demonstrations one is privy to through engagement in the interaction. That sensitivity comes from the taken-for-granted expectations on everyone's part that since the learner belongs to the community of language users, she will of course learn the language the other users use (F. Smith, 1981b). No need, then, to deliberately elicit language just to see how well she is doing.

THE 1980s PROPOSAL

The 1980s proposal grew out of my attempts to find a basis for distinguishing examples of reading and writing that seemed obviously artificial from examples that did not. I collected these examples from classroom observations, teachers' manuals, research reports, my own experience as a reader, and conversations with colleagues. I tried—and rejected—such contrasts as in-school/out-of-school, assigned/unassigned, official/not official, purposeful/ not purposeful. Some of these contrasts did not differentiate all the examples; some were poorly conceived (e.g., nothing has no purpose; what matters is whose purpose and what purpose). Eventually, what I took as the central factors were theoretical features of the reading process.

It was a comment by Harste et al. (1982) that supported that decision as well as my central point; that is, there is a distinction between reading and "reading"—something that merely masquerades as reading. Harste and his colleagues claimed that responses to unpredictable, nonfunctional graphic displays (e.g., isolated words in workbooks, syllables as prompts in a research setting) simply do not count as reading. That comment was based on what Ken Goodman (1969, 1984), Jerry Harste and Carolyn Burke (1977), and Frank Smith (1982a) had theorized about what people do when they read; that is, they engage in a process that consists of predicting with interdependent cuing systems in order to create a text meaning for some purpose. It was these features of the reading process—predictability and predicting, cues from interacting cuing systems, creating a text meaning, and reader's purpose—that I proposed were what distinguished literacy from reading and reading from something that only resembled reading.

The 1980s proposal (Edelsky & Draper, 1989; Edelsky & Smith, 1984) can be summarized as follows: Literacy, the superordinate category, is any use of print as print; reading is a particular kind of literacy. Literacy includes every use of print as print, but not, for instance, as material for wrapping fish or washing windows. Some uses of print as print do not result in the creation of a text meaning for the user; for example, naming the letters on a chart during an eye examination is an instance of literacy but not reading. Reading is an act of predicting with cues offered by simultaneously present, interactive, interdependent cuing systems (graphic, orthographic, syntactic, semantic, pragmatic) to construct a text meaning. Reading, in other words, is defined in terms of an interior process. By implication, if a person is not engaged in the reading process—if she is not constructing a text meaning, or if she is not using cues from all systems (because she does not know how or because the graphic display does not offer them), or if the interactivity among systems is severed—what is happening is an act of literacy but not reading. It is something that only looks like reading—a simulation, an exercise, "reading." The reason researchers should not be studying, evaluators should not be evaluating, and teachers should not be teaching responses to print that do not invoke the reading process (sense-making through the use of cues from all cuing systems interacting appropriately) is that such responses are acts of "reading" but not reading.

Real reading, reading with no quotes around it, can be mundane (reading one's grocery list) or special (reading a telegram announcing one has won the lottery). It can involve short texts or long; socially acceptable or unacceptable ones (e.g., hold-up notes); it can have single or multiple purposes, be direct or full of innuendoes, well or poorly crafted. What matters is the creation of meaning through the use of cues from all written language cuing systems interacting "normally" with each other. Reading one-word texts (like single word bumper stickers or signs on doors) counts as reading because pragmatic cues help one predict syntax (e.g., location on a car signals *this genre is bumper sticker* which in turn makes syntax predictable [e.g., eliminating the possibility that the word on the bumper sticker would be an article or preposition]); genre also helps predict semantic cues so that, with graphic and orthographic cues, a reader can guess a one-word bumper sticker offers *Fore* but not *For, Tea* but not *The.* A word on a flashcard in a lesson, however, can be *for, the,* or any part of speech, any meaning that isn't obscene, blasphemous, or unpatriotic. Decreased predictability due to missing systems (no syntactic cues) is what makes a response to a flashcard a reading exercise but not reading.

Decoding the graphics of a language one does not understand is not really reading because one is creating no text meaning for oneself (e.g., my oral decoding of the transliterated Hebrew in a prayer book is culturally meaningful for me and others, and constitutes an interpretable text for a Hebrew speaker, but is not textually meaningful for me since I know no Hebrew, and is therefore, for me, a simulation of reading).

But, according to the proposals from the 1980s, even when all systems are being used and a text meaning is being created, something can still be only a simulation of reading if all the language cuing systems are not interacting. The reader's purpose is what might prevent the systems from interacting. Two purposes have that potential. Either using print just to take part in instruction for instruction's sake or using it simply to be evaluated for evaluation's sake creates distortions or outright severs the connections among pragmatics, syntax, and semantics. For example, when letters are produced only to be evaluated but not mailed, normative expectations about genre and audience are violated, and expected connections (e.g., among purpose, genre, and semantic and syntactic choices) are not made.

This earlier proposal distinguishing varieties of activity with print according to whether they constitute reading or merely something that looks like reading was a helpful one. It offered a theoretically principled guide for changing classroom literacy instruction, since it was based on an empirically supported, theoretical model of the reading process. It helped explain why children who spent an entire school year writing for publication reverted to resistance and finally shoddy production when confronted with a school-district-wide writing test at the end of the year (Edelsky & Smith, 1984). It made sense of the fact that many people who can read adequately for their own purposes do poorly on reading tests. What it said was this: These are different phenomena—authentic reading on the one hand, "reading" on the other. Learning or researching or evaluating one was not the same thing as learning or researching or evaluating the other.

THE 1990s PROPOSAL

The Dilemma

By the mid-1990s, although I still believed there was a difference between reading and reading exercises, I was having second thoughts about the character of that difference.[6] One of the distinguishing features still seemed right; the reading-process-derived requirement that, to be reading,

[6]I owe shifts in my thinking about this topic to conversations with Steve Gelb, some nudges from Larry Friedman and Allan Luke, and the influence of Dell Hymes. They may well contest what I've done with their views, but I remain grateful to them.

a person has to be creating a text meaning for herself (not just for someone else, as in the case of copying an address in a foreign alphabet without knowing which marks signal the street and which the city). But the other defining criteria for exercises (decreased predictability, missing cuing systems, lack of connections among cuing systems, leading to all-around phoniness) simply did not hold up. There were too many occasions when the criteria did not permit me to sort exercises from nonexercises. Take all-around phoniness. When normative expectations regarding genres such as letters or reports are violated, the result is a "pragmatic setup." The writer of a report is expected to have more information (and report it) than the audience, and the norm is that reported information is to be used for something outside the report. In school reports, however, the norm is violated. The teacher audience is more expert than the writer, and reported information is used only as "evidence" to be graded. Similarly, the person named in the salutation of a letter is the expected reader of the letter, but in school letters the expected reader is the teacher, not the named addressee. Writing a report or letter for school is thus more often an exercise in writing a report or letter. It is true that these are exercises— but not because of their phoniness. After all, it is a frequent occurrence in language that events, acts, and texts are not what they seem. Requests can be complaints, questions can be directives. *Is that a threat or a promise?* is a comeback that highlights language's pragmatic ambiguity. In other words, "phoniness" is not what makes something an exercise. And straightfor- wardness (e.g., self-proclaimed workbook exercises) does not prevent it.

Predictability was one of the requirements for authentic reading, but there are cases when print is being used with utter predictability yet the activities are clearly exercises. It is highly predictable, based on pragmatics and graphics, that the mark to be made after the 17th capital *T* in a hand- writing exercise will be another capital *T*. A youngster who has gone through a set of flashcards often enough can predict the next flashcard in the sequence without any cues from syntax or semantics (S. Gelb, personal communication, April 6, 1990).

In the 1980s proposal, reduced predictability due to missing cuing sys- tems or missing connections between cuing systems made an instance of print use an exercise. The earlier proposal took note of the fact that sys- tems that seemed to be missing might actually be deleted. For instance, lists and other texts of single words were not necessarily texts with missing sys- tems. They were more like performatives with the performative verb deleted; for example, *I state* is deleted from *it is raining* (Fromkin & Rodman, 1983). Thus, grocery lists offer syntactic cues because that genre signals but then deletes *buy the following items*. Pragmatic conventions were what led people to expect only nouns or adjectives on doors of public restrooms (the frame *this facility is* sometimes appears before the adjective in the slot: *vacant* or *occupied*).

Unlike these cases of deleted systems, there are examples in which whole cuing systems are missing, not merely deleted. According to the 1980s proposal, these should be exercises. But they do not always seem to be. For instance, when the 4-year-old holds up a scrap of paper, with one word on it (e.g., *building*) and says *Mom, what's this say?*, Mom has no syntactic cues to help her predict. Now it is true that word identification in such a context entails attention to different language phenomena than does word identification in connected prose, and it is also true that the meaning the reader creates with that single word (*building*) must remain vague without confirmation from other systems (Is it *building a house* or *the building?* What kind of building is it? Why was the larger text written in the first place?). Nevertheless, the mother who responds *it says "building"* is not just simulating reading. And when people look at Frank Smith's (1982b) examples of ambiguous print, or when they work puzzles for fun, or when they read personalized license plates—all of which deliberately eliminate cuing systems to require "tricks with print"—doing those tricks constitutes a special (tricky) kind of reading, not something that merely pretends to be reading.

The 1980s proposal also classified print use as non-reading if cuing systems were present but did not interact (if pragmatic purpose did not help someone predict syntax, if genre did not predict semantics, etc.). That proposal recognized that people could use genres non-normatively. For example, someone could write a thank you note, not to thank, but to make the addressee feel guilty. The writer's syntactic and semantic choices would then be fitted to this purpose as well as to the genre demands. Sincerity—being "true" to the genre—was, thus, not a requisite for "really" reading or writing in the 1980s proposal, because cuing systems would still be interacting, but in ways that would fit the atypical purpose. There was only one exception when the cuing systems failed to interact: when a reader's sole purpose was to take part in a literacy lesson for its own sake or to be evaluated on literacy for the sake of evaluation.

It was hard to admit, but the only reason that can account for this exception must have been a double standard about interactivity. I must have been demanding more obvious interactions among syntax, semantics, and purpose if the purpose was being instructed or evaluated than for syntax, semantics, and other purposes. It became apparent to me—finally—that the high school student reading a chapter in the biology textbook only to answer the questions at the end is making her own connections, selectively using graphic, orthographic, syntactic, semantic, and pragmatic cues to fit her purpose—to spend as little time as possible in order to be finished with the biology reading exercise. If someone can be using all cuing systems interactively when reading a mystery novel from an efferent stance (Rosenblatt, 1978) to learn about a character so she can dress accurately for a costume party, then so can a student who is reading a mystery novel to learn about a character to score well on a test. Rather than cutting off the interactivity among systems, the purposes of participating in literacy instruction or proving literacy proficiency (purposes that do not usually go with certain genres or particular semantic or syntactic choices) do not sever connections among systems; they simply create non-normative inter-activity. And it is not non-normativity of interactions that makes a literacy activity an exercise.

Nor is it distortions in cuing systems. Reading an auto license plate *BRD4GZS (Be ready for Jesus)* requires one to allow graphics to contradict semantics in order to overemphasize grapho-phonics while eliminating orthography—certainly a case of distortion and disconnection. However, all of those overrides and contradictions stem from, serve, and are intensely tied to pragmatic conventions about this particular kind of print and what one does with it. Moreover, after the reader gets the trick, she confirms using the systems that were seemingly eliminated or discon-nected. In other words, not only is the reader reading but the systems are connected after all.

The major reason, then, that the 1980s proposal for what distinguishes reading from reading exercises did not hold up was that in emphasizing one key feature of language (predictability arising from cuing systems), I had for-gotten two others: arbitrariness and ambiguity. Given the right circum-stances, any text (and perhaps any language resource) can be used for just about anything. And, of course, if the defining criteria in the original pro-posal did not stand the test of subsequent examples, then neither did the single two-part division: authentic reading versus simulations of reading.

My sense remained, however, that there were important differences between reading a list to be evaluated on reading and reading a list to remember what to buy at the grocery store; that those differences may have been more social than I had previously thought; and that they were impli-cated in whether a person learned to read and, therefore, in whether he or she would ever be able to use reading as a tool for societal change.

The Solution

The 1990s proposal relied on a conception of reading as both an underly-ing process and as part of a variety of social practices. Processes and prac-tices alike have social and psychological dimensions. Neither processes nor practices are strictly within or strictly between people. Social practices include psychological processes (memory, categorizing, predicting, etc.); underlying processes rely on social norms. While that inseparability was noted in the proposal from the 1980s, and while normative expectations regarding genres, audiences, and so on reflected an implicit accounting for social practices, those practices still took a decided back seat to an underlying interior process. Although underlying processes still appeared in the 1990s proposal, it was social relations and meanings that were foregrounded.

The 1990s proposal can be summarized as follows. Three distinctions should be considered in teaching, researching, and evaluating literacy: reading/ NOT-reading,[7] exercises/nonexercises, and literates-as-Subjects/literates-as-Objects. Not considering these distinctions makes it all too easy to think one is researching reading but to actually be researching NOT-reading, to promise reading but deliver exercises, to promote literacy as a tool for empowerment but offer school literacy practices that disempower.

Reading/NOT-reading maintains the 1980s process-based distinction between whether or not a reader is trying to construct a text meaning for herself. Someone might pronounce print in a foreign language "without understanding a word" to someone else who does understand the language and therefore interprets a meaning for the text. The pronouncer, however, is not reading even though he or she may be taking part in creating a meaning for the event.

As in the earlier version, purpose is still crucial, but purpose is now seen as an outgrowth of a broader meaning of events, not just texts: What is this event *about?* And meanings (and, therefore, purposes) of events are shaped by social relations. These two dimensions working together—event meaning and social relations—distinguish exercises from all other reading

---

[7]A pervasive problem in writing this chapter is the absence of an easy-to-understand, short label for what I am calling *NOT-reading* (repeating "use of print with no aim of creating a meaningful text" is clear but cumbersome). Putting pen to paper with no intent of making a meaningful text might be called *scribbling* or *doodling.* There is no comparable term for looking at print or pronouncing it aloud with no intent of making any text meaning (except in schools, on tests, or in laboratory research projects where that activity might either be called *decoding* or even *reading* itself—which is part of the situation that prompts this chapter.) The absence of such a label is part of a more general phenomenon: There are few folk terms for different reading activities; far more for different speaking activities. Ask people what they are doing when talking and they might say: talking, just talking, conversing, gossiping, joking, lecturing, debating, arguing, holding forth, chatting, shooting the breeze, interviewing, confessing, conferring, consulting, rapping, reporting, schmoozing, and so on. Ask them the same question regarding writing and the possible list grows shorter: writing, just writing, jotting, scribbling, doodling, transcribing (in schools, I've heard journaling and composing; among researchers, I've heard memo-ing), filling out a form, taking notes ("dashing off" is about manner rather than type of activity). When it comes to reading, the choices are also few: reading, just reading, studying, scanning, skimming, perusing, speed-reading. The list can be lengthened with objects: reading a letter, book, note, message, magazine, and so on. The shorter lists for reading and writing probably reflect a folk theory: Reading and writing are relatively undifferentiated, though the objects connected with the activity are varied. It is precisely this folk theory I counter with the present proposal.

(i.e., nonexercises) and literate Subjects from literate Objects. If the event is about learning or evaluating reading (so that the reader's purpose is to comply with an assignment simply for the sake of doing the assignment, or to show how well she can read simply for the sake of being evaluated), those are sufficient grounds to experience that event as an exercise (i.e., it is not necessary to make a further appeal to what is happening to cuing systems). If the event is instigated, ended, shaped, paced, assessed, and so on, by someone other than the reader—if the relative control is in the hands of another—the event positions the reader as an Object. The difference between the literate person as Object and the literate-as-Subject is social and political, not individual. It requires a look at who else is involved and how and at the role and power of the literate in relation to the role and power of the other(s).

The difference between literacy as an exercise and all other literacy reflects a difference in the meaning of the literacy event. When literacy events primarily mean instruction or evaluation (where purposes of the literacy used in the event are instruction for instruction's sake or evaluation for evaluation's sake), the literacy is experienced as an exercise. Nonexercises have other (communicative) purposes and occur in events that have other meanings.

This proposal assumes that people are either aware of these dimensions or that they at least orient to them. People using print know whether they are creating meaning for themselves with the print, know what the event is about from their perspective (even if they dispute or dislike what it "should" be about), and know (or are made to know) when they are not in control of certain aspects of the event. If they are "wrong" (e.g., if students believe they are writing to the President but the teacher has no intention of mailing the letters and will, instead, be evaluating them), it is their perspective that stands during the activity itself, though duplicity in one event will most likely affect how other events are perceived.

Like the earlier version, the 1990s proposal says nothing about length, prestige, or involvement with or import of the print use. A person can write a note of a dozen lines or do a writing exercise of dozens of pages, read a poem in the position of either Object or Subject, and write a phone message with no involvement or a classroom essay with intense involvement. Nor does quality of the reading or writing enter into the difference between reading and NOT-reading, exercises and nonexercises, or Subject or Object positions. A person who does not see how the clues led to the villain in the murder mystery is, nevertheless, reading (making a text-meaning), doing a nonexercise, and reading as a Subject. A young child stumbling over words or an even younger one using at least some features of the print to reconstruct the story in a well-loved book is reading. Using print cues to make any text meaning is reading (though it may not necessarily be

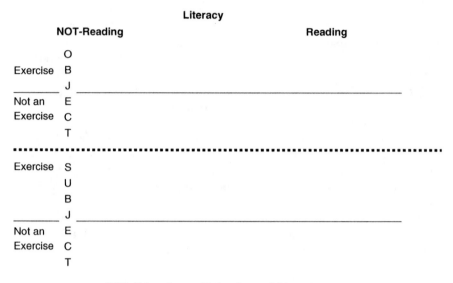

FIG. 5.1.   Some distinctions within print use.

"good," "deep," "sophisticated" reading, according to her community's standards). Nor are the divisions confined to Western technological society. The Hanunoo whittling courtship messages on bamboo (McDermott, 1977) were writing, not doing a writing exercise. On the other hand, the literate Vai, pronouncing Qur'anic verses during a religious ceremony in a language they did not understand (Scribner & Cole, 1981), were most likely not engaged in an exercise with no purpose other than instruction or evaluation, but they were not reading, either. Doing reading exercises should not be associated only with school, just as nonexercises should not be associated only with the out-of-school world. In classrooms where teachers were trying (in the 1990s) to buck institutional pressures and create whole language environments (see chaps. 7 and 8), children read and wrote with considerable control over their nonexercise activity. Writing a sample movie review as part of applying for a job as movie critic, however, with no expectation that the review will be published but solely to be evaluated on one's ability to write movie reviews, is an exercise.

Figure 5.1 offers a schematic summary of the 1990s proposal. Some of the examples and their placement in Figure 5.2 will be referred to in the discussion of social relations, meaning of the event, and fuzzy examples.

SOCIAL RELATIONS

The social relations among participants in an event may not highlight control (e.g., empathy, affection, or reciprocity may be more salient). Nor is

Literacy

		NOT-Reading	Reading
Exercise	O	• letter-naming, flashcard lesson • nonsense syllables, experiment • ?self-initiated calligraphy practice	• take reading test • read essay to answer questions • fill in worksheet to be checked off
	B		• write essay for application • read word on flashcard • do puzzles/tricks with print on worksheets as a lesson
	J		• ?tricks with print for prizes
	E		

Not an
Exercise
	C	• naming letters on eye chart
		• ?pronouncing foreign language
		  print in rituals
		• ?copying address in foreign
		  alphabet
			• parent orders child to write
			  thank you note
			• ?tricks with print for prizes

	T		

****

		NOT-Reading	Reading

Exercise	S	• ?self-initiated calligraphy
		  practice
			• worksheets in 'open classroom'
			• writing trial movie review to try
			  out for job as movie critic

	U	• ?Freire's pedagogy	• practicing writing 'purpose' statements in grant-writing seminar • ?Freire's pedagogy
	B		

Not an
Exercise
	J	• doodling decorative letters
		• ?pronouncing foreign language
		  print in rituals
			• reading essay to be entertained
			• writing movie review for
			  publication and to try out for job

	E	• ?copying address in foreign
		  alphabet
		• ?Freire's pedagogy
			• reading word in response to
			  'Mom, what's that say?'
			• drafting purpose statement for
			  grant proposal

	C		• reading known language in rituals • ?Freire's pedagogy
	T		

FIG. 5.2. Some examples of distinctions within print use.

control the only consideration in terms of what meanings are constructed. As Gilbert (1991) argued, readers are positioned historically to construct gendered, raced, classed, ethnicitied, cultured, aged, and able-bodied meanings, not just meanings reflecting their relational position in the literacy event itself. Still, control does matter (and, indeed, it is implicated in those dominance-related constructions of meaning). If the print user is being controlled in her use of print—if someone else decides what literacy event will occur, how it will begin, what it will be about, when it will end, and so on—then the print user is positioned as an Object.

It is not control over any single aspect of an event, such as who initiates the reading or writing, that renders someone a Subject or an Object. In Hudson's (1988) study, for instance, teacher initiation of writing resulted in children feeling powerless in some assignments but in charge in others. More likely, it is control over some combination of several aspects of the event. Moreover, control over literacy is a peculiar continuum; that is, both ends (total control and total freedom) are impossible. While there are social conventions—and therefore constraints—for every minute aspect of language, the conventions are not handcuffs. People are agents in their own language use, giving that use a highly personal character (Becker, 1988, p. 31). Yet neither can people have total freedom in print use since, through following, violating, or modifying conventions that are social, the social is always a part. In other words, people's experiences, including their language experiences, "can never be entirely their own" (Barone, 1990). Nor does an overall hierarchical relationship between the parties guarantee that the subordinate person will read or write in the Object position throughout a particular literacy event. That relationship impinges on the Subject-ness or Object-ness that is created, but it does not mechanically determine which general position a reader or writer is in during a specific event. Thus, a mid-level manager can write a report for a chief executive officer and have considerable control over the writing. So can a writer writing a letter of apology, feeling decidedly one-down in the relationship and wanting desperately to appease by meeting the expectations of a perhaps controlling significant Other. Whether the other participants are physically present is not what determines who controls the event. Test-takers can be in a room all by themselves, but an absent test writer and absent policymakers have great control over the reading that takes place during that test-taking. *Social relations,* then, means the particular relations among participants as they are played out concerning the reading or writing in a literacy event. While the broad outline of what those particulars might be can be sketched out, the specifics probably can be identified only after the fact.

Social relations that position the print user as Object may also include the relationship between the reader and the print—the ways in which the print itself and its use control the reader. Certain genres, like transliterations of foreign alphabets, charts of randomized letters, and tricks with print (puzzles, clever license tags, nonsense syllables for experiments that announce *let's see what you can do with this*), exert excessive control. To be used successfully, they must be used perfectly rather than plausibly. They have a combination of "controlling devices." If they elicit NOT-reading, they omit whole systems of cues and also do not permit the meaning-making that could help the print user confirm her response. With eye charts, handwriting practice, nonsense syllables in an experiment or on a worksheet, or transliterations of foreign language syllables, there is no way, using one's own knowledge of language conventions, to know if one "got it right." If the tricky print can be read (i.e., given a text meaning), something about it controls how and when the reader confirms predictions. For example, instead of confirming periodically (constantly?), the vanity license-tag reader suspends confirmation of all but the graphic system (and sometimes, when numbers are used for words—e.g., *2* for *to*—that, too, must wait) until the reader "gets it" and the event is over. Not only does such print sometimes omit systems, but it is stingy with cues from the systems it does provide. Moreover, it allows the reader no leeway. The puzzle reader (e.g., the Scrabble player or the five-letter-word game player) and the reader of some worksheets and test items must supply more than his or her share of the orthographic or syntactic or semantic cues and then, to add insult to injury, must produce a perfect response. In other words, when the relations between print-user and print help create the literate as Object, those relations also distort the underlying process.

Print use outside of school usually positions people as Subjects. But not always, as the examples of tricky print show. There are other out-of-school examples in which the participants (or the print) make the reader an Object. Ordering a child to write a thank you letter to a grandparent, making sure he begins, overseeing his production, and telling him when he can be finished is a case of the writer-as-Object. Using print as part of the curriculum in school often creates literates-as-Objects. But it doesn't have to. Literature study sessions (Edelsky, Altwerger, & Flores, 1991; Edelsky, Smith, & Wolfe, 2002; K. Smith, 1990) in which children turn to the novel they have been reading as they initiate topics, ask questions of each other and the teacher, and establish the topic of next meetings, are events in which students are literate Subjects.

MEANING/PURPOSE OF THE LITERACY EVENT

The overarching theoretical justification for considering the purpose of literate activity (which contributes heavily to the meaning of the event) is Soviet activity theory (e.g., Leont'ev, 1978). This theory argues against the idea of the individual-as-such (with particular abilities and traits) in favor of the individual-in-action.[8] Goals and motives (purposes) are not separate

---

[8]Minick (1985) identifies three kinds of theories about human functioning. *Isolating* theories assume an individual whose "psychological characteristics can be defined in isolation from the concrete characteristics of the external world" (p. 18). *Contextual* theories attribute psychological characteristics to the individual but maintain that these characteristics cannot be understood in isolation from the tasks or contexts in which they are manifested. *Activity* theories, on the other hand, presume that the individual has no psychological characteristics in isolation from actions that are themselves part of larger action systems constituting the social system in which the individual finds himself or herself.

from but are key features of action. A change in goals, motives, or conditions of the action is a change in the total activity itself (Minick, 1985).

The 1990s proposal (as well as the 1980s proposal) singled out two purposes: instruction and evaluation. Print use may well be incidentally instructive (*Oh, that's how that word is spelled!*); it may indeed be spontaneously evaluated (*What a bumbling reader she is!*). However, when people use print for the purpose of being instructed in using print in an event which is itself about instruction, or when they use print for the purpose of being evaluated on print-using ability in an event that is about evaluation, that use of print is an exercise. Now exercises may, ultimately, have very "real-world" purposes. For example, many function as gatekeepers, giving or denying people access to jobs—a real-world purpose indeed! But though exercises may subsequently serve to gate-keep or to diagnose, their first purpose is to evaluate print use for the sake of evaluating the print use, or to provide instruction in print use for the sake of instructing in print use.

Bloome and Bailey (1990) maintain that all activity in school comes into being for the purpose of instruction, that nothing can be "authentic"—not even a vocational education project like building a house in which someone will live. I disagree. Some projects (like building a house or publishing a newsletter or organizing a science fair or lobbying for better playground facilities) have the potential to override their instructional *raison d'être* so that other purposes can be foregrounded. If a big, multitask project subordinates learning to production (a characteristic of apprenticeships; Minick, 1985), then the embedded tasks are not exercises. For instance, in the case of producing a newsletter, though the "because motive" (what instigated the whole enterprise) might be instruction, the "in order to motive" (the hoped-for outcome) of some of the embedded tasks (Schutz, 1962) can become more tied to producing the newsletter. Instruction in writing headlines, then, would not be instruction for the sake of instruction but instruction for the sake of the newsletter. In other words, school tasks do not have to be academic (i.e., instruction- or evaluation-focused exercises).

Two special conditions for some exercises should be mentioned. One set is that of a person voluntarily and deliberately seeking out instruction or practice in order to learn or to improve performance (e.g., self-initiating calligraphy practice or willingly practicing writing headlines for the class newsletter). Such practice, while an exercise, can be helpful if the reader or writer clearly sees herself using what is practiced in the near future. There is also a conflux of conditions that is especially detrimental. When exercises elicit NOT-reading by someone positioned as an Object, they deliver a triple whammy. They violate all the usual conditions of language and language learning (making meaning, having some purpose other than instruction or evaluation, having relative control). No wonder people feel the discrepancy between reading a torturous test item and reading a letter from a friend. No wonder children in remedial classes, deprived of chances to read as Subjects for some purpose other than getting a reading lesson, remain poor readers.

The exercise/nonexercise distinction may seem as though it duplicates the Subject/Object distinction. But actually the two dimensions can be separated, if with some difficulty. It is possible to find examples where someone is doing an exercise but still has considerable control over the event and the activity, as Figure 5.2 shows. The reverse—not doing an exercise but still being positioned as an Object (i.e., having one's reading controlled by peculiar print or by another person)—is more difficult to find. Probably, this is because relations among participants and meaning/purpose of the event interact. That interaction can be seen most clearly when considering the role of the person who responds to the writing or reading. (In speech, the contrasting roles of the other party are seen in the difference between the exchanges *What time is it?/Two -o'clock./Thanks* and *What time is it?/Two- o'clock./Good answer.*) The other person in a literacy event might accept the written apology, try out the written recipe, read the book a reader just praised, and so on. When the other participates in these ways as a co-literate, the reader or writer can become active in the post-event event (e.g., restating the written apology, asking for a recipe in return, checking the respondent's responses to the recommended novel). However, when the other's role is simply to evaluate the print use, the print user is out of the picture at the end.

FUZZY EXAMPLES AND WHAT THEY REVEAL

There are several examples preceded by a question mark that appear in more than one category in Figure 5.2. Categorizing something as reading or NOT-reading—as making a text meaning or not—was not a problem. Nor was deciding whether examples of NOT-reading were exercises (literates respond to eye charts to have their vision evaluated, not their literacy). Except for the Freire items, all the double categorized items in the left-hand column (the NOT-reading category) are double categorized because I am unsure of the designation of Subject versus Object in those examples in which the literate person has reasonable control over the event in relation to other parties but is held on a short leash by the print itself. For example, the member of the congregation who joins with others to pronounce foreign language syllables in a prespecified ritual is collaborating with other participants in order to make the event "go right" but is being tightly constrained by minimal cues from the print, absence of opportunities for any confirming triangulation from other cuing systems, and little latitude for interpretation. The 8-year-old who self-initiates practice in cursive script has a similar problem. These conditions do constitute a short leash, but there are circumstances that could offset this bind. The examples with question marks all include voluntary participation, ignorance of the quality of one's own performance, and no evaluative consequences for poor performance (though there may be penalties; e.g., a poor copying job in a foreign alphabet could well result in nondelivery of the letter). These conditions cast some doubt on whether these examples should be considered "positioning the literate as an Object."

Regarding the right-hand column of Figure 5.2, tricks with print (scrambled letter games, puzzles, etc.), the question is: Should these be considered exercises or not? When the tricky reading is done for prizes or points (e.g., on quiz shows) and not just for "fun," is the activity an exercise? That is, does the awarding of prizes constitute evaluating? If so, is the quiz show event about proving proficiency?

The other set of repeated entries involve peasants reading in Freire's circles of culture. In Freire's pedagogy, nonliterates voluntarily seek out instruction in learning to read. In some of the meetings (classes), they respond to nonsense syllables, thus NOT-reading. In all meetings, there are discussions that are shaped by the peasants' questions and comments. The larger topics of the meetings, however, are controlled by a sequence of pictures and a set of conclusions to which the coordinator (deliberately not called "teacher") leads people. (Two of these conclusions are: Some things are natural while others are cultural; people can make culture, but animals cannot.) At the same time, the coordinator is trained to refrain from setting up hierarchical relationships that discourage dialogue among equals (C. Brown, 1987). Given the preordained conclusions, the peasants might be considered to be positioned as Objects. However, the latitude they have in attending and contributing intermediate ideas (if not conclusions) leans toward positioning them as Subjects. But are they doing exercises or not? They seek out and willingly engage in instruction for its own sake. However, the literacy instruction is not for its own sake. Freire's pedagogy, after all, is about *conscientization*—a change in how one views constraints so as to encourage taking action to transform situations. Do the peasants know this purpose? Do they appropriate it? Moreover, while it is difficult to imagine Freirian coordinators saying *good* in response to a correct decoding of a word, it is easier to imagine more subtle evaluation, such as immediately repeating the student's response in the ongoing dialogue for liberation. Nevertheless, the evaluation (if it occurs) would not be for gatekeeping or diagnosing and would not, in any case, be the reason for eliciting the reading in the first place. Yet at least some of the reading in the culture circles certainly takes place for the purpose of instruction in reading. At that moment, are the peasants doing exercises in reading to have their reading evaluated? Or are they reading for some communicative purpose?

The difficulty in categorizing some instances of print use according to these dimensions—meaning-making for the distinction between reading versus NOT-reading, purpose/meaning of the event for exercises versus nonexercises, relational position for Subject versus Object—reflects the nature of conceptual categories. That is, categories in any scheme have prototypical and also fuzzy members; boundaries between categories are often fuzzy (e.g., when is a chair a stool?); and the defining features of any conceptual scheme are not self-evident (e.g., just what counts as evaluation?). Difficulty in categorizing some instances also reflects the purpose of the entire proposal. It was formulated for politico-educational purposes; therefore, its three dimensions are more pertinent to literacy in educational practice (classroom life, educational policy, educational research, educational publishing, etc.) than to literacy in other domains. And while this proposal reveals some important features of these dimensions, the difficult-to-categorize examples show that it hides other features because it makes only one gross division within each dimension—that of *yes* or *no*.

THEN WHAT GOOD IS IT?

Despite its limitations, the 1990s proposal was an improvement. The 1980s version, while helpful because it too was an attempt to point out and then analyze a major distinction, was too easy to discount. After all, it is hard to tell a student she has not really written that friendly letter for her English class even though she recognizes that writing the letter to a friend who just moved felt very different.

More important than how this proposal compared to the first one, however, is how it was able to address educational practice. With its three dimensions, it cautioned against two traps: the myth of total generalizability—that any use of print counts as reading, and the myth of total particularism—that no print use is comparable to any other. The former (that there are no important differences) leads to mistakes such as believing an experiment on responses to nonsense syllables is an experiment about reading. The latter (there are no important similarities) provides no direction for anyone interested in connecting literacy education to projects of social transformation.

Although the 1990s proposal did not address just how the social relations of literacy events and the features of the reading process impinge on each other, it did show the value of including both perspectives. *On reading process grounds,* it steered us away from mistakenly substituting NOT-reading for reading. It argued that teaching, testing, and researching print use where a text meaning is not being created or where the print itself positioned the reader as an Object by preventing her from confirming predictions appropriately or by forcing her to supply too much was not the same as teaching, testing, and researching reading. In each case, basic characteristics of the reading process would either be absent or distorted. And *on social relationship grounds,* the 1990s proposal made a case for avoiding reading exercises (i.e., they entail purposes unlike those for which people generally use language) and for avoiding the position of literate-person-as-Object (i.e., using print for examining and critiquing taken-for-granted conditions in one's own life within one's own society requires the position of the literate-as-Subject).

The major benefit of the proposal, however, is that it raised the most critical question of all—a question of value. Just what is it a student, a researcher, a literacy educator, a community wants? Print use with no meaning-making? Exercises in reading? Reading for submission? Because it assumed that the practices people participate in are the ones they acquire, the proposal promoted the question: What *should* school and research practices be? And, therefore, what *should* be acquired? (Axiomatically, it discouraged worrying about whether certain practices transfer to or predict others.)

PART THREE: 2005—AND STILL FIDDLING

A decade later, the overall distinctions still seem right. Almost. I still believe that making text meanings with considerable control over one's own reading in events that are about something other than instruction for instruction's sake or evaluation for evaluation's sake should predominate in classroom instruction, in research on literacy, and in evaluation of literacy. But I have begun to question certain aspects of the 1990s proposal. I close this chapter, then, by leaving it open, putting forth my dialogue with myself—questions, answers, rebuttals, more questions.

One original and continuing assumption, as I stated early on, has been that, in general, people do not learn language by using it for the purpose of learning it or for the purpose of showing how well they use it. Instead, they learn language by using it for some noninstructional, nonevaluational intent. But, in fact, babies do ask *wha dat?* Parents do prompt *say "kitty."* Beginning readers and writers do ask *what does this say?* and *how do you spell _____?* Second language learners do ask *how do you say _____?* A young child does read the handwriting strip near the classroom ceiling to see how to make a *G.* Adults do read a word in a dictionary to find out how to spell it. Not only do these examples not fit neatly into one of the major distinctions in the 1990s proposal, but they are also making me rethink this premise and another (that learning a [first] language is learning a [written] language is learning a [second] language).

The above are all examples of using language to learn or teach language. According to my proposal, they should be exercises. Are they? Maybe not. Even though they create mini-events that are about learning or teaching language, they are often embedded in a larger event that is about something else; for example, soliciting a present (*how do you spell 'tobaggin?' I want to put that in my letter to Santa*) or entertaining oneself (e.g., reading

Eats, Shoots and Leaves [Truss, 2003], a witty treatise on punctuation). Moreover, they do not "feel" like exercises. On the other hand, maybe they are. Meta-linguistic examples that are for learning (rather than for playing, arguing, complaining, etc.) might be a small, special class of exercises. But I am still wondering if they are exercises at all—and when that matters. However, no matter the answer, it is clear to me now that, even considering the following mitigating *in general,* I have been overstating the claim that, in general, people do not use language for the purpose of learning it. Sometimes, they do. (Chap. 6 explores the differentiated nature of "sometimes" by distinguishing first language learners from second and written language learners.)

Being unable to ignore the examples that counter the two basic premises above has not been my only problem with the 1990s proposal. I have become increasingly aware that my distinctions do not address an important part of my own agenda. Reading to make a text meaning, reading as a nonexercise, and reading in Subject position may be prerequisites for using written language critically, but they do not require it. However, positing a critical/noncritical distinction would undermine the notion of multiple literacies and, with it, the relativity necessary for considering culturally specific literacy practices. Trackton residents (Heath, 1983), for instance, or village Athabascans (Scollon & Scollon, 1981) make text meanings (i.e., they are not NOT-reading) as nonexercises while having relative control over the literacy event (being Subjects). But they do not necessarily question texts against the yardstick of systems of privilege and domination. Nor, most of the time, do I (not, for instance, when I write my grocery list or read the instructions on a package or write an e-mail to a friend). The distinctions in the 1990s proposal are meant to be general enough— "true" enough—to apply to all instances of literate activity and to all communities.[9] Being true to my agenda—adding a distinction pertaining to critical literacy—would render the proposal unusable for making claims about written language in general. Does maintaining the integrity of the proposal undermine my political agenda? That is, is it sufficient, given my agenda, that the proposed distinctions are at least prerequisites to using written language critically?

My overriding concern, though, is related to wrestling with those meta-linguistic examples I noted above. It is not only that they poke holes in basic premises or that they are difficult to classify. After all, I could just

---

[9]In making the 1990s proposal, I was not concerned about potential charges of essentialism. After all, (oral) language use shows enormous variation from one speech community to another, and yet statements can be made about general characteristics of (oral) language use. Why, then, despite comparable cross-community variation in literacy practices, should it not be acceptable to posit general, cross-culturally valid distinctions for written language use?

refer again, as I did in the 1990s, to prototype theory (Rosch & Lloyd, 1978); it predicts fuzzy examples. But sweeping those examples under that particular theoretical rug is not as reassuring as it once was. All along, I have been trying to establish a principled basis for the "feeling" that there is a difference between reading a passage to answer questions on a test and reading to find out who made the most points in last night's basketball game. My intent has been to provide a literacy-oriented theoretical justification (rather than a linguistic or sociolinguistic or curricular or pedagogical or ethical or political or sociological one) for changing literacy teaching, research, and evaluation.

I was not so naive all along as to think that my theorizing would change the predominant, commonsensical view of undifferentiated literacy. But I did think the distinctions in the 1990s proposal could provide fresh energy or arguments for those already predisposed to an alternate view. However, as those difficult-to-categorize examples increasingly gnaw at me, I am wondering if that proposal would serve even an admittedly limited number of others. I am brought back to the question posed in an earlier subheading: Then what good is it?

Comber and Nixon (1999) and A. Luke, Freebody, and Gilbert (1991) would answer: It simply is not useful. Instead of arguing for changed practice by applying theoretical criteria, they prefer looking at the consequences of various instructional practices for particular students. But which consequences? Dropout rates can be correlated with certain kinds of instruction but, to be fair, the kinds of instruction have to be consistent across years, and the correlation should track cohorts instructed in particular ways from kindergarten through graduation. To track other long-term consequences (e.g., college enrollment, income level, etc.) of particular written language educational practices requires, obviously, many years—too many for the research to be used to justify demands for timely change. How, then, would someone look at consequences in the short term so that instruction, research, or evaluation could be changed if the consequences were detrimental? Should test scores be used as consequences? Should reading levels of particular students as determined by basal reader packages be used as consequences? Should miscues count as consequences? What about qualitative analyses that show students becoming engaged writers, producing extraordinary writing, but not getting spectacularly better test scores (Edelsky & Smith, in press)? What about changes in curriculum leading to abandonment of complex projects in favor of school days full of "test prep" (Amrein & Berliner, 2002a)? How about students' ability to articulate how particular texts position them as readers or how those texts serve particular interests? Choosing any of these as "consequences" is, knowingly or not, based on some theory. How is using a theory to choose consequences different from using a theory (in the form of distinctions) to choose practices?

Back to what good is it. In an earlier draft of this postscript, I let that question lead me to ask if theorizing about literacy education in a time of severe crisis (e.g., mandated instruction in, research on, and evaluation of exercises, many of these exercises in NOT-reading—a situation causing some of the best teachers to leave teaching and some of the most innovative practices to be abandoned) has any value.[10] That momentary slide— from asking about effects on prevailing theory in the 1990s to asking about a direct impact on the world of policy and practice in 2005—reflects my anxiety about this crisis. But it was an error. Academic theorizing (mine and others) about written language may be susceptible to a "show me" demand for effecting wider views because, as described in the Introduction, literacy figures so prominently in various political agendas. But theorizing about written language should not be held to such a requirement any more than anthropological or psychological theorizing should be required to directly affect dominant perspectives on culture or emotions. Moreover, it is a truism that "theories leak"; holes are not sufficient to devalue them. Thus, I return to my optimistic answer from the 1990s to the question of value. Even if my somewhat leaky theoretical distinctions will not directly affect the current crisis in literacy education, they can still take a role in transformative activity by informing the efforts of activists. And activism is certainly called for on behalf of a new meta-narrative for what literacy *should* be for—for learning how knowledge and interpretations are constructed, for challenging inequities, and for repairing a society that works only for the few. Recognizing the differences between reading and NOT-reading, exercises and nonexercises, and literate Subjects and literate Objects can be central to this meta-narrative.

---

[10]After all, my distinctions will not change the minds of corporate producers whose agendas drive federal legislation to mandate reading instruction comprised of exercises in NOT-reading done by students-as-Objects; they will not change the minds of those who find nothing wrong with National Institutes of Child Health and Development-sponsored research on NOT-reading exercises performed by research subjects positioned as Objects; nor will they change the minds of politicians, editors of corporate media, and members of the public who support evaluation by means of exercises completed by test-takers-as-Objects.

On Second Thought

AT FIRST

For many years, I thought the best way to think about learning to read and write was to use the analogy of learning to talk. Both written and oral language seem to begin as acts of meaning (Clay, 1975; Halliday, 1993) that produce whole texts (whether oral or written texts; Harste, Burke, & Woodward, 1983; Lindfors, 1987). From the start, both are highly social and functional. Both implicate identities, with neophytes becoming "the kind of people who speak like us" or "the kind of readers and writers we are [or aren't]." Early examples of both learning to talk and learning to write reveal overgeneralizations that reflect an active learner constructing hypotheses (Cazden, 1972; K. Goodman & Goodman, 1981). Moreover, the earliest "teachers" of each— more mature users of oral or written language in ordinary settings (as opposed to school settings established for the purpose of teaching and learning)—seem to do similar things. They use language, oral or written, in front of and with the learner. They provide information and feedback—Gee (2004b) refers to this as information "on demand" and "just in time;" in earlier years (F. Smith, 1973; Edelsky, 1978; Edelsky, Altwerger, & Flores, 1991), it was described as what the learner needs in the course of social life, rather than as what a curriculum determines for a course in school. Others have agreed that people "learn to read and write the way I learn to talk." In fact, Marlene Barron (1990) wrote a book with just that title. And various scholars have posited that important features of first language acquisition offer a guide for thinking about learning in general, including learning to read and write (Edelsky et al., 1991; Gee, 1994; Halliday, 1993; F. Smith, 1983).

BUT, ON SECOND THOUGHT ...

I am shifting gears.[1] It seems that a better analogy for written language learning is second language learning. Of course, it might be argued that analogies

---

[1]Actually, the gear-shifting was mentioned, but not developed, in Edelsky (1996, pp. 207–210).

are not necessary, that it is best to try to see written language learning on its own terms. But given the human tendency (need?) to think of one thing in terms of another—that is, metaphorically (Lakoff & Johnson, 1980; 1999)—it would be difficult to view written language learning or anything else solely in "its own terms." Instead, we would see it as "taking on" "something"—with "taking on" viewed as learning or acquiring[2] or participating with, and with "something" viewed as a set of skills, a technology, a set of cultural practices, or language.[3] I want to reject my earlier analogy and claim that learning written language is like—or is, perhaps, a case of—second language learning. But in order to make that proposal (as well as justify it and present its benefits), I need to explain why I am claiming that writing is language.

IS WRITTEN LANGUAGE LANGUAGE?

Some scholars agree that it is. Ken Goodman (1984), whose theory of reading grew out of his conception of reading as a language process, is one who sees written language as language—not just as a graphic expression of an oral language. But that view is not shared by all who have pointed to first language as a model for other learning (e.g., Gee, 1994).

The Hard-Wiring Argument

Having cut their linguistic teeth on Chomskyan linguistics, MacSwan and Rolstad (2003), Gee (1994, 2004b), and others argue that humans as a species are "hard-wired" for language. Thus, language, having a biological basis, would appear throughout the species. Speech certainly meets that criterion. Moreover, all biologically unimpaired humans learn oral language "completely" (i.e., it is not the case that some people simply cannot learn relative clauses or that others have trouble with negation). If reading/writing were language, the brain would be as hard-wired for writing as it is for speech or sign. Therefore, people would be as successful with reading and writing as they are with speech or sign. Moreover, if brains had evolved so that writing were part of its hardwiring, then all communities would have writing systems.

I think there are three possible directions for arguing against this position that refuses to acknowledge reading/writing as language.

---

[2]In general, I will use the term *learning* in a nontechnical sense. Occasionally—and this is one of the occasions—I will differentiate *learning* from *acquiring*. When I do so, I will use Gee's (1992b) adaptation of Krashen's (1982) distinction based on consciousness and intent, with acquisition being out of awareness and learning being conscious and deliberate.

[3]The choices within each set are not all contradictory, although some are. For instance, it would be possible to think of learning literacy as participating in cultural practices and also as acquiring a language, but not to see learning literacy as both acquiring a language and also as learning a set of skills.

What Is Hard-Wired?

One possibility begins with the facts as presented: Speech is universal, but writing is not; successful learning of oral language is universal, but successful learning of written language is not. Taking this direction, I would not be disturbed by the appeal to biology. It is the nature of that biological inheritance that I would question. Those who appeal to biology in refusing to accord writing the status of language indeed refer to various aspects of language as "wired in" (e.g., Jackendoff, 2003, p. 697). The brain, in their view, comes equipped with "something" that specializes in language learning independent of other learning. That "something"—related to the brain's neurological structure—enables (contains? determines?) the acquisition (existence?; even proponents such as Jackendoff, 2003, acknowledge that much is unknown here) of a Universal Grammar (UG).[4]

There is, however, another way to look at our biological endowment in relation to language without appealing to UG for explaining both first language learning and commonalities across languages. According to Terrance Deacon (1997), referring to work in evolutionary/biological anthropology, what is hard-wired or, as he writes, what has evolutionarily derived neural support, is symbolic reference. In a fascinating account of the co-evolution of brain and language, Deacon describes how, in crossing the symbolic threshold, Australopithecines might have begun the evolutionary trek to language-adapted-for-brain and brain-selected-for- language. The earliest simple symbolization would have made "computational demands" that would have then selected evolutionarily over thousands of generations for a number of brain developments (e.g., greater prefrontalization, more efficient articulatory capabilities). Each development in the brain would have enabled even more complex symbol systems, which in turn would have selected for greater prefrontalization, and so on. If it is symbolic reference, rather than syntax or semantics[5] or phonology,[6] that is what is hard-wired, then humans should be

---

[4]UG is not to be confused with language universals. *Language universals* are abstractions common to all languages (e.g., a Subject/Predicate division). By contrast, UG is more like a toolkit for constructing language, for example, instructions about linguistic probabilities or about how to shape a tone system if the language has a tone system (Jackendoff, 2003).

[5]Jackendoff (2003) now disputes the "syntactocentrism" of earlier linguistic theories while explaining why they would have been necessary in the history of linguistic scholarship. He proposes a syntax–semantics interface and reasons that, evolutionarily, meaning was the first generative component of language.

[6]Recent studies in the neuropsychology of reading funded and/or touted by the National Institutes for Child Health and Development, a key player in the corporate/government efforts to promote phonics as a tool in its agenda to control education, purport to show that people diagnosed as dyslexic have a "glitch in the wiring" of the brain, specifically in the area concerned with "sounding out words." Gerald Coles (2000) and Steven Strauss (2005b) have written detailed critiques of that research.

especially adept at learning systems for representing "synthetic logical relationships." Not just speech but writing, sign, musical notation systems, and others. And indeed that is the case.

If language universals and a UG were genetically determined, they (or rather, their linguistic consequences) should use the same neural circuits from individual to individual no matter the language. But, according to Deacon (1997, p. 333), the parts of the brain involved in seeming universals (e.g., distinguishing Subjects from Predicates or formulating questions) vary depending on the "kind" of language (e.g., a relatively inflected language as compared with a relatively uninflected one). That is, it seems to be the surface representations of syntax, not the deeply abstract hypothesized language universals or the "toolkit" UG, that have neural support.

Other evidence from various cognitive and social sciences offers additional reasons to question the hard-wired-for-language hypothesis in its various forms (the older Language Acquisition Device, the newer UG and language universals). If language depended on innate neural structures, those structures should not be present in species that do not have language. And yet, language's "central aspects arise via evolutionary processes from neural systems that are present in so-called 'lower animals'" (Watson-Gegeo, 2004, p. 333, citing Bates, Thal, & Marchman, 1991). Moreover, non-language-using species should not be able to learn language even under artificial conditions. But a bonobo (pygmy chimpanzee) named Kanzi has learned, without explicit training, to use lexigrams to express meanings and to comprehend normal spoken English (Savage-Rumbaugh & Lewin, 1994).[7] Instead of being invariant preconditions for learning language, human brain structures related to language, then, may be *outcomes* of learning (Watson-Gegeo, 2004).

Rather than innate language universals and a UG, an evolved genetic capacity for symbolic reference and language adapted to fit that capacity could help explain the facts of language acquisition and commonalities across languages (Deacon, 1997). More help comes from the fact that the human brain is profoundly embodied. Commonalities of experience across cultures, resulting from human skeletal anatomy and physiology rather than innate linguistic structures, could be responsible for deep commonalities across languages (e.g., the tendency of languages to treat agents as Subjects,

---

[7]In a videotape (Niio, 2000) from the chimp language studies laboratory of Sue Savage-Rumbaugh and Duane Rumbaugh at Georgia State University, Kanzi, sitting in a room by himself, observed through a one-way window, hearing English through headphones so there is no possibility of aid from visual cues offered by lab workers, follows complex oral directions. On that same videotape, Panbanisha, another bonobo at the lab, without ever having been trained to write, took a piece of chalk and wrote the abstract symbol for the lexigram representing what she had been previously pestering her trainer for: *walk outside.*

and the tendency for *front* [of the body] to be metaphorically positive and *back* to be metaphorically negative [Lakoff & Johnson, 1980, 1999]).

Does a Second Have to Be a First?

If the symbolic-reference argument is not convincing, a different argument in favor of seeing reading/writing as language accepts a brain hard-wired for language. In this argument, however, that hard-wiring—those neural supports that permit babies to begin using "impoverished" input to figure out abstract patterns of a complex system—is instantiated only once: for acquiring the first language. Biology does not seem to help with subsequent language learning; the universal success of first language acquisition is not repeated for second language learning. However, the fact that I have been only minimally successful in learning Spanish as a second language—or that Spanish is not found in every speech community—does not lead to the conclusion that, therefore, Spanish is not a language. The writing-is-not-language position could well counter with an appeal to native language; that is, those who would disagree with me could well say that while a language may not be learned universally as a second language, it is learned somewhere, in some speech community, as a first language. A symbol system that counts as a language, in other words, has native speakers. But evidence from new Englishes[8] discredits that argument. Many African, Indian (Mufwene, 1998), and Central American (P. Sayer, personal communication, October 16, 2004) varieties of English, spoken by adults in the workplace or at school, are not learned by anyone "from the crib" (Singh, 1998). Despite the lack of first language speakers of, say, Oaxacan English, we do not refuse to count that variety as *language*.

How Does Western Bias Figure in This Argument?

A third direction in arguing against the opponents of seeing writing as language is disciplinary bias. Historians who have studied writing systems have been steeped in Western literate traditions that include certain assumptions about the relationship between writing and speech and about the alphabet as the evolutionary endpoint of writing systems. Thus, some well-respected historians refer explicitly to written language as "a technology for decoding and reproducing ... printed materials" (Graff, 1987, p. 4) or as a secondary representation of language (Stewart & Vaillette, 2001, pp. 140–141). The

---

[8]To be more precise, "no native speakers" should be couched as no first language users. "The native speaker" is a political designation used to disqualify non-native speakers, as Canagarajah (1999), Mufwene (1998), and Singh (1998) have shown. The term *native speaker*, seemingly referring to individuals, actually implicates varieties of language. Worldwide, *native speaker* often means imperial varieties of, say, English as opposed to colonial varieties.

authors of File # 140 in an encyclopedic reference, the Language Files (Stewart & Vaillette, 2001), say that writing is "based on units of speech"—with no sensitivity to the historical diversity in cultural practices that might include graphic metaphors and an interest in "writing as writing" rather than "what it sound[s] like" (Harris, 1986, p. 119).

In a remarkable early discussion of this bias, Roy Harris (1986) maintains that historians of writing have confused the origins of writing with the genesis of scripts. Moreover, they have succumbed to what he calls "the tyranny of the alphabet." Thus, writing (with script and process conflated) is depicted historically and taxonomically with the alphabet as the major dividing line—nonalphabetic systems on one side, alphabetic on the other. In that bifurcation, the rebus is given a pivotal role. But the rebus, according to Harris (1986), is "not what it's cracked up to be" (p. 67). Using the same symbol for *bee* and *be* does not mean one is semantic and the other is phonological. It just means that a single symbol has now acquired a second word meaning. The rebus, based on a random identity of forms, is nonsystematic. Systematicity, however, is what is needed to represent pronunciation. What puts *bee, be, bean,* and *beak* in the same system is "not an extension of the rebus principle but a complete break with it" (Harris, 1986, p. 68). Elevating the rebus over other developments is an example of an unwarranted projection "into prehistory of a conceptualization of writing which is itself the product of the uses of literacy in a highly sophisticated civilization" (Harris, 1986, p. 53).

Unlike these historians of writing criticized by Harris (1986), Coulmas (1999) claims that writing has significance "equal to speech," is partially autonomous, and is "a means of expression in its own right" (p. 28). Both Coulmas and Harris emphasize the importance for historians to investigate where writing is located within an overall system of language and how writing relates to other systems. They are joined by Halliday (1993), who refers to language as a semiotic—oral language as one form of expression and written language as another. Harris, Coulmas, and Halliday seem to be supporting the position that undergirds my categorization of writing as language. That position is that *language is a semiotic ecology with various modalities of expression (oral, written, gestural) in various relationships to each other, depending on the particular community of users.* Speech may be the most common medium for instantiating language (Deacon, 1997), but writing and sign are also mediums for language.

If, on the other hand, writing were merely the technology some claim it to be, a reasonable question to ask is: technology for what? It cannot be a technology for representing speech, since it is clear to anyone who has ever transcribed an audiotape of conversation that speech written down is quite different from writing. Even sermons written out for oral delivery, extemporaneous formal monologues, and other examples of formal speakings are often revised for publication so that written syntax, for instance, can be recruited to substitute for oral prosody. For centuries, classical written Chinese was unrelated to spoken varieties but was nevertheless the language of literary prose (Coulmas, 1999). Written French has a preterite tense that does not appear in oral French (Harris, 1986). Moreover, learners of English as a foreign language in many parts of Asia who are reported to learn to read and write written English without learning to speak or understand oral English are not using a print technology to represent oral language. Neither are deaf users of Sign who become literate in written English without learning oral English. It would require considerable theoretical contortions to maintain that literacy is a technology for representing an oral language and then to assume that the non-English-speaking Asian and the non-speaking/hearing Signer have learned written English as a graphic representation—a relexification—of Japanese, for instance, or Sign. Nor is it likely that what writing-as-a-technology would be representing is subvocal speech. Scholarship in writing over the past many years has shown that writers do not merely take dictation from themselves. Instead, considerable meaning is created in writing at the point of penstroke or computer key, just as it is created at the point of oral utterance (Britton, 1970).

Seeing writing as language means seeing that, like other forms of language (speech, sign), it is an ordered way of making meaning—a semiotic. It is social, conventional, symbolic, intertextually tied to other instances, reflexive with contexts, predictable, ambiguous, and redundant. Along with other forms of language, its learning and use may well establish neural networks in the brain.

BACK TO THE PROPOSAL: LEARNING LITERACY IS LIKE (OR, IS A CASE OF) LEARNING A SECOND LANGUAGE

If I can maintain that writing is language, then it makes good sense to see literacy learning as a special case of second language learning. After all, that is the sequence; written language learning happens after a person has begun to learn a first language. This is the case even for nonaural, severely involved cerebral-palsied youngsters whose first productions are in writing with the help of computers and headwands but who, from birth, have been exposed to and at least minimally interacted with through speech (Edelsky & Rosegrant, 1981).

If literacy is seen as a second language, certain arguments vanish. It is second languages that are not found in every community, second languages that are not learned with universal success. Second languages—classic "dead" ones, modern live ones, oral ones, written ones—are the ones generally recognized as being learned with variable success. (Indeed, variability of learning in regard to literacy is an explicit part of the it's-not-language argument.) That speech is present in all cultures but writing is not also loses its clout as an argument against considering writing as language. Communities have taken on additional languages as they have needed them. Writing systems too have been invented as communities have needed them, and they have changed historically through borrowing, innovation, error, and other avenues of language change. Just as traces of gestures and cries can be found in the syntax of oral language (Deacon, 1997), so are various signs from earlier periods embedded in the pragmatics of written language.

Aside from greater accuracy, seeing literacy learning as a case of second language learning has potential tactical and certain pedagogical value.

TACTICAL VALUE OF SEEING LITERACY LEARNING AS A CASE OF SECOND LANGUAGE LEARNING

It is clear that literacy learning has become a site of struggle, a pawn in political agendas. Those of us at odds with the view of literacy embedded in recent legislation such as the Reading Excellence Act and No Child Left Behind have been losing in this struggle. Media representations of both the struggle and of literacy as a set of hierarchical skills beginning with the ones closest to the sounds of speech have contributed to our difficulties in attempting to change the common sense about reading and writing. But an analogy to second language learning might help. Not because prevailing views would take up the idea that written language is language. In fact, public conceptions of written language are ambivalent. On the one hand, the product of written language use—a written text—is frequently seen as a more "true" instance of language than an oral text with its hesitations and backtracking (Lippi-Green, 1997). On the other hand, learning to use written language is widely seen as merely learning sound–letter relationships that, once turned into speech (i.e., language), are then comprehended. For that matter, popular conceptions of first language learning— supported by early 20th-century studies of child language development— are not models of sophisticated understanding either; they tend to equate first language learning with the learning of countable words. When such notions prevail, trying to persuade the public that learning to read and write is like learning to talk is not an easy argument. Making a case that learning to read and write is like learning a second language would also be difficult. After all, popular ideas of second language learning are also word bound (travelers are more likely to buy bilingual dictionaries and phrase books than grammar books). It is not the particulars, then, of the "common sense" about language, written language, written language learning, first language learning, or second language learning that can be enlisted because, in fact, they work against us.

But what is more widely understood for second language learning than for first—and what might be able to be used tactically on behalf of learning and teaching written language—is one piece of a common stereotype for second language learning: That is the general belief that the best way to learn a second language is to go to where it is spoken. In other words, the public has faith in immersion experiences for second language learning.[9] People "know," from firsthand experience or from hearing it from others, the difference between, on the one hand, studying German as a foreign language in high school, then going to Germany after high school and not being able to understand or be understood; and on the other, living in Germany for a year and learning enough German to conduct daily life through German. What I am proposing is that while an important detail may be refused (that written language is language), it might be possible, tactically, to rely on stereotypes of second language learning in order to insert into the public discourse a gestalt: enough of a similarity between literacy learning and second language learning to warrant the benefit of immersion experiences.

Immersion Experiences

What immersion experiences provide that make them so attractive as people think of second language learning is conditions for language acquisition. Krashen (1982), with important modifications by Gee (1992b, p. 113),[10,11] distinguished two major ways people "come by" what they know: acquisition and learning. It is a crucial distinction in the present discussion. *Acquisition* is subconscious; it happens without formal training, through exposure to models and through trial-and-error practice within social groups in natural settings where what is to be acquired is needed for

---

[9]Ironically, it is first language learning that is actually the prime exemplar of the immersion experience for language learning, but first language learning is ubiquitous. It does not provide the contrasts of learning through being immersed "on the street" versus learning in a classroom. It is second language learning, with its variable success rate, that offers the advantage of that contrast.

[10]Gee (1992b) eliminates Krashen's hypothesized Monitor and some of the proposed constraints on learning (e.g., that what is learned cannot eventually become tacit knowledge, as though it had been acquired). He also adds a major dimension to the discussion. Acquisition, in Gee's adaptation, brings in its wake not only the phenomenon of interest (e.g., a second language, a skill) but an identity replete with other behaviors, values, and beliefs.

[11]Gee (2004b) now claims there are three ways people come by what they know: biologically supported acquisition, learning, and cultural processes. In this scheme, a person's first language is the only knowledge that is acquired. Much is learned by overt instruction. What is important to a culture (e.g., cooking, reading) is learned through cultural processes wherein "masters," with socially significant identities, create environments that offer rich support for learners. In this chapter, I do not insist that acquisition requires biological support; my discussion includes under *acquisition* what Gee is calling *cultural processes*.

functioning and where the neophyte wants to so function. *Learning,* by contrast, involves conscious knowledge gained through teaching or conscious reflection, involves comparison or analysis (focusing on analytic parts) and the attainment of at least some degree of meta-knowledge. It is primarily acquisition, rather than learning, that accounts for initial enculturation (Gee, 1992b) into what is variously called *culture* (Geertz, 1973), *communities of practice* (Lave & Wenger, 1991), and *primary Discourses* (Gee, 1990). It is also acquisition that enables taking on secondary Discourses. Whether a primary or a secondary Discourse, whether the practices of a culture or a of community of practice, when someone is acquiring it, what she or he is acquiring is, at minimum, "characteristic ways of acting-interacting-feeling-emoting-valuing-gesturing-posturing-dressing-thinking-believing-knowing-speaking-listening (and, in some Discourses, reading-and-writing, as well"; Gee, 1999, p. 38).

There are two key elements in acquiring this stew: immersion and identity. That is, one has to be *in* it—immersed in that culture or that community of practice or that Discourse—with others who are also immersed in it, enacting it, living it. In addition, one has to want to become (like) and be recognized as one of "them," one of those others with whom one is immersed.

While any daily lifeworld immerses those who are a part of it, the term *immersion experience* almost always refers to an intentional learning experience, not to the experience of simply being caught up, willy-nilly, in ongoing life. In common usage, *immersion experience* is not even used in reference to what, theoretically, would seem to be the prototypical case—being born into a culture/language. For this discussion, I will follow common usage and reserve *immersion experience* for those that happen after initial enculturation.

An important question to ask about the notion of an immersion experience is: Immersion in what? The answer is: in (the practices of) a community of practice (Lave & Wenger, 1991), a group of people who take part in certain activities and, in so doing, share an identity for some piece of their lives. Immersion experiences have three key features that together promote acquisition: meaning, time, and support.

Meaning.   *Meaning* refers to what the experience is *about* for the neophyte, what it means. Someone's original purpose for spending a year in Italy may be to learn Italian but, once there, if the experience shifts from being about learning Italian to being about living through Italian (living through the second language and second culture—buying food; making friends; going to the dentist; doing one's job; perhaps as a high school exchange student or as a volunteer in a neighborhood clinic), it becomes an immersion experience. The neophyte is not, then, a tourist, there to be entertained by "the natives." The neophyte is, instead, trying to join "the natives" in "native" pursuits, trying to become part of the Discourse, to take on the value-embedded, worldview-infiltrated practices of the community of practice. For the present discussion, it is important to note that these practices include using social languages. Despite the commonsense view that learning Italian as a second language amounts to learning some general entity in and of itself, Italian (or any other language) as a second language or a first does not exist except as embedded in social languages ("styles of language that communicate socially situated identities [who is acting] and socially situated activities [what is being done]"; Hawkins, 2004, p. 17).

An immersion experience does not have to entail foreign travel. Joining an ongoing book club in Tucson, a Weight Watchers group in Minneapolis, a bowling league in Newark, a weekly writing group in Boise, a teacher inquiry group in Philadelphia, or entering mid-year as a new student in a worksheet-driven classroom in Oakland each provide an immersion experience in particular ways of doing/believing/valuing concerning books and book talk, weight loss, bowling, writing, teacher inquiry, or student-ing. (Below, I return to the complicated case of classrooms as communities of practice.)

A traveler stranded for 2 days in a foreign country, however, may be "immersed" there, but she is not having an immersion experience. The experience is not about joining a lifeworld; it is about trying to leave one. While getting her needs met, she may be sharing a physical/interactional space with members of a community of practice, but she is not likely to be trying to share an identity (unless it is with other stranded travelers), not likely to try to become (like) a member. (In fact, she may well highlight her nonmembership in order to elicit help.)

Some aspects of the central work or activity of a community of practice may have to be consciously learned (e.g., bus routes and bus fares in Italy, titles and authors of books, points and exchange values for food on the Weight Watchers program, rules for scoring in bowling, names of other teacher inquiry group members, in-group terms for writing techniques, certain worksheet tasks). But the ways of fulfilling what the immersion experience *means*—doing daily life in that community of practice, being like those who are members of that community of practice—have to be acquired (how to talk about what one is doing, how to get a turn at different parts of the central activity, how the activity is organized, who to see as having more and less status, what to see as funny and what as sad, what to give importance to and what not—in short, how to talk, think, act, feel, value like a book club member, writing group member, Weight Watchers group member, etc.). In other words, the material, behavioral, emotional, interactional, linguistic, ideological medium in which and through which and with which daily life in these communities of practice is constructed is, on the one hand, what a neophyte is immersed in and on the other what he or she acquires.

Time. It takes a long time for such acquisition to occur. Time, indeed, is a second feature of an immersion experience. An immersion experience is long. A community of practice with only a short life span (e.g., a 2-week summer school class) will also develop its own ways of doing and being, and students who participate wholeheartedly and do not hold back will acquire those ways within that short time. My guess, though, is that the practices of a community of practice with a short life span will be less complex and less entangled than those of ongoing, cross-generation communities of practice.

Support. An immersion experience also offers emotional, intellectual, and social support—in the form of comfort, hand-holding, offering venting space, information, advice, introductions, and "vouching for." The stereotype is that an immersion experience is a matter of sink or swim, that the immersed person is on her own, fending for herself, figuring out the ways of doing and being in the Weight Watchers group or, in the most extreme case, learning an entirely different language and culture by herself out of dire necessity in order to survive. Actually, in Weight Watchers groups, book clubs, writing groups, and classrooms in mid-year, old-timers initiate newcomers. Universities provide staff to help international students. More long-time immigrants advise newer ones. Host families help exchange students with information about the local scene. The Peace Corps provides intensive training prior to in-country immersion. And neophytes seek out support—a friendly face, a sympathetic ear—where such is not already built in to the experience (Siefer, 1989).

Attention to Form. So far, these three features of an immersion experience could describe conditions for infants' acquisition of their first language, embedded in their primary Discourse. But something else happens in a second language immersion experience. Occasionally, that second language is extracted from its function as a resource for living and is treated as a subject for explicit teaching and learning or an object of conscious reflection. In the prototypical immersion experience of, say, going to Germany to work, some relatively small amount of time would be spent in a language school or at home studying German, doing language exercises, or writing down constructions and vocabulary in a notebook for reflection and study—that is, explicitly focusing on the bits and pieces. To the neophyte, these exercises would not seem artificial or out of context because they would be immediately useful in daily life. This attention to form might be limited to a conscious awareness of "intrasystematic relations" of language, or it might extend to conscious critique of aspects of language in relation to the "workings of power, politics, ideology and values" (Gee, 1994, pp. 350–351). In any case, important though it may be, only a relatively small proportion of a neophyte's time and energy in an immersion experience would be devoted to such attention to language as an object of study or reflection; most of the time would be spent living through the language (working, going to school, volunteering, going out with friends, doing the laundry, buying food, dealing with bureaucratic offices, etc.).

PEDAGOGICAL VALUE OF SEEING LITERACY LEARNING AS A CASE OF SECOND LANGUAGE LEARNING

As I said earlier, I see two main benefits from looking at literacy learning as a case of second language learning. One is tactical; as just discussed, widespread approval of the idea of a pivotal role for immersion experiences in second language learning might be beneficial in arguments about optimal conditions for literacy learning. Immersion experiences are also pivotal in another sense; that is, they pivot, they turn—from a tentative, potential tactical benefit to more certain pedagogical benefits.

Immersion experiences for second language learning are not generally associated with educational settings. In fact, prototypical immersion experiences for second language learning contrast classrooms with a "real" world. But looking at literacy learning as (like) second language learning directs us to consider immersion experiences for literacy and how these might occur in classrooms. The first question, again, is what would literacy learners be immersed in. The answer, again, is (the practices of) a community of practice. But extending such notions as *community of practice, immersion,* and *acquisition* to classrooms presents some complications.

First, members of a community of practice identify as members, want to be, and are recognized as such. The same cannot be said for all students in a classroom. Some want to be insiders, some are ambivalent, and some actively resist. They resist the identity,[12] resist the practices, and reject the values and beliefs embedded in the practices. It is an open question whether or to what extent students who are present but who reject membership still acquire (even as they reject) the practices of a community of practice.[13]

Another complication has to do with the practices in which students are immersed. All classrooms immerse students in a "medium." By *medium,* I mean what makes schoolwork happen—the value-laden, worldview-bound, emotion-infused, ideology-supporting activity and material props. That

---

[12]Even though I am shifting between talking of identities and membership, identities are actually not reducible to membership or to individual autobiography (Holland & Lave, 2001) but to some combination.

[13]Labov (1972) showed that children who were marginal to their social groups ("lames") had not acquired the same sociolinguistic knowledge as more central peers.

includes how to "act" (e.g., how to get turns, when to talk and when not to, to what extent examples can be personal, what to wear, how to sit and how close, etc.) and how to "work" (e.g., when to begin, which cues signal the end of a work period, what work really counts, who can help, etc.). But not all classrooms offer an immersion experience in <u>literacy</u>. The primary literate-related practices of every classroom do not entail *using* written language communicatively, functionally, and interactively. If the central focus of classroom work is worksheets and other reading and writing exercises (see chap. 5 for a discussion of exercises), the written language that is actually *used* with students might well be limited to directions at the top of the page or on the blackboard and to texts used for management (of time, curriculum, and behavior; e.g., posted schedules, classroom rules, students' names written on a public space for special privileges or punishments). Student members of such a community of practice might *use* written language outside of school, but inside their worksheet-driven classroom their "immersion" in literacy would be only toe deep.

By contrast, if the central focus of classroom work is publishing a newspaper to be distributed in the community, or, in a kindergarten if the central focus is creating original alphabet books, the written language of the central work is functional, communicative, and interactive. So is the written language used in activities related to the newspaper or the alphabet books (e.g., ads, cartoons, articles and editorials used as models for genre and style; reporters' notes; plans for articles; documents providing information for articles, etc.; other alphabet books as models; plans and sketches appearing in student journals responded to by the teacher). This is an immersion in literacy that the worksheet classroom barely begins to provide. And it is even more. Just as Italian, for instance, cannot be acquired as some autonomous entity but must be acquired as part of social languages, so must reading and writing be acquired as part of social languages, that is, reading and writing something as certain kinds of people doing certain things. The social languages students have the opportunity to acquire via immersion in the newspaper/alphabet book classroom are more powerful social languages than those available in the worksheet classrooms. They entail "kinds of people" who have more agency doing "kinds of things" that have some impact, through literacy, on the world.

As noted above, it is not only immersion that enables acquisition. It is also identity—a desire to become a member of the community of practice. But when the classroom is the community of practice, taking on a new identity adds yet another complication. The desired identity needs to be double: a member of a community of practice composed of "initiates" and also one composed of literates. After all, it could well be said that the only person within the kindergarten classroom who is already a full-fledged member of "the literacy club" (F. Smith, 1985) is the teacher. For students to believe there is a literacy club and that they can join it, they have to reach outside the classroom and conjure up an imagined literate community of practice. Some students, of course, only have to look to their families to find people who are already in such a club. For others, it is a stretch and a possible betrayal of identity. (Do "people like me" expect "people like me" to be literate in these ways with these particular social languages?) Adding a new identity dependent on literacy, that is, is not simply a free choice equally open to all. People construct identities based on current identities as well as how they understand their possibilities for the future (Norton, 1997). But in order to acquire certain literate social languages, students *must* want to become (like) a member of the classroom community of practice and also an out of school, more or less imagined literate world. What can be done to promote that desire and ease its problematic aspects?

Two examples from fourth- and fifth-grade classrooms (Edelsky, Smith, & Wolfe, 2002; Edelsky & Smith, in press) offer some direction. Each appealed to that double identity (member of the classroom community of practice which, in turn aligned its work with an imagined out-of-school community of practice). In both classrooms, the practices (of the communities of practice) were hybrids. They belonged partly to the world of school (the teacher established the schedule for the day, announcements on the public address system interrupted the discussions, the teacher initiated and ended most activities) and partly to the imagined world of, in one case, literary critics and, in the other, memoirists (e.g., topics in book discussions were deemed unimportant if they would, presumably, be unimportant to literary critics; memoirs were studied to see how memoirists deal with the problems students were having, such as how to make a moment memorable for the reader as well as the writer).

In the memoir classroom, identity was an explicit concern—does this particular literate social language seem like a possibility for "people like me"? Students were lured into identifying not only with the community within the classroom but also the imagined one outside: memoirists. The lures were set out the month prior to asking students to write their own memoirs. For example, school adults took on the work of memoirists themselves and teased students with occasional glimpses of that work. The teacher read aloud several book-length memoirs by memoirists who matched students in Latino ethnicity and social class origins (indeed, who highlighted ethnicity and social class in their memoirs). Long daily time periods were allotted for students to talk to each other in pairs about times they remembered when they were surprised, frightened, worried, tended to, teased—later to share with the entire group and thus experience the pleasure of resonance (*oh, that happened to you too!*). By the time students were asked to write their own memoirs, they were willing to join the imagined community of memoirists, willing to try on the identity of memoirist.

Students in both classrooms experienced an immersion in real and imagined communities of practice that made extensive use of communicative, functional written language. The meaning of the immersion experience to the students was not learning literacy. Instead, learning literacy was a by-product of what the immersion experiences were about: focal work that required literacy in order to participate (discussing literature, writing a memoir). In each case, the focal work continued over a long period of time (each literature study lasted for 2 weeks; the memoir unit lasted for more than a month). And students had support; for example, one feature of interaction in these classrooms was the extent to which the teachers used discursive strategies to make students appear "smart" and to offer solidarity.

Similar to second language immersion experiences, these immersions in literacy also provided explicit attention to reading and writing "skills." This is the kind of focus on form described in the whole language literature as teaching skills at the moment they are needed (Edelsky et al., 1991) and as teaching strategies as they are needed (Gilles, Bixby, Crowley, Crenshaw, Henrichs, Reynolds, & Pyle, 1988; Goodman, Watson, & Burke, 1996); it is the kind discussed in the writing process literature as having interesting conversations about skills (Calkins, 1986); it is similar to what Gee (2004a) refers to as offering explicit help "on demand" and "just in time." Focus on form in these two classrooms included studying differences between the syntax of written memoir and everyday talk (e.g., written *how does that feel?* vs. spoken *what does that feel like?*) just at the moment students were revising drafts, finding different means of representing the speech of bilinguals as they were trying to insert dialogue into their memoirs, studying punctuation as a tool for disambiguating confusing passages when having trouble while reading, talking about the relationship between the spellings of root words and related words when polishing up final drafts, trying out written language resources (e.g., punctuation, capital letters, fonts) to create particular effects when writing early drafts.

The pedagogical value of seeing literacy learning as a case of second language learning thus pivots, again, on the immersion experience but with the addition of an explicit focus on form. The focus on form is immediately useful to what the immersion experience is about—some project that is already (or that becomes) interesting and important to students and that is heavily dependent on literacy for its execution. That is, the literacy/second language learning comparison directs priorities: Immersion (and its partner, identity) is first; attention to form is enlisted in the service of the immersion experience.

Thinking of literacy learning as second language learning also leads to reaping some of the benefits of recent theoretical developments in second language acquisition (SLA) scholarship. These developments have been brought together by Watson-Gegeo (2004) in what she calls a language socialization (LS) paradigm for SLA. They imply lenses for looking at literacy pedagogy. Now what I am calling *lenses,* suggested by Watson-Gegeo's language socialization paradigm and by work in critical English as a second language (ESL)/SLA (e.g., by Hawkins, 2004, Norton, 2000, Pennycook, 2004, Toohey, 2000), do not represent entirely new issues. For example, *the learner as whole person* (the first lens presented below) is an idea that predates Dewey (Froebel, 1826) and receives considerable attention in the literature on open education (Ashton-Warner, 1963; Weber, 1971) and to a lesser extent, in the whole language literature (Y. Goodman, 1978; Newman, 1985).[14] But these ideas and issues are intensified and made more urgent by relating them to second language learning. After all, it is "expected" that everyone (in the United States, at least) will become literate (therefore, much is made of the percentage, questionable though it may be, of adult illiterates).[15] And while there is a similar expectation regarding learning English, no such expectation exists (again, in the United States) for learning any other language as a second language. Second language learning is seen as problematic in another way, too; it more obviously requires not just new ways of talking but also new ways of thinking and doing within new social networks. With literacy seen as second language learning—less certain results and more problematic requirements—these issues and these lenses might be taken more seriously, more consistently, in more quarters.

The first lens Watson-Gegeo proposes in the LS paradigm for second language learning is the *learner as whole person.* This lens includes an embodied mind that does most of its work unconsciously and in conjunction with other people (i.e., distributed cognition) and that inherently fuses thinking with emotions, desires, will, and beliefs. This whole person constructs cultural models that are infused with emotional valences and values and brings these cultural models to bear on specific tasks. Using this lens to look at literacy as a second language would prompt asking questions about students' and teachers' cultural models—where these merge and where they collide.

---

[14]As I mention earlier work in literacy that corroborates aspects of these lenses, I do not intend to imply that the ideas are "the same." Frequently, they have roots in other disciplines, therefore bringing along other assumptions. Some are not as fully developed as the research cited by Watson-Gegeo. Many have both points of congruence and points of incongruence with theories that provide these lenses. Nevertheless, the kernels of these ideas have been early guideposts in "progressive" discussions of literacy and should be recognized as part of a broad intellectual history.

[15]A recent reassessment by Matthews (2001) of the National Adult Literacy Survey (Kirsh, Jungeblut, Jenkins, & Kolstad, 1993) shows that 70% of those judged illiterate said they read a newspaper once a week—hardly a sign of illiteracy. Although the project director of the original study now claims the results were "misunderstood," headlines at the time did and continue to do considerable damage. That nearly half of America's adults are functionally illiterate is now an accepted, but erroneous, truth.

Above all, it would remind educators, researchers, and parents that the body (health, physical comfort, hunger, thirst), feelings, and desires are inseparable from learning and using written language (Coles, 1998).

Identity is another one of those lenses that is discussed in relation to literacy but that takes on added weight in relation to literacy as second language learning. Frank Smith (1983) and Nancie Atwell (1987) each wrote about the need for learners to see certain kinds of literacy as something done by "people like me." In the critical ESL literature, identity as a theoretical construct is more fully developed, but it retains the notion of "people like me." (In more recent work in literacy, the construct is also theorized along critical lines. For instance, the research of Christian and Bloome, 2004, in a primary classroom serving English speakers and English learners, arguing that learning to read is "who you are," discusses identities as related to cultural capital.)

In recent scholarship, identity does not mean stable, core characteristics. Instead, it is a matter of being recognized by others as "a certain kind of person" in that particular context (Hawkins, 2004). It is not only fluid (potentially varying from context to context) and plural (allowing for multiple identities); it is also thoroughly social. It is others who both invite or hail (*interpellate* is Louis Althusser's word, as cited by Janks and Ivanic, 1992) people into identities, and others who recognize identities entered into. If such recognition does not occur, the identity does not "work" (Hawkins, 2004).[16] Identities might be seen as formed within the ongoing performance rather than pregiven and taken up (e.g., as discussed by Pennycook, 2004), or they might be conceived as ways of being that exist, perhaps, in schemas and cultural models and that can be recruited for particular tasks (e.g., as discussed by Hawkins, 2004). In either case, to repeat, identities are profoundly social—made possible, on the one hand, by a person's prior experiences and assessments of future possibilities (related to the distribution of material and cultural capital; Norton, 1997) and, on the other, by the extent to which the identities are recognized in that context.

Looking at literacy through the lens of identity makes certain questions salient: Which students are hailed—and how—for which literate identities? Who recognizes whom in which literate identities, and how is that recognition displayed or withheld? Why are certain literate identities (like certain second language identities) sought after by some and resisted by others? How is cultural capital distributed among students, and how does that distribution influence their identities as literacy learners.

---

[16]A person may, of course, continue to think of himself—identify—as a comedian even if no one laughs at his jokes. But that unappreciative audience is more likely to provide him with a different identity; wannabe (but failed) comedian is only one of the possibilities.

A lens closely related to identity is *situated learning*. Although situated learning is a general theoretical perspective on learning, it actually backgrounds learning because it conceptualizes learning as a by-product. What it foregrounds are participation and membership and identity. Once again, writings about literacy resonate with pieces of these ideas. For example, Frank Smith (1981b, 1983, 1985) proposed that to become literate a learner has to join "the literacy club" (has to be invited and has to want to join), seeing herself as a literate among literates, participating with those already "in the club" in a particular way. That is, more expert literates have to actually *use* literacy in front of and with learners—a kind of participation that "teaches" inherently though implicitly, showing learners—in the use—how written language works and what it's for.

As developed by Lave and Wenger (1991), *situated learning* focuses on people entering cultural activities (communities of practice) with the intent of "joining the club"—participating as and becoming members (becoming butchers, midwives, tailors, members of an Alcoholics Anonymous group, etc.). Participation is a key construct. In order to participate, they must have access to the activity; they have to be privy to its enactment by those who are already central members of the community of practice. As newcomers, their earliest legitimate participation (i.e., participation that contributes to the activity) is peripheral. For example, young girls in the Amazon basin may plait grasses into mats for midwives; young boys in Liberia may carry bolts of cloth for tailors. As they become more central members, neophytes' participation changes; that is, neophytes learn. Situated-learning theory depends on certain tenets; for example, people are always learning,[17] and all learning occurs through and is colored by particular local contexts.

A situated-learning lens offers extended theoretical support for various aspects of immersion experiences in learning any second language, including written language. It also magnifies certain issues and questions. For instance, the idea of learning as ubiquitous prods the question: What *are* students learning about literacy (especially those who are not learning the official objectives)? What constitutes legitimate peripheral participation in literacy practices for neophytes? Instead of thinking of how someone acquires literacy, situated-learning theory urges a shift: How does a community of practice (or a "literacy club") go about acquiring—or not acquiring, shutting out—new members? What kinds of participation does it permit as legitimate, and what kinds does it exclude?

The language socialization paradigm for SLA makes much of the lens of *culture*. In bringing together insights from cognitive sciences, human

---

[17]Frank Smith (1981b), too, talked about the ever-learning brain, and Ray McDermott (1993) also pointed out that cultural learning is ubiquitous.

development, language socialization, cognitive anthropology, cognitive linguistics, cultural and cross-cultural psychology, feminist studies, and ethnic studies, the paradigm itself, as well as each of these fields of study, appeals to culture at many critical points. Culture, of course, is also a familiar issue in discussions of literacy (e.g., Gee, 1990; Faltis & Hudelson, 1998; Martinez-Roldan, 2003; Nieto, 2004; D. Taylor, Coughlin, & Marasco, 1997). An intriguing point made in relation to several others in the language socialization discussions of culture is that culture is formative (Watson-Gegeo, 2004, p. 337). That is, the effects of culture on child development are not only pervasive; through the family, culture influences every aspect of human development. Therefore, as mentioned in the language specialization paradigm, the unit of analysis for human development should be the family rather than the individual child. Reconceptualizing the unit of analysis would have major implications for observing (and educating) second language learners, including learners of written language as a second language. Whether or not the family as unit of analysis should be augmented for older learners by the peer group or social network, the change in focus would be stunning. Family literacy (Auerbach, 1989; D. Taylor, 1983, 1997; D. Taylor et al., 1997; D. Taylor & Dorsey-Gaines, 1988; Weinstein-Shr, 1993) would move from the periphery to the center in education. And instead of seeing families in need of teaching or improvement, families and family organization would be seen as epistemological agents with knowledge and practices that must be accounted for.

If culture is crucial in the language socialization paradigm, so is context (as I [Edelsky, 1986] noted for literacy). However, the lens here is *context-as-the-thickest-imaginable*. No matter how much context is explicated, more remains. The LS paradigm argues that nothing is learned outside of specific contexts, even the most general knowledge. All knowledge, all learning, all activity, is shaped by context, even as every interaction partially renegotiates the context. Contexts cannot be subdivided into variables or components (although theoretical models in second language acquisition theory and sociolinguistics too often present them as such). They are indivisible complexities of real lived situations—all the interrelationships within which an experience is situated. This lens directs us to consider literacy learning within the full thickness of contexts. It confronts us with the folly of attempting to reduce literacy activity to a person, a text, and a setting— taking the life out of it.

One more lens (though there are actually many others) is *knowledge and learning as political.* What constitutes knowledge, who can be a knower, and how evidence is turned into truth are always social, cultural, and political. And all interactional activities (e.g., learning) are socially organized and therefore inherently political (entailing anything from moment-to- moment shifts in power to power hierarchies that, even though they are interactionally accomplished, are nevertheless stable and enduring). Recognizing the political nature of second language learning is a hallmark of critical SLA and critical ESL scholarship. Norton (1997), Singh (1998), Canagarajah (1999), Pennycook (2004), and others have interrogated notions such as *the native speaker, the proficient speaker,* and *applied linguistics* in the context of colonial and postcolonial teaching and learning of English. These interrogations are not for the sake of celebrating the diversity of multiple Englishes but for the purpose of exposing insider/outsider, colonizer/colonized, central/peripheral distinctions. And these exposés, in turn, are not merely for scholarly purposes but because the globalization of English—producing multiple Englishes yet sorting the new varieties in a colonial-inspired hierarchy—has material consequences. It is a key but underanalyzed undercurrent in decisions about who is qualified (to teach English, to study abroad, to advance in a career).

The multiplicities and hierarchies of Englishes have a counterpart with literacies. Certainly, literacy and literacy instruction have been seen as political (A. Luke, 1991; Shannon, 1985). But using this political lens to look at literacy as a second language raises new questions and emphasizes different dimensions. It leads to interrogating constructs associated with literacies. The term *literate* (with its implied *illiterate*), for instance, may be similar in some respects to *native speaker* (with its implied *non-native speaker*). The political lens, when associated with second language learning, also urges interrogating the hierarchies of texts and of literacies. The location of a text, a literacy, an English in a hierarchy is even more revealing when other relationships are also uncovered—not only the particular rung and not only the more and less direct beneficiaries of rungs in the hierarchy but also by what means benefits are distributed. Seeing literacy as a case of second language learning not only encourages immersion in literacy as a major pedagogical condition, including pragmatic attention to form; it also promotes critical literacy.

Viewing written language learning as a case of second language learning would thus raise important new questions as well as providing tactical and pedagogical benefits.

Chapter 7

Whole Language: What's New?

This chapter begins by presenting a new discussion that begins with occasional summaries and quoted sections of the original chapter. The new discussion is followed by a narrated condensation of the original chapter. The concluding section is new.

When Bess Altwerger, Barbara Flores, and I began writing the article in 1985 upon which this chapter is based, we were worried about the tension between the growing popularity of whole language and the persistent confusion about its meaning:[1]

> Those of us who want to see fundamental change in schools—the kind of change that improves all children's educational chances, the kind that does more than simply offer a traditional curriculum in two languages rather than one, the kind that resists centralized control over teachers, that resists practices that perpetuate societal inequities, that democratizes classrooms and encourages pluralism—are, in turn, gratified by this increased popularity for a pedagogy with just those intents. But the gratification is tinged with worry, because, as often as not, the same statements and activities that support whole language reveal outright confusions about it. So while we are delighted with the increasing popularity, we wonder what it is that is popular: The idea of whole language? The label? Innovation per se?

Our early version went on to describe why such tensions worried us; that is, popularity often distorts innovations and guts them of whatever radical

---

[1]Throughout, I will be alternating between material I am writing in 2005 and indented quotes from the original chapter.

(i.e., system-threatening) qualities they may have.[2] And whole language certainly had system-threatening qualities.

> It has the potential not only to change educational histories of a token few who might otherwise have failed in school, but to change the terms of educational discourse itself—to change what is meant by *literacy, achievement, educated, evaluation,* and so on.

We knew then that whole language undermined sorting and ranking people through testing and tracking, demanded teacher autonomy for developing their own curricula with students in their own classroom, decreased reliance on commercial reading programs and commercially prepared assessment systems (decreasing profits for giant educational publishers), and promoted the questioning of authority (through theories that argued for multiple interpretations of texts). But we did not follow the implication of our understanding; that is, an innovation that threatens "the system" will be attacked by "the system" whether or not there is confusion about what the innovation is. Instead, we focused on clearing up the confusion. Meanwhile, "the system" was gearing up to use whole language for its own political purposes. While we were taking up sense and nonsense about whole language (e.g., why would people equate whole language with a "whole word" approach to teaching reading, and what is wrong with that equation?), corporate interests with ties to governmental and right wing organizations were beginning to enact their education agenda. Whole language became a code word they used to accomplish their aims.

THE CAMPAIGN TO ACCOMPLISH THE CORPORATE/ GOVERNMENT EDUCATION AGENDA

The campaign actually began prior to the announcement of any agenda. In 1985, the first of the highly influential federally commissioned reports appeared—*Becoming a Nation of Readers* (Anderson, Hiebert, Scott, & Wilkinson, 1985). As Altwerger (2005c) argues, that Report, the ensuing "phonics furor" in the media, and the subsequent prominence of phonics in requests for proposals for federal funding for research on reading prepared the ground for the focus on phonics in the campaign for the agenda-to-be. So did the efforts (dating from at least the 1970s) of the radical religious Right to mandate phonics and control instructional materials (Altwerger 2005d; Coles 2003b). In the same period, the federal government began funneling funding for research on reading failure through the

---

[2]Edelsky and Cherland (in press) provide a lengthy discussion of the problematic effects of popularity.

prestigious National Institutes of Child Health and Development (NICHD), thus ensuring federal "control over the direction of reading research while maintaining a façade of scientific neutrality" (Altwerger, 2005c, p. 36). By 1989, when the National Business Roundtable (BRT) announced its education agenda (the BRT Education Initiative) in response to President George H. W. Bush's call to reform K–12 education, the phonics focus of the campaign and the positioning of NICHD had already been established.

The agenda itself had (and still has) three "pillars": standards and standardized curricula, high-stakes testing, and punitive accountability (Altwerger, 2005c). While these pillars of the agenda are stated explicitly in BRT Web pages and publications, the goal is not. That goal is to control education for corporate interests. (The goal is shared by both the federal government and the corporate world [increasingly, U.S. corporations are equated with the United States itself];[3] thus, it is more accurate to talk of a government–corporate agenda.) The corporate interests are profit (in the short term), privatization, and the spread of a market ideology to public spheres (Engel, 2000) in the somewhat more distant future and, most fundamentally and for the long term, maintaining a competitive edge for U.S. corporations in the global economy (Altwerger & Strauss, 2002). That edge is to be maintained by a "21st century workforce" equipped for the information technology labor market (Strauss, 2005a, citing a report by the Congressional 21st-Century Workforce Commission).

Presumably, the three pillars help achieve the goal. Standards and standardized curricula afford considerable opportunity for profits for publishing integrated instructional and assessment materials (basals, workbooks, teachers' manuals, tests, and test preparation materials) (M. L. Smith, 2004). High-stakes tests, with their politically engineered cut scores (Glass, 2003), along with punitive accountability, undermine the public's trust in its schools and help to soften up the public for charter schools and, eventually, vouchers. Privatizing public schools offers an additional avenue for corporate profits. And the kind of literacy curriculum that lends itself most easily not only to standards and high-stakes testing but, importantly, to the goal of preparing the right kind of labor force to maintain the world power of U.S. corporations, features phonics embedded in a behaviorist instructional environment that teaches students to read for technical information (Strauss, 2005a).

---

[3]Charles E. Wilson, president of General Motors, is often cited here, but what Wilson actually said in 1952 was not that GM's interests should stand for U.S. interests but that "what's good for the country is good for General Motors and vice versa." The difference is slight but important: The country and the corporation do not have identical interests. And the order matters, even if Wilson was only being "politic": the country's interests (arguably, the polity's) come first.

The campaign to push this government–corporate education agenda picked up steam in the 1990s. Many in the public at large, at first perceiving only the pitting of phonics against whole language, dismissed what was happening as merely another inevitable swing of a natural pendulum. If a pendulum is to be invoked, however, it was certainly not natural. (Wolfe & Poynor, 2001, argue that the pendulum metaphor is flawed at the core, failing to reveal either the political nature of educational innovations or the pressure to resist innovation from the status quo.) Rather than a swing, there was a push—a campaign. Altwerger (2005c) identified strategies in that campaign, for example, government-commissioned reports (*Becoming a Nation of Readers* [Anderson et al., 1985; *Preventing Reading Difficulties in Young Children*, a report of the National Research Council/National Academy of Science [Snow, Burns, & Griffin, 1998]; Marilyn Adams's [1990] *Beginning to Read;* Bonita Grossen's [1997] white paper synthesizing NICHD research, "Thirty Years of Research: What We Know About How Children Learn to Read"; *Report of the National Reading Panel* [2000]); conservative foundation and think tank reports (e.g., the Heritage Foundation's Policy Review reports on reading, in particular "See Dick Flunk"); media blitzes and campaigns; NICHD-funded research (e.g., the Houston study by Foorman, Francis, Fletcher, & Schatschneider, 1998); legislation (creation of the 21st-Century Workforce Commission to develop 21st-century literacy skills; the Reading Excellence Act, passed in 2000; No Child Left Behind, passed in 2002); and political appointments (e.g., Reid Lyon as director of reading research at NICHD, later as Bush's "reading czar"; Hans Meeder as head of 21st-Century Workforce Commission; appointments of panelists for commissioned reports). Altwerger (2005c) also identified key events in a timeline running from the publication of *Becoming a Nation of Readers* to the passage of the No Child Left Behind (NCLB) legislation. The strategies and the events are marked by suspicious coincidences and outright conflicts of interest at every turn.

The Media

The campaign to push the government–corporate education agenda relied heavily on the media, controlled almost entirely by 10 conglomerates made up of corporations that, by and large, are members of the Business Roundtable. The campaign established that there was a literacy crisis (falling test scores, employer complaints), and it blamed whole language—along with lack of uniform standards and uniform curriculum (as editorial writers complained, without uniformity how could students who move from one school to another keep up?) and lack of accountability. It is no coincidence, then, that the media launched a "blitz" wherein, during the week of October 27, 1997, and just prior to Congressional consideration of the Reading Excellence Act (designed by phonics proponents Douglas Carnine, coauthor of

DISTAR, and Hans Meeder), *Time, Newsweek, U.S. News & World Report, Atlantic Monthly,* and many newspapers all ran stories pitting phonics against whole language. Nor is it a coincidence that, despite lengthy interviews in which whole language spokespeople tried to impress upon reporters the underlying theoretical, philosophical, and political principles of whole language, the media persisted in representing the whole language/phonics struggle "as one of methodology rather than ideology" (Altwerger, 2005c). Nor that whole language was consistently distorted (e.g., as being the same as a "whole word" approach to reading, or as amounting to nothing more than giving children books with no help in making them comprehensible [Krashen, 2001a], as being opposed to teaching phonics, etc.).

The fact of a media cartel (Miller, 2002) aligned with the BRT is not the only source of such misrepresentation. Characteristics of reporting are also responsible. Crawford (2000a) refers to *reportage by template.* In education, one method versus another is a familiar storyline—a template—for reporters to use. One ideology versus another may be a familiar storyline for reporting the Cold War and now the War on Terror, but when applied to education it is so strange as to be unreportable. (The dominant view is that teaching is methods. Period.) Additionally, those tapped by the media as reading experts during this campaign have been singularly without expertise or experience; most have never taught reading; "never authored an original study on reading, at least not one published in a refereed research journal"; and never served on the editorial board of a premier literacy journal (e.g., *Reading Research Quarterly, Journal of Literacy Research, Research in the Teaching of English*), "although they have served on the boards of the *Annals of the Orton Dyslexia Society* and other special education journals" (Allington, 2001a). The kindest explanation is that "shallow media reporting in a he said/she said style, prompts a media outlet to simply call the person last cited, with little regard for actual expertise" (Allington, 2001a, citing Lieberman, 2000). A darker reason is that those anointed as experts have been approved by a government office such as the NICHD or by the BRT Education Task Force. Certainly that would account for the government's own designation of experts: witnesses to testify at Congressional hearings (Coles, 2003b; D. Taylor, 1998); researchers selectively recruited for conducting research (e.g., Foorman), reviewing it (e.g., those on the National Reading Panel [NRP]), and advising policymakers about it (M. L. Smith, 2004); the head of the Task Force to work on 21st-century literacy skills, and the director of the NICHD himself (Strauss, 2005b).

The Research

The media's impressive contribution to the campaign on behalf of the government–corporate education agenda frequently featured research that showed that "phonics won" (Strauss, 2005b). National Assessment of

Educational Progress (NAEP) results from 1992 (the first time scores were reported state by state) were used relatively early in this regard. California had come in last. Since its 1987 English Language Arts Framework included literature-based reading instruction (equated with whole language), a state government/media circus blamed whole language for the dismal results—completely ignoring the fact that high-ranking Maine was even more thoroughly in the whole language camp (Altwerger, 2005c) and that factors identified with whole language (e.g., reading for fun every day, access to libraries and other sources of reading material) were associated with higher NAEP scores for fourth-graders. (After whole language was banned in California, replaced by rigidly enforced phonics programs, phonics was not blamed for the continued bottom ranking of California in the 1994, 1998, 2000, or 2003 NAEP results) (Krashen, 2001b; 2005.) The case of California is instructive here. It was whole language (villain of choice) that was held responsible for low test scores, not (compared to other states) California's overcrowded classrooms, its lack of certified teachers, its inadequate school and public libraries, its high number of students in poverty, its huge percentage of students who speak English as a second language, and other factors—all of which have at least as much to do with low test scores as an instructional method (Altwerger, 2005c).

In 1997, another piece of research that "proved" the superiority of phonics appeared in headlines across North America and in policymaking chambers—not only before it appeared in a peer-reviewed journal but before the study was even completed. The Houston study conducted by Barbara Foorman and her colleagues (1998) proved that "direct code" phonics first was better than "implicit code" whole language and "embedded code" phonics. There were numerous problems with the study, not the least being that its authors violated professional norms by refusing to provide other researchers with the data and analyses for independent evaluation (Coles, 2000; D. Taylor, 1998). More substantive problems included: the research was not independent (i.e., Foorman coauthored *Open Court*, one of the treatments used in the study); there is considerable evidence that classrooms designated as whole language did not in fact represent whole language; and reanalysis of the data (obtained largely through the Freedom of Information Act after the authors dragged their feet in providing it to other researchers) showed that, contrary to the claims on its behalf, "direct instruction phonics" did not result in superior reading achievement (Coles, 2003b).

At about the time that Denny Taylor (1998) was documenting in exquisite detail the spinning of the Foorman research by the media, NICHD, other state and federal government offices, and some major corporate performers, notably McGraw-Hill, were warming up in another ring of this circus. The National Research Council was the first panel of "outside" experts (though their status as "outsiders" is certainly questionable given that more than half of them received funding from NICHD) appointed to "stand above the fray of the reading wars," look at all the research, and puts its stamp of approval on NICHD-directed research (Coles, 2003b, p. 16). But the report it produced was too judicious for NICHD; it left "too much wiggle room" (Coles, 2003b, p. 17, citing Louisa Moats, an NICHD-funded researcher). The next national panel would be entirely "chosen by the NICHD chiefs and the Department of Education" (Coles, 2003b, p. 17). This one (the National Reading Panel/NRP) conducted a meta-analysis using only experimental research (excluding qualitative research, case studies, and observational studies) on selected categories (it excluded studies on silent reading, reading for pleasure, comprehension of extended texts, effects of phonics on writing, effects of writing on reading, and other topics). Its full Report was satisfactory enough to warrant a Summary and promotional materials that were sent to school districts, textbook publishers, and policy-makers across the country (M. L. Smith, 2004). Aside from the Panel's narrow conception of research, science, and reading itself, a big problem this time was not "wiggle room" but contradictions. Claims that appeared in the Summary and the promotional materials were contradicted by the full Report (Garan, 2002). To take but two examples: (1) contrary to phonics-promoting headlines around the country (e.g., "Reading Panel Urges Phonics for All in K–6") based on "facts" from the Summary, the Report itself stated that there were insufficient data to draw conclusions about phonics instruction above first grade, and (2) systematic phonics instruction did not improve spelling, as claimed in the Summary; instead, *Open Court* phonics instruction in particular had negative effects on spelling (Garan, 2002).

The discrepancies between the spin-off promotional materials and the full Report might be attributed to the fact that the former were not produced by people with research experience but rather by a public relations firm, Widmeyer Communications (more on that shortly). The closed-minded character of the Panel's process, however, cannot be explained by lack of scientific research experience since the panelists were almost all scientists, though not all in the field of reading. The one notable exception, Joanne Yatvin, a former school principal, eventually became a whistle blower, courageously writing a dissenting report that exposed the Panel's undemocratic and unscientific process (Yatvin, 2002). Given the ideology behind commissioning the Report and selling it via a public relations firm, and the multiple roles played by the corporate media in pushing this education agenda, it is no surprise that Yatvin's report received little attention. Coming on the heels of the previous research that "proved" the superiority of phonics, the NRP Report seemed to show that there was now a consensus in the field. (Allington and Woodside-Jiron argued that in the 1990s they were already seeing the political use of expertise. The political use of expertise is a strategy in *policy as political spectacle* [M. L. Smith, 2004]. It is what occurs when policy advocates promote "the appearance of an external professional consensus ..., often achieved by using highly selective research teams whose advice may not be easily dismissed" [Allington & Woodside-Jiron, 1999, p. 11].) The NRP Report—the "expert consensus"— with its narrow, mechanistic conception of reading—was highly influential in the passage of the No Child Left Behind legislation. Indeed, in Title I of NCLB, Congress arrogantly elbowed aside professional research organiza- tions (e.g., the American Educational Research Association) to outdo itself with a legislated definition of research, using language appropriated from NICHD (M. L. Smith, 2004).

Questionable Connections

The connections between and within the players and the actions in this very brief history of the campaign to achieve the government–corporate education agenda should already appear too numerous for coincidence. The problem is not quantity, however; it is probable illegality. Many of those connections involve conflicts of interest. Elaine Garan (2005) and Gerald Bracey (2005d) have each documented the connections among requirements written into federal legislation, developers of criteria for materials that meet those requirements, creators of the materials that meet the criteria, and high-level politicians (e.g., the President, among others) sponsoring the federal legislation that imposes those requirements. For example, researchers who wrote the criteria to evaluate materials named in Reading First applications also were authors of the *Voyager Expanded Learning* series, one of the few approved Reading First curricula. Officers in *Voyager* have close ties with President Bush (Bracey, 2005d). There are also researchers who profit from the policies that rely on their research. Both Foorman and Adams are coauthors of *Open Court* (published by McGraw-Hill). Foorman's research presumably proved the superiority of *Open Court*, leading to increased sales for *Open Court*. Foorman was the sole reviewer of the phonics section of the NRP Report, a section in which Foorman's research figured prominently. Both the Reading Excellence Act and then the NCLB legislation relied on the NRP Report, including its section on phonics (Garan, 2002).

Research on *Open Court* and *Direct Instruction* has not been independent as it should have been according to the criteria for "independence of the research team from the program/product being studied" as set forth in the Reading Excellence Act (Allington, 2001b). Instead, authors of those pro- grams were key figures in the research teams. Their research on these pro- grams has been used to influence state policy on textbook adoptions, national legislation on instruction and assessment, and, in turn, helped reap profits from the purchase of those materials (Allington & Woodside- Jiron, 1999; Garan, 2002). Moreover, if it doesn't account for why features of *Open Court* figured so prominently in the materials prepared by Widmeyer Communications, the contract with Widmeyer to prepare the Summary and other promotional materials still smells of conflict of interest since Widmeyer is also the public relations firm for McGraw-Hill's *Open Court.* Another probable conflict of interest are the connections between "outside experts" (called to serve as panelists, give testimony, or act as government advisors or consultants) and the agencies (e.g., NICHD) and companies (e.g., test processor NCS Pearson, McGraw-Hill) with which they are affiliated (Garan, 2002; Metcalf, 2002) and which stand to profit from the testimony and advice.

If not illegal conflicts of interest, the connections involved in "buying the press" are severely damaging to a democracy. The ability to buy (or sell one's perspective to) the press further diminishes whatever independence remains of an already corporate-owned press. For example, McGraw-Hill gave a $1 million grant to the Hechinger Institute at Columbia University to provide seminars to train education reporters in "reporting methods, story ideas, and in depth background from leading experts on critical issues" (Garan, 2002, p. 79). It is not too farfetched to imagine that these experts would lead reporters to provide good press for McGraw-Hill products such as *Open Court* and *Direct Instruction.* What *is* illegal is using public funds to buy the media (through bribes and contracts) to sell or market government policies. Congress defined such activity as *covert propaganda.* As investigated by journalist Greg Toppo and reported in *USA Today* on January 7, 2005, the $240,000 contract with a syndicated commentator by the Department of Education to promote NCLB appears to be a case of *covert propaganda*—propaganda masquerading as news.[4]

In each aspect of the history of this campaign to control education in order to keep corporations internationally competitive, the topic of interest—what the research has been about, what the laws have concerned, what the headlines have been about—has been largely reading. Scientific research-based reading instruction. Reading instruction supposedly supported even by brain research using new imaging techniques (Strauss, 2005b). Reading instruction that put phonics first. Throughout, the foil— explicitly at first but now so expected it can be implicit—has been and remains whole language. And by now, whole language has been so egregiously misrepresented that the term has come to stand for anything not sanctioned by federal law (K. Goodman, 2002). Of course, whole language is not just "anything," certainly not an "anything" in the realm of "methods" for teaching reading. But does it really matter that people understand what

---

[4]Education is not alone in being the subject of *covert propaganda.* The George W. Bush administration used promotional videos designed to look like news broadcasts to promote a federal drug policy and also its new Medicare law (Kurtz, 2005).

whole language is? Given the mere sketch above of phonics-as-hero and whole-language-as-villain in a coordinated campaign on behalf of a much larger agenda, would understanding what whole language is make any difference? I think the answer is yes, but contingent upon who *people* are and what *any difference* is.

By *people*, I do not mean those pushing the government–corporate agenda. Nor, at this time and most immediately, do I mean the general public. Steve Strauss (2005a) maintains that in the face of the current education agenda juggernaut, the choice is between resignation and resistance. The *people* I mean here are the resisters. They are the ones to whom understanding whole language will make a difference. They are the ones who, at first, need to become very clear about what is wrong with the kind of education imposed by NCLB and what is wrong with the campaign's presentation of its favorite foil, whole language. Many of the resisters will be educators who already claim a whole language heritage. Others will be those who are whole language educators without knowing it—for example, the extraordinary teachers and teacher educators working with young children with significant disabilities in inclusive early childhood settings, documented by Kliewer et al. (2004). (Kliewer and his colleagues described observing children and responding imaginatively, working from children's strengths, giving meaning primary consideration in literacy instruction, honoring individual differences, using authentic texts for communicative purposes, using multiple semiotic systems, being sensitive to the subterranean culture of children—all whole language "principles," phrased in just those ways—without a single mention or citation of any whole language literature or educators.) Still others will be noneducators who are part of a coalition of resisters. Knowing what whole language is and how it has been misrepresented (as well as what phonics is, what its supporting research is actually about, and how it too has been misrepresented) (Coles, 2000; Strauss, 2005b) will not substitute for learning how to organize and how to resist the powerful, dominant, multitentacled opposition. But resisters also have to learn about what they are opposing: what the government–corporate agenda is ostensibly about versus what it is really about, what it takes to oppose it, what code words (e.g., whole language) are used by those in control and how they have been misused. Paraphrasing Susan Eaton (2005), who was referring to civil rights, when government–corporate ideologues get to set the terms of public discourse about whole language, it is important to restate what whole language *means*.[5]

---

[5]The difference between the present attempt to clear up confusion and the earlier one is that, originally, we expected that ensuing clarity by itself—if sufficiently widespread—might offset attacks on whole language. Clarifying whole language now is for the benefit of resisters; I have no illusions that it can directly affect the dominant campaign for control of education.

RESTATING WHAT WHOLE LANGUAGE MEANS

The original statement began with our brief description of what whole language is.[6]

> First and foremost, whole language is NOT merely practice. It is a set of beliefs, a perspective, a theory-in-practice. It must become practice (i.e. it must turn into ways of handling error, interactional choices, instructional behavior, materials, curricula, schedules, etc.), but it is not the instructional behavior, the materials, the curricular choices themselves.

In the 1980s, districts wanting to appear up to date were mandating whole language (imagine that!). We cautioned that since whole language is a viewpoint, districts may mandate practices (e.g., writing centers, book publishing, etc.), but they cannot mandate the viewpoints required to turn practices into whole language.

In identifying whole language beliefs, we began with the most basic, the one that constitutes whole language's political stance:

> Systemic social inequality is undesirable; ... education must work to end rather than to perpetuate a stratified society. Much educational activity (e.g. that which goes into testing and tracking) contributes to stratification. Whole language opposes that activity as well as the theory that supports it.[7]

Key beliefs about language and language learning followed:

- Language is for making meanings, for accomplishing purposes,
- Written language is language; what is true for language in general is true for written language,
- The cuing systems of language (phonology in oral, orthography in written language, morphology, syntax, semantics, pragmatics) are interactive and interdependent,
- Language has the potential for multiple interpretations because language use always occurs in a situation,

---

[6]Today, I would maintain that whole language is a Discourse with a capital *D* (following Gee, 1999)—a set of values + beliefs (some of those being formal theories about language and literacy) + behaviors + ways of talking specific to a community of practice (Lave & Wenger, 1991).

[7]Even though we did not emphasize the political nature of whole language in the original chapter, we did note its importance at various points, including right at the beginning. Later in this chapter and elsewhere, I will mention the strategic failure of the whole language movement to adequately identify and position itself as a political movement. The original version of the chapter may have contributed to that failure by not claiming that identity for whole language.

- Situations (small, local face-to-face situations and larger ones that concern what is happening culturally and historically) are critical for making sense of and with language …
- The world over, babies acquire a language through actually using it, not through practicing its separate parts or practicing with only one or two systems until some later date when the parts are assembled or the system is reintegrated and the totality is finally used.
- Language acquisition (both oral and written) is natural—not in the sense of innate or inevitably unfolding, but natural in the sense that when language (oral or written) is an integral part of the functioning of a community and is used around and with neophytes, it is learned "incidentally" to what else is [going on] (Ferreiro & Teberosky, 1982; Lindfors, 1987).[8]

We then identified two major educational implications of these beliefs:

1. "If language is acquired through use, and if written language is language, then written language too is learned through use, not through practice exercises[9].... (e.g., cake mix directions [are] used for actually making a cake rather than for finding short vowels); and …

2. If language is a tool for making sense of something else, then the "something else's" must have prominence …" [i.e., social studies issues, themes in literature, and science investigations are what the school day is mostly about, providing] "contexts for much of the reading and writing."

---

[8]I would no longer state it this way—that written language is learned *incidentally*. In fact, even early on, descriptions of whole language pedagogy did not show a total reliance on "incidental" learning. Instead, they showed teachers strategically demonstrating the use of written language, teaching a particular skill as a child needs it for something the child wants to communicate (see such comments in this chapter and in the 1991 version of this chapter), providing strategy lessons in reading (Y. Goodman & Burke, 1980), talking about decisions authors make during literature study in reading and attention to aspects of writing in writers' workshops. Whole language proponents today are more likely to talk about written language being learned through "immersion" in an environment in which (1) written language is used by others in front of and with neophytes, showing them how it works and what it is for, and (2) aspects of written language conventions are made the focus of explicit attention in conversations and play.

[9]In chapter 6, I argue that the analogy between first language learning and written language learning should be replaced by one that sees written language learning as a case of second language learning. The admonition against exercises, following from the first-language–literacy learning analogy, is less true for a second-language–literacy learning comparison. Still, exercises (how much, what kind, when), balanced against "use," remain an issue.

COMMON MISUNDERSTANDINGS
ABOUT WHOLE LANGUAGE

We identified six common misunderstandings, framing them as questions, and presented what was sensible about the faulty equation, followed by the whole language position. We should have added a seventh, an omission that will be corrected at the end of this chapter.

IS WHOLE LANGUAGE A NEW TERM FOR
THE WHOLE WORD APPROACH?

It Could Be ...

We pointed out that a common misconception is that reading is a matter of "getting the words," and that The Great Debate (Chall, 1967), which was supposed to be between two distinctly different conceptions of reading—look/say and phonics—is[10] actually just variations on one theme: a phonics approach to "getting the words" and a look/say or whole word approach to "getting the words." This matches conventional wisdom about language learning—language development amounts to learning words. Much in the general culture (vocabulary as a means of social gatekeeping) and school culture (vocabulary exercises and tests) supports the idea that "getting the words" is what matters, that there are only two ways to "get words," and whole language might be one of them.

But It Isn't

> The whole language view of reading is not one of getting words but of constructing meaning for a text in a situation (see the development of this view in the writings of K. Goodman) (Gollasch, 1982). Word boundaries and lexical features are indeed used as cues, but meaning is created with many other cues too—syntax, semantics, and pragmatics (including the reader's purpose, the setting, what the reader knows about the author's purpose). To believe that reading means getting words assumes that words have constant meanings; yet words like *Mary, lamb, had,* and *little* in the following examples derive meaning from the sentences which follow them.
>
> 1. Mary had a little lamb. Its fleece was white as snow.
> 2. Mary had a little lamb. She spilled mint jelly on her dress.
> 3. Mary had a little lamb. It was such a difficult delivery the vet needed a drink.
>
> (example adapted from Trabasso, 1981).

---

[10]The present tense is deliberate: The Great Debate continues today.

Reading as getting (and saying) a word implies that we have to know a word orally in order to read it (get its meaning) but, in fact, we learn words through reading just as we learn them through conversing (surprising us when we later discover that *Penelope,* for example, does not rhyme with *antelope*). Knowing a word is knowing:

> a set of potentials (e.g. meaning potentials, word class information, morphological possibilities, possible metaphorical usages) related to other sets of potentials, embedded in a variety of schemas for social life. It is the set, the range, and the schema-type storage that permit us to create different meanings for *Mary, had, little,* and *lamb* in [the above examples].

A whole word approaches assumes that:

> word meanings, once "gotten" are added up to produce a text meaning. In fact, the whole far exceeds the sum of the parts. Print provides a text potential (Harste, Woodward, & Burke, 1984; Rosenblatt, 1978, 1985). When we read, we turn that potential into an actual instance—a text-in-situation, with details of meaning that must be inferred from, but do not appear in, the printed cues.

IS WHOLE LANGUAGE ANOTHER TERM FOR TEACHING SKILLS IN CONTEXT?

It Could Be ...

We pointed to the widespread view that literacy consists of isolatable skills (e.g., decoding skills, comprehension skills, etc.), separately learnable and separately teachable (DeFord, 1985; Harste & Burke, 1977). This view is part of a more general assumption: If it is possible to identify subactivities in the proficient performance of any complex activity, then those subactivities should be taught separately. Some whole language educators in the 1980s added to the confusion by talking about their whole language practice as teaching "skills in context" so as to lessen the threat to the status quo of what they were doing. So, we noted, people might well think that whole language is simply teaching skills in context with an emphasis on comprehension skills.

But It Isn't

> According to a whole language perspective, any separate skill or sub-activity performed outside the total act of reading functions differently from the way that sub-activity works when it is part of the total activity. In other words, the

"skill" of decoding for decoding's sake (as on a worksheet or a test) is a different activity than decoding [while reading a letter from a far-away relative].

It is a different practice. The former is for the purpose of instruction or evaluation and positions the reader as Object, the latter is for some communicative purpose and positions the reader as Subject (see chap. 5).

> Moreover, the sub-activity is not merely the behavior. It interacts with other sub-activities ... [the isolated behavior is] meaningless in itself. It would be as if separate pedaling, handlebar-holding, steering, and brake-applying did not need to be integrated, as if they could simply be added together to produce bike-riding....
>
> In written language use, cues from one system have an effect on cues from the other systems. Thus, syntax influences phonology, permitting a reduced vowel when *can* is part of a verb (*the garbage /ken/ go over there*) but not when it is a noun (*the garbage /kaen/ is over there*). Syntax influences graphophonics so that the unit initial th+vowel is voiced for function words (*this, their*) but voiceless in content words (*thing, thistle*). Semantics controls syntactic parsing in such sentences as *flying planes can be dangerous.* Pragmatics is what permits variation in orthography (*lite/light; through/thru*). It should be noted that the direction of influence is from high to low: Information from the higher system is required in order to make a decision about the lower. This is just the opposite of the basic skills hierarchy which begins at the supposed beginning—the smaller units and lower levels....
>
> When whole language teachers point out and teach language skills as a child needs them during actual language use, the instruction is not for instruction's sake—not just so that the child will learn the skill—but for helping the child achieve [a purpose] (getting permission from the principal, entertaining his or her classmates, informing another class, persuading the City Council, etc.). A whole language framework insists that we become "skilled language users," not that we "learn language skills."

IS WHOLE LANGUAGE A METHOD? A PROGRAM? A "SLANT" FOR BASALS OR OTHER PACKAGED PROGRAMS?

It Could Be ...

We acknowledged that method (and its accessories, such as packaged materials) is what many people think constitutes professional expertise. Colleges of education in the United States contribute to this idea by separating theory courses from methods courses and positioning the methods courses immediately before student teaching. Authoritative sources such as state reading instruction guides that (used to) cite whole language as one of many methods, advertising pitches for "whole language basals" (when such were permissible), and teachers' general preference for eclecticism

(choosing from a grab bag of methods) all compound the error. It is easy
to see how whole language comes to be (mis)understood as a method.

But It Isn't

We noted that equating beliefs or orientations (a whole language orientation, a skills orientation) with methods is an error in level of abstraction.
Conducting spelling drills and holding writers' workshops are methods,
not theoretical viewpoints. Examples of theoretical viewpoints are: skills;
whole language. Neither of these is a method.

Moreover, there are no essential "methods" for a whole language
viewpoint:

> Some practices [are an easy fit with whole language beliefs] (e.g. journals,
> reading aloud to children, silent reading, literature study, publishing books,
> content logs, small group science projects). However, none of these is essen-
> tial. It would be possible, though impoverishing, to emphasize science pro-
> jects and exclude literature, yet still have a whole language classroom....
>
> [On the other hand, a] teacher who uses the "method" (*practice* is actually
> a more apt term) of literature study and who views reading as a collection of
> separate skills will turn those literature study sessions into skills lessons....
> Like a liquid, practice takes the shape of, and represents, whatever belief-
> container it is in. (C. Browne, personal communication, February 23, 1985)

If thinking of whole language as method confuses levels of abstraction,
common claims of eclecticism amount to magical thinking—to pretending
to a professional idyllic dream world where teaching practices have no
premises and (nonexistent) premises do not clash. But a basic premise running through basals (reading consists of separate skills) contradicts a basic
premise of whole language (reading does not consist of separate skills):

> The only way basal readers or phonics programs could be congruent with
> whole language beliefs would be for children to use these materials as data
> (e.g. as documents in an historical study of changes in school culture
> [Edelsky, Altwerger, & Flores, 1991], or as instances of discourse to critique
> [Baker & Luke, 1991]).[11]

Of course, whole language teachers do use methods. And they are eclec-
tic in one sense: They have a large repertoire of materials, modes of interacting, and ways of organizing classrooms, so they can vary their approaches

---

[11]The stories in basal readers can also be read simply for enjoyment—no vocabulary worksheets, no comprehension questions, just reading and, probably, talking about them with others.
Such use would make them congruent with whole language.

with different children for different purposes. But this is not the eclecticism of borrowing surface forms without examining their underlying premises.

IS WHOLE LANGUAGE A NEW TERM FOR
THE LANGUAGE EXPERIENCE APPROACH?

It Could Be ...

We mentioned a number of similarities. Both whole language (K. Goodman, 1986; Newman, 1985) and language experience approach educators (Allen, 1976; Ashton-Warner, 1963; Lamoreaux & Lee, 1943; R. Peterson, 1981; Veatch, Sawicki, Elliott, Barnette, & Blakey, 1973) paint images of rich classroom environments, emphasize the importance of literature, treat reading as (at least in part) a personal act, accept and work with whatever language varieties a child brings to school, and use a variety of symbol systems. There would be good reason, therefore, for thinking that whole language is a synonym for the language experience approach.

But It Isn't

An important difference concerns premises about the relation of oral and written language. The language experience approach presumes that written language is a secondary system derived from oral language. Whole language sees oral and written language systems as structurally related without one being an alternate symbolic rendition of the other. Moreover, written language learning need not wait for oral language acquisition. People can learn vocabulary, syntax, and stylistic conventions directly through written language (Edelsky, 1986b; Harste, Woodward & Burke, 1984; Hudelson, 1984).

Dictation provides a symptomatic difference. The reason language experience teachers so frequently take dictation from students while whole language teachers do not is related to the evolution of theory. At the time the language experience approach was being developed, the belief was that writing was a matter of composing first, then transcribing the composed meanings (taking dictation from oneself). By the time whole language theory was being developed, writing was seen as meaning-making occurring during the act of writing (Smith, 1982b). Thus, in a whole language view (and with the benefit of better theory), taking dictation deprives language learners of a key context for making meaning—the act of writing.

The language experience approach assumes that reading entails knowledge *about* written language (Allen, 1976; R. Peterson, 1981; Veatch et al., 1973). Thus, after a child's experience is dictated to the teacher, the transcription is often used to teach word attack or phonics skills. In contrast, whole language disputes that such metalinguistic knowledge is best gained through fragmented exercises:

> The main distinction, however, between whole language and the language experience approach concerns theory. The language experience approach made major breaks with established reading pedagogy. It taught reading without basals ... relying mostly on children's literature. It gave up the assumed sequence of reading before writing. It contradicted the presumed need to group children for reading instruction. It recognized the importance of children's own purposes and children's own language patterns. But it appealed to no developed theory to support these breaks with conventional wisdom.

Given the limits of linguistic and psycholinguistic theory in the mid-20th century, all it had was structural linguistics and some naive views about the size and type of vocabulary acquisition. Still, it was the most progressive (i.e., undermining oppressive literacy practices in schools) and comprehensive (i.e., explicating assumptions and suggested practice) view of written language teaching and learning at the time. Its weaknesses reflect historical limits on knowledge rather than failure of vision. Indeed, the language experience approach may have been a necessary precursor to whole language.

IS WHOLE LANGUAGE A NEW TERM FOR THE OPEN CLASSROOM?

It Could Be ...

Whole language and the open classroom of the 1960s and 1970s (also known as the *British Infant School model* or the *Integrated Day*) certainly bear a family resemblance (see Gross & Gross, 1969; Lucas, 1976; A. S. Neill, 1960; Nyquist & Hawes, 1972; and Silberman, 1970). Both open education and whole language note the active character of learning; both consider the "whole child," understanding (with early critical theorists; Gibson, 1986) that emotions and bodies cannot be separated from learning and thinking. Both see learning as rooted in firsthand experience, genuine problem-posing and problem solving. Both see the need for a curricular focus on significant content. With so many resemblances, no wonder whole language is seen not as a cousin, but as an identical twin of, open education.[12]

---

[12]For these comparisons, we looked at the ideal rather than distortions. For instance, in the name of open education, some classrooms were organized so children rotated in rigid time blocks among so-called "learning centers" at which they worked on worksheets. Whole language has its own examples of "whole-language-in-name-only" where teachers make up "whole language" comprehension questions to go along with the "whole language" basals.

But It Isn't

One minor distinction we noted concerns the role of the teacher. The open education teacher is painted as a facilitator, a provisioner of the environment, and a resource person. So are whole language teachers—but to a different degree. The literature on open education (e.g., Bussis & Chittendon, 1972) puts more emphasis on the physical environment (Loughlin & Suina, 1982); whole language puts more weight on teachers and learners constructing meaning together.

A more important difference is the view of the learner. Despite the stress placed by Dewey (and A. S. Neill, 1960) on communities, the learner in open education is seen primarily as an individual, making individual choices (e.g., about what to study). Whole language views the learner as profoundly social:

> Participating in a community of readers (and speakers) during small group literature study, a community of writers in peer writing workshops, a community of learners in group social studies projects with built-in plans for collaborative learning.

Another key difference we discussed concerned approaches to standardized tests. Both open education and whole language oppose them, but for different reasons. To open-classroom proponents, standardized tests fail to test what teachers are teaching (e.g., self-directedness, problem solving). The tests, in other words, are insufficient. To whole language educators, the tests fail to test what the tests themselves claim to be testing (i.e., reading); that is, they are invalid (see chap. 12). The source of this discrepancy lies in the origins of open education and whole language. Whole language takes its direction from a particular theoretical view of language acquisition and literacy. That view not only invalidates standardized tests; it also delegitimizes a variety of school practices (e.g., test-based grouping for reading, tracking, admission criteria, etc.) that deny people access to cultural capital, and it lends theoretical support to whole language's political goal: a more just, equitable society.

Open education and whole language also have distinctive meanings because of their varying historical contexts. Open education experienced a rebirth in the 1960s:

> a time of both relative prosperity and widespread criticism of endemic, structured social inequities, a time when the modernist faith in technology and progress still had a hold on the public consciousness.

Whole language, on the other hand, developed as a movement during meaner times:

> when the homeless are increasing, when government social programs have suffered many cuts, when freedom to criticize, even to create, is threatened

by rightwing groups, when a growing postmodernist mentality acknowledges the damage done by "progress" harnessed to technology.

IS WHOLE LANGUAGE A SYNONYM FOR WRITING PROCESS?

It Could Be ...

Writing process classrooms are largely workshops. Children choose their own topics for writing; they choose their own books for pleasure reading and for study; they work as colleagues, responding to each other's work (Calkins, 1986; Graves, 1983). Whole language classrooms often exhibit the same workshop atmosphere. Both writing process teachers and whole language teachers see themselves as "kidwatchers" (Y. Goodman, 1985), responding in informed ways to what the student is trying to do (Atwell, 1987; Graves, 1983; F. Smith, 1982b). Many writing process teachers meet regularly in grassroots groups to promote their own professional growth. So do whole language teachers (see chap. 11).

Whole language and writing process distinguish between writing exercises and all other kinds of writing (see chaps. 5 and 8, this volume; Atwell, 1987; Hansen, 1987). In fact, a fundamental premise shared by both is that children in school should be doing what real writers do—they should write, not do writing exercises. Rather than seeing unconventional spellings as mistakes or bad habits that will interfere with correct responses, whole language and writing process teachers know that errors are necessary for learning and illuminating for teaching.

Both writing process and whole language also share another similarity: Each has become a movement. As such, their informing frameworks are often misunderstood, ignored, or adapted (co-opted) so as not to disturb dominant assumptions about language and learning.

With such apparently identical beliefs, practices, and even undesirable reactions, it seems right to consider whole language not just an identical twin of writing process but another name for the same thing.

And It Is ... Almost

Writing process and whole language are each frameworks, though not identical ones. Whole language includes both an *explicit* theoretical base (about language and language learning) and pedagogical implications. It takes key features of the way language is learned as a "best model" for all learning in school. In other words, whole language is an umbrella *theory-in-practice*.

Writing process is a perspective on writing pedagogy that includes an *implicit* theoretical base (about the nature of writing). It takes key characteristics of the contexts writers rely on for their own growth as a "best model" for learning to write in school. It offers those characteristics (time, ownership, and response in a workshop setting) as the best context for all learning in school. In other words, writing process is an umbrella *pedagogy*-with-implicit-theory.

In the original chapter, we mentioned that this somewhat subtle distinction between a theory-in-practice, on the one hand, and a pedagogy-with-implicit-theory, on the other, is reflected in how writing process treats reading and how whole language treats writing. In the absence of an explicit theoretical tie between writing and reading, writing process educators either ignored reading at first or treated it as pedagogically separate from writing (see Calkins, 1983, for an example). When writing process educators began to make connections between writing and reading, they gave curricular rather than theoretical reasons for the connections. They seemed to be saying that literature was a means for teaching reading, as opposed to the whole language idea that reading is a means for learning literature (Edelsky, 1988; R. Peterson & Eeds, 1990). We noted that as writing process educators continued their study of reading, they began to present what whole language had advocated from the beginning: Schools should have students doing what readers do when they read, just as they have students do what writers do when they write.

In its early years, writing process was only about writing; whole language, however, was not only about reading. From the beginning, whole language educators looked at children's writing as well as their reading because they put the two into the same theoretical category: language. Thus, young children's invented spellings (Read, 1975) and their writing (Harste, 1980) provided evidence for whole language beliefs about children's language strengths in constructing the system of written language. From the start, whole language educators welcomed writing process as providing a rich pedagogy for their own whole language theory of learning language through actual use.

Another difference concerns the political implications of becoming a whole language or a writing process teacher. When whole language teachers first took control of their teaching, they explicitly advocated and acted to overthrow the established reading technology (basals, workbooks, and packaged programs tied to tests with stakes attached). Such an action had immediate political consequences (e.g., some teachers were threatened with dismissal for insubordination if they refused to use the basal reader). Such actions unmasked the relationship of big business and class ideology to curriculum and to teacher autonomy. Writing process teachers, on the other hand, had comparatively little to overthrow. While there were required language arts texts and spelling series, there were (and still are) no counterparts in writing that carry the same weight as the entrenched basal technology does in reading. Deciding to take control of one's teaching of writing, therefore, was less of a threat within the big business of education. Such actions lack the built-in potential for revealing teachers' roles in relation to the structure of the institution and the larger society.

IS WHOLE LANGUAGE AN EXPLICITLY POLITICAL MOVEMENT?[13,14]

It Should Have Been....

Whole language educators from the early 1970s to the early 1980s were aware of the radical path they were taking and the obstacles they faced in rejecting basals, tracking, testing, and their respective foundational premises. Through their work in teacher study groups, they came to understand the ideologies embedded in whole language ideas (e.g., about learning as comprehending, meanings as multiple, and reading as imprecise). As the weight of power and authority began to bear down upon them, they saw that being a whole language educator meant learning about "the politics of schooling in America" (Altwerger & Saavedra, 1999, p. viii).

These whole language educators argued explicitly for the rights of all students to their linguistic and cultural heritages as they sought out multicultural literature and devised culturally linked units of inquiry so that all students could see themselves in the curriculum. They formed networks of teachers (Teachers Applying Whole Language) and, later, a confederation (the Whole Language Umbrella) "to continue learning and agitating for change" (Altwerger & Saavedra, 1999, p. viii). With its early proponents seeing that corporate and political interests merely pretended to a concern for the educational welfare of children, experiencing the "displeasure" of the power structure when faced with the threat posed by whole language, being committed to improving educational equity for those with a history of failure in traditional education, and linking themselves through informal networks, whole language should have been identified as a political movement for educational and social justice.

---

[13]If only this had been a frequently asked question! When we wrote the first draft in 1985, whole language had just barely passed the moment of its great potential for being a political movement. Thus, we probably would have framed our response in terms of obligation (*it should be* ...) rather than possibility (*it could be* ...), even though the ability to act on the obligation would have been slim. However, with the passage of 20 more years, it seems necessary to account for the loss and to use the perfect tense (*it should* have been ...)

[14]This entire section owes most of its content and shape to Bess Altwerger's and Elizabeth Saavedra's (1999) Foreword.

But It Wasn't

What happened instead was what prompted the writing of the original draft of this chapter in 1985; that is, "'whole language' became too popular" (Altwerger & Saavedra, 1999). In whole language's early history, its political nature had not been made center stage. Nor had whole language been explicitly and *primarily* framed as liberatory politics—as a struggle for the rights of teachers and students, rather than government bureaucrats and corporations, to control teaching and learning. Thus, as the movement grew, it was easy (through both self-identification and misrepresentation by others) to lose whole language's original political concerns. When teachers and district administrators began flocking to whole language (without much knowledge about language and literacy theory or about the politics of education), it was not as a way to act politically but as a way to make literacy instruction more enjoyable and more *au courant*. And when entire districts began mandating whole language and corporations started selling whole language basals with whole language end-of-unit tests, whole language was further diluted, made "safe and impotent" (Altwerger & Saavedra, 1999, p. ix) so it would cause little disturbance to existing practice.

Although some whole language educators continued to talk about whole language as a liberatory political movement, the new vast majority had little interest in such a project. By the time the whole language movement had ballooned to a size to be reckoned with, it was no longer a threat. Appropriated for profit and fashion, stripped of its equity-and-justice-seeking goals in the materials and programs sold (literally) under its name, most recently exploited as a foil for phonics by those pushing the government–corporate agenda to control education on behalf of corporate competitiveness, converted from principled movement to trendy bandwagon to ghost ship as the political winds shifted—whole language, as it became a broad movement, was/is certainly no explicitly political movement.

But It Still Can Become One

Or, at least, it can become a small and important part of a much larger one.

Nearly two decades of an intensifying government–corporate campaign has made the politics of literacy and education more obvious. What was understood by a few early whole language educators is now becoming increasingly clear to many; that is, that a political struggle is being waged over who will control education (a government–corporate alliance or parents, teachers, and students) and for what purpose (to serve corporate interests or to serve the public's interests). If, in 2005, through the machinations described at the beginning of this chapter, the government–corporate alliance appears to be winning hands down, it is because a movement has not yet coalesced to oppose it. To be sure, though few in number and limited in resources, people have been working against the campaign—primarily local groups of teachers and parents organizing around high-stakes testing. Whole language groups have been part of these efforts (e.g., the Teachers Applying Whole Language network [while considerably reduced in size, it remains connected through email] and national political action committees of whole language teacher educators). And particular whole language educators have been tireless in resisting various aspects of the campaign (e.g., Stephen Krashen and Ken Goodman in writing almost daily letters to editors of local and national newspapers, Susan Ohanian in building and maintaining an exceptional Web site of resistance [www. susanohanian.org], Susan Harman in organizing the California Coalition for Authentic Reform in Education [www.calcare.org], Gabie Gedlaman in organizing the Arizona group against high-stakes testing [www.azstandards.org]). What is needed is for these whole language resisters to not only join forces with each other but, more important, to form a coalition with other progressive education organizations (e.g., the National Coalition of Education Activists, Rethinking Schools, anti-high- stakes-testing groups in states from Virginia to Washington State and from New York to Florida) and with noneducation organizations whose issues touch upon but are not limited to education (e.g., progressive labor unions, race/gender/ sexual orientation minority organizations, environmental activist groups, etc.). The objective is to bring together enough people (huge numbers are crucial) from enough directions to beat back the government–corporate agenda and successfully install in its place an education that will serve the interests of citizens in a democracy. The role of whole language educators in such a movement would be to educate their fellow resisters about the politics of pedagogies and of views of language and literacy. Whole language, then would not constitute a political movement; it would be an integral part of an explicitly political movement—which is what it should have been all along.

Chapter 8

Hookin' 'Em in at the Start of School in a Whole Language Classroom

with Kelly Draper and Karen Smith

> This is the original chapter, slightly revised.

It is the afternoon of the first day of school for sixth-graders at Laurel School. Twenty-five children, many of whom have failed two different grades somewhere between kindergarten and today, several of whom have reputations as "bad kids" in this inner-city school, have an assignment. They are to take potting soil and plant a bean in each of two milk carton containers. They will use their plants to begin the first of many experiments. The teacher tells everyone where to find the soil, seeds, and scissors. Children are to pace themselves for coming to the sink for planting: "If there are five people at the sink already, use your own judgment about what else to work on. Work in your journals or decorate your folders."

Forty-five minutes from the presentation of the assignment, with no reprimanding, no step-by-step directions, and no close teacher monitoring of the cleanup, the children have filled 50 milk cartons with soil and seed, put them on trays near the window, cleaned the sink area, and put finished journal entries on the teacher's desk. By the end of the first school day, these children look like self-directed, conscientious "good kids," able to perform an intricate, efficient dance choreographed (but seemingly not directed) by the teacher. How did they learn the steps so quickly?

This chapter summarizes a study of how the school year began for one teacher and 25 inner-city students. This classroom was unusual because of its effectiveness[1] and because it reflected a whole language conception of literacy and language development (see chap. 7 and Edelsky, Altwerger, & Flores, 1991, for lengthy descriptions of a whole language viewpoint). Although there have been many observational studies of the beginning of the year in classrooms with a skills view of literacy (see, e.g., Moskowitz & Hayman, 1976; Sanford & Evertson, 1980; Tikunoff, Ward, & Dasho, 1978), there have been no examinations of "the establishings" in a whole language classroom. We contend that literacy instruction has such an impact on elementary school curriculum, on daily time allocations, and on assessment of learning that the failure to account for views of literacy in studies of classroom phenomena (e.g., in studies of how interaction is structured, how key events are organized, how school begins, how effective teachers teach, etc.) is a systematic omission of prime significance.

Of course, it is not only conceptions of language, literacy, learning, or other topics in the school domain that remain unarticulated in classroom research. Unless the phenomenon of investigation is clearly related to class, gender, race, authority, and so on, it would be unusual to find researchers identifying and describing a teacher's beliefs about these topics. Yet just because the research phenomenon (e.g., research on teacher knowledge or on effective teaching) does not seem to be immediately affected by gender, race, class, or ethnicity does not mean beliefs about such issues are irrelevant. The relevance of prevailing ideologies cannot be gauged, however, if they remain hidden. Yet they (and their classroom effects) most often remain hidden because atypical, "alternative" ideologies are not even considered. This state of affairs permits the fiction that the prevailing ideology is not ideological—that it is simply the way things are (see chap. 4 for a similar point in regard to the relationship between language proficiency and a particular definition of academic achievement; see also chap. 1 for a discussion of the depoliticizing of second language research when the political relationship between native and second languages is not considered). What happens, then, is that classroom phenomena are portrayed as generic rather than political (e.g., effective teaching is portrayed as effective teaching in general rather than as effective teaching by a teacher who believes his Whiteness is not a "color"). We too do not identify Karen Smith's (KS's) political beliefs about social structures[2] (nor do we try, for comparison's sake, to infer these beliefs for teachers in other

---

[1]Karen Smith (KS) was the teacher. Draper and Edelsky were the participant observers. All three took part in video viewing and coding of Edelsky's and Draper's field notes. Edelsky and Draper put pen to paper and thus were the ones who assumed and proclaimed KS to be an effective teacher. Therefore, what might look like continuous bragging on KS's part was not.

[2]In 1989, I wrote about "social structures." In 2005, I would now say "socially structured systems of privilege." The latter signals more agency; the former, an entity that exists separate from human activity.

beginning-of-the-year and effective teaching studies), but that does not mean such an effort would be out of order. What we do here, however, is to at least begin to problematize notions about starting the year—and, by implication, notions about effective teaching—by claiming that the teacher's ideology of literacy is an important research consideration. A basic assumption of this study of a teacher getting children to adapt at the start of school, then, is that the children are adapting to *something*.

One of the key "somethings" is the teacher's theoretical orientation to what written language learning is and how it occurs. As mentioned in chapter 4, Harste and Burke (1977) identified three such theoretical orientations: decoding, skills, and whole language. The present discussion requires some elaboration of these orientations as they pertain to what happens in classrooms. The decoding orientation views the sound–symbol relationship as the key to reading. Meaning is something arrived at after sounds are translated into larger units, such as words and sentences. Function and purpose are not important issues. A teacher operating from the decoding orientation typically introduces each letter and assists students in associating letters and sounds. In the skills orientation, the word is the basic unit in reading and writing. Assorted separable skills (decoding, word attack, comprehension) are learned and used separately. A teacher with this view typically uses grade-leveled, vocabulary-controlled basal reading texts and workbooks. New words are introduced and drilled. Assignments use stories and workbook activities containing those words.

According to the whole language orientation, meaning-making (and transactions among readers, writers, and texts) is the central focus of reading and writing. The complex, context-bound skill of reading or writing cannot be broken into component subskills. Thus, the whole language classroom looks different: There are no spelling books, no sets of reading texts with controlled vocabulary. Whole, meaningful texts are the materials, not isolated words, sounds, or paragraphs. The reading program is, more accurately, a literature program. Children write for real world (rather than instructional) purposes. Significant content and interaction about that content (talk between teacher and student and among students) are essential to the whole language orientation.

The skills theory is the prevailing orientation in the United States.[3] The dominant pattern of reading instruction involves relatively homogeneous groups working out of a basal reader and the accompanying workbooks. The time spent on skill and drill activities outweighs the time spent reading (DeFord, 1981). Writing instruction consists primarily of exercises on isolated aspects of penmanship, spelling, punctuation, capitalization, vocabulary, and grammar; little writing is required (Graves, 1978). Virtually

---

[3]It was in 1989 and remains so in 2005.

all commercial programs for teaching reading, writing, or language arts assume the existence of separate skills. Even in classrooms where creative teachers try to "integrate skills" (with each other and with subject matter) by instructing for comprehension or word identification in conjunction with literature or social studies content instead of basal readers, the skills orientation is what is driving the curriculum. In fact, "the culture's implicit task analysis" of reading (decode first, comprehend later) stems from a skills orientation (the skill of decoding, the skill of comprehending; Laboratory for Comparative Human Cognition, 1982).

What confronted the sixth-grade students in this study, however, were the expectations of one of a minority of teachers who work from a whole language view of literacy.[4] KS's assumptions about language, language learning, and learning played a significant role in her curricular plans and in her interactions with students at Laurel School. From interactions over the course of many years, it was clear that KS held the same assumptions that are identified in chapter 7 and in Edelsky et al. (1991) as basic to whole language.

Laurel School had a student population of approximately 75% Latinos, 10% African Americans, and 15% Caucasians. Over 80% of the children qualified for free breakfasts and lunches. Absentee rates were high; test scores were low. By sixth grade, approximately one third of the students had failed at least one grade in school.

Despite these students' prior histories, KS and the students succeeded together. Absentee rates were low in her room. Visitors frequently commented that students were almost always engaged in appropriate tasks. Parents reported a sudden and dramatic turn to book reading and story writing as at-home activities. Students whose September journals had entries such as "I don't got nuthin' to write" were writing full pages by October. Previous "nonreaders" read award-winning children's literature and revised and edited multiple drafts of long, involved stories. By spring, children spontaneously discussed the literary merits of their own writing and of books they read, commenting on style, point of view, plot structure, and other literary elements.

We knew about KS's beliefs about literacy and had seen similar activities in her room the preceding years, so we were prepared for these successes. It was all new to the students, however. Most of these children began the

---

[4]KS was a strong advocate of the whole language view in 1989. In 2005, she remains committed to the theoretical underpinnings, in particular, a transactional view of learning (Rosenblatt, 1985). She continues to conduct workshops and teach courses based on this view of learning. Her teaching has also been videotaped by me and by Jerome Harste to teach others about practice growing out of such a viewpoint.

year as "low achievers," having experienced education according to a "skills" perspective in prior years. Under ordinary circumstances there would have been no reason to expect them to make a dramatic change. But circumstances were not ordinary. Instruction was not based on prevailing assumptions about the need to present a hierarchy of decontextualized literacy skills (Heath, 1982; Shuy, 1981). With such a discrepancy between students' past experience and KS's approach, how was the gap ever bridged?

OBSERVING EFFECTIVE TEACHERS

The phenomenon we were attempting to explore was how, at the beginning of the year, teachers "coerce" children (following McDermott, 1977) so that classroom life becomes what they want it to be.[5] However, we were interested in more than just how that happens in any classroom but in how it happens in a classroom with an effective teacher who has a whole language view of literacy.

Studies of teacher effectiveness almost always investigate teaching from a skills orientation to literacy. These studies follow steps outlined by Rosenshine (1971), including developing an instrument for systematically recording specified teaching behaviors, ranking classrooms according to measures of pupil achievement, and relating teaching behaviors to class achievement scores. Effective teaching is equated with high scores on standard measures of achievement—all of which are based on a skills theory of literacy. The focus of beginning-of-the-year studies is usually some variant of the question: How do effective teachers differ from ineffective ones during the first days of school? Since beginning-of-the-year studies define effective teaching in the same way teacher effectiveness studies do, these too can be considered skills-orientation studies.

---

[5]We considered the term *enculturate* but found it lacking. It implies a group with a culture to transmit, not just one individual with a viewpoint. Though new members are not passive recipients when becoming enculturated, they get information about how to be members from many sources. In this school, the only source of KS's expectations, demands, or goals was KS— and what she provided. Others, too, have noted that the metaphor of classroom as culture has its limits, a serious one being that the teacher is the only native (Cazden, 1979; Florio, 1980). We wanted a term that allows for flexibility and active response on the part of all participants, such as *negotiation*—but negotiation implies that the outcome is more up for grabs than it is in this classroom. We also wanted a term that means the learning of a general underlying structure that can guide choices from a repertoire, such as *internalization of norms*, since it wasn't any mere surface matching of behaviors that was going on. But internalization tends to focus on an interior process and to skim over what is happening that promotes that process. We settled on *coercion* because it acknowledges that it is the teacher's view that will prevail, but we recognize its limitations (e.g., a sole focus on KS—only one party in the enterprise).

Our study of how the year begins, however, was not focused on finding correlations between prespecified behaviors and ranked classrooms. Rather, our aim was to discover and describe factors integral to one classroom. We relied on numerous markers of effectiveness: KS's reputation, our prior knowledge of student performance in her room in other years, observations of interactions, observations of children's actual work (their writing, projects, improvised dramas, discussions of literature) and spontaneous reports from parents. None of our markers was linked with a view of literacy as a set of separable skills. Moreover, our question itself accounted for a contextual feature that is usually ignored: teachers' theoretical views. Our intent was to produce a description that might enlarge the view of (and how to view) effective teaching at the start of school.

PROCEDURES

Our main data collection was through participant observation of teacher–student interaction all day, every day, for the first 2 weeks of school and then 3 days per week for the next 3 weeks. Video- and audio-tape recordings, made periodically, were used to confirm and modify the focus of further observations. We took field notes during classroom observations and videotape viewings. Students were interviewed during the 1st and 3rd weeks. We also interviewed KS prior to the beginning of school and during the 4th week. We returned in December and again in January to verify whether the kinds of interaction observed in September were still occurring.

No researcher looks at everything. Decisions about what to look at are based, in part, on the researchers' prior knowledge. Since we began with considerable prior knowledge of this teacher, both the data collection and analysis were informed by this prior knowledge; one cannot un-know what one knows. We began with the question: How does this teacher get children to meet her unusual expectations? Our initial observations were guided by an assortment of questions: What are the norms here for reading and writing? How does the teacher get students to expect to write? How are certain procedures (e.g., journal and book writing) established? What student–teacher relationships are in evidence?

We expected to see gradual change occurring over the first few weeks of school, with some students wavering in accepting KS's uncommon demands, some adapting to the new concept of school and literacy almost immediately, and others taking considerable time to adjust. However, during the first day of school it was evident that the students were already becoming what the teacher wanted them to be. By that afternoon, they were cleaning up without being asked, helping one another, and taking responsibility for making decisions and completing assignments. Here were children in a relatively new environment almost immediately performing like "natives."[6]

Obviously, it had been an error to assume that adaptation would be gradual. The original plan had called for student interviews the 2nd week of school, but now that it was apparent that the object of interest was rushing by, we interviewed children on the second day. Yes, they recognized this class was different: no spelling books, no textbooks. Yes, they had "known all along" it was going to be "hard" but "fun" (they eagerly anticipated constructing a haunted house and putting on plays for the entire school). No, they couldn't say what KS expected or how they knew what she wanted them to do. And no, despite conducting science experiments, participating in discussions, rehearsing reading performances they would later give for first graders, and so on, they thought that so far they had not done any "work."

INTERPRETING THE DATA

The question: How does this teacher coerce? (and the related question: coerce to what?) led to using the teacher's stated goals for organizing the data. Other studies have used daily or weekly goals or lesson objectives as organizers (e.g., J. Green & Wallat, 1981). KS's goals, however, were for the entire year and beyond, rather than for the week or the lesson. She described three goals that we used as organizing categories:

1.   *To get students to see opportunities for learning everywhere.* "To get them to see learning as more than just books and school, and that out-of-school and fun things have purpose and can provide learning."
2.   *To get students to think and take pleasure in using their intellects.* "To get them to seek out learning, to pique their curiosity."
3.   *To help students learn to get along with and appreciate others.* "That they'll see you can get along with all kinds, to accept people, to look at the good in everybody."

With these goals in mind, we examined the teacher interviews for statements explaining what she does to try to accomplish these goals. To get students to see that learning is everywhere, KS stated she used what they

---

[6]Ease of adjustment to a new system has been observed with much younger children in a study at the beginning of the year in a reception class in England (Willes, 1981). That researcher, too, was surprised to find immediate rather than gradual adjustment, with children seeming to learn to meet new demands in the course of a single session.

know and their experiences, emphasized functional learning, used sources of information besides teachers and books, and related in-school learning to out-of-school learning. To get students to enjoy using their intellect, KS included setting up thought-demanding projects; providing minimal help until the student first did some thinking; reinforcing students for coming up with good ideas or questions; dealing with high-level content; and modeling that work is serious, important, fun, and exhilarating. To develop their ability to get along with others, KS said she emphasized grouping for interaction, encouraged them to help one another, tried to build group cohesiveness and a sense of room ownership, and demanded that they respect one another.

Based on other statements she made, we inferred three additional goals:

4. *To manage the day-to-day environment smoothly so other goals could be accomplished.* KS's statements relating to this inferred goal included ignoring inappropriate behavior, being prepared and organized, getting processes or routines established, checking up and reminding, giving directions, making reprimands in private, and stating official rules.

5. *To get students to relate to, and identify with, the teacher.* Through respect, trust, and identification, KS believed that her sixth-graders would take on her values. Her stated ways of achieving this goal included helping children be successful in developing their ideas and interests, modeling appropriate adult behaviors, letting them in on her thinking, talking to and treating them like adults, and being an "authentic person" herself.

6. *To get students to be self-reliant and sure of themselves and to trust their own judgments.* The means KS stated in interviews for accomplishing this goal included using student work and behavior as examples of what to do, giving students responsibilities, assuming competence, giving encouragement, and suggesting alternative behaviors.

KS's stated means for accomplishing these six goals were reflected in her behavior in the classroom. Although her statements do not account for everything she did, they show that she was exquisitely aware of her goals and intentions and the means she used to reach these goals.

We added two other major organizing categories:

7. *Teacher's knowledge and understandings.* This category includes KS's assumptions, beliefs, and understandings of children, curriculum, and human relationships. It was prompted by notes on observations and interviews and our prior knowledge of the teacher.

8. *Implementing a whole language writing program.* This category
    includes any entry in the field notes that concerned writing.

These eight categories provided a basis for addressing the questions:
What are students being taught to adapt to? and How were they being
taught? What we saw in field notes, interview transcripts and videotapes
were the embodiment of particular values, the imposition of a few rules,
the enactment of various roles, and the provision of cues. We sorted these
values, rules, roles, and cues according to the eight goals to see if certain
roles, for instance, clustered with certain goals. Our primary interest, however, was in characterizing the values, rules, roles, and cues.

VALUES

Those values derived from interviews and found most frequently in the
field notes were collapsed to make the following categories (the original
glosses are in parentheses):

- Respect (respect others; consider needs of others; see the good in
  all—all are equal but special; children's ideas are important);
- People are good (people are well intentioned; people are compe-
  tent; people are sensible);
- Interdependence;
- Independence;
- Activity and work (work is enjoyable; work is purposeful; work is
  real, serious, good; being busy is good); and
- Originality.

It is important to note that we did not find that KS's interview comments
reflected common classroom values of obedience, correctness, or silence.
Nor did we find assumptions about "human nature" such as "children will
try to get away with what they can" or that "children have to be motivated
to do schoolwork." Instead, the values and assumptions consistently played
out directly contradicted those frequently held.

RULES

KS seemed to be using four implicit rules: (1) Do Exactly As I Say, (2) Use
Your Head, (3) Do What's Effective, and (4) No Cop-Outs. The Do Exactly
rule was used frequently during the first days of school to give directions
and to indicate what not to do. On the third day of school, when the
teacher asked the students to come and sit on the floor, a couple of

students attempted to bring their chairs. The teacher corrected, "If I say 'Floor,' I don't want chairs. If I say 'Chairs and floor and table,' I want chairs, floor, and table."

Often, Do Exactly was noted in the breach, as the previous example shows. After the 3rd week of school, Do Exactly requirements seemed to disappear. Along with these explicit commands there was a push from the very beginning for independence. This was reflected in the Use Your Head and Do What's Effective rules. Use Your Head commonly was related to responsibility for independent work—whether in or out of school ("You know what to do," "You're on your own").

Do What's Effective was a rule often revealed by what the teacher did not say. Students in this classroom did not have to line up and wait for the bell to ring before entering the room (even on the first day); they entered the classroom at will. The school day usually began with students sitting on the floor in the front of the room, some reclining under a desk, others leaning against the wall, others sitting with folded legs. For viewing films the criterion was "as long as you can see."

The last rule identified was No Cop-Outs. Students were expected to use their heads and do what was effective, but that did not mean they could weasel out of responsibilities. We saw no examples of the teacher relaxing her requirements because a child had not performed; instead, she just kept demanding. If a child said "I don't know," the response was "No 'I don't know's!'"

The rules were not in force evenly throughout all the events of the day. Children were required to Do Exactly in events called *total group* and *scheduling*, while No Cop-Outs operated during small-group work. Do Exactly instances pertained largely to the goal of managing the day-to-day environment; No Cop-Outs related primarily to the goals of self-reliance and using the intellect.

ROLES

KS did play the stereotypical part of teacher as Lesson Leader, but infrequently. More often (as well as more interesting) was the total range of her roles: Lesson Leader, Information Dispenser, Scout Leader, Consultant/ Coach, Neutral Recorder, and Preacher. Of course, KS's roles were enabled and supported by a reciprocity on the part of the children who themselves took appropriate roles. However, because our recording was inadequate for preserving subtle features of language interaction for both teacher and child, and because our focus was on the teacher, it is KS's roles we highlight.

Unlike Lesson Leader, a role marked by talk structured by initiation–response–evaluation (IRE) sequences (Mehan, 1979), the role of Information

Dispenser seemed to emanate from an FYI (For Your Information) posture. Here, KS delivered long explanations, drew diagrams, or offered factual tidbits. Children could take the information or leave it; they were not evaluated with it (no "Now what did I just say?" check-ups). This role was associated only with the goal of using the intellect.

Contrasting with Lesson Leader on several dimensions was Scout Leader. This role occurred most often during transitions. When the children were moving from one event to another, KS looked at individuals rather than surveying and supervising the crowd, stayed put for awhile, and otherwise signaled accessibility. Children approached, usually individually, and they and she seemed like peers. Interaction could be initiated by either teacher or child, and the talk was conversational. Scout Leader was an affectionate friend who teased (and was teased back) and who shared anecdotes with her students. A sense of comradeship ("We're in this together") pervaded these exchanges. Not surprisingly, Scout Leader occurred most frequently with the goal of getting children to identify with, and relate to, the teacher.

The Consultant/Coach offered advice on schoolwork or helped students out of an academic dilemma (even if it was KS who had made the assignment and had thus created the dilemma in the first place). Focusing on what the student was trying to do, the Consultant/Coach elicited the student's perceptions, then gave advice or tips. The message was "I want you to do well." Conveying this message sometimes took the form of a pep talk or an offering of expertise: "If anyone wants to stay in and practice reading for the first-graders, I'm available after lunch."

The Consultant/Coach role ran through every goal except managing the day-to-day environment. The management in this classroom was done with dispatch; the teacher was in charge. No coaching.

Both Scout Leader and Consultant/Coach roles dominated for KS's goals of relating to the teacher and relating to others and for the category of implementing a whole language writing program.

Neutral Recorder was distinguished by the absence of evaluation. The Neutral Recorder offered her abilities at organizing and recording but did not make final decisions. When a student asked the Neutral Recorder what to do, she replied, "You decide," or "What do YOU think?" Given this characteristic, it was not surprising to find the Neutral Recorder only in segments of field notes we had sorted as being about the goal of using the intellect.

When interviewed before school started, KS explained that she used "preachy talk" only at the start of the year to emphasize cooperation and mutual respect. And in fact, the only instances of Preacher occurred the 1st week of school and only in connection with goals concerning relationships. True to form, there was no preaching about schoolwork or study habits.

CUES

Cues from KS were certainly needed to help students follow rules they had to figure out by Using Their Heads. We identified 12 different cuing devices KS used for showing children how they should behave in relation to peers, teacher, academic content, and materials. Although many of these exploited language, not all did. The cuing devices were: Using the Work of Others as examples, Giving Directions (which included directions about desirable behavior), telling what not to do (Don't Do X), Ignoring Inappropriate Behavior, Reminding, Behaving As If the desired were actual, Modeling how to be, Structuring the Environment and Curriculum to provide the cues, providing Minimal Guidance, Privatizing Reprimands, using Written Cues, and providing an Exaggerated Display of desired ways to be.

Ignoring Inappropriate Behavior may seem like the absence of a cue; however, by attending with studious concentration to what she desired (e.g., refusing to interrupt a writing conference to reprimand others; continuing a discussion, as if blindered, with no attention to silliness or groaning), KS gave information about what she desired. Sometimes, she gave some form of Minimal Guidance such as a nod or the "evil eye" to direct a student to stop misbehaving. This served to get the erring student back on track without disrupting the flow of classroom activity. Why something as objectively benign as a "look" should have been an effective technique with low-achieving "bad kids" is a key question. For the "evil eye" to work requires that the student was already identifying with KS, already trying to live up to her rules. Thus, the minimally intrusive "evil eye" had a double function: It was both a cue to how to act and, when acknowledged, a display that children were already acting that way.

When students were reprimanded at length about their behavior, the reprimands were usually Privatized. The teacher took the offender out of the room or asked the child to remain while others left the room. Public reprimands during which all could hear everything were almost nonexistent.

An especially interesting cue was Behaving As If—as if the students were competent, sensible, and well intentioned. KS did not call attention to new responsibilities; she simply behaved as if the children had shouldered these all their lives. She did not line children up and walk them to art, music, physical education, and lunch; they were trusted to go on their own. She did not instruct on how to order the movies from the district audiovisual department; she gave two children the district forms and the catalogue and told them to do it. Props were part of Behaving As If students were already capable. They were used deliberately and matter-of-factly as concrete symbols of KS's belief in children's competence and good intentions. Examples of using props were: giving two boys a camera to photograph classmates on the first day, providing a clipboard for a group leader, supplying folders so

students in charge of collecting money for book orders could organize
their orders, offering flowered pink stationery (instead of lined school
paper) to a child for the final draft of her letter. Props also signaled that
the responsibility was really theirs. This was not "playing at it"; it was the
real thing.

KS's preference for Minimal Guidance covered both academic areas as
well as comportment. As she roved around the classroom, working with
groups or individuals, she would offer support but would refuse to take
over ("You decide"; "Whatever you want to say"; "Spell it the best you can").
Nonverbal examples include an outstretched hand or shifts in posture to
signal "handing over" or a shrug to signal "don't ask me; use your head."

Directions also provided cues. KS's directions were effective (i.e., they
were usually followed) but unusual. They were often minimal and frequently not delivered until an activity was already underway. The effectiveness of minimal directions is understandable here; when students carried
out their own rather than the teacher's tasks, they needed no more than a
scheduling signal, since they already knew what they would do.

KS Structured the Environment to show the children how to view learning and schoolwork in this classroom. As she explained:

> I want them to feel like they have too much to do that they want to do. When
> I say they don't have time to do the experiments they're talking about, that's
> deliberate now. I'll give them more time later. But now they have to come in
> before school if they want to do things or stay later, so they see it's serious and
> I'm here to help. I want them to see that learning is urgent and that ideas are
> tension-producing; you can't wait to try them out!

Another cue was Routines, which were also deliberately included as part
of the planned curriculum—routines for writing projects, literature
studies, science experiments, and so on. However, the teacher did not
break the routines into steps and make each an "objective." Use of Others
(or students' own experiences) as Examples was yet another device for
"coercing" students so that KS could accomplish the goals she set. These
were always affectionate references:

> The teacher reminds Gloria of the time when abstract notions of measure-
> ment seemed to click for Gloria in an "aha" experience. "I think it was the
> first time in your life you ever really knew what a ruler was for—when we did
> the pinhole camera!"

The tone, topic, and effect of such moments were like "family stories"
about learning—past incidents, fondly remembered, making connections.

Exaggerated Display was a feature of many of KS's responses. She took
special delight in only the slightest hint of a well-turned phrase in a child's

writing; she showed intense attention when helping a child with an idea and prolonged interest in items children showed her. KS's Exaggerated Display of concentration (i.e., The Thinker posture) effectively fended off students who might have interrupted a writing conference. Her stern expression, giving full attention to the performer, effectively dispelled any giggling during creative dramatics.

Like exaggerated concentration, the teacher's Modeling served to show students how to behave in a particular context. She modeled expressive reading, how to confer about children's writing, and how to be a serious, interested student:

> The teacher and all the students are reading during sustained silent reading time (SSR). The teacher glances around just once, then goes back to her reading. The bell rings, signaling that SSR is over, but the teacher keeps on reading. Some students get out their folders; others, following the teacher's model, keep on reading.

When we examined how these 12 cues were sorted in relation to goal categories, we found that the goals for managing the environment and for establishing a whole language writing program seemed to be cued the same way; management and curriculum were a tight fit. There was also some similar cuing for building a relationship with the teacher and establishing a whole language writing program. This clustering of similar items in the goals of relating to the teacher and implementing an important part of the curriculum occurred for KS's roles as well as her cues. Climate (cues and roles) and curriculum, indeed were interrelated.

DISCUSSION

This effective teacher provides a clear contrast with the picture painted in the literature on effective teaching (both during and at the beginning of the year). The research literature presents the effective teacher as stating clear expectations for behavior (Evertson & Emmer, 1982; Moskowitz & Hayman, 1976; Tikunoff et al., 1978), yet KS established ambiguous rules requiring judgment rather than mechanical application. KS largely ignored inappropriate behavior; effective teachers nip it in the bud (Evertson & Anderson, 1978; McCormick, 1979). KS often gave minimal directions after many children were already engaged in the activity. Effective teachers wait for everyone's attention and then give complete directions before students begin working (Denham & Lieberman, 1980; Tikunoff, 1982). Effective teachers maintain short, smooth transitions because these are seen as "down times" when nothing important happens

(Brophy & Evertson, 1976; Denham & Lieberman, 1980). By contrast, transitions in KS's class were few but long, included considerable movement and conversation, and served as important contexts for achieving a major goal (building a close relationship with the teacher). Effective teachers are portrayed as ensuring students' success by making simple, unambiguous demands (Emmer, Evertson, & Anderson, 1980); KS set tasks that were long, complex, and potentially ambiguous.

These are not contrasts in isolated features; they are contrasting gestalts in which interacting features can be isolated, contrasting total Discourses, according to Gee (1989a). Similar discrepancies can be seen in how KS and "effective teachers" begin the year. Beyond showing children the idiosyncracies of life in this classroom (where the paper was, whether ink or pencil was allowed, etc.), KS also had to get them to go along with a whole new and generally unshared set of underlying patterns derived from a whole language orientation to literacy. How did she do it?

Overall, what KS did was maintain particular values, impose particular rules, play particular roles, and provide particular cues—all very deliberately and self-consciously in the service of accomplishing a few goals. Three of the goals were associated with the same values, roles, and cues. For the goals of building a relationship with the teacher, getting along with others, and implementing a whole language curriculum, KS played the roles of Scout Leader and Coach; foregrounded the values of Respect, People are Good, and Interdependence; and tipped children off with cues including Behaving As If, Using Others as Examples, and providing Exaggerated Displays. Certain roles contributed greatly to the character of this classroom. KS did not depend on the power of the stereotypical Lesson Leader role to coerce students. Effective work depended on students having access to her through roles in which the balance of power was more equal. The Scout Leader role was especially significant during transition times, embodying the offer "I'm available," which seemed crucial to relationship-building.

And as for our question: How did it all begin? The only certain answer is that it happened very fast. During the first 3 hours of school, children's timing seemed to be slightly "out of sync" as they looked around the room and to each other for guidance. Few answered questions; none ventured opinions. Nevertheless, during the first hour, when KS (Behaving As If they could) gave them a copy of the same complicated schedule she gave to us, with the time blocks filled in for each day of the week, and told them to change the Tuesday 10:45–11:30 block from "reading" to "literature study," they rose to the occasion. Some of these poor readers glanced around quickly but then "got hold of themselves"; all made at least some kind of mark somewhere on their copy of the schedule. Three hours later, they were having conversations with the teacher, cleaning up materials unasked, wondering aloud about scientific principles, and generally making themselves "at home" in the room.[7]

We can account for the speed with which these children picked up on KS's desires and demands by positing that they came to school the first day primed to look for signals about how to survive there. Perhaps that is how people enter any new situation, actively searching for signals. Moreover, teachers who have been at a school for more than 1 year have a "book on them" (to borrow a term suggested by Ralph Peterson), a reputation. Entering students thus come prepared not just to figure out a way to survive but a way to interact from the first moment with the teacher's reputation as well as with the teacher. The phenomenon that intrigues us, however, is that, more than being ready to figure out just any way to survive, the children all came quickly to the same conclusion: Do what KS wanted. If the answer to "How did she do it?" is "Quickly, because the children's antennae were out for cues about how to make sense," that still leaves unexplained the issue of why they did what KS wanted. Why didn't they just as quickly devise ways to beat rather than follow her system? Why did something like the "evil eye" work with them? To answer this, we have to return to the theory that undergirds KS's approach to literacy.

What KS offered these students on the first day was purposeful assignments and a chance to read and write in a setting that acknowledged all the participants' "ownership" of tasks, texts, and contexts. Moreover, she proffered relationships based on respect and interdependence. It was an offer that fit her goals. Perhaps on the first day of school, every teacher offers a "deal." If the offer seems reasonable, if it seems to be in the students' interests, if the teacher does not undermine her own offer through ambivalently giving contradictory messages but instead keeps demonstrating the sincerity of the offer, the children do not make a counteroffer. They accept the teacher's offer while still learning and negotiating the details.

---

[7]We do not know to what extent children came to share KS's views on reading and writing, just that they acted increasingly in accord with them. Through the year, KS's demands (but not her theoretical conception) changed. For example, she raised her requirements for what qualities in writing she would applaud, and she changed the focus and intensity of writing conferences. In addition, the character of some of the activities changed as children invested the tasks with intentions that went beyond complying with an assignment. Perfunctory journal entries available to any reader became private conversations with the teacher, hunched over and covered up if anyone glanced over the writer's shoulder. Children moved from supplying a response to the teacher's questions about pieces of literature to asking questions of their own and discussing each other's questions. What started as mumbled, awash-in-giggles dramatic portrayals became serious attempts to make particular characterizations "believable." But regardless of the changes in demands and the changed stance with which the children came to meet the demands, the process of "buying in" began on the first day.

These sixth-graders entered expecting a difference and expecting the difference to be positive. Their initial stance, in addition to their supersensitivity to cues available in new situations, speeded their adaptation to strange expectations. What the children came with (a favorable disposition toward KS and openness to cues from the new situation) and what the teacher offered (her "deal") were what allowed them to take the initial leap and accept KS's offer before the first day was over. Accepting the overall offer meant a willingness to enter into a particular relationship with the teacher and also to believe in the substance of her promise—in this case, that she would have them engaging in real world reading and writing in projects largely under their control, often with consequences extending beyond the classroom. The substance (not merely the lack of ambivalence) in such an offer is what we think held children so powerfully to their part of the bargain. Thus the "evil eye," a subtle reminder tied to a human relationship, could work very early in the school year, even with "tough cookies." Once the abrupt leap was taken, KS continued slowly and profoundly, via rules, roles, and cues, helping the children make sense out of the particulars of the deal.

In describing how teachers let children know how to act in their classroom, how teachers attempt to get students to achieve teacher-established goals and, ultimately, how teachers and students make sense of school during the first days or the last, we cannot ignore what they are making sense *of.* We have to take into account what kind of literacy, subject matter, and relationship "deal" is being offered. We have to come to understand that the most ubiquitous deals—whether a skills deal for literacy, a patriarchal deal, an elite social class deal or any other—are not givens. There are (or could be) contrary deals in just those areas that are pervasive in classroom life. Until we seek out those contrary deals, we can never understand to what extent such purportedly generic activity as beginning the year or effective teaching is actually contingent upon the deal and is thus ideological.

Chapter 9

Risky Literacy

New material appears in the Prologue, an interlude,
and footnotes. The original chapter has been
condensed, with those spots marked with [...].

PROLOGUE

This chapter began life in 1989 under a different name ("Risks and
Possibilities of Whole Language Literacy: Alienation and Connection").[1] The
original version reflected concerns for alienation (or culturally based identity
conflicts) associated with whole language instruction, and it offered what
amounted to critical literacy as a way to offset some of those tensions. But
literacy instruction has changed since then. On the one hand, critical literacy
has joined the remnants of a media-battered whole language to form the only
genuine theoretical and political alternatives to dominant literacy instruction.
Sometimes, these are separate, in which case the whole language alternative
ignores or hides its underlying politics and the critical literacy alternative fails
to examine its underlying literacy theory. More often, the two merge into critical whole language literacy instruction (Edelsky, 1999; Edelsky & Johnson,
2004). In any case, despite the increasing (though still minute) existence of
critical literacy in U.S. classrooms, the potential for literacy-related alienation
or struggles over identities remains, so it is clear that the solution we proposed
in 1989 neither prevents nor resolves those tensions.

---

[1]The original chapter was coauthored with Susan Harman. Many people commented on
earlier versions of this chapter, especially Stanley Aronowitz, Nan Elsasser, Michelle Fine,
Hannah Fingeret, Yetta Goodman, Gregory Tewksbuy, and John Wolfe, none of whom are
responsible for how these ideas were finally worked out.

On the other hand, the regime of No Child Left Behind (NCLB) has exacerbated "worst practice" in the majority of classrooms. In many school districts, the only "legal" instructional materials are packaged programs that require the teacher to use a prepared script and that keep all students moving at the same mechanized, antihuman pace. The time devoted to (mandated for) literacy instruction has increased (sometimes, it is an entire morning); the range has narrowed ("test prep" for standardized tests of reading skills and writing conventions now has a monopoly). This kind of literacy instruction, promoted by NCLB, is actually a tool in a larger neoliberal project featuring "free" markets, deregulation, privatization, and commodification. Under neoliberalism, education in general and literacy in particular must be controlled. The control (to be achieved through rigid standards and high-stakes tests) is for two related purposes: to produce a sufficient number of information technology workers to enable corporations to prevail in the global market (Strauss, 2005a) and to ensure that education that is "off market"—that is, public—provides only "basic" literacy, since providing anything more would disrupt the market and the neoliberal belief that people should only get what they can pay for (Gee, 2004a). Both purposes thus lead to a hierarchy of literate genres in public schools: worksheets at the bottom; the technical manual at the top (Strauss, 2005a).

Under such conditions, literacy instruction that actively subverts NCLB by refusing its separate, low-level skills theory of literacy and its unquestioning stance toward society—whether separate whole language, separate critical literacy, or merged—is understandably rare and certainly risky. It is clear how such transgressive instruction might be risky for teachers: They feel pressured to give up what they believe is right in favor of what NCLB demands; they are demoralized; some are even pushed out of the classroom (Edelsky, 2005). It is less immediately obvious that instruction that is simultaneously welcoming, engaging, and provocative—whether whole language literacy instruction, critical literacy instruction, or critical whole language literacy instruction—might also put students at risk. Thus, this chapter.

LITERACY AS LIBERATION

There is a long, honorable, and articulate literary and political testimony to the mixed blessings of "the immigrant experience." Abandoning one's social class roots and moving "up" into the American Dream, leaving home, has always been risky business. And whether the journey is from the old neighborhood to the suburbs or a condo; from the father–son union to a desk and white collar; from Kinder, Küche, and Kirche to the schoolroom or real estate office; or from church picnics to dinner parties, the distance is rarely covered without leaving someone or something behind.

The achievement of literacy, however, unlike changes in social class and cultural identity, has been viewed as politically neutral, a tool, unambiguously positive, and universally powerful. Just as language lifts one's dreams out of the inchoate and makes them articulate, so literacy can possibly multiply those dreams by the factor of each that has ever been written down; it can allow the reader to borrow, steal, and adapt as his or her own every dream ever inscribed. Literacy potentially provides the ability to enter others' worlds, whether through novels or through political analyses, and that entrance immediately presents contrasts, alternatives, and choices and, hence, the possibility of change. There is, of course, no guarantee that the mere presentation of choices will result in a reader choosing something new, but without the data—the images of possibility—that literacy gives a reader, there is less likelihood he or she will invent entire new worlds out of whole cloth.

One need only consider to whom schooling has traditionally been denied (Blacks, women, the underclasses of every culture) to recognize the awe in which literacy has been held and the frugal and discriminatory way in which it has been allocated. The legends of stolen literacy speak for its magic: Abraham Lincoln studying law in the flickering kerosene light of his log cabin, Frederick Douglass teasing White boys into spelling out words for him, Hassidic girls shearing their hair and binding their breasts to sit as boys in yeshivas, George Eliot creeping out of bed before dawn to write and then hide away what she had written before she lit the kitchen stove for the day, Hispanic cigar workers in New York at the beginning of this century listening rapt as professional "readers" read aloud the news and the classics.

But literacy is not necessarily liberating. First, merely knowing how to read and write guarantees neither membership in the dominant culture nor the concomitant political, economic, cognitive, or social rewards of that membership (Graff, 1986, 1987; Street, 1984). The consequences of literacy have always been related to how it is used and what it is used for, what value is placed on it, and who is permitted to become literate. Although one of the powerful meanings surrounding literacy in the Western world today is a belief in its liberatory power, in fact literacy is a necessary but hardly sufficient passport to the mainstream. If other stigmata—such as color, gender, or class—betray subordinate status, one may not be able to talk (or read or write) one's way across the frontier.

Second, traditional approaches to literacy instruction can fetter students, not liberate them. Mastery of traditional literacy instruction sometimes permits access to certain societal resources. But these traditional curricula depend on: one single interpretation of one prescribed text; the use of conventional Standard English as the only criterion for evaluation of writing; and the standardized, multiple-choice reading tests, which have only one right answer per item, as the passport to the next grade. Therefore, these literacy curricula inordinately favor middle-class speakers who simply acquire Standard English at home, as contrasted with those who have to learn it deliberately in school (Krashen, 1982). No wonder these curricula tend to maintain, rather than improve, the status of subordinate groups. Members of such groups are held behind gates in elementary grades, kept from graduating high school by tests of supposed competency, and reminded one last time (if they didn't understand before) when they score poorly on the standardized tests in adult basic education (ABE) classes, that they do not belong in the mainstream. As Villanueva (1988) describes his experience:

> I do not believe I had a problem with English after kindergarten. I could switch from Spanglish to Street to Standard at will. I read. I didn't fear writing. I could mimic the prestige dialects—both the spoken and the written. I could even add *however* to essays on the basis of sound, although not often on the basis of sense. I was, however, apparently unable to mimic the school's way of viewing the world, the ways reflected in rhetorical patterns. The literacy we [Puerto Ricans] acquire tends to be of the wrong sort, even when the dialect is right. Basic literacy wields little power. (p. 3)

Despite the currently widespread, unreflective faith in the benefits of literacy, neither the ability per se, the method by which it is acquired, nor the materials used to teach it, is neutral. Both the methodology and the content of the traditional curricula center on obedience and acceptance; for example, there is only one English that is Standard and only one right answer for worksheet blanks and on multiple-choice tests. This kind of curriculum is therefore more likely to be stifling than liberating, although it paradoxically may have one ambiguous advantage over more creative curricula—it shows the enemy's face. That is, the traditional, fragmented, authoritarian, and narrow approach to reading and writing is so plainly nonsensical and unrelated to life outside school that it permits students to make a clear choice between conforming to its standards or rejecting them (going to special education, dropping out of school, or simply not allowing oneself to be recruited or coerced into joining ABE classes). Of course, this "choice" is less likely to be empowering, resistant, and liberating for the individual making it (and for his or her community) and more likely to be defeating for them both (Aronowitz & Giroux, 1985).

At the moment, there is much talk, considerable money, and an indefensible pedagogy (the same traditional assumptions, sometimes even the same traditional materials) aimed at "curing illiteracy" in both adults and children. Government leaders, social scientists, corporate executives, publishers, and educators are united in calling for universal literacy,[2] although the instructional methods they support practically guarantee failures. Our

---

[2]Strauss (2005a) argues that this universal literacy is to have a ceiling—the ability to handle texts appropriate for information technology workers. The "indefensible traditional pedagogy" from 1989, now having become extreme under NCLB, is perfectly suited to such a ceiling.

purpose in this chapter, however, is not to explain why these traditional approaches to teaching reading and writing usually fail; there is a large and growing body of literature on that (K. Goodman, 1986; Goodman, Freeman, Murphy, & Shannon, 1988; Harste, Woodward, & Burke, 1984). Nor do we attack the eccentric and peculiar kinds of reading, writing, and talking that go on exclusively in school (Edelsky, 1986; Lindfors, 1987). We do not chant a misty-eyed paean to the supposedly automatic, revolutionary political and personal potential of literacy *per se;* after all, George Babbitt could read and write. Nor do we explicitly criticize the monomaniacal, Eurocentric, trivial curriculum proposed by Bloom and Hirsch[3]—although our nontraditional view of literacy is a clear and implicit antidote to their attack on pluralism. Finally, we do not join the broader issue of whether the institution of school is either necessary to literacy or good for anything or anyone at all (see, e.g., Bowles & Gintis, 1977; Graff, 1986; Illich, 1970; Scribner & Cole, 1978).

Instead, we will look unsentimentally at the third reason why literacy may not be liberating: the price demanded by so fundamental a personal change may be too high. Rather than poke at the straw man of traditional language arts, we will focus on the unintended, ironic underside of an optimal classroom theory-in-practice: whole language *[and critical practice].*[4]

THE PROBLEM

Our contention is that the acquisition of the kind of ideal literacy[5] promoted in educational rhetoric but rarely in actual practice may have unanticipated repercussions in the lives of some learners. It is the kind of literacy that emphasizes reading and writing for expanding personal horizons, for understanding how texts have the effects they have, for considering alternate ideas. In more progressive rhetorical statements, it is the kind used for critically analyzing conditions in one's life and finding effective

---

[3]In 1987, Allan Bloom and E. D. Hirsch Jr. had made such a splash with their respective books that there was no need to further identify them. Their prescriptions (Bloom's in *The Closing of the American Mind* and Hirsch's in *Cultural Literacy: What Every American Needs to Know*) made a popular case for a conservative canon of knowledge, right in step with the standards movement that was soon to take off with support from the Business Roundtable.

[4]Wherever it seems appropriate to include critical instruction, I will do so by adding *[and critical practice]* in brackets and italicized to show that it was not part of the original version.

[5]Given the imposition of high-stakes testing, "ideal" in 2005 in some quarters has reverted to the kind of literacy needed to score well on standardized tests. But some of those tests, especially those for older students, now identify proficiency levels, with the highest (presumably, the ideal) entailing the ability to infer, evaluate, and reflect on one's reading. Not even the ideal of the highest proficiency level, however, includes critiquing texts for their support of systemic privilege.

ways to work with others to change those conditions—the kind promoted in actuality in at least some classrooms through the -theory-based pedagogy known as whole language *[and critical practice]*. As students in these classrooms (whether adults enrolled in basic education programs or children in elementary school) become literate in these ways and begin to feel the liberating effects of their ability to use written language, to wonder, analyze, argue, critique, escape, or envision, they may paradoxically begin to feel the constraints of estrangement from their roots.

Because the explicit purpose of education has been the assimilation of subordinate groups into dominant American life, much has been written about the implied demand on those groups to reject their home communities and of their ways of responding to that demand. Labov (1970) and Ogbu (1987) have described black teenagers' refusal to succeed in school in order to avoid becoming "White"; Fingeret (1987) has reported adult illiterates' fears of losing their common sense or "mother wit" and becoming "educated fools," of "forgetting where I came from." Kingston (1976) has written movingly about her difficulty reconciling the myths of her Chinese culture with those of the American educational establishment; academics who grew up in the working class have testified to their marginality in both worlds (Ryan & Sackery, 1984); and, most notoriously, Rodriguez (1981) has argued for actively rejecting one's cultural and linguistic past as the price of "making it." Less has been written from the community's point of view about how it feels to watch children or adult relatives grow distant, become "familiars" in another worldview that operates in a "foreign" school and that threatens to invade the home as well; but the anguish is still there. Well documented or not, these are examples of conflicts induced by the "otherness" of the school as a mainstream institution. Our concern is that whole language, with its ability to get more students to achieve the "ideal" literacy through classrooms structured democratically, may have an even greater alienating potential.

WHOLE LANGUAGE *[AND OFTEN CRITICAL PRACTICE]* PRINCIPLES: PROMISE AND PREDICAMENT

The primary principles of whole language are that learners are actively constructing meaning all the time, not just passively absorbing information, and that this language learning takes place in a coherent, sensible, predictable, purposeful environment in which coherent, sensible, predictable, purposeful language is being used—not merely practiced—both with and in front of the learner (see chap. 7, this volume; Edelsky, Altwerger, & Flores, 1991; K. Goodman, 1986; and Newman, 1985, for discussions of whole language). That is, whole language intends *theoretically* for reading and writing to be seen by students as useful and relevant, as both possible to acquire and worth acquiring.

The choice between accepting and rejecting assimilation into the dominant culture is muffled in a whole language classroom, since the home cultures of all students (what Gee [1989a] defines as their primary Discourses—their "ways of using language, of thinking, and of acting"[6]—are welcomed there. Whole language *[and critical practice]* is geared to the creation of texts for use; *[they both]* encourage multiple interpretations of existing texts-in-the-world, but *[they]* honor and use the language norms students arrive with; *[they]* not only accept *alright* and *ain't* as linguistically legitimate, *[they]* also accept differing discourses and worldviews; *[they]* focus on the ideas students have rather than the ones they lack; *[they]* assume the expansion of roles so that students teach and teachers learn; *[they]* set high but flexible standards; *[they]* emphasize language repertoires rather than right answers; and *[they]* foster questioning, analyzing, speaking up, and writing down.

In addition to its philosophical and political stances, whole language is a set of theoretical beliefs and educational practice based on a sociopsycholinguistic model of reading and writing (K. Goodman & Goodman, 1981; Harste et al., 1984) and an interactive model of language acquisition (Halliday, 1977; Teale, 1982). It tries to create the conditions for literacy acquisition that exist for language acquisition: little formal instruction, authentic use of language within specific contexts, no apparent suffering, and essentially universal success.[7] Like talking, reading and writing must be seen by learners as having obvious functions in the lives of those around them and those they want to be identified with. That is, the attention of talkers (and readers and writers) must be on something else, on what the talk or print is about, on the social work it is doing.

Actual classroom practice emanating from this whole language set of beliefs avoids workbooks, basal readers, controlled vocabularies, and kits. Center stage is occupied by what the language is about and what the adults and children do with it and why: cook, plan, build, experiment, make contact, label, organize, analyze, remind, play, imagine, threaten, inform, persuade, insult, entertain, interrogate, soothe, and so forth. The school day is spent using language rather than doing exercises with its parts and working with texts that have some function other than evaluation; for example, recipes, letters, directions, labels, notes, tickets, games, maps, memos, magazines, newspapers, lists, reports, songs, journals, order forms, poems, menus, and stories.

---

[6]Gee (1989a, 1990, 1999) distinguishes between small *d* discourse for speakings/writings and big *D* Discourse for communities of practice—shared worldviews + beliefs + values + behavior (including using oral and written language).

[7]Some of these conditions for literacy learning—in particular, those pertaining to little formal instruction and essentially universal success—as well as the analogy itself between first language acquisition and literacy learning—are questioned in chapter 6.

It is this set of beliefs about language acquisition and these and other implied classroom practices that are what we mean by whole language. And it is this set of beliefs and practices—this challenging yet responsive, accepting whole language *[and critical practice]* atmosphere—that may lull some learners out of their habitual wariness of the dominant culture, setting them up for disaffection from their communities.

Traditional skills-based curricula create a different context. Such curricula are central components of a mainstream institution that has had the historical function of teaching mainstream ways of being and doing and then sorting the assimilated successes from the unassimilated failures. Subordinate groups have rightly had an ambivalent relationship with mainstream education; deliberate success in school—learning the ways of The Man—is often perceived as both an opportunity and a betrayal. Since traditional curricula in mainstream education devote so much time and importance to literacy exercises, to be successful in school means to learn to perform those exercises. Performing them well not only generates fears that the ensuing school success will mean becoming alienated from the home community; such successful performance also requires that students lose touch with their own boredom and anger—that they become alienated from themselves. Between the smell of danger that emanates from mainstream school in the abstract and the mind-numbingness of the daily curriculum in the concrete, many students refuse to buy in. They reject the literacy exercises of the traditional curriculum, taking the ultimately self-defeating but common route of maintaining personal integrity and a connection to their communities by rejecting and alienating themselves from school. In fact, in New York City over half the students drop out of high school and drop back into their home communities, with little to contribute from their years in school.

Whole language, with its attention to students' interests and *[both whole language and critical practice's]* valuing of students' home cultures, are not so likely to alienate students either from themselves or from school. Because *[they]* are so attractive, *[they]* entice students to connect with and succeed, sometimes almost in spite of themselves, not as reading/writing exercise-doers, but as readers and writers. In providing more students with at least this part of the entry fee to greater efficacy in the world, whole language *[and critical practice]* benefits students as well as their communities. An unwanted stowaway in students' success through whole language *[and critical practice]* classrooms, however, may be the tension between school and community that creeps out unexpectedly after the successful literacy-learning journey is well underway.

Now, it is not whole language's *[and critical practice's]* success in promoting literacy per se that is the problem; after all, the traditional skills approach does help some people learn to read and write (though we believe learners' own reading—during rare opportunities to read in school and abundant opportunities to read outside—as well as interaction with others who read in front of and with learners is what "teaches" most people to read). The problem arises when, on the one hand, people learn to read how they shouldn't (e.g., to read and question in some communities, to write and imagine in others) or, on the other, when the contexts for learning (and therefore the meaning of the literacy that is learned) conflict with community norms.[8] Except for the case where a community's norms prohibit certain categories of people from attaining any kind of literacy (so that even the deciphering of a mark if one were a woman or the making of a mark if one were a man of a certain status would contradict those norms), instructional activity in workbook-dominated skills classrooms is unlikely to violate community literacy prohibitions. Not so with whole language *[and critical practice]*. The very beliefs and daily activities that make *[these]* so successful (not merely in getting people to learn to read and write but to become readers and writers) also make *[them]* revolutionary—are at once a welcome threat to the stability of existing hierarchies and also a potentially disturbing threat to the stability of individuals' relationships to their home communities.

Perhaps the most powerful of these beliefs and practices, and therefore both the most liberating and potentially the most alienating, is the commitment to a collaborative, democratic relationship between the student and the teacher, and between the student and the text. Unlike traditional skills approaches, whole language *[and critical practice]* teachers strive to demystify written language, texts, and learning. In whole language *[and critical practice]* classrooms, students choose curricular areas to explore, negotiate activities with the teacher, collaborate with other students, take risks and chances with the structure and the content of their projects, work with and create texts they control, and learn to value varied "readings."

It is, of course, tremendously rewarding for teachers to see their students more excited about publishing a book than bothering the child next to them, or more engrossed in writing their autobiographies than watching TV. It may not, however, be quite so rewarding for parents of young children or for spouses of adult students to see those same students

---

[8]Recent reports in the press and in memoirs (e.g., Nafisi, 2003) show just how dangerous it was/is for women to read critically in Iran and how literacy is used symbolically in international affairs (e.g., as a sign of victory for Western democracy when permitting girls to attend school was foregrounded by the mainstream press after U.S. bombs routed the Taliban in Afghanistan). (That this was more a sign of propaganda than of reality is attested to by the fact that soon afterward, under the new U.S.-backed Karzai government in Afghanistan, married women were not permitted to get an education, sexual violence increased to an all-time high, and women were increasingly subject to "chastity checks" by roving street gangs) (Ingalls & Kolhatkar, 2004.)

practicing at home the democracy and daring they have learned in class. Children in some communities may begin to feel cramped (where before they didn't notice) when the space that exists in school for multiple interpretations of a story shrinks at home because the family holds to the idea that a text is decipherable but not interpretable. Parents may perceive their children's new self-confidence and intellectual curiosity as talking back and arguing too much with them (*She always has an opinion on everything; He thinks he's so smart*). Husbands may resent their wives no longer needing to have newspapers read to them and even having their own opinions about the articles they've read on their own.

Clearly, life in many mainstream homes is not democratic; moreover, many mainstream homes do not promote analysis, lively discussions, or respect for divergent opinions. Nor is life in non-mainstream families necessarily authoritarian and oppressive. But the ideal of the critically thinking, experimenting, aware and reflective, independent man (and woman—a late 20th-century amendment to the ideal), educated to participate literately in a democracy, has a hold in mainstream culture. While it is an ideal found in the rhetoric of traditional mainstream schools, where it is actively sought after in practice is in whole language *[and critical practice]* classrooms. On a daily basis, conditions are enacted that promote that ideal (as well as many others concerning social responsibility, feeling, aesthetic response, etc.). Even if its real-life enactment may be foreign to many mainstream students, its position as an ideal, at least, is not. Students from non-mainstream communities in which the critical thinker is part of community ideals will also find a significant point of contact in whole language *[and critical practice]* classrooms. So will many non-mainstream students accustomed to a community of arguers, discussers, storytellers, interpreters, and interpreters of the interpreters.

But for others, the discrepancy between school and community ideals and discourse practices is great. Since the whole language *[and critical practice]* classroom is welcoming and supportive, such a student may well begin to learn to use language in these new ways. Learning to read as a reader, as a Subject, can then catapult that student out of his or her family, community, class, or ethnic group, because he or she has learned, not simply a new way of using language or of comprehending text, but a new way of viewing the world—a new Discourse. And, like the student in the traditional classroom who sees a forced choice down the road, the student in the whole language *[and critical practice]* classroom too may believe he or she must choose between the old and the new Discourse. Only in this case, he or she has already begun to learn (and choose?) the new.

Entering a new Discourse is not the only strain on a student's loyalties. Teachers may reinforce unwittingly the student's conflict by holding affectionately and unreflectively to a melting-pot mythology that romanticizes rejection of one's roots as a prerequisite to upward mobility, self-improvement, and financial success. And even in whole language *[and critical practice]* classrooms, the teacher's warm acceptance of the learner's home language is not unconditional; certain written language situations demand conformance to Standard English conventions. The continuity between home and school that welcomes and reassures young children and beginning ABE students, that frees them to take the risks necessary to learning, begins to vanish when demands for conventions increase. The invented spelling that was charming in first grade is worrisome in sixth. No fifth grade or ABE teacher wants her Black students to write *He been knowing that* in an article for the class newsletter without clear awareness of its sociolinguistic import. The prescribed text of the traditional classroom reappears as the text that prescribes success in the world.

At some point the road forks, and the same choice must be made by whole language students as is made by students in skills classrooms: whether to adopt mainstream ways or not. As F. Smith (1986) says, to become literate one must "join the club" and decide that reading and writing are things that "people like me" do. But what kind of literacy club do I join, and who am I like: my parents or husband, or my mainstream teacher?

There is a major difference, however, between asking *who am I?* in a traditional classroom and asking that same question in a whole language *[or critical practice]* classroom. The whole language *[and critical practice]* teacher has sought out materials that support the study of folk categories, histories, stories, and literature told and written by "people like me." Thus, the student in a whole language *[and critical practice]* classroom is more likely to see himself or herself as like others already in the club, and more likely to decide to add Standard written English conventions to an existing repertoire rather than to trade old ways for new. Still, there are students who could well see literate discourse as a threat to who they are.

If a minority language group is not literate, the children's literacy in the second language may threaten existing relations between the generations. Or the child may come from a literate minority community with norms that limit, by gender or social class, who writes what. Or, appropriate ways of relating to text may contradict what the child is learning. No matter how or whether the conflict is reconciled, there will be a challenge to the community's sociolinguistic norms. And the challenge will be played out within the student, as well as between student and school, and student and home.

So, despite the progressive pedagogy, good intentions, and success of whole language *[and critical practice]*, *[their]* students might arrive at the same crossroads as students in traditional literacy programs, thinking they have to choose between the mainstream and home. In fact, because of what they have experienced in whole language *[and critical practice]* classrooms, including a taste of democracy and power, the choice for these students may be even more painful.

For some students, then, their growth in competence as language users may bring to them and to their families a confused and confusing mix of pride, loss, and pain. This pain has at least two sources: one coming from outside the student, and the other from within. The child or adult who has put one foot into the exciting new world where language is power may feel a strong tug on his or her other foot from those left behind. Family and friends may express resentment, jealousy, abandonment, or simply incomprehension at their loved one's movement away from them. And the student may ache with embarrassment at what he or she now sees as his or her family's inadequacies. Anna, a competent 10-year-old, watches her mother struggle with math problems for a high school equivalency diploma course, and brags that in her fifth-grade class she does much harder work (J. Wolfe, personal communication, October 9, 1988). Although it may have been Anna's very success in a whole language *[or critical practice]* classroom that inspired her mother to earn a high school diploma, there is now a gulf between them, across which the child mocks her mother's Puerto Rican-accented English and her efforts to educate herself.

And because adults' relationships with family and friends are probably less fluid than children's, the adult learner's world may be even more shaken by the consequences of reaching for a literacy explicitly intended for empowerment. N. Elsasser (personal communication, November 10, 1988) describes a woman whose husband kept her from attending her adult writing class at knifepoint.[9] And Breslin (1987) writes the sad story of a young woman's need to educate herself (perhaps even become a doctor) and her hard-working, hard-drinking husband's baffled and limited response (that she should get pregnant).

At the same time, the student may have internalized the mainstream culture's disdain for his or her old world (after all, the larger society, as well as the classroom, communicates which discourse, which cultures, which people are legitimate), but he or she may not yet have mastered the new. He or she may not only suffer alienation from family and friends but may also become suspended in self-doubt between the two Discourses, especially as the ante is raised for more competence and more conformance to mainstream standards.[10] Johnston (1985) describes his adult students as

---

[9]A more recent, fictional example was written by Zuhara (2005), translated by R. Krishnan, and appears in the Literary Review section of *The Hindu*.

[10]Kate Miller, the copyeditor for the first edition of this book, cited other examples and a more general point. While we do not gloss education for empowerment as education for upward mobility, and while we do not mean that becoming literate is the same as learning a standard dialect, we appreciate the way Miller made the following point: Women can suffer double alienation in acquiring a literate discourse or even a prestige dialect.

expressing "concern over the increased responsibility that improved reading skill might engender. If they were to improve they might be *expected* to read, even by those who are close to them and know that they have difficulty" (p. 173).

2005 INTERLUDE: CAN WE TALK?

The suggestions below spotlight the local community and its discourses and Discourses. Because these suggestions have the potential to uncover ideologies and to, literally, bring curriculum home, they are valuable for those interested in critical literacy and in critical whole language practice. But they were originally intended as suggestions to help ameliorate alienation caused by conflicts between the Discourse of the classroom and the literacy norms embedded in a student's home/community Discourse. In 2005, I no longer see how it is possible to offset alienation from one's community by further violating community norms. If those norms include literal interpretation of written texts, not questioning the authority of texts, or treating written texts as not having value, it seems to me that doing just the opposite in a whole language or a critical literacy or a critical whole language classroom will not defuse the conflict. But if doing the opposite is accompanied by awareness that all such conflicts have repercussions, that repercussions must be respected (rather than surrendered to), and that critical and whole language educators are obligated to find ways to work with the repercussions, then

---

"... [This is] reminiscent of the situation in the film Educating Rita, in which the female protagonist's husband would rather have babies than a wife who is 'educated out' of her class. The same author who wrote that screenplay, Willy Russell, also wrote two other plays/screenplays in which a woman liberates herself [but alienates peers and/or family]: Shirley Valentine and Dancing Thru [sic] the Dark. Melanie Griffith's character in [the film] Working Girl manages to get promoted (in part by losing her thick New York accent and pretending she is upper middle class) and keep her best friend (female) but loses her partner (male). And, of course, the granddaddy of the literary concept of education alienating peers is George Bernard Shaw, in whose *Pygmalion* Eliza Doolittle is tutored in the intonations of Standard English. As a result, she is fettered, unable either to return to her Cockney roots and sell flowers or to participate in the upper middle class ladies' pastime of selling themselves (society calls it *marriage*). Finally, *blue-stocking* is a feminine pejorative term without a male parallel, and if the term is not now widely used, the concept of educated women being "unwomen" remains. An educated woman thus not only loses her class discourse; she is traditionally held to lose her feminine discourse as well.

... [It seems that] in the media, a person (usually portrayed as a woman) who loses her class roots through education is offered a tradeoff that more than outweighs what she left behind (i.e. upward mobility). However, the reality often seems to be that she loses her same-class peers and position without gaining anything but a posh accent and alienating ideas. No Cinderellas in real life!"

perhaps the conflicts can be sites of learning. They would still remain sites of personal risk. And so, I return to the suggestions we developed in 1989—not, this time, as suggestions to resolve alienation but as suggestions for promoting deeper, more significant learning.

BACK TO THE ORIGINAL CHAPTER[11]

We are certainly not promoting illiteracy or failure in school in the face of literacy-related alienation. Nor are we recommending a retreat to basal readers and worksheets, which produce exercise-doers rather than readers and writers and which, besides, can easily be dismissed as nonsense. Nor do we advocate abandoning core whole language *[and critical practice]* notions (e.g., multiple interpretations of texts, readers and writers as socially constructed) because they may conflict with literacy norms of particular communities.

Rather, we propose four alternatives:

1. Treat all discourses as if they were equally interesting and legitimate objects for scrutiny or inquiry.
2. Act on the results of those inquiries.
3. Stretch dominant discourses into accommodating more subordinate discourses.
4. Reconnect literacy learners with their communities.

OBJECTS FOR SCRUTINY/INQUIRY

In *Ways With Words,* Heath (1983) describes how three different discourses were collected like specimens and brought into the classroom, where they were examined as if in a laboratory. The fact that one of the discourses belonged to Black working-class farm children, another to White working-class farm children, and the third to the Black and White townspeople/teachers did not stand in the way of the children's evenhanded examination of them. Through their examination of the characteristics and complexities of the three discourses, the children's appreciation of, respect for, and fluency in their own—as well as the other two—discourses grew. They began to become bi- and some even tridiscursive.

[...] Borrowing from Heath would help make curricular connections with students' roots. If teachers can persuade children and adults that it is

---

[11]Not quite the entire original chapter. I am removing statements about how these curricular suggestions can resolve alienation caused by conflicts in the Discourses of home and school. A pair of brackets [.] indicates that I have removed a phrase or sentence.

safe to bring their home discourses into classrooms, and if students and teachers can examine and explore that collection of subordinate and dominant discourses together, with the same objectivity and care they would give to a collection of seashells or snake skins, then perhaps they too can create multidiscursive classrooms.

It is already integral to whole language *[and critical practice]* classrooms that students' questions, perceptions, histories, background knowledge, and preferred ways of making and expressing sense (important aspects of their primary Discourses) are used and respected. But we are suggesting going beyond merely using these as vehicles for the study of something else, to making the study of the various discourses themselves into a "science of language" curriculum.[12] Jordan (1985) provides a moving example of this curricular shift which results, like Fiore and Elsassers's (1982), in a letter to the editor, in Black English, occasioned by the death of a student's brother at the hands of the police.

We join Gee (1987) in proposing that school should enable students to investigate and critique primary and secondary Discourses, including dominant Discourses and the discourses within them. [...]

ACTING ON THE RESULTS OF EXAMINING AND CRITIQUING DISCOURSE

An even bolder step, one more in keeping with the political progressivism embedded in whole language *[and critical practice],* is that taken by Martin-Jones and her colleagues at the Center for Language in Social Life (CLSL) in Lancaster, England. The language scholar–activists there[13] criticize liberal mainstream programs for treating discourses as neutral data or "objects of nature" (as Heath did). Instead, concurring with Aronowitz and Giroux (1985), who make the same case for cultural knowledge in general, the CLSL group maintains that all discourses (subordinate and dominant) are social practices that must be subjected to close "interrogation." But interrogation leading only to a heightened awareness of, a "critical relation" to, increasing one's own knowledge of, is insufficient if action does not follow. CLSL members, along with Aronowitz and Giroux, insist that asking questions (e.g., Who has access to what knowledge? To which ways of using language? Why is access to certain discourses unequally distributed? Who benefits or suffers from the unequal access?) without tying that investigation to action can be disempowering. It can generate feelings of impotence, and even increase alienation.[14]

---

[12]Y. Goodman (2003) offers a book-length treatment of such a language curriculum.

[13]Norman Fairclough's (1992b) work on Critical Language Awareness is closely related.

[14]Several *Rethinking Schools* educators make the same point (e.g., B. Bigelow & Peterson, 2002; Christensen, 2000).

On the other hand, the investigation can be made "purposeful" (according to the CLSL), creating both a "language of possibility" and a context for "transformation (according to Aronowitz and Giroux), by linking it "to a vision of the future that not only explode[s] the myths of the existing society but also reach[es] into those pockets of desires and needs that harbor a longing for a new society and new forms of social relations" (Giroux, 1984, p. 38). These visions, desires, and needs could lead to:

- investigations of the possibilities for changing both the discourses and their social contexts and
- investigations of the contexts and the particulars of other struggles for change (e.g., studying various literacy campaigns or campaigns for instituting antiracist/antisexist language policies).

We believe the best place to begin such an enterprise is with the mainstream culture's discourse. We can explore, for example, how the asymmetries of doctor–patient or teacher–student talk or of boss–employee written exchanges "contribute to [people's] understandings of what [they] are allowed to say and therefore allowed to be" (CLSL, 1987, p. 30). Such a critique, requiring as it does a stepping-back and examining as if from the outside, is especially possible for students who have already come from outside. Their journey from home to the mainstream may have given them the tools for this interrogation: the knack of putting one world into perspective from the distance of another and the customs of democracy brought from their whole language *[and critical practice]* classrooms.

The dominant Discourse should be the first to be interrogated, because it is more impervious to criticism and because critiquing it will be less likely to separate students from the Discourses in which they are rooted. However, all Discourses, subordinate as well as dominant, offer comforts and constraints in unequal measure for different categories of people. Therefore, the ultimate aim is not only to legitimize primary Discourses and the community's cultural knowledge but to critically analyze these, too, for their strengths as well as their weaknesses (Aronowitz & Giroux, 1985).

Students who take part in such an education would certainly not be able to continue to participate unconsciously in either their old or their new Discourses. This consciousness could itself lead to alienation—students could well be doubly alienated, from both their home Discourse and that of the mainstream—or it could lead to examination and action. A scientist, after all, one who studies something consciously and objectively, doesn't love his or her subject less because he or she sees it clearly. Acting—working with others from both dominant and subordinate groups to change what is oppressive in both Discourses—[...] would bring learners together into a new community, sharing a common responsibility for effecting change.

STRETCHING DOMINANT DISCOURSES

Subordinate Discourses could challenge dominant Discourses to accommodate to their literacy—to their language, to their topics, to their worldviews. Zora Neale Hurston (1979) began publishing in the 1920s—too early for Black English (and Black lives) to dent the mainstream. It took Walker's (1982) *The Color Purple* to expand the boundaries of acceptability. Soto's (1973) *Spiks* is written in English, Spanish, and Spanglish, but it is not on many freshman English reading lists, even in colleges with substantial Hispanic enrollments. Gilman's (1892/1973) *The Yellow Wallpaper* was first published in 1892, after many rejections, despite her reputation as an accomplished economist; Chopin published *The Awakening* (1895/1972) 3 years later. Both of these profoundly feminist stories had to be rediscovered by the recent women's movement, since they had not been continuously read as part of mainstream discourses.

If whole language *[and critical practice]* educators are serious about helping child and adult learners find their voices, then it seems to us we have a concomitant obligation to provide forums for those voices in the mainstream. It is not enough to welcome subordinate Discourses into our classrooms; we must also wrest space for them in the dominant literate world.

RECONNECTING LEARNERS WITH THEIR COMMUNITIES

Although the Schoolboys of Barbiana (1970) held the naive belief that literacy always meant power, they were quite sophisticated about the politics of the distribution and use of literacy. They carefully documented how few peasant children were allowed by the schools to graduate from the university, in comparison to children of the "big shots." Their solution to the dual problem of literacy distribution and use was to have two school systems: one, called the *School of Social Service*, for those who decided to dedicate themselves to serving "the family of man"; and the other, called the *School of Ego Service* (those we have now), which would perpetuate the status quo.

We can borrow from the Schoolboys [...] but forgo their innocent confidence in the power of literacy per se. Their recommendation that each new literate feed his or her knowledge back into the community (although rigidifying if all students were to follow it in that it does not allow for geographic or social mobility) can help both students and communities [...]. [...] It would respond, for instance, to fears that learning school literacy requires leaving home. Graduates of whole language *[and critical practice]* environments are well suited to this kind of investment in service, having already been members of democratic learning communities.[15] Instead of feeling like

---

[15]Esther Sokolov Fine (2003) has written about (and with) former students in her whole language classrooms who have become social workers and community leaders in the communities in which they lived as children.

graduation demands moving on and moving out, tearing up roots and leaving home communities ever more impoverished, some graduates might well prefer staying as important and connected members, creating new learning communities at home. (Horton, 1990, gives many examples of community education projects stemming from a community leader's attendance at and then return from the Highlander Folk School, a school sharing many features with whole language *[and critical practice]* classrooms.)

THE DUAL POTENTIAL OF WHOLE LANGUAGE

Learning to read and write can be both empowering and alienating, but learning to read and write in a whole language *[or critical practice]* classroom carries with it special potential—for both more power and more alienation. This is because whole language *[and critical practice]* are simply more successful than traditional approaches in developing thoughtful, confident readers and writers. It is because, being more successful, whole language *[and critical practice]* are more likely to put some students into the position of experiencing discontinuities between the kind of literacy they learned in school and the sometimes covert, sometimes overt literacy expectations and desires of their communities. It is because democratic, critical, analytical work is intrinsic to the practice of whole language *[and critical practice]*, and learners may turn these tools against their home Discourse. It is because the collective dialogue and individual critique characteristic of whole language *[and critical practice]* classrooms are likely to lead to personal and political change, and change can be exhilarating—but it can also be painful.

[...] Those teachers who will help students cope with the pain and solve the dilemma of the negative consequences of literacy success are more likely to be whole language *[and critical practice]* teachers, with their commitment to respond to students' needs. And the liberation of learners from the confines of the either-home-or-mainstream Discourse dilemma into active struggle with the issues of literacy, community, identity, and social change is more likely to come from the power of the critical thinking and collaboration learned and practiced in whole language *[and critical practice]* settings.

Chapter 10

Criticism and Self-Criticism[1,2]

This chapter borrows heavily from the first two sections of the original chapter.

Whole language has certainly had more than its share of troubles. First there were attacks fomented by the religious Right. For instance, in 1996, I described scenes from a protest at a nearby school: "Picketers marching around an elementary school with placards reading 'Whole language: The culprit behind your child's failure,' and 'Whole language is the Devil's work'" (Edelsky, 1996, p. 182). As whole language gained popularity, mainstream parents with more secular but still traditionalist preferences demanded that their neighborhood schools reject whole language for its emphasis on multiple interpretations rather than single right answers ("I don't want my kids to think; I want them to learn," one father shouted, smacking a table for emphasis.) At the same time (as described in chap. 7 and elsewhere in this volume), there is a campaign to put education under corporatist control. One tactic of this campaign has been, first, to show that education was failing and, second, to blame that failure on whole language. Adding insult to injury, those with whom, presumably, whole language shares a political stance regarding social justice and equity, have also criticized whole

---

[1]This chapter borrows from the chapter entitled "Critique, Critics, and Self? Criticism" that appeared in the 1996 edition of *With Literacy and Justice for All.*

[2]It is touchy to engage in self criticism when we've already been so roundly—and unfairly—attacked. Touchier still to be providing more ammunition to the attackers. But whole language has always had its own words turned against it. This response to criticism and self criticism fits our character (an evolving pedagogy, given to self reflection and change). It is for our own benefit and the benefit of the progressive/radical educational community. Our ideological enemies will misuse it as they have misused our other statements. So be it.

language. It is the arguments of these should-be-allies, those I am calling "left critics of whole language," that are the focus of this chapter.

WHO ARE THESE CRITICS?

In the category of "left critics of whole language" I am including those who refer explicitly to whole language (e.g. Baker & Luke, 1991; Gee, 2004b; B. Green, 1991; Luke & Freebody, 1997), those who critically analyze practices associated with whole language but who do not name whole language (e.g., writers' workshops critiqued by Gilbert [1989]),[3] and those who critique favored premises like child-centeredness (Walkerdine, 1990) and the individual-as-separate-entity (e.g., as reflected in positing an individual, interior "nature" for cognitive processes and learning [Lave & Wenger, 1991; A. Luke, 1995]). All of the members of my category, then, do not make whole language their major concern. Some do (e.g., those invited to critique whole language in the Winter 1994–1995 issue of *English Quarterly* [Church et al., 1994–1995]). But most never mention it. Rather, in the process of proposing and elaborating their own ideas, they point out what they see as flaws in current progressive pedagogies (a category that often includes whole language) or in current theories that are important in whole language (even if these writers don't identify them as such). They are as often developers of theory and models as they are critics. But, for my present purposes, because the ways in which they contradict/criticize whole language is what I am making most salient now, I will call them *critics*. And if one's presumed allies are criticizing, it is important to take the criticism very seriously, to try to understand where it is warranted and where it is not.

Among the criticisms are three I will address below: individualism, a status quo curriculum, and essentialism.

WHOLE LANGUAGE AS INDIVIDUALISTIC

Portelli, a contributor to an article on varying perspectives on whole language (Church et al., 1994–1995), is one who explicitly criticizes whole language for its excessive individualism, leading to "the illusion that freedom has no limits, that somehow there is the possibility of making choices in a neutral context, that any individual choice is acceptable" (p. 8). The entire social practices perspective (e.g., Gee, 1999; Lave & Wenger, 1991; Street, 1984) constitutes an implicit criticism of one aspect of a whole language perspective in both practice and research.

---

[3]Others (e.g., Henkin, 1998; Lensmire, 1994) have been critical of favored whole language practices such as writers' workshops and various kinds of sharing (author's chair, sharing time), but these critics do not attribute the problems they identify—inequities, difficulties in interpersonal dynamics—to something inherent in whole language.

Whole language's theoretical foundations do focus on interior processing—individuals predicting and hypothesizing—just as scholars of child language acquisition have focused on individual hypotheses. Whole language theory encourages viewing students' productions as emanating from individual preferences or styles rather than from social positionings or membership in communities of practice. It promotes considering students' interpretations as individual transactions. While it permits a social practices view of literacy (to be added to but not thoroughly integrated with its socio-psycholinguistic perspective), it does not entail such a view. And although the *socio* in that perspective emphasizes the social nature of literacy conventions and contexts for literacy, it does not sufficiently emphasize that meanings are not infinitely variable but rather are constrained by history (writ large, and also the history of local interpersonal dynamics), culture, and power arrangements.

However, whole language has a political agenda that includes changing some of those constraints by promoting justice and equity. Therefore, whole language theory could well impel teachers to work with students on interrogating the social origins and consequences of various conventions of language use, text construction and interpretation. Too often, however, it does not. Thus, the critics are right; whole language does need to shift its theoretical frame so that it highlights two areas: (a) relationships of language and power (Fairclough, 1989, 1992b; 1992c); and (b) literacy as a social practice with inherently ideological dimensions (Rowe, 2005).

The scholarly work on relationships between language and power is indeed illuminating and, if integrated into a whole language perspective, it would compel whole language educators to look at issues of power in texts and language registers. But promoting such an integration does not imply that whole language should entirely relinquish its existing conception of language as systems of conventions instantiated in performance. Relating power and language is not all that is happening as language is used or learned. There is also the learning and use of contrasts such as "*the* girl has a truck" versus "*a* girl has a truck." Focusing on language and power should not require giving up serious consideration of the learning of abstractions entailed in such a distinction as *a* versus *the* and other "small" linguistic/pragmatic phenomena.

If a language/power dimension is necessary but not all encompassing, the same can be said of viewing literacy (actually, multiple literacies) as a social practice. Whole language does indeed need to saturate its current conception of literacy with that view (for one thing, it would illuminate the cultural and historical character of reading instruction, as well as contesting ideologies about reading). But the sociological character of literacy practices is not all there is; social practices are not *only* social. Foregrounding the social does not have to mean refusing to consider the various sociocognitive and linguistic processes that are simultaneously entailed in making textual meaning with print.

Rethinking whole language theory so that it profoundly integrates language and power relations and literacy as social practice into its view of language and literacy—making it less individualistic—would change what whole language "makes something of." McDermott (1993) discussed "making something of" (as in "wanna make sump'n' of it") in relation to school failure and learning disability. It isn't, he said, that there are no differences in people's rates or ease of learning; what matters is that our culture has made these differences important (e.g., with the labels it establishes and the professionals it employs to deal with those so labeled). Whole language has "made something" of meaning-making. In the process, it has discredited the fuss made over word-getting, precise oral reading, and assorted other sound- and word-focused skills. A whole language fuss over meaning is also a considerable improvement over making something over test scores or rank orderings or failure—a fuss brought back with a vengeance by the No Child Left Behind (NCLB) legislation.

But making something over meaning is not enough. As Deborah Rowe (2005) discussed, it is necessary for whole language educators to shift research on literacy (and, I would add here, pedagogical concerns) to make something over participation. That does not mean abandoning old issues (e.g., readers' hypotheses, transacted meanings, etc.). It means embedding those issues within more complex understandings. This would entail understanding the positioned, local, ideological, material, and spatial nature of participation (Rowe, 2005). Thus, whole language should be highlighting what literate positions are open to students and what cultural models of learning to read and write are implicit in events children participate in (Rowe, 2005), how texts work on readers and in society and on what political work they do (Luke & Freebody, 1997), how texts position readers and how readers resist or take up already available meanings (Mellor, Patterson, and O'Neill (1991), and what social work is done to devalue or exclude certain texts (Trimbur, 1989). Whole language has indeed made something of who gets to read for meaning (the Robins—the high scoring, more mainstream, more affluent students—but not the Pigeons). It must continue to make something of the ideological and social nature of taken for granted classroom practices.

WHOLE LANGUAGE AS PROMOTING THE STATUS QUO

Another criticism: Not only does whole language theory fail to demand that teachers and students question texts for their social import and their "interested" production, it also does not offer theoretically principled criteria for choosing to study one topic over another. With "the child's interest" as the major engine for curriculum but with little explicit recognition of the social construction of children's interests, with meaning-making in the foreground, but not which meanings are made about what, the manifest whole language curriculum is as likely to concern ethnic clothing as it is ethnic cleansing. When topics for study avoid anything "controversial" (i.e., anything over which there is a struggle for meaning tied up with questions of power and knowledge), or when they avoid interrogating all positions on whatever topic is studied, that avoidance amounts to silent support for dominant positions and the dominant side of controversies.

The critics may be right about whole language as it was typically practiced during its heyday, but not as it is practiced now (more about that below). Moreover, even if the criticism is correct, some holistic educators dispute the reasoning. Explicit critique, they argue (e.g., Dyson, 1993a) is not a mode through which children play and learn. Children's own participation, their own struggles, is what does and should engage them most— whether or not those struggles are ever critically interrogated. According to these educators, my own urgings, along with those of other critical whole language and also some just-plain critical educators (e.g., B. Bigelow, Harvey, Karp, & Miller, 2001; B. Bigelow & Peterson, 2002; Christensen, 2000; Edelsky, 1999; A. Luke, O'Brien, & Comber, 1994; B. Peterson, 1994) for a more head-on approach, are simply adult-centric. Dyson (1993a, 1993b), for instance, offers examples of children's struggles over gendered power distributions while negotiating story writing and dramatic play. She convinces me that even without explicit critical inquiry, these children did indeed learn to make new connections among gender, access, and power and to disrupt powerful cultural stories about gender. I am not convinced, however, that such learning substitutes for that which comes from guided critique. Nor am I yet convinced that just because children benefit from play they would not also benefit from sustained critical inquiry (see Vasquez, 2004, for detailed examples of such inquiry among 4-year-olds).

Despite the theoretical voids I acknowledge above—the one that allows students to read and write without questioning the social consequences of the texts they create and the one that provides no principled criteria for choosing what to study and how to study it—I am not convinced that whole language does not disturb the world-as-given. Many of its theoretical premises run counter to the status quo. For instance, its aversion to misrepresenting skilled performance as a collection of subskills helps resist commodification of learning. Whole language's theory-based rejection of literacy exercises frees considerable classroom time for questioning the status quo through authentic language use. That same theoretical notion (demanding that children be engaged in actually using written language rather than doing exercises with it) is behind the idea that science should be learned through "doing science" the way scientists "do" it, "doing social studies" the way social scientists "do" it, and so on—asking multi- and interdisciplinary questions of messy phenomena and, therefore, interrupting the boundaries of disciplines.

The whole language conception of reading as a transaction between a situated reader and a text in a net of embedded contexts necessarily acknowledges the contribution of readers' home discourses and personal histories (including histories with other texts). That conception overturns a faith in single interpretations that transcend history, a view of the moral superiority of standard dialects, and a privileging of single canonical traditions. The view of reading as transaction interrupts the status quo; it promotes pluralism and more democratic classroom relationships (among students, teachers, and text). By refusing to sort students into high, medium, and low reading groups and fast and slow tracks, whole language educators undermine a major educational contribution to social stratification.

It is not only that whole language's theoretical premises challenge dominant practices; they also contradict prevailing premises: that language in use is composed of separable components, that learning a language entails practicing its separate parts, that evaluating language ability is best (or even possibly) accomplished by testing people on their manipulation of separate parts. These dominant premises underlie the justifications of differential access to cultural capital. In refuting them, whole language threatens the entire arsenal of language-based testing weapons currently used against people so efficiently and so "objectively." Contrasting whole language premises about the wholeness of language-in-use and its important role in Discourse (an identity kit made up of words, acts, beliefs, gestures, attitudes, and values) (Gee, 1989a) implies that to evaluate people's use of language requires watching them actually use it with others.

Whole language precepts also work against the status quo. "Trusting teachers," and—for theoretical reasons concerning whole language's rejection of separate reading skills—withholding trust from published reading instruction technologies, encourages teachers to reclaim their professional autonomy from usurpers like publishers and policymakers. In so doing, whole language teachers become part of the struggle to help subvert the usually unacknowledged, uncontested control of schools by a corporate system of domination. "Attend to students' language strengths" (and assuming, axiomatically, that all people indeed have language strengths) is more than a theoretical preference; it is a political tactic. It counters the prevailing political tactic of making it look like the knowledge that high-status people have already learned outside of school as a function of their privileged status, knowledge that serves them well as they use it as a basis for further learning of class-biased knowledge inside of school (Gee, 1989a), is evidence of their superior innate ability. "Honor the home discourse" lessens the privilege of dominant discourses. "Knowledge is social" opens all knowledge (including whole language precepts) to critique and could encourage key critical questions, such as What struggles lie behind this knowledge? Who benefits from this view?

Given the extent to which a whole language theoretical perspective challenges the sociopolitical status quo, how has whole language effected change? Here, I must distinguish between whole language as a principled theory-in-practice and a motley, mostly co-opted movement that took the label "whole language" (to be discussed below)—a movement which, because of the successful corporatist demonizing of whole language (as discussed elsewhere in this volume), now exists only in rhetoric—and, even there, only as a foil. Teachers who taught with a principled whole language perspective certainly felt its influence, as did their students. For these teachers and their students, whole language brought greater access to rich, complex curriculum for all students; diminished hierarchies in the classroom; promoted greater respect for more varied literacy and language practices; and increased the likelihood that more students would try on academic literate identities and see that they fit. Unfortunately, aside from having an impact within their classrooms, genuine whole language teachers (i.e., those well grounded in a whole language theoretical perspective) were too few to unseat injustice and inequities in education even within their own school districts, let alone within a wider arena. Despite its name recognition (resulting from the activity of the movement that took its name and, later, the campaign to demonize it), whole language as a principled theory-in-practice was, in fact, always marginal; now, it is even more so. Its premises do not now and never did underlie dominant curriculum projects, most educational publishing, national assessments, or even the bulk of educational research.

By contrast, the whole language movement—a bandwagon that extracted surface details from the integrated theoretical–political–philosophical whole while, not coincidentally, stripping away its radical intent—did have an impact. In one sense, the impact was minor. Fittingly—since the movement (unlike the theoretically principled whole language perspective-in-practice) was never opposed to bringing a market ideology to public education—it was the market where that minor impact was felt. Sales of children's literature increased because one of the features the movement borrowed from the genuine theory-in-practice was the use of trade books instead of basal reader packages. Dramatically increased classroom exposure to children's literature also led students, parents, and grandparents to buy more trade books. And, at the height of the movement, "trendy" whole language terminology was used as a marketing tool in basal packages put out by publishing companies (e.g., *theme study, shared reading, strategies, invitations, the writer's craft, predicting and confirming*, etc.; Edelsky, 1994a). The major impact of whole-language-as-movement, however, was to provide a demon (occasionally converted to a buffoon) for the media circus that figured prominently in the political spectacle surrounding recent educational policy and legislation (M. L. Smith, 2004).

The movement labeled as whole language did not survive the corporatist assault described in chapter 7. But it was that movement that was what was destroyed, not genuine whole language theory-in-practice. Teachers who were deeply knowledgeable about whole language's theoretical premises and who were committed to their democratizing character did not forsake their beliefs in the face of the attacks. And while those attacks certainly did not create a welcoming climate for other teachers to learn about whole language, neither did they completely close the doors to newcomers. Thus, whole language teachers today are those who would have been considered the genuine article 20 years ago, not followers of a fad they barely understand. Because of their knowledge, political analyses, and commitments, current whole language teachers are more likely to be actively undermining the test culture of NCLB and working from a critical stance in the classroom (see examples in Comber, 2001; Edelsky, 1999; Edelsky & Johnson, 2004; Leland & Harste, 2005). Whole language theory regarding curriculum and literacy does indeed need to be revised to *entail* critical practices, to make critical questions commonplace, and to hold up quality of critique as an index of success.

But current whole language teaching and whole language as a theoretical perspective-in-practice do not deserve to be criticized for preserving the status quo.

WHOLE LANGUAGE AS AN ESSENTIALIZING MODERNIST PEDAGOGY

Left critics tend to identify whole language as yet another liberal modernist pedagogy, outdated by postmodern, poststructural understandings.[4] It is

---

[4]Modernism and postmodernism are pervasive (if, paradoxically, somewhat overlapping) social conditions and mentalities. Modernism was/is marked by faith in Progress, Reason, and Science (Berman, 1989). Its dominant analyses appeal to some underlying comprehensive theoretical system (e.g., behaviorism, Marxism, Freudianism). It presumes a reality that exists outside of culture and history—essential qualities that pertain across time and after culture is stripped away (that's the way women/the poor/Jews/pieces of literature/great paintings *are*) (Peller, 1987).

With the cataclysmic disasters of the late 20th century (world wars, threats of nuclear war, catastrophic pollution), change as Progress and improving the world through Science are no longer such certainties (Lyotard, 1984). Indeed, certainty itself seems unwarranted (T. Morgan, personal communication, September 14, 1990b). Postmodernism is, thus, marked by a profound skepticism. No Truth lies beyond interpretation or culture; everything (including people's subjectivities—their identities and sense of those identities) is socially constructed. There is no essence to great art or to women's nature or to anything else. What makes a text *literature* is the way it is treated (Eagleton, 1983). Cynicism is rampant. So is alienation—not

true; whole language does refer to a seemingly essentialized teacher or student (*the student, the teacher*). But whole language teachers also have a considerable history of attending to individual differences among students (e.g., Rhodes & Dudley-Marling, 1988; Weaver, 1994). Whole language writings take pains to point out that what is often claimed as typical of classrooms in general (e.g., patterns of classroom interaction) is actually associated only with teachers who have particular (though predominant) theoretical orientations. Moreover, books about whole language are full of vignettes of classroom scenes (e.g., Crafton, 1991; Edelsky, Altwerger, & Flores, 1991; Routman, 1991), offered in part, at least, to show that practice is always locally contingent—that there is no single way to "do" whole language.

What is probably most troublesome to the left critics, however, is whole language's theoretical view of reading. The critics prefer conceptualizing literacy as a multiplicity of literacies (as though saying reading *is* social practice(s) is somehow not as essentialist as saying reading *is* a sociopsycholinguistic process). In fact, whole language does claim an "essence" for an activity called *reading*. I want to offer some historical reasons for the theoretical and strategic correctness of that claim.

Many whole language educators (e.g., Edelsky & Draper, 1989; Edelsky & Smith, in press; K. Goodman, 1992; Harman & Edelsky, 1989; Lindfors, 1987) appreciate and cite scholars such as Gee (1999), Graff (1987), Kress and van Leeuwen (1996), McDermott (1992), Street (1984), and Szwed (1981), who have written about the ways reading has been variously defined and socially allocated in different places at different times; that is, scholars who see literacy as situated, historical, and sociological. Whole language is particularly interested, however, in one of those views, the one that is currently predominant in North America: making sense of/with print. If there is some current popular consensus that a goal in being able to "read" means being able to comprehend a written text (evidence for that consensus appears in a wide range of institutional documents as well as in ordinary

---

being fully present, always both participating yet holding back a bit to watch oneself participate. And so is nostalgia—a deep yearning for a time when one did not hold oneself back, when what is now smiled at condescendingly was taken in earnest innocence (Birkerts, 1989).

Postmodernism has given birth to several approaches to analyzing social life—poststructuralism, deconstruction, critical sociology, critical theory, and others. Despite major differences among these, they share certain postmodernist premises: Meanings are fundamentally unstable, meanings have their opposites embedded within them, what is put forth as neutral knowledge by dominant groups supports existing power arrangements and thus is far from neutral. They also share a project: to unmask what is hidden within dominant knowledge structures. And they share a position: to unseat class as the privileged category in analyzing social life and instead install a triumvirate—gender, race and class, followed by other subjectivities (ethnicity, sexual orientation, etc.) (Morgan, 1990).

people's complaints about their own or their children's problems with reading), it is reasonable to then ask: What does it mean to "comprehend a written text?" What is "reading" in that sense? How do people learn to do that?

That doesn't mean no attention should be paid to questions like who gets to read for meaning and who doesn't, or to questions like where do meanings come from or what kinds of literacy practices are common in various communities. In fact, some whole language educators do attend to such questions (Altwerger, 1993; Harste, 2004). But at the time of "The Great Debate" (Chall, 1967), it was historically important to highlight the question: What *is* reading?

Although that debate about two methods for teaching reading did not ask that question, it answered it: Reading is a collection of skills, the main one being "getting words." After readers "get enough words," they comprehend. In Chall's famous Great Debate, the only interesting question was which is the best way to teach people to "get words," a phonics way or a sight word way. And an implication of the word-bound position on reading in that debate was that reading failure (i.e., poor performance on school reading tasks) can be traced to trouble with "words" (nonmainstream lexicon or nonstandard word order). Ken Goodman (1969) argued, with backing from linguistic theory and data on oral reading, that reading is not a matter of "getting words," that it is instead a process of constructing meaning by predicting with cues from linguistic systems (orthographic, syntactic, semantic) in a particular context. Thus, a Black child's miscuing of *he asked his mother if he could go* as *he axed his mother could he go* is a sign of comprehending and then "recoding" into a more familiar dialect; that is, the child's miscues are evidence of strength in reading, not weakness in word-getting.

Goodman's (and others' since) definition of reading as a psycholinguistic process still holds for the activity I am referring to as "making sense of written text." It has been supported by research involving miscues (oral deviations from the print) in a number of languages and cultures (Al-Fahid, 2000; J. Brown, Goodman, & Marek, 1996; Flurkey, Paulson, & Goodman, in press; K. Goodman, 2005; Wang, 2005). It is not a sufficient definition. But it is a necessary consideration. Harste, Burke, and Woodward (1982) amended the psycholinguistic definition to include social influences, naming that kind of literacy activity a *socio*-psycholinguistic process. At first, what was social was merely tacked on. Later, the idea of reading as social practices (Cook-Gumperz, 1986; Heath, 1983; Street, 1984) expanded whole language educators' understandings (e.g., Flores, Cousin, & Diaz, 1991; chap. 5, this volume). Whole language now views the psychological and linguistic processes involved in reading-as-making-text- meaning as also simultaneously social.[5] They are social in at least two senses: (1) the processes work with cues that are conventionalized within a social group and (2) the processes always operate within layers of social contexts. Thus, it is not the case that first we make sense of print and then we note its and our place in the world—a sociocognitivist version of the behaviorist notion that we decode first and comprehend later. Instead, we cannot make sense of print in the first place without identifying its key social features (e.g., its genre, its function, the worldviews embedded in it) and without locating ourselves in relation to it (Gee, 1990).

Of course, there are other perspectives on the "truth" about reading as making sense of print, but that doesn't mean all those perspectives are equal. It isn't only that each has different social implications; it is also that some perspectives are better; for example, the idea that people make text meanings and social meanings at the same time as they decode is a better idea than that they make them after they decode—better because it receives inferred support from readers' oral readings, better because it could underpin more equitable reading instruction and assessment.

Now there are certainly other kinds of literacies and literate practices to investigate. But I think it is a tactical error to attempt to discredit inquiry into reading-as-making-meaning-with-text. The various publics in North America are not concerned with the full range of what constitutes literacy in the many communities around the world. Public concern is for one part of that range, the part having to do with making sense of print. The dominant response in education, policy, and testing has been to concentrate on a different part of the range, the part focusing on separate skills—those skills that supposedly add up to being able to comprehend print. Whole language tries to offset that dominant response by arguing that reading to make sense with print has an "essential" nature; it *is*—or *requires*—predicting based on cultural/linguistic knowledge in the service of making meaning. This "essentialist" definition needs to be read in context. It is not located at the center of educational or cultural power. (Susan Bordo, 1994, makes a similar argument about the relatively inconsequential essentializing aspects of feminist theory compared with the enormously consequential theorizing

---

[5]Seeing these mental processes as social (as well as psychological and linguistic) is not the same as seeing them as social practices. As processes, they are "in the head" even if they are shot through with culturally conditioned meanings and even if they occur while during the local, social practices of reading. Practices highlight participation. They may include "in the head and heart" phenomena such as emotions, values, and ideologies, but they more obviously include interactions, bodily postures, roles and activities of various people, physical locations, and so on. Rowe's (2005) work on shifting the initial focus from process to participation is an example of a current change underway among some whole language educators regarding a theoretical view of literacy.

of gender within the meta-narrative of Patriarchy.) Rather, it tries to unseat a different and dominant definition, one that hegemonically supports rankings in various hierarchies. To dismiss a whole language view of reading on the basis of "essentialism" does not attend to its strategic potential in education: to counter the oppressive uses of the dominant, separate skills views of reading.

The left critique of whole language that concerns essentialism is related to a larger critique of modernism.[6] In a particularly insightful challenge to postmodern critiques of education, Aaron Schutz (2004) argues that postmodernism's "fascination" with criticizing "pastoral" aspects of various forms of progressive education overlooks the "blunt discipline experienced by those at the bottom rungs of society" (p. 16). While he acknowledges that practices such as having students interact with each other about multiple interpretations of texts (practices I am associating with whole language) discipline students by co-opting their creativity and recruiting their desires and motivations, he also points out that this softer kind of discipline when connected to learning is yet one more privilege of those already privileged. Whole language should indeed be sensitive to the fact that, for all its liberatory aims, it nevertheless engages in "discipline." At the same time, it must continue to attempt to initiate all students into "robust postmodern forms of democratic engagement" in learning (Schutz, 2004, p. 18), not merely short-circuit student resistance by making school "fun." Critics, therefore, should note that whole language classrooms offer the softer "discipline" of minds, hearts, and bodies in whole language classrooms to all students, not only the already privileged, and that this softer discipline is surely an improvement over that which is blunt and Dickensian.[7]

Whole language does indeed hold the modernist goal of improving "the world." It aims to do so by improving education. I believe whole language cannot, must not, let go of that aim. Nor must it let go of a concomitant, modernist, unashamedly old-fashioned hope. That aim, that hope—for improvement in the direction of greater justice—is shared by whole language and critical pedagogies too, even postmodernist ones (Gore, 1993).

---

[6]The postmodern critique of modernism "unmasked the way universals suppress difference" (Fusco, 2005). In the current context of rollbacks of four decades of hard-won gains in civil rights for the poor and disenfranchised, conservatives discredit these "discourses of difference" as coming from "special interests." Postmodernists, too, are turning their backs on their original critique by claiming these discourses of difference are also "essentialist." Ironically, both criticisms— the conservative accusation of special interests and the postmodern charge of essentialism— justify dismantling legislation protecting civil rights. (Fusco, 2005).

[7]I do not subscribe to the position that conditions should be made as miserable as possible to encourage the greatest resistance.

HOW DID WE GET TO THIS POINT?

A Tactical Error

The left critics rightfully point to some flaws in whole language. But there is also a major flaw in their criticism: It implies that whole language is an adversary, or at least outdated and worth discarding. That is both a substantive and a tactical error. Whole language educators frequently share overlapping history, aims, pedagogical practices (e.g., reflective journals, firsthand data gathering, etc.), and some topics of study (e.g., fairness on the playground and beyond) with educators identified as "critical" (Shannon, 1990). But, more than that, if the left critics hope to convince others to join in their political project, they should consider who would be their most likely converts. Wouldn't it be those educators who already eschew textbook-driven curricula, who try to avoid assigning exercises (even in this period of education-as-test-preparation) and so free up time for students to conduct sustained inquiries about what is *really* on their minds, who look for ways to get students to have an effect on their communities? Strategically, it is a mistake to treat one's most likely allies as either "the enemy" or as complete has-beens. How did whole language get into either of these positions *vis à vis* the left critics?

It's Their Fault

An unfortunate series of misunderstandings may be one source of the problem. Whole language educators and left critics of whole language are often associated with different academic disciplines and endeavors and thus participate in different discourse communities. Whole language comes out of Curriculum and Instruction (formerly Elementary Education and Reading) in Departments or Colleges of Education; many of the left critics are in Sociology of Education or Anthropology of Education, Educational Policy, or disciplines more tightly tied to those associated with Colleges of Liberal Arts. Thus, left critics may understandably be ignorant of ongoing arguments and developments in distant disciplines. (Jennifer Gore [1993] gave a similar explanation for the lack of articulation between feminist pedagogy in Women's Studies and feminist pedagogy in Education.) Even those left critics housed in Departments of English Education or Reading Education often have looser ties to day-to-day life in K–12 classrooms than do whole language educators, whose professional concerns are usually tightly enmeshed with those of student teachers and mentor teachers.

A darker explanation is that the omissions and misconstruals are related to the individualism of academia, that is, to the practice of maximally differentiating one's own position from others in order to gain recognition and status. Gore (1993) referred to this phenomenon as she discussed the "struggle for pedagogies in feminist and critical pedagogies." In maximally differentiating one's own position from others, one may underdifferentiate the others. In the case at hand, whole language is often lumped together with open education, "process writing," cooperative learning, the language experience approach, and reader-response theory.

It is not surprising that mainstream academics who are untroubled by positivist research assumptions and premises of a basal technology would not bother to distinguish the above pedagogies. But it is odd that, when it comes to whole language, scholars such as the left critics, with a principled sensitivity to history and discourse, should be ahistorical and blind to discourse. That is, by not distinguishing these various alternatives to dominant practices they fail to discuss what the alternatives are historically alternative *to* and in which discourses those contrasts appear. For instance, the critics rightfully argue that in foregrounding students as authors, "process writing" (one of the practices used by whole language) fails to examine the ways authors' works are social constructions (Gilbert, 1991). But these critics neglect the historical reasons for such foregrounding. Whole language and writing process were countering two conceptions that were dominant at the time: (a) that text construction is not the province of ordinary students, but only of experts who are authoritative, and (b) that students are to "consume" texts (by comprehending the meaning-in-the-text put there by the author), not create them. Positioning students as authors rejects this conception.

We Don't Get No Respect

Part of distinguishing whole language from other progressive pedagogies is distinguishing whole language from "whole language," that is, what is theoretically framed as whole language from what is merely called whole language. At the time of the heyday of whole language, the term had come to mean anything from a time slot ("we 'do' whole language on Tuesday afternoon") to a method of teaching reading to any even slightly humanizing variation on the prevailing skills-based theme. As Allan Luke (personal communication, March 25, 1990) aptly put it, "whole language" became "an empty semantic set" meaning anything anyone says it means. (A particularly egregious instance here is Bergeron's, 1990, attempt to extract a "definition" of whole language from all published definitions, including those devised by avowed opponents of whole language.)

Now, whole-language-as-movement is certainly worthy of analysis and critique. So is whole language as a self-consciously theoretical perspective-in-practice. But in order to adequately critique either one, it is necessary to distinguish them and to respect the latter enough to study its nuances along with its clichés.[8] That would mean believing that whole language writings present valuable ideas and that whole language educators are legitimate intellectuals. Unfortunately, whole language is generally considered "liberal" or "bourgeois" by these critics and therefore worthy only of being looked at from above (as critics) but not from below (as students) or on a par (as colleagues). A rare example of left critics favorably citing holistic education, as though it had indeed made a contribution to the critic's thinking, is Giroux's (1987) extension of Graves's work on writing workshops. Another is Gee's (1994) limited approval of the use by "immersion pedagogies" (a category Gee devised to include whole language, open classrooms, inquiry, and "cooperative" approaches to content areas, among others) of first language acquisition as a guide for learning in school.[9] The more usual case, however, is an absence of such citations.

---

[8]Another example of an educational reform that turned into a movement and lost its "soul" is the small-schools movement. More precisely, the small-schools movement was turned into a new movement by others—privatizers and bureaucrats who destroyed or simply ignored the issues of central concern to early small-schools educators. Instead of the "radical principles" that grounded the original small-schools efforts (access, participation and democracy; commitments to equity; sophisticated systems of assessment to support rich, deep learning; schools for social justice and social responsibility), the new small-schools movement focuses on size. By taking up the surface and skipping the central meanings, the new movement has brought along with it, depending on the city, gentrification, union busting, privatization, self-imposed budget austerity, and faith-based public education (M. Fine, 2005).

[9]Gee (1994) argues that, in school, an acquisition model of learning (via immersion) must be supplemented by instruction. But he writes as though it is his own analysis that allows him to say that first language acquisition is used by whole language (and other pedagogies) as a guide for learning in school ("In fact, this analogy, between first language acquisition and other forms of later learning is, I believe, a large part of what constitutes the basis of modern 'progressive' 'immersion' pedagogies such as 'open classrooms,' 'whole language,' 'process writing,' and various 'cooperative,' 'project,' and 'inquiry'-based approaches to content areas [Edelsky, 1991; Goodman, 1986; Graves, 1983; Smith, 1983, 1988])" (pp. 330–331). Unfortunately, not one of these citations appears in his references at the end of the article. But in my bookcase is Frank Smith's (1983) *Essays into Literacy* in which he discusses learning to read ("The general requirements of immersion in the problem, of making sense, and of getting feedback to test hypotheses would seem to be just as easily met with written language as with speech" [p. 47]). In the book I coauthored with Bess Altwerger and Barbara Flores (1991), there are entire sections about first language acquisition being used as a guide for learning in school. Here are two statements ("It means that *whatever* is language [we had just been claiming that written language is language] is learned like language and acts like language" [p. 9]; "So far, we may have contributed to the general misperception that whole language is only about language learning [we had just discussed views of language, language development, and reading and writing]. It is true: the theoretical bases of whole language do concern language and language learning. But those bases are relevant to learning in general, not just learning to read and write" [p. 23].) And the title of Marlene Barron's (1990) "very first book about whole language" is *I Learn to Read and Write the Way I Learn to Talk*. Thus, Gee (1994) gives with one hand (being a rare academic who recognizes a theoretical basis for whole language) while taking away with the other (withholding credit from whole language for positing that theoretical position).

But it isn't only that whole language educators and left critics of whole language come from different academic homes or are associated with different endeavors (the left critics with policy and "theory"; whole language educators with "practice"—no matter that practice is theoretical and that theorizing and policy analysis are practices). It is also that the homes (departments, faculties, journals, discourses) are in different neighborhoods, and the endeavors have different status. The academic hierarchy puts education near the bottom, below sociology and anthropology; it puts curriculum and instruction below sociology of education, educational policy, and educational foundations; it puts reading education methods below critical literacy theory. The left critics are usually connected with either the more elite academic departments or the "classier" academic endeavors. Thus, they may not be so willing to read with an intent to learn from those with lower status, such as curriculum and instruction workers who associate closely with classroom teachers—especially if the critics themselves are tainted by being in a low-status field like education. They may not even be willing to take notice of, or acknowledge, cases where whole language educators have already been working with ideas similar to those they themselves advocate. For example, all the following appear in whole language writings, even if they are not always named as I name them here: the importance of meta-narratives for literacy (Edelsky, 1990); the explanatory value of communities of practice (F. Smith, 1983); the necessity of participating with others in the practices one is to learn (F. Smith, 1983); the difference between skilled practitioners and learning skills (Edelsky et al., 1991); the need to see reading and writing as transitive verbs (one always reads or writes *something;* Calkins, 1994) rather than as a free-floating skill; the notion that all texts, regardless of how seemingly original, are intertextual since they respond to, or rely on, other texts (Harste & Short, 1988); and the importance of considering multiple sign systems and transmediation of signs (Harste, Woodward, & Burke, 1984). It isn't the lack of citation that is the problem here; it is the implication that whole language does not work with certain ideas favored by the left critics, and yet these ideas do indeed appear—sometimes centrally—in the whole language literature.

Now clearly, some of the above ideas, in fact discussed by whole language educators, are contradicted by other whole language ideas. For example, the idea that reading is a transitive verb and therefore it doesn't make sense to talk of reading in the abstract is in tension with the idea that reading is a transactional process no matter what text is being read. Moreover, similar ideas discussed by whole language writers and by the left critics do not necessarily mean the same thing; they do not occupy the same epistemological positions (they sit in different webs of meaning, differently weighted and spotlighted). Even so, the seeming invisibility of whole language ideas is disturbing.

I do not think this invisibility stems from malice on the part of critics. Rather, I believe the phenomenon is due to stereotypical academic categorizations (e.g., insisting on categorizing whole language as a "method," thus being blind to its theoretical statements; seeing whole language as "bourgeois liberal" and, therefore, not worth learning from on political grounds); academic pressure to maximally differentiate new theoretical proposals from preceding, possibly competing ones; and academic hierarchies that lead to associating (by citing and thus learning) "up" rather than "down" the status ladder. What both left critics and whole language educators describe as systems of dominance are at work in the academic institutions in which we work; thus, they are also at work in us.

We Have Met the Enemy and It Is ...

The blame for misunderstandings cannot be laid entirely at the feet of the critics, however. Whole language proponents bear much of the responsibility. We did not sufficiently distinguished movement from perspective. We oversimplified complex ideas and discouraged analysis by creating buzzwords. In highlighting what seemed most theoretically salient and strategically necessary at the moment, we neglected what came back to haunt us. We too often failed to make explicit the connections between our political and theoretical premises. Let me take these in turn and include my own culpability.

Not Distinguishing Movement and Perspective. As I said earlier, *whole language* is the name for both a perspective-in-practice and a movement. Anything anyone called *whole language* became part of the whole language movement. The whole language response to this lack of theoretical integrity was ambiguous. There were some efforts (Edelsky et al., 1991; Harste, 1989; Pace, 1991) to distinguish whole-language-in-name-only from practice congruent with the theoretical and political premises discussed in this volume. But there were also presenters at whole language conferences who argued for not creating new orthodoxies (i.e., this is whole language; that isn't) and for being inclusive (after all, theory/practice will always exhibit internal contradictions).

Probably, the ambiguity accurately reflects a genuine ambivalence; achieving movement status had double-edged consequences for whole language. The existence of a nameable movement gave some legitimacy to those who had tried for years to oppose oppressive traditional education and also to those newly interested in experimenting with a different viewpoint. Whole language as buzzword and as movement also gave people the sense that they were "part of something larger" (Clarke, 1990). But buzzwords and movements are also dangerous to the very phenomena they name (Edelsky, 1987; chap. 7, this volume). They announce a substantive change that most often has not occurred. Unprincipled, co-opted spread of a label can doom both the principled practice and the movement. The same instrumentalist discourse (*it works*) used to help "sell" the label is now used to discredit it (*well, that didn't work*).

Some whole language educators used to laugh among themselves about sending in the whole language police to stop the most outrageously un-whole-language-like "whole language" practices from false advertising. But the idea of policing ran counter to the anti-elitist stance of whole language. To avoid seeming elitist, not open to all comers, whole language educators too often refrained from policing or drawing lines. I believe that was a strategic error. It would have been one thing to close the door to newcomers; it was quite another to let others define us—not only those who were merely looking for some new fashion to spice up their drab practice but also those who only opportunistically appropriated the label as well as those who did not identify as whole language educators at all but who wrote about it. Whole language as perspective-in-practice is very easily confused with what may look like similar practice but is guided by different perspectives. Even as a retrospective activity (the movement, but not the perspective, having been killed off as part of the corporatist agenda), I think it is important to renew early sporadic efforts to draw lines. We give our critics no reason to make what they may see as too fine distinctions if we ourselves fail to make them with clarity and consistency.

Oversimplifying Complex Ideas.   Whole language is certainly complicit in general misunderstandings of ideas important to whole language. In contrast to "the pedagogy" of the writings about critical pedagogies (as Jennifer Gore, 1993, analyzed it), "the pedagogy" of whole language writings is meant to be accessible to a wide audience, to use familiar discourse to explain new ideas rather than to expect an audience to learn a new discourse first. The problem is that complex whole language ideas remain oversimplified and favorite whole language terms underanalyzed.[10]

Terms like *ownership, voice, child centered, teacher centered, invitations, natural,* and so on, are used in whole language writings as descriptors but not as objects of analysis. For example, *take ownership* does not have the meaning of "acquire private property" that Moorman, Blanton, and McLaughlin (1994) claim; in whole language writings it is closer to a meaning that

---

[10]Curt Dudley-Marling (personal communication, November 20, 1995) suggests that, to some extent, whole language writers do not thoroughly and theoretically explore whole language terminology because such explorations would not easily suit the publications that welcome whole language writings, that is, practitioner journals such as *Language Arts* and *The Reading Teacher.* Whole language writers have much more difficulty being published in "scholarly" journals because, in part, as noted above, the "scholarly" community fails to take whole language seriously. (The chicken/egg nature of this situation should be evident.)

combines the ideas of joining or adopting with the notion of student self-empowerment. Another example: The space between *teacher centered* and *child centered* is too often undeveloped territory. Laminack and Lawing (1994) describe how one "child-centered" teacher "directs" activity in the classroom. What kind and how much teacher direction undermines *child-centeredness?* As Featherstone (1995) said about the progressive educators at Central Park East Secondary School, whole language teachers have "important and even necessary things to teach kids" (p. 891). How does that claim fit notions of *child centered?*

Unfortunately, fine-tuning such ideas is often instigated by outside criticism rather than self-scrutiny. For example, Edelsky et al.'s (1991) explanation of *natural* as meaning "entailed by" or "incidental to" but not "inherent" appeared only in response to anthropological criticism that took *natural* to mean inherent and thus universal (cross-cultural variety in reading practices contradicts such a notion). More extended analyses should develop internally, from reflexive self-criticism. If they did, whole language educators might abandon some positions or rename them; certainly such activity would deepen our own understanding of them.

Return of the Silenced Ones. Another aspect of the problematic nature of whole language, according to the left critics, may be our fault, but it cannot be helped. That is, it is not only that "everything is dangerous" or has an underside and that "every theory leaks" or has internal contradictions. It is also that everything cannot be simultaneously highlighted. By foregrounding anything, we automatically background something else. And these "voices from the margins" (Bordo, 1994) come back to haunt us. At a time when reading instruction was consumed with teaching phonics and when language arts instruction was overwhelmingly concerned with handwriting, spelling, and punctuation, whole language de-emphasized decoding and editing skills in favor of interpreting and revising. It was a correct choice according to whole language theory; it was also a correct choice for the time.

So was the choice of de-emphasizing teaching in favor of learning. Learning had been (and continues to be) confused with teaching (Lindfors, 1984), so that what and how teachers teach is equated with what and how students learn. In order to budge basals and other textbooks out of the curricular driver's seat, it was important to separate teaching and learning conceptually and to focus on interesting learnings (such as saying *goed* for *went* and spelling *chair* as TAR). At a time when *a priori* checklists and imposed scope and sequence charts controlled instructional decisions, it was important to argue for the value of observing rather than imposing, that is, for *kid-watching* (Y. Goodman, 1985).

But a price was paid for those theoretical and historical choices: Teachers in some classrooms labeled as whole language abdicated teaching. I am not referring here to nontraditional, whole language teaching of phonics, spelling, punctuation, and so on. Whole language teachers are often accused—unjustly—of neglecting these literacy practices. From early on, whole language educators talked about teaching phonics and other skills as students needed them (K. Goodman & Goodman, 1981). Book-length treatments on phonics (K. Goodman, 1993; Mills, O'Keefe, & Stephens, 1992; Weaver, 1990) and detailed descriptions of how whole language teachers teach spelling and punctuation (Calkins, 1994; Wilde, 1992) as well as detailed descriptions (Calkins, 1994; Crafton, 1991; all issues of *Primary Voices K6*, a journal of the National Council of teachers of English) of how and where whole language teachers directly instruct (e.g., in whole class mini-lessons, in small group and individual conferences, in composing chart stories with a class, in coaching sessions, etc.)—all these show that whole language gives the teaching of skills considerable attention. But because it was not "typical" attention—not the weekly spelling list and weekly spelling test, for instance—it often faded from view.[11] It was not only traditionalist observers who failed to see that whole language did indeed concern itself with "local conventions" (Smith, 1982b). It was also teachers who jumped on the whole language bandwagon without studying whole language. For many of these teachers, the messages about not emphasizing spelling in old ways, for example, were interpreted as "don't teach spelling at all." The messages about kid-watching were heard as "only watch; don't intervene."

As I noted above, these misconceptions were partly prompted by whole language's own choices of what to foreground and background. For example, as I look at a book I cowrote (Edelsky et al., 1991), I find only a few mentions of how whole language teachers teach. In that book (as well as in chap. 7, this volume), my coauthors and I were trying to persuade readers that teaching is not nearly so much "method" as it is perspective or ideology. We wanted readers to understand that the dominant conception of teaching as method promotes a willful blindness to underlying theories, ignoring the fact that methods are always shaped by implicit theoretical beliefs. Since we believed "how-to's" change according to local conditions, it made sense to us to refrain from offering those "how-to's" and instead to provide scenes so readers could envision what we were talking about. We meant to depict the teacher as a thinker-in-action. But by concentrating on the thinking and downplaying the action (in order to offset the dominant focus on action/method), we probably contributed to the misconception that, in general, whole language teachers don't teach and that, in particular, they don't teach skills.

---

[11]Faded not only from view but also, apparently, from memory. Despite Gee's (1994) citations of whole language writings that included considerable discussion of what the teacher does to instruct literacy learners, a decade later Gee (2004b) claims that whole language advocates argue that "no instruction is needed or helpful" as children acquire literacy (p. 10).

Not Making Politics Explicit. Finally, whole language must share responsibility for being critiqued as "apolitical" or even conservative. With rare exceptions (e.g., Edelsky et al., 1991), until recently, whole language educators did not make explicit the connections between their political stance and their theoretical positions. Whole language opposition to standardized testing, for instance, is not just a theoretical stance; it is also a decades-old political position. Performance-based or "authentic" assessments, if used for old purposes of ranking and sorting, would simply be richer, more theoretically defensible but even less assailable means of perpetuating societal inequities. For another example, whole language teachers treat content seriously, not merely as glue to hold school subjects together (e.g., writing about dinosaurs, doing arithmetic problems about dinosaurs, reading about dinosaurs, etc.). But without explicit connections between political projects and theoretical positions on the sources of curriculum there is no principled push for treating content critically.

Until 1990, when an entire strand of the first Whole Language Umbrella Conference was devoted to whole language's political stance, this topic was generally ignored or avoided. But by the mid-1990s, whole language educators became more explicit about the political nature of their work. Increasing numbers of whole language workshops and articles in mid-decade focused on the "interested," gendered, cultured nature of positions that texts offer readers and that those readers take up. More recently, despite the near destruction of whole language at the hands of the corporatists (via "common sense" about literacy education as created by the corporate media paving the way for government policies, in particular NCLB), whole language survivors have made politics explicit. They have written analyses of the business behind testing (Altwerger & Strauss, 2002), the marketing of fear in education (Poynor & Wolfe, 2005), and the corporatist agenda as reflected in reading instruction (Altwerger, 2005c; chap. 7, this volume). And they have pushed whole language—at last—into the sphere of critical teaching (Edelsky, 1999; Edelsky & Cherland, in press; Edelsky & Johnson, 2004; Heffernan & Lewison, 2003; Leland & Harste, 2005; Leland, Harste, Ociepka, Lewison & Vasquez, 1999).

In sum, whole language may well deserve some of the criticism it has received from the left critics, but it never did deserve all of it, and recently, as whole language has evolved, it deserves it even less. In the current context of assaults on education as well as on necessary conditions for education (e.g., access to ideas, tolerance of dissent, freedom to teach and to learn), whole language, though greatly diminished in number and strength, remains committed to education for greater justice and equity. It deserves respect—for its increasingly politically aware classroom work; its activist struggles against high-stakes testing, scripted reading instruction, and commissioned reports on reading; and its openness to criticism, self-criticism, and subsequent change. And it deserves allies.

Chapter **11**

Resisting (Professional) Arrest

Updated material in this chapter appears in a few
footnotes and in the Postscript.

Teaching is a profession, and teachers are professionals—or so we are told.
A variety of practices, however, puts teachers' status as professionals in
question. Standardization of curriculum and of criteria for assessing teachers as well as children, school policies that turn teachers into clerks,
teacher preparation programs being reorganized to provide training in the
narrowest sense rather than education—the moves to deprofessionalize
abound. Nevertheless, there are some small but brilliant (not merely
bright) lights in the darkness. Scattered around the North American con-
tinent are clusters of teachers who are part of what I call a *grassroots teachers' movement,* teachers actively resisting deprofessionalizing forces, teachers
who are acting with determination to make a reality of the rhetoric about
being professional. Before describing a bit of this activity, I want to elaborate on the context in which it is occurring.[1]

---

[1]The first version of this chapter was written in the late 1980s. Someone who had looked
into a crystal ball could well have said about my description of the context, "You ain't seen
nuthin' yet." "Nuthin'" in terms of damage from an intensifying neo-liberalism worldwide;
"nuthin'" in terms of damage from the related corporatist agenda on education. Instead of
toasting its future, someone with my proclivity for angst should have predicted that the glow-
ing energy from the grassroots teachers' movement highlighted in this chapter would be
dimmed (the adjective *dimmed* rather than the verb *dim* is a deliberate choice since the dim-
ming was imposed). That dark prediction would have been correct—but not completely, as I
note in the Postscript.

In important ways, these are terrible times (despite recent astounding events in Eastern Europe[2]). Global economic, political, and social problems seem to be worsening (ecological destruction made even more visible to the West now that the Iron Curtain is down; whopping trade deficits for some nations; increasing monetary crises; increased proliferation of nuclear arms, unemployment, homelessness, drug traffic—the list is long). In recent history, education has been a convenient scapegoat during uncontained crises. The current time is no exception. (After all, if the United States imports more Toyotas than it exports Chevrolets, it *must* be the kindergarten teacher's fault, right?!) Anxious for quick, politically acceptable analyses of, and solutions to, horrendous (and horrendously intertwined) problems, federal and state governments identify education as the arena for attention.[3] Governments appoint commissions that write reports that influence courts, legislatures, and state and local education agencies to take more control over what happens in schools. Most of this pressure for change and increased control is aimed at teachers (their skill, their training) and teachers' domains (curriculum, assessment). Few recent criticisms of education, for example, have critically spotlighted decisions by state agencies. No commissioned reports have faulted the ties between corporate sales practices and schools' reliance on textbooks and packaged curricula. None have complained about the role of the media in misinformation about tests and test scores. Neither the cause of the previously mentioned problems of war, poverty, and environmental destruction nor the means for reversing them reside in classroom practices. But no matter— problems are redefined simplistically, and the finger is pointed at schools.

Connecting trade deficits with kindergarten teachers could be a matter of deliberate obfuscation—an attempt to keep hidden the ways in which financial finaglings (junk bonds, leveraged buyouts) and corporate decisions impinge on both national and personal life. On the other hand, the purported connection between international drug cartels and homework could be less willful—"merely" another instance of a dominant ideology at work (one that excludes any consideration of business interests and profit motives from an analysis of problems, one that defines the interests of business as "national" but the interests of women and minorities as "special"). Deliberate or not, the most charitable explanation for linking international problems with educational solutions is that people feel impotent in the face of overwhelming problems. In what has the psychoanalytic look if not the psychodynamic origin of classic displacement, they substitute what is

---

[2]Among the hopeful events one might note in 2005 would be increasing numbers of protests against neoliberal institutions and somewhat more pro-people governments in parts of South America.

[3]It is now clear (in 2005) that the focus on education is not the distraction I read it as in 1987 but a deliberate part of a neoliberal agenda.

amenable to relatively immediate blame or control for what is not. And among all public domains, it is education that is eminently controllable.

Michael Apple's (1983) analysis of efforts to control education through controlling teachers is helpful here. According to Apple, educational "reforms" of the 1970s and early 1980s amount to deprofessionalizing—decreasing teachers' autonomy through the deskilling, reskilling, and proletarianization of teaching. *Deskilling* is a process in which occupational skills are redefined so that former skills entailing judgment and intuition and a sense of start-to-finish control over large work spheres become atomized, then behaviorally described, then appropriated by management. The purpose is to cut costs and increase efficiency as well as enhance management's ability to assess the execution of the now-atomized skills. The older, more global skills atrophy since they are no longer needed. *Reskilling* refers to substituting mechanical, clerical, and management skills for the older, more global skills. Along with reskilling comes intellectual deskilling (e.g., relying on experts to create curricular and teaching goals) and intensification (e.g., increased demand for routine work, such as grading more and more pre- and posttests and worksheets, managing "systems" of objectives and packaged lessons, and organizing and reorganizing multiple subgroups of students according to frequent mastery test results). Intensification frequently leads to "burnout." *Proletarianization is* a process of declining autonomy in an occupation. Decreased autonomy separates conception (e.g., development of instructional goals) from execution (e.g., instruction). As Apple notes, when such a process is underway in education, teachers' efficiency as managers increases while their control over curriculum decreases.

The irony is that such processes are now being called *increased professionalism.* Although deliberate misrepresentation might be at work here, it is also the case that confusing decreased autonomy with professionalism actually has some basis in teachers' day-to-day experience. *Professional* includes the meaning of increased responsibility. With deskilling, reskilling, and intensification, teachers indeed have increased clerical responsibilities. In an extensive qualitative study, teachers felt so beleaguered by increased demands for testing and then organizing their lessons on the basis of the test results that their major goal had become "getting done." Nevertheless, they thought the longer hours spent on such clerical and managerial tasks were evidence of their increased professionalism (Gitlin, 1980, cited in Apple, 1983). But enhanced professionalism is not an increase in just any responsibility. The question that has to be asked is: Increased responsibility for what? (Erickson, 1986, criticized the time-on-task mystique with the same question. That is, from an anthropological perspective, everybody is on task 100% of the time. The question is: What's the task?)

The error in equating deskilling with increased professionalism gets support from the multiple, possibly contradictory meanings of the words *profession* and *professional. Profession* (from Latin *pro* [forward/before] + *fateri* [to confess/to own]) variously means a declaration; a vocation; an occupation that is not commercial, mechanical or agricultural; a calling (*Webster's New Collegiate Dictionary*, in fact, gives the example of "the calling of teaching," which it distinguishes from "the Learned Professions" of theology, law, and medicine). The *Oxford English Dictionary* adds that a profession is more than a noncommercial, nonagricultural, nonmechanical occupation; it is also one that has as a major activity the giving of advice or service (implying that a member of the profession professes). *Professional* not only means acting in accord with the norms and ethics of a profession. It also connotes being efficient, prompt, methodical and businesslike on the one hand; remunerated (doing for pay what amateurs do for noncommercial satisfaction) on the other; and, on yet another, having an insider's expertise (vs. being a layperson). Thus, while teachers' experience of deskilling/reskilling/intensification is not related to the meaning of having autonomy over a large sphere of activity, it is certainly related to being methodical and efficient—another meaning of *professional.*

I have left an important factor out of this discussion of the definition of a professional—and so have the dictionaries. That factor is gender. In thinking of the meaning of *professional,* and in discussing how deprofessionalization is now being called *increased professionalism,* it is critical to consider that teaching has its ranks composed mostly of women. And that teaching—and women—are subject to frequent and successful attempts at external control. It is not coincidental, then, that the professional status of teachers—who are mostly women—is ambiguous. Apple (1983) cites Hearn (1982), who notes that full (i.e., unambiguous) professional status is granted only to activities dominated by men—in both management and the ranks.

So far, the context presented for the current grassroots teachers' movement includes: severe, widespread noneducational problems; attempts at partial solutions to noneducational problems through "improving" education; efforts to improve education by controlling teachers (who are mostly women); control of teaching that entails proletarianization; "selling" proletarianization as enhanced professionalism—that sale made easier by the existence of contradictory meanings for *professional.* In such a context, teachers' professional activities that run counter to proletarianization are acts of real resistance.

PROFESSIONAL RESISTANCE

One of the most optimistic and optimism-generating examples of professional resistance is a networked (rather than an organized) grassroots teachers' movement. Teachers in this movement know full well the oppositional nature of their activity; that is, they are not unwitting resisters. They know they are reclaiming control over their teaching and, depending on the particular grassroots group, control over more or less of what goes with teaching (e.g., curricular decisions, assessment, choice of materials, placement of students, and the right to hire their own administrators as well as their new colleagues). They know they are joining with others so they can learn even more about their own professional field (teaching and learning) and its key topics, especially language in education and knowledge as a social construction. Many in this movement focus more on their growth in understanding theoretically informed practice and less on the struggles that come when teachers confident in their own professional knowledge confront theoretically flawed and deprofessionalizing bureaucratic and legislative policies. Still, even those with this professional-growth-oriented focus on theory know that such a focus constitutes a profound opposition to institutional definitions of the "professional" teacher as efficient clerk. If few teachers in this movement make any grand political analyses of *why* it is not they who are responsible for trade deficits, acid rain, and the like, they are nevertheless aware that they are refusing to take the blame for these horrors. Thus, while teachers in these grassroots groups may not see themselves as "political," their activity contradicts and resists prevailing currents.

Befitting its local, on-the-ground character, grassroots teacher groups are many and scattered. They can be found across North America, in small, isolated school districts; in rural regions cutting across district and even state boundaries; and in huge unified districts in large industrial cities. They are composed of teachers with a particular perspective who have come together on their own initiative, to work together to improve education in their own communities. Some of the sites of such activity are: New York City; Philadelphia; Grand Forks, ND; Prospect, VT; Bloomington, IN; Tucson, AZ; Columbia, MO; Winnipeg (Manitoba), Montreal (Quebec), London (Ontario), and Edmonton (Alberta) in Canada; Redwood City, CA; Chicago; Fresno, CA; Calexico, CA; Phoenix, AZ; Detroit, MI; Albuquerque, NM; Norman, OK; Boone, NC; and Boothbay Harbor, ME.

Some of the groups have names; some do not. Most are autonomous, although teachers in a grassroots group in one city often have connections with people in similar groups elsewhere. What are these grassroots groups like? They meet regularly—once a week for some, monthly for others. Meetings may include discussion of a prearranged topic or article, or they may consist of participation in some theoretically grounded process such as "reflective conversations" or "staff review of a child" (see Carini, 1982, for a description of these processes). Meeting time may also be devoted to planning strategies (to help individual teachers or children, to try to change district policies) and to working on organizational activities. Organizational activities include such things as writing articles and books, selling books, publishing newsletters, offering workshops, and lobbying for changes in state laws.

The content of all of this activity incorporates particular assumptions about learning (e.g., people actively construct what they know; culture is both the goal of learning, the prerequisite for, and the medium through which all learning occurs; whole activities—reading a book for escape, writing an apology to a friend—are greater than the sum of their parts; meaning and interpretation are central in all knowing). These assumptions directly challenge prevailing ideas that construct learners as passive recipients of ready-made knowledge, that decompose activities (including teaching) into "manageable" subskills and that use proficiency with those subskills as a basis for sorting and ranking people.

A prime example of a group within this grassroots movement is s.m.i.l.e. (Support and Maintenance for Implementing Language Expression) in metropolitan Phoenix, Arizona. It has a newly created nonprofit corporate relative, the Center for Establishing Dialogue in Teaching and Learning, Inc. (CED).[4] Both groups are based on the following premises:

- State and district policies often impede rather than enhance learning and language development;
- Teachers already know more (and can learn even more) about language development and learning than do many who impose programs for teachers to follow; and
- Teachers can function as teachers for each other.

Since 1979, s.m.i.l.e. has offered semiannual workshops on Saturday mornings, attended now by 600–800 teachers, administrators, and parents. After a keynote address by a noted educational leader (past keynoters have included David Booth, Lucy Calkins, Ken Goodman, Yetta Goodman, Donald Graves, Jerry Harste, Frank Smith, and Dorothy Watson), 30 or more teachers present individual hour-long workshops to share ways they have been working with holistic teaching in their classrooms (Christine, 1987). In 1982 at its workshops, s.m.i.l.e. began to sell books congruent with s.m.i.l.e. teachers' views on language and learning. The aim was to make it easier for teachers not close to a university bookstore to obtain texts such as Aronowitz and Giroux's (1985) *Education Under Siege;* Calkins's (1986, 1994) *The Art of Teaching Writing;* Goodman's (1986) *What's Whole in Whole Language?;* Harste, Woodward, and Burke's (1984) *Language Stories and Literacy Lessons;* Rosen's (1988) *And None of it Was Nonsense;* Shannon's

---

[4]The description of s.m.i.l.e. and CED, in particular, as well as many of the other groups in this movement now must be read in the past tense, as is noted in the Postscript. S.m.i.l.e. no longer exists; neither do its Arizona spin-offs (WOW, WILD, and the others). CED's activities and presence is now sharply diminished, as is discussed in the Postscript.

(1989) *Broken Promises;* Shor's and Freire's (1987) *A Pedagogy for Liberation;* F. Smith's (1986) *Insult to Intelligence;* and over 50 other titles. The hope was that such texts might help loosen the hold of opposing ideas prevalent in education. Additionally, members of s.m.i.l.e. have worked together as adjunct faculty, teaching a course on whole language at Arizona State University.

Four other groups in Arizona have modeled themselves after s.m.i.l.e., starting out with discussion/learning sessions for a small group which then organizes workshops for others in its own locality. These are WOW (Way Out West); WILD (Whole Integrated Language Development); GRIN (Greater Reservation Interdisciplinary Network), on the Navajo reservation; and RIMTALK, located on the Mogollon Rim of the Grand Canyon. Two other groups of Arizona teachers have different primary activities but share s.m.i.l.e.'s general stance on language, learning, and teachers controlling their own professional lives. These are Tucson Teachers Applying Whole Language (TAWL) and Glendale SHARE (a group of holistic bilingual educators).

In 1985, Carol Christine, one of the teacher–founders of s.m.i.l.e., taught herself enough about written legal discourse to write two important documents on behalf of the founding of a new Center: (1) articles of incorporation and (2) a legal application for nonprofit status. The State of Arizona approved these in 1986. The new nonprofit corporate Center (CED) was initiated not only to relieve s.m.i.l.e. of the bookkeeping tasks involved in book sales but for two other more pressing reasons. First, it would create an entity more capable of responding to an increasing number of requests for in-service sessions in between the two yearly s.m.i.l.e. workshops. Second, it would divide at least some of s.m.i.l.e.'s former work along "educational" and "political" lines. Nonprofit status would prohibit CED from engaging in "political" activity such as lobbying for changes in state laws and campaigning for candidates; but that work could now be done by s.m.i.l.e., since its load was lightened by having CED take over the professional development activity.

As might be expected, CED in-service differs from the usual top-down variety imposed by central administrators. The latter, compulsory and aimed at the presumed needs of a wide audience, rarely makes its theoretical positions salient. Instead, it usually concentrates on new ideas for subject matter activities, tips for controlling groups of children, or "instruction" that often amounts to no more than managing the movement of children through preplanned curricular packages. By contrast, attendance at CED in-service is voluntary; it is teacher requested and offered to meet specific teachers' needs. In fact, CED-sponsored in-services are often conducted by local teachers who are known in the community for particular expertise. They are attended primarily by teachers but also by parents and administrators (the latter have increased their participation significantly in the past two years). People who attend CED workshops frequently know the workshop-giver, and they are certainly aware of the theoretical position on language and learning taken by the Center. In electing to attend, they seek out practice associated with that theoretical position. Instead of walking away with new activities or theory-blind "tips," they are likely to walk away with new ways of thinking.

While each grassroots teachers' group is somehow unique (few sell books, many offer in-services, some work only on local school problems, a few restrict themselves only to conducting child-study sessions, etc.), they share certain characteristics. First, members of these groups see teaching as a career rather than a job; *teacher* is a major part of their identity. They are people who want control over who they become within their profession and how they will act as professionals. They are determined that they will not be defined by publishers' marketing notions or by bureaucrats' mandates.

Second, as one would expect, given the makeup of the teaching ranks, most members are women. But given teachers' generally moderate voting patterns, few are likely to identify themselves as *feminists*. Still, these women have created groups that embody principles remarkably like those proposed as feminist organizing principles (Stanley &Wise, 1983). For example, the groups are relatively small and nonhierarchical. Although responsibilities are frequently divided among members, there is shared control over topics to be dealt with, activities to be pursued, and ways to operate. TAWL groups are loosely organized (no dues, no officers) into a national group that holds a meeting in conjunction with the annual meetings of the National Council of Teachers of English and the International Reading Association; and a new international organization (Whole Language Umbrella)[5] connects TAWL groups with some of the others. With these exceptions, the various grassroots teachers' groups are organizationally independent of each other. Decentralized and shaped according to local visions, the "movement," then, is both organizationally feminist and also postmodernist in spirit. There are at least two other feminist organizational principles these groups share. In each, the individual teacher's experience and voice is heard as valid, and personal teaching experience is treated as part of a larger picture—often a political one.

Another important feature the groups have in common is that they are consciously theoretical. They take an explicit position on the nature of learning (seeing it as holistic and as occurring primarily through productive activity rather than through exercises). They knowingly work from particular theoreticians' views (e.g., Carini, Dewey, Freire, Goodman, Vygotsky). Indeed,

---

[5]Whole Language Umbrella is now (2005) a part of the National Council of Teachers of English.

the primary aim of working with one of these grassroots groups relates to the fact that they are consciously theoretical. They aim for praxis—bringing theory and action together and improving education by resisting policies, programs, and materials that contradict holistic principles and that restrict teachers' autonomy. A by-product of this work is the teachers' own professional growth. In other words, by acting as the professionals they already are, teachers grow as professionals.

As mentioned at the outset, the activities of these groups constitute acts of resistance, in Aronowitz and Giroux's (1985) terms. That is, the activities incorporate a *language of possibility* (they propose and show what *can* be), they are *intellectual* (they depend on a critical, creative questioning of authority while holding to principles), and they have the *potential* for changing oppressive structures through opening up opportunities for analyzing what is often hidden.

What is especially noteworthy, however, is that not only are these acts of resistance; they are acts of detailed *curricular resistance*. They certainly do not constitute romanticized rebellion—some grand, if futile, gesture. These teachers are engaged in a principled struggle over what they will teach as well as how they will teach it—and they are in it for the long haul. As they work, their theory becomes more solid, their strategies shift, their influence grows. Side by side with the deskilling that is now going by the name of *increased professionalism* is this professionalism that asks the right questions: Responsibility for what? Expert at what? Education for what? It is The Resistance. Its primary purpose is not to increase professionalism (which is a by-product) but to change educational contexts through praxis. To repeat: A brilliant light. May it shine ever brighter.

POSTSCRIPT 2005

Alas, as is clear to any observer of the educational scene, that "brilliant light" has become almost invisible. Almost, but not totally. With accelerating corporatist victories that put more and more of what goes on in classrooms under the control of politicians and corporate publishers, resistance and resistors have been forced to retreat. Unwittingly, CED bumped into the corporatist agenda on corporate turf—the market. Teacher-led CED's idea (actually originated by s.m.i.l.e. in the late 1970s) had been to sponsor workshops with well-known consultants on topics teachers requested for their own professional learning. Once private corporations appropriated that idea from CED (and s.m.i.l.e.), not for the ultimate benefit of teachers but for their own profit, they priced CED out of the market. That is, corporate entrance into "professional development from a teacher's perspective" (a niche market originated by the grassroots teachers' movement), with corporate pricing capabilities, underpriced CED. When CED had to price its workshops competitively with corporate workshops, it could not earn enough to cover the costs of space and staff. Thus, while CED remains a legal entity, and while it still offers an annual summer professional development workshop on Carini's processes (Himley, 2000) for small numbers of teachers who already know the CED perspective, CED had to close its physical location that served as a bookstore and meeting place. It no longer offers workshops on a broad scale or sells professional books to teachers. It no longer serves as a friendly, personal way to link people together (e.g., a teacher new to a district who wants to find another like-minded teacher in her own district, a student teacher who wants to find a holistic teacher to observe, a bilingual teacher looking for another bilingual teacher as an online teammate, etc.).

If CED retreated under market pressure, other independent resisters were driven away by corporatist-inspired pressures on daily life in classrooms. Oppressive legislative mandates and a government-sponsored phonics-based view of reading (presumably supported by "scientific research") not only sapped teachers' energy for learning more about providing the richest classroom contexts for literacy but also caused districts to withdraw their prior support for teachers to direct their own learning about students' literacy. Frightened for their own survival (under the terms of No Child Left Behind), and with shaky histories to begin with when it came to trusting teachers, districts brought in scripted reading instruction programs that made no pretense about who was in control: It was not teachers.

It is no wonder, therefore, that teachers' enthusiasm waned for seeking out colleagues with whom to study questions about young children's literacy. After all, the federal government had already handed down the answers—in government-commissioned reports such as the National Reading Panel Report that, in turn, buttressed legislation such as NCLB that was, subsequently, promoted by paid-off media commentators (as reported by Toppo, 2005). Rather, the wonder is that some teachers (though certainly fewer than before) continue to find others who also refuse to be completely taken over by mandates, and, together, try to keep their professional development in their own hands.[6]

Those teachers currently involved in such professional development work seem to have a history of participation in one of several activities: s.m.i.l.e. workshops, TAWL, Pat Carini's descriptive review processes (Carini, 1982; Himley with Carini, 2000), or the Rethinking Schools Collective in Milwaukee, Wisconsin, and Portland, Oregon. Some combination of two

---

[6]The discussion of current grassroots teacher group activity is based on my own professional connections over the years as well as interviews and e-mail exchanges that took place in 2005 with 15 teachers from Arizona, California, Georgia, Indiana, New York, and Pennsylvania.

main emphases is visible in their work: a holistic view of literacy and conscious political analyses. While some groups are certainly troubled by the mandates of the last decade and may even have originated because of them, the mandates themselves remain marginal to the group's focus on students' learning and classroom practice. Other groups lean toward a holistically oriented focus on literacy and learning but have been developing greater political awareness and engaging in some explicitly political activity. Still others foreground their political analyses of education and its contexts as well as their goals for social and economic justice in their study of learning, teaching, and curriculum.

Teachers in these groups have a deep interest in the topic of learning and a serious commitment to keeping "the real thing" alive—whether it is "real teaching" or "real equity" or "real change." It is as though they see themselves as protectors of "what teaching *ought* to be about" or as providers of "what is *really* needed to give kids a quality education." Thus, when some of the teachers talk of their professional study groups as "a reprieve from NCLB" and a place to "forget the pressures" from the mandates, it is as though these groups constitute, not a space free of NCLB, but a space of "post-NCLB" (except that, unfortunately, NCLB is not [yet] a thing of the past). In the same sense that postmodernism and poststructuralism respond, respectively, to modernism and structuralism, grassroots teacher groups are "post-NCLB" in that NCLB saturates the ground of their activity. It is in these groups that members focus on "why we are *really* here" (as contrasted with ensuring that their school makes Adequate Yearly Progress by making certain "eleven kids get four more questions right" on the test). Or on "what kids are *really* doing with print" (as contrasted with coaching students to do exercises with print). Or on "what *real* education equity means and how to struggle for it." It is against the backdrop of these contrasts—all implicating NCLB—that the groups currently do their work.

As they did in the 1980s, current grassroots teacher groups provide an antidote to the isolation of atypical (holistic or critical or critical–holistic) teaching. Even though teachers in these groups have considerable confidence in their beliefs about their focus of study (learning, teaching, literacy, antiracist curricula, etc.), they benefit from interactions with like-minded colleagues. Validation and support help even the strongest feel—and be—stronger (e.g., developing arguments to convince an administrator to turn down federal Reading First dollars). Peers with similar beliefs are optimal sources of suggestions, advice, and criticism. And with such colleagues, teachers can intensify the power of their efforts through collective action.

It is in these groups that teachers have their most satisfying professional conversations—where they can "talk *to* colleagues rather than being talked *at*," conversations that differ from talk in the teachers' lounge (grassroots group talk is more focused, demanding, sustained, more likely to cause rethinking rather than retrenching). These conversations are also different from talk in nonvoluntary school district groups with assigned member-ships, where a teacher often has to "tiptoe around certain ideas in order not to offend" when beliefs about literacy, learning, and political perspectives are not shared. Grassroots teacher activity is also a site for identity work—for formulating professional selves, with others acting as coformulators and as mirrors—articulating stances and interests and defining who and how one is as a teacher.

In chapter 12, there is a call for an Education Rights Movement requiring a variety of kinds of resistance, including grassroots teacher groups that, in their very existence, turn their backs on the corporate agenda to control teachers and teaching. Contrary to what I said with hope and naiveté at the end of the original version of this chapter, these groups do not constitute The Resistance. But they are indeed one part of it. My hope is that these groups come to understand more acutely how their resistance fits within a larger movement for educational rights.

Sorely Tested

Standardized tests have been around for more than 150 years.[1] Almost from the start, they have been linked with reform. Reform of civil service employment—after President Garfield was assassinated by a disappointed office seeker, Congress passed legislation to require test scores rather than political patronage for deciding who would get federal jobs (Haney, 1984). Reform in immigration policies—standardized test scores of Army recruits in World War I (showing the "superior intelligence" of native-born recruits as compared with the "inferior intelligence" of immigrants whose birth-places were far from northern and western Europe) were used to justify new polices to limit immigration by "mentally inferior races" (Sacks, 1999). Reform in education—in the 1890s, pediatrician-turned-educational-reformer Joseph Rice called for more objective ways to assess schools rather than relying on reports by school personnel. For nearly 100 years, testing has been seen as having commercial value (World Book Company and Houghton-Mifflin entered the testing field in 1914 and 1916, respectively, with the publication of a standardized test of arithmetic and two intelligence scales; Haney, 1984). For almost a century, standardized tests have also been criticized. And for longer than that, the federal government has played a role in generating public interest in mental tests as well as in the proliferation of testing. Thus, it may well seem as though the general story about testing—as solution, problem, profit source, and policy—has been fairly stable.

In actuality, the story changes over time. The claims and counterclaims, the critics, the critiques, the urgency of the problems, the solutions, the role of corporations, the role of government, the nature of policy, and the uses of tests have all changed in concert with each other and with other historical phenomena. This chapter concerns the part of the story that focuses on critiques of testing but, as I will show, that story brings in the

---

[1]A few passages in this chapter appeared first in chapter 9 of the first and second editions of this volume.

rest. I have divided the critique-of-testing story into three periods based on the kind of critical response to standardized testing that illuminates the historical character of the social/political/educational scene. Thus, there is the period of proprietary or professional fixes, the period of pedagogical concerns, and the period of organized resistance. This division is not a clean one. During the period marked by proprietary fixes, there were criticisms centered on instructional and curricular values, that is, on pedagogical concerns. Likewise, proposals for authentic assessment (an example of what I am calling a *pedagogical concern*) appear in the current period when significant critiques are more overtly political and responses increasingly include organized resistance. Nevertheless, different themes in critiques of testing become clearly visible, if not predominant, in these three periods.

THE PERIOD OF PROPRIETARY OR PROFESSIONAL FIXES

Context and Fixes

A famous critique by journalist Walter Lippmann on the dangers of IQ tests appeared in *The New Republic* in 1922 (Sacks, 1999), indicting hereditarian thinking. Other than criticism around this issue (joined by some psychologists and cultural critics), however, much of the criticism of tests prior to the late 1950s came from testing professionals themselves. As Haney (1984) discussed, the professionals had witnessed and benefited from the development of: empirical item selection (by Binet); the conversion of test performance into an age level (extended later to a grade level) for the Binet scale; statistical techniques of reliability (by Spearman), correlation (by Galton and by Pearson) and factor analysis (by Spearman); the multiple-choice exam (for the first Scholastic Aptitude Test [SAT]); and optical scoring equipment enabling large-scale testing programs. But they had also seen egregious misuse of tests, such as the publication in local newspapers of the names and IQ test scores of individual students. Thus, in 1953, the American Psychological Association developed professional testing standards (*Ethical Standards of Psychology* [Hobbs et al., 1953]). A year later, the APA issued *Technical Recommendations for Psychological Tests and Diagnostic Techniques.* The *Ethical Standards* were aimed at preventing nonprofessionals from giving and interpreting tests; the *Technical Recommendations* were intended to ensure that professionals could evaluate and use the tests properly. Thus, in this period, it was not so much the tests that were criticized as it was who was using them (laymen and outsiders) and the way they were used and interpreted.

This period of "proprietary or professional fixes" was marked by a huge increase in demands for testing (the government's decision to test all Army recruits in World War I, the influx of immigrants into schools—with testing holding the promise of helping with grouping [i.e., tracking] these students for instruction and for vocational guidance). There was widespread public interest piqued by publicity surrounding the Army's testing program accompanied, not surprisingly, by a proliferation of tests prompted by a growing gullible market for even a "poorly constructed test of unknown validity. . [promising] to do all sorts of things which no test can do" (Buros, 1961, pp. xxiii–xxiv, cited by Haney, 1984, p. 618). Countering this sudden popularity was the skepticism in scientific circles about testing in particular, and also about the entire (and relatively new) field of psychology. It had not been so long, after all, that Science itself had wrestled Religion for the role of ultimate Authority—and won. The recency of that victory meant that Science had to protect itself—could not admit just anyone to its ranks nor permit just anyone to have a say about its dramatically modern new tool. It is understandable, then, that criticisms of testing and responses to criticisms during that period would be tangled up with protecting the legitimacy of testing's claims to being "scientific."

The Period of Pedagogical Concerns.   Although there had been rumblings in the 1920s and 1930s about testing's fatal flaws (not merely that tests were misused but that they were misconceived), significant criticism of tests in the first half of the 20th century emanated from testing professionals and concerned the uses of tests. That situation changed beginning in the late 1950s. Critics of testing from mid-century until the 1990s tended not to be testing professionals; their criticism concerned the tests themselves (in particular, their pedagogical consequences), and they argued instead for alternative modes of assessment.

The period of "pedagogical concerns" began with the launching of Sputnik in 1957 and the ensuing frenzy in the United States to catch up with and surpass the USSR in space. The response to this crisis of the Soviets "getting there first" involved policymaking as political spectacle (M. L. Smith, 2004)—theatrics (backstage activity by power elites, onstage symbolism, and storylines) aimed at reassuring the audience (the public) that something was being done on the audience's behalf (see chap. 3 for a description of policy-as-political-spectacle regarding bilingual education and chap. 7 for an instance applied to reading instruction). The major post-Sputnik policy "spectaculars" involved "improving" math and science education by mandating increased testing.

This period also saw student political activism around the world questioning established societal structures and demanding justice on various fronts. Oppressed minorities in the United States (Blacks, Latinos, women, gays and lesbians, physically handicapped, poor people) and their more privileged allies took to the streets, demanding equity. Their activism was matched at first by hundreds and then by millions (Zinn, 2004) demonstrating in the streets against the U.S. war in Vietnam. This activism, with these demands, was the backdrop for War on Poverty legislation, Voting Rights legislation, and policies legitimizing bilingual education and equity for women in education. In education, this spirit was reflected in questioning traditional curriculum, opening the literary canon, putting student interests at the center of curriculum, and offering a decade of Open Classrooms. These shifts also prodded the U.S. Congress to create Title I as part of the Elementary and Secondary Education Act of 1965, providing funds for special educational assistance for children from low-income households. Title I came with strings—a requirement that local education agencies measure educational achievement annually and "objectively." In 1974, for the sake of greater uniformity in reporting, Title I was amended to encourage local education agencies to use, as an "objective" measure, norm-referenced tests with scores based on normal curve equivalents (Haney, 1984).

The Elementary and Secondary Education Act of 1965, Title I, and its amendments helped create one of many out-of-sync historical moments. Just as the federal government was establishing rules of the game in program evaluation and federally funded research that required standardized testing (with its roots in positivist, quantitative research), the direction of educational research in general and literacy research in particular took a qualitative turn. Ken Goodman's (1969) theory of reading as an imprecise language processing activity (rather than a behaviorist product), with a focus on the active process of comprehending (not on the completed "fact" of comprehension; Dombey, 2004), figured in this contradiction and also in another that developed in the 1980s. Using Goodman's insights and research on readers' miscues, a practitioner movement (whole language) developed that reached its zenith in the late 1980s. Thus, on the one hand, increasing numbers of knowledgeable teachers were courageously taking professional control of their classrooms But, on the other, the federal government began sponsoring "a decade of Reports" that would undermine such professional activity. Reports such as *A Nation at Risk* (National Commission on Excellence in Education, 1983) and *Becoming a Nation of Readers* (Anderson et al., 1985) provided reasons to worry about the quality of education and to call, once again, for reform-by-testing. The consequence was that control over education was taken away from teachers and put in the hands of bureaucrats, policy makers, and importantly, test publishers.[2]

The Criticism

While certain tests had long been accompanied by high stakes for individuals (e.g., college admission tests), and while some tests had begun to have consequences for programs (e.g., scores had to be submitted for renewing

---

[2]By 1990, 100 million standardized tests were given annually—a rate of 2 to 4 per year for every child in the United States (FairTest, 1990).

funding of local Title I programs), federal mandates for testing had not yet become a stranglehold. Thus, "high stakes" were not often the focus of critiques during this period of pedagogical concerns. Instead, what was at issue was how tests impinged on what was salient in the larger context—equity; conceptions of thinking, learning, and teaching; and views about curriculum, reading, and knowledge. Often included in these critiques were alternative proposals for curriculum and for assessment.

Test Items. In this period, test items were critiqued for bias, triviality, and for the kind of thinking they promote. Researchers found cultural (Deyle, 1986), racial (Meier, 1981; Nairn & Nader, 1980; Owen, 1985), gender (R. Adams, 1985; Hale & Potok, 1981; Tittle, 1973), social class (Owen, 1985), and curricular (Webster, McInnis, & Crover, 1986) biases. Because external validity of a new test is established by correlating it with older tests, the biases built into past tests are passed on to more recent tests (Gould, 1981). Biased or not, test items were seen as reflecting trivial content since they are chosen for how well they discriminate among test-takers, not for the importance of the knowledge or skill demanded by the item (Haney, 1984). The favored format, multiple choice, was criticized for penalizing depth and critical acumen (Hoffman, 1962) and for confounding product and process (eliciting wrong answers for the right reasons and vice versa; Meier, 1981).

Claims About General Ability. Critics during this period argued that standardized tests and test-users make false claims—both implicitly and explicitly. Regardless of disclaimers in the fine print, tests are treated at least some of the time, by professionals and nonprofessionals alike, as tests of ability. Ralph Nader and his colleagues (Nairn & Nader, 1980) discredited this claim. If, as Nairn and Nader (1980) documented, SAT scores can be changed through coaching—a surprise to many in the more innocent 1970s–1980s before the huge growth of the commercial test coaching industry—then clearly the Educational Testing Service's assertions that the SAT tests aptitude (and the public's erroneous view of the SAT as a test of raw ability) are wrong. The problem with the SAT being coachable derives from the problem of what a test is supposed to be a test of.

A test of reading, for example, implicitly claims to be about a general ability to read. but, actually, a reading test can only be about reading the particular items on that particular test. Some items test similarities in dialect between the test writer and test-taker—in vocabulary (e.g., an item asking young children to consider *teeter-totters* is foreign to children in some areas who play on *see-saws*) or pronunciation (e.g., a phonics item asking children to mark the word with the same vowel sound as in *for* and offering choices of *wart, drop, roll,* and *farther,* does not account for the fact that in parts of Texas and New Mexico, *for* is pronounced as /far/). Others test factual information (e.g., "The frequency of a sound determines its (a) treble, (b) pitch, (c) volume, or (d) harmony"). Moreover, many items on reading tests test reading test strategies. The key overall strategy, of course, is to be able to think like a test writer (Cook & Meier, n.d.; Edelsky & Harman, 1988), a feat more easily accomplished if one is of the same social class, the same ethnic and cultural group, and the same gender as the test writer. James Gee's (1992a) students, for instance, could choose the correct answers on a reading test without ever reading the passages because, belonging to the same general social class as the test writers, they could tap into the "right" values, worldviews, normative expectations, and language behaviors.[3]

Claims About the Standardness of Situations.   Standardized tests explicitly claim to provide all test-takers with the same testing situation (directions, time allotment, tasks, test materials). But situations are not so trivial; they consist not only of what is outside the head, but also *how what is outside is interpreted.* The color of test booklets affects how people respond to and interpret the testing situation (Orasanu, McDermott, Boykin, & the Laboratory for Comparative Human Cognition, 1977). So do changes in meteorological climate, let alone emotional climate. Humans, that is, inter-pret constantly (see Mehan & Wood, 1975, for a discussion of the role of interpretation in human activity). Since no two people interpret identi-cally, there is no such thing as a standard situation. Young children in par-ticularly have decidedly nonstandard interpretations of how to take a test (e.g., 6-year-old Jesse picks answers for the appeal of the picture; 8-year-old Nicky thinks it is cheating to look back at the passage, so he covers it up). What the critics showed was that the entire testing situation—from inter-pretation of item content to "proper" attitudes toward answering—can never be standardized.

Claims About Scores.   The numerical nature of standardized test scores, along with the statistical procedures applied to scores on norm-referenced tests, combine to create the impression that scores have scientific precision and objectivity. But that aura masks some interesting instabilities and imprecision. For one thing, test scores do not mean the same thing across time. People taking a 1940 edition of a test in 1970 did much better on that test than people who took it in the 1940s (Harste, n.d., citing work by Roger Farr and Leo Fay). Reading achievement test scores tend to improve

---

[3]The major reason that using "quick intuition" when guessing test answers works for middle-class mainstream students but not for poor and minority students is that the class- and culturally based worldviews, values, normative expectations, and language behaviors of the latter will lead them astray (Meier, 1981).

not because of any increase in the ability tested but because curricular materials are geared to the tests. Over the years, hard items (more people get them wrong) become easier (more people get them right as they learn from materials geared to the tests). Until recently, most standardized tests were norm referenced. In the norming process, scores are converted statistically so that they fall into a bell-shaped curve. Therefore, in newer editions of a test, either items must be made more difficult so the average test-taker gets the same number right, or the norms must be changed so that it takes more right answers to attain the same converted score (e.g., grade-level equivalent). Norming makes it impossible to continue to raise scores for the entire population for which a test was normed. Over time, half the people have to be below the midline, and half above, no matter where the midline is. Scores on norm-referenced tests are simply stand-ins for rank ordering (Meier, 1981; Owen, 1985).

Passing scores (or *cut scores*) are another story. A score on any test (whether a converted normed score or a raw score) can be further qualified by whether or not it meets the cut score. A passing score is determined not by the shape of the curve or the midpoint of scores but by factors external to the test itself. For instance, market demands for teachers were what determined Delaware's passing score on the National Teachers Exam. In years of high demand, the passing score was lowered to allow more to pass through the "moveable gate" (Owen, 1985); when fewer teachers were needed, the passing score was raised.

If what counts as a passing score changes, so does the distance between raw scores. On standardized, norm-referenced reading tests, the difference between raw scores of 34 and 35 and between raw scores of 42 and 43 is not 1 point in each case. In the middle of the bell curve, one more question answered right does not matter very much. A raw score of 34 and a raw score of 35 are both converted to a grade equivalent of 2.8 in the test scores presented by Cook and Meier (n.d.). It takes many additional correct answers to change a grade equivalent or percentile in the middle ranges. For high- or low-scoring students, however, only one more right or wrong answer can result in a difference of several percentiles or months in grade equivalents. Cook and Meier documented for at least one test that a raw score of 42 counted as Grade 4.4 while a raw score of 43 translated to an entire year more in grade equivalence (5.4). It should be obvious, then, why both high and low normed scores are less reliable than middle scores and how test-based criteria for entrance to, or exit from, programs aimed at high- or low-scoring children (e.g., programs for the "gifted" or the "at risk") are suspect.

Claims About Predictive Power.   In the 1970s, critics such as Ralph Nader and Allan Nairn charged that despite claims to the contrary, the SAT does not predict how well students do in college or in life after schooling (Haney, 1984). Instead of predicting, standardized tests reflect—and what they reflect most accurately is differences in experience as related to membership in social categories such as race, culture, gender, and particularly socio-economic status. A prime example is the relationship of SAT scores to family income. Data for 2005 college bound seniors show that SAT scores rise steadily with income, with the increase ranging from 12 points to 56 points for every additional $10,000 in family income (College Board, cited by www.fairtest.org[4]

Claims About the Nature of Reading. Implicit in any test is a conception of the phenomenon the test is testing—intelligence, math achievement, aptitude for law school, and so on. Because standardized tests are so often reading achievement tests, it is worth singling out the conception of reading embedded in such tests. One implied claim (Altwerger & Resta, 1986; Edelsky & Harman, 1988) is that reading consists of separate skills (reflected in separate sections on word analysis as separate from vocabulary as separate from sentence comprehension as separate from passage comprehension). However, just because an activity can be analyzed after the fact into parts does not mean that the separate parts add up to the total activity, or that a part (like recognizing words) performed outside the total act of reading works the same way as it does during actual reading.

Another implicit claim is that reading offers a conduit (see Lakoff & Johnson, 1980, for a discussion of the conduit metaphor) for moving meaning from print to a reader's head. But reading is more aptly seen as a *transaction* (Rosenblatt, 1978) between what the reader supplies (cultural/historical knowledge of written language cuing systems) and what the print and the context offers. What is transacted—what is created anew through predicting and confirming—is meaning-in-context. When we read, we use cues from higher level cuing systems (e.g., pragmatics—is the print on the wall of a public toilet? or is it on a satin banner?) to predict possible general meanings. At the same time, we use the lower level systems to start to specify that meaning (Is it many words or a few? Sentences or just a phrase? What orthographic cues appear?). We predict more particular meanings, using all the systems (pragmatics, semantics, syntax, orthography, graphics) simultaneously as we construct particular context-bound meanings for particular communicative purposes (Harste, Burke, & Woodward, 1983). When

---

[4]In 2004, College Board tried to prevent FairTest from publishing data about score differences between different groups as well as between various racial, ethnic, and gender groups). The College Board lawyers claimed publication of such data "significantly impacts the perceptions of students, parents, and educators regarding the services we provide." FairTest said that was exactly its goal—to show that the SAT is not a "level playing field" (FairTest, 2004b).

print is used for evaluation only, sometimes without even any intent to create a textual meaning, the activity is merely an exercise (as discussed at length in chap. 5).

Of course, reading exercises are easier to control, measure, and test than more complex processes like written language-in-*use*. But ease of measurement does not guarantee that the way one does reading exercises relates to how one reads for one's own purposes. A study of 1,000 children showed no particular relationship between their actual reading and their scores on the California Test of Basic Skills. Some children scored high but read poorly; others scored high and read well; some low scorers read well; others did not (Altwerger & Resta, 1986). However, a person's score on a test does have a relationship with how well that person does on test-like literacy tasks in school because both the tests and the class work entail the same thing—doing exercises.

Negative Effects.   Critics attacked the multiple-choice format as detrimental to learning and thinking; it pushes learning to take a back seat to cramming and teaching to be overshadowed by coaching on test-taking. That format also promotes superficial thinking and discourages the development of complex cognitive abilities (Hoffman, 1962). Moreover, testing *per se* changes conceptions of education for the worse. Scores become the goal rather than mere indicators. Textbooks devolve over time to match the format and content of the tests (Madaus, 1988). Deficiencies become the lens for viewing students (Harman, 1990). Magical thinking supplants reason (e.g., thinking that the measurement tool improves education is as silly—and as wishful—as thinking that eye charts improve vision; Meier, 1981). Testing drives out student-centered, integrated projects (Darling-Hammond, 1991) in favor of curriculum that more closely matches what is on standardized tests, so that reading instruction, for instance, becomes a barely disguised reading test (Meier, 1981). A particularly egregious example of testing dominating the curriculum comes from Australia, where rigid high-stakes exams in chemistry, instituted in the 19th century, prevented changes to the chemistry curriculum. Despite significant new knowledge, the chemistry curriculum was not changed until over a half-century later, in 1959 (Madaus, 1988). The stakes were so high that the fit between the curriculum and the field of chemistry took a back seat to the fit with the exam.

Measurement-driven curriculum (or what Madaus, 1988, p. 84, calls *psychometric imperialism*) limits teachers' creativity and spontaneity (Meisels, 1989) and demeans their professional judgment. Indeed, as control over what is taught shifts from teachers to testing companies, everyone in the educational encounter (students and teachers) is demeaned because their interests, talents, and questions disappear from the scene. Even testing professionals become devalued as psychometric principles (e.g., admonitions against using a test score as the single factor in decisions regarding retention, graduation, admission) are ignored in the momentum of testing.

The most devastating effects are borne by the most vulnerable. While ascribing merit to those favored by various biases (one meaning of *privilege*), the tests damage life chances for those not so favored. During the period of pedagogical concerns, low scores (associated disproportionately with minority status and poverty) on increasing numbers of standardized tests was related to placements in low-level tracks with impoverished curricula, denial of admission to particular programs and institutions, and high dropout rates (Haney, 1984).

Suggested Remedies

Some of the above criticisms of test items led to tinkering with the tests (e.g., efforts to develop culture-fair test items). And some of the criticism (e.g., about particular negative effects of testing) led to efforts to reform the processes of testing (e.g., legislation to ensure "truth in testing" for college admission). But as late as 1978, the foremost bibliographer of testing, Oscar Buros, could complain that achievement tests were still being constructed the same way they were 50 years before—mistakes and all (Haney, 1984).

Concerns that measurement was driving education prompted calls for a reversal in that relationship. Harman (1990), Meisels (1989), and M. Neill and Medina (1991) urged that curriculum—especially a rich, integrated, complex curriculum—should guide testing rather than vice versa. Critics also argued that, as bad as the tests were, their uses (and misuses) were even worse. According to Haney and Madaus (1991), using the same test for multiple purposes (for diagnosing student learning, for evaluating programs, for evaluating teachers, and for making systems accountable) was the prime misuse; it was this that "warped and corrupted" test results and also curriculum and instruction. Other critics (e.g., Meisels, 1989), focusing on the damage done by linking tests to high-stakes educational and life decisions, urged limiting the use of tests to low stake decisions—with consequences only within one classroom.

But, motivated by fears that tests were playing too big and too negative a role in education (that "the servant" had become "the master"; Meisels, 1989), most of the criticisms during this period were accompanied by recommendations to bypass standardized tests altogether. There were alternatives, and these would more closely reflect the complexity of the phenomena assessed, value diversity among students, honor teachers' professional judgment and their knowledge of individual students, and encourage in-depth learning and critical thinking. Prominent among the alternatives was authentic assessment—assessing tasks that are "worthwhile, significant and meaningful," that are "not contrived only for the purpose of assessing knowledge," and that have "value beyond evaluation" (Archbald & Newmann, 1988). In addition to portfolios, theoretically informed observations and authentic assessment (Bridges, 1995; Meier, 1981; S. Valencia, 1990), Harman and I (in the second edition of this volume, 1996) proposed using instruments that make language processes visible. We urged reflective interviews such as the Burke (1980) Reading Interview and Atwell's (1987) writing interview along with a simplified version of the Reading Miscue Inventory (Y. Goodman, Watson, & Burke, 1987) for parents, teacher, and student to examine together during family conferences.

We also argued that the various audiences with legitimate rights to information about how well students and schools are doing—the public, the state, school administrators, parents, teachers, and the children themselves—do not all need the same data. Just as parents cannot give a babysitter explicit instructions for every imaginable contingency but ultimately must trust his or her references and his or her good sense, so parents and the schools' other audiences can impose only so much oversight before they demoralize and immobilize the professionals responsible for their children. Instead, audiences at different distances from actual classrooms should have different kinds of information. The audiences farthest from the classroom—the public, state administrators, and parents—need information about *the school* (the condition of the physical plant; the teacher–child ratio; children's attendance rates; staff turnover; the racial balance; enrichment programs available, such as violin or gymnastics; the content of the curriculum; orderliness in the halls; observable engagement of the children in class; etc.). The model for this kind of assessment is the routine site visit for accreditation performed at intervals by independent reviewers. Those closest to classroom performance—school administrators, teachers, children, and parents again in their dual role of concerns for both the school as a whole and their own individual children—need information about *the child,* each individual child's learning in that school.

All the critical arguments and the accompanying remedies during this period were presented as though testing policies were backed by "honorable intentions." The critics, myself included, acted as though the ostensible purpose behind these mandates—to assess what particular students had learned based on what their teachers had taught—was the ultimate purpose.[5] Further, in proposing alternatives, the critics presumed that the most basic reason for wanting to know about educational quality was to improve it. For students. Not for politicians. Not for testing companies. And

---

[5]Meier (1981), for example, argued that, just as it was not necessary to call the weather bureau to find out if it was raining, it was not necessary to look at a test score to find out what one's own children could do—as though the test were actually for local use.

not for any ulterior motive (e.g., for promoting the agenda of a powerful interest group). Now several critics (e.g., Edelsky, Altwerger, & Flores, 1991; Edelsky & Harman, 1988; Madaus, 1988; Meier, 1981; M. Neill & Medina, 1991) were aware that behind the tests was a big business of testing becoming ever bigger and that it would take more than arguments to offset the influence of these giants. Nevertheless, critical efforts during this period were aimed, on the one hand, at developing clear, convincing arguments about the fact that tests do not show how well schools (and teachers and students) are doing, and on the other hand, at providing vivid descriptions of alternative assessments that would improve the quality of education by giving all students richer, deeper, more coherent learning experiences.[6] It was as though if only the argument were stated well enough, if only the alternatives were presented with enough appeal, surely standardized testing would lose its support.

THE PERIOD OF RESISTANCE

But the intentions were/are not "honorable." It turns out that: (1) testing is a major tactic in a neoliberal corporatist agenda to control education, (2) testing policy mandates are little more than "scenes" in a political spectacle, and (3) what is required to dislodge the tests from their prominent position is an organized political movement for educational rights. But I am getting ahead of my story.

The Context

The period of resistance began as neoliberalism was already shifting into high gear, turning the social world into a giant market where every act is converted into a competitive market transaction (Treanor, 2004)—where "every sphere of economic, social, cultural, and biological life [becomes] a commodity, open to privatization" (Lipman, 2005). By the 1990s, the consequences were already apparent: market interests trump democratically approved policies (e.g., North American Free Trade Agreement regulations override state antipollution measures); corporations move capital and production to obtain the cheapest labor and the least regulated conditions,

---

[6]One notable exception was the different direction taken by a handful of politically aware testing professionals who established the National Center for Fair and Open Testing in 1985, with a mission to "end the misuses and flaws of standardized testing and to ensure that evaluation of students, teachers and schools is fair, open, valid and educationally beneficial" (www. fairtest.org). FairTest has been particularly concerned with eliminating racial, class, gender, and cultural barriers to equal opportunity posed by standardized tests. FairTest's activities have included developing the Assessment Reform Network, filing amicus briefs and suing to stop misuses of tests, providing technical assistance, and monitoring the testing industry.

thereby incurring a "race to the bottom" in wages; income disparities grow obscenely to produce the largest gap in wealth since the 1920s. This is also the period of the attacks on September 11, 2001, a grotesque tragedy for the victims and a tragedy as well for the future of democracy since the attacks are being exploited to suppress civil liberties and to corrupt democratic practices in the name of security. Education in this period—policies, agendas, critiques, and remedies—must be understood within this context.

There is currently a desperate need for serious educational reform. Not because of bad teachers (the old "favorite villains"). And not because of bad teacher preparation institutions (the new "favorite villains"). Real reform is needed because, by and large, the United States is "in denial" about the fact that it has two public education systems—one for the poor and one for everyone else. This divided system is achieved through the primary means for funding public schools in the United States: local property taxes.[7] The Poor People's Education System, as Gerald Bracey (2002) wrote, is the one where, according to a legal brief filed in Alabama in 1990, there are significant numbers of schools with too few as well as obsolete textbooks, no guidance or support staff, pupil–teacher ratios of 43 to 1, teachers who encourage students to bring headphones from home to block out the noise from nearby machines, condemned septic tanks burble under playgrounds, termite-eaten shelves hold termite-eaten school records; and, according to a class action suit filed in California in 2001, where young children are excused from reading instruction to remove beer bottles, condoms, and bullets from the school grounds; rats run through cafeterias with food in their mouths; chemistry labs have no chemicals and computer labs have no computers; and one substitute teacher after another fills in for the lack of a regular teacher. The Poor People's Education System—not the one for everyone else—is the system whose students are at the bottom of international comparisons (e.g., Trends in International Math and Science Studies and the Program for International Student Assessment and on "the nation's report card," the National Assessment of Educational Progress [NAEP]; Berliner & Biddle, 1995).

Of course, poor people's children suffer from more than an insufficient number of chairs in classrooms (another detail in the 2001 class action lawsuit filed in California; Bracey, 2001). Aside from poor nutrition to outright

---

[7]Since poor people live in poor neighborhoods with lower tax valuations, poor people's schools receive fewer funds—even though poor people's children often have higher educational needs. Funding schools through local property taxes, with all its inequities, has been fought in courts in the United States for at least 25 years and been ruled either illegal or in need of remediation (School Finance Overview, 2005) but, for the same period of time, state legislatures have resisted those courts' instructions to change the means (or formulae) of funding.

hunger, and besides a lack of adequate housing to—in an increasing number of cases—a lack of any housing at all, one third of poor people's children have untreated dental cavities (most likely producing throbbing toothaches on test days), and 10% have dangerous, IQ-lowering levels of lead in their blood (Rothstein, 2001).

Genuine educational reform *ought to* address such basic student health problems. Certainly, it *must* address grossly unequal material conditions in roofs, toilets, labs, chairs, cafeterias, class size, and in numbers of teachers and support staff. But real reforms such as these would require changing the ways schools are funded (through inequitably allocated property taxes and state budgets that appropriate less for schools than state statutes provide). And, of course, real reforms would require acknowledging the fact of the two school systems. But, as Mary Lee Smith argued (2004), educational policy in modern times, supposedly geared to reform, is almost entirely a political spectacle, given neither to such honesty nor to genuine reform.

The neoliberal move to step up efforts to control education began in the preceding period with various opening acts in the policy spectacle intended to promote anxiety as well as calls for tougher test-based accountability: a Republican policy paper in 1989, a provision in the Adult Literacy Act of 1990, and the Reading Excellence Act in 1998 (G. Coles, 2003b). But the headliner in the policy extravaganzas belongs to the current period. It is the Elementary and Secondary Education Act passed in 2002, better known as No Child Left Behind (NCLB).

NCLB has all the components of policy as political spectacle: attendant crises (often manufactured [Berliner & Biddle, 1995], such as threats of widespread illiteracy), actors and a plot (the black hat education establishment [a special interest group wanting to preserve the status quo] pitted against white hat reformers [corporate-minded leaders and phonics-promoting researchers]), symbolic language intended to evoke confidence in science (*scientific, evidence based, research based*) and hard-nosed business (*accountability, performance standards, inducements, quality control*), and hidden strategies (paying for covert propaganda that masquerades as news in the mainstream media to endorse the Bush education policy [Toppo, 2005; Spivak, 2005], hiring the same public relations firm, Widmeyer-Baker, to write and disseminate the Summary of the National Reading Panel Report that also acts as the public relations firm for McGraw-Hill, the publishing company that profits from the way the Summary misrepresents the Report [Garan, 2002; Strauss, 2005a]). High-stakes testing figures prominently in all of the components, either as tool or as evidence.

NCLB requires all students in Grades 3 through 8 to be tested each year. Scores must be disaggregated according to race, gender, poverty, language background, and ethnicity in order to determine adequate yearly progress (AYP). Each subgroup within a school must make AYP or the entire school faces sanctions (i.e., one subgroup—frequently, the school's special education students or English Language Learners—can scuttle the ship). Because a few low scores have more of an impact on the average score of a smaller group, the more diverse the school (the more small racial, ethnic, linguistic subgroups), the more likely it becomes a failing school—and the more likely racialized blaming occurs (Lipman, 2005). If a school fails to make AYP for 2 consecutive years, that school can be restructured (its administration replaced, its faculty moved). Students attending a school that fails to make AYP can transfer to one that does—with transportation costs borne by the failing school with funds that might have been used to improve instruction. Failing districts (criteria for which vary from state to state) can be abolished entirely or taken over by outside entities. The punitive character of NCLB is hard to miss.

NCLB is not some anomaly. It is one of many achievements of corporatism ("the fusion of corporate interests with government"; M. L. Smith, 2004, p. 201). The corporatist agenda under neoliberalism is to install its ideology (the worldview of the market along with its metaphors of production, consumption, profits, and losses) into all social domains (Engel, 2000), to privatize public spheres, and to control social processes such as education for its own interests. Thus, the NCLB regulation that requires an overcrowded high-performing school to accept students transferring from failing schools increases the likelihood that public opinion will begin to favor vouchers in order to handle the overload. In fact, according to the National Conference of State Legislators, 70% of all schools will soon be designated as failing, augmenting pro-voucher sentiment (Schemo, 2002), to the delight of privatizing neoliberals.

The corporatists also assert their control over the content and intent of education through pressing for rigid state standards written by committees that deliberately by-pass professional educators. They follow up by posting (on www.statestandards.com) lesson plans for standards-linked state assessments (A. Cole, 2001). A "public/private collaboration" among the U.S. Department of Education, Standard and Poor (owned by McGraw-Hill), and Just for Kids now provides a national online database on students' test results disaggregated by every student subgroup and grade level for cross- and within-state comparisons (M. Neill, 2003). Teacher education also becomes part of the agenda: Maryland's bill (Higher Education Teacher Education Reading Programs Alignment with Federal Law) will require professors of reading instruction to revise their teacher education courses so that these match the results of the flawed National Reading Panel Report (Altwerger, 2005b).

With NCLB, the corporatists not only benefit from moving closer to their goals of controlling and privatizing; some also make handsome profits. After all, between 2002 and 2008, states are expected to spend between

$1.9 billion and $5.3 billion to develop, score, and report NCLB-mandated tests. That money goes primarily to the big three test publishing companies (Harcourt, CTB/McGraw-Hill, and Riverside) and the giant data processor, Pearson Educational Measurement (Miner, 2004–2005). A $2.5 billion test prep market benefits related companies—the established Princeton Review and Kaplan, as well as newer companies, such as William Bennett's K12 and SmarterKids.com (Brandon, 2001). Indeed, the market for tests and their accessories has grown much faster than the market for textbooks (Bacon, 2000). No wonder, then, that to these corporations NCLB looks like "their own business plan" (Metcalf, 2002).

While the corporatists have enjoyed huge benefits in profit and control, no such gains have accrued for the public and its schools; instead, these are being sorely tested. The political spectacle of recent education policy does acknowledge one small piece of the problem of having two public school systems—the test score piece. "Closing the Black/White achievement gap" (Hispanics and Native Americans are rarely mentioned) is a frequent refrain. But in its obsession with testing, the spectacle ignores what screams out for change: the material facts of a Poor People's School System. This time, however, the corporatists may have overstepped a line. It isn't just that the test-obsessed current policies damage the Poor People's School System (historically, that system counts for so little in corporatist schemes that its most egregious features can be ignored). It isn't even that NCLB damages everyone else's public school system (after all, middle-class disenchantment with its schools could give wings to corporate calls for privatization). The danger for corporatists is that their convoluted, test-based regulations have pulled the curtain away, revealing some of the activity backstage, ending the innocence of spectators—perhaps too many for corporatist taste.

The Critique: The Same and Then Some

The same criticisms are being presented in this period as in the last, with some important additions. First, the criticisms are now offered with a different purpose and a different audience: no longer arguments to convince policymakers but analyses for use by political resisters. Second, the old criticisms are now transformed (in intensity and urgency) by virtue of forces that appear to many to be strangling public education.

Items.   State tests now include especially "loony" test items (e.g., a fourth-grade test item asks if it is more likely to find information on the history of pretzels in an encyclopedia or a newspaper; Ohanian, 2001), as well as items and answers that contain factual inaccuracies (Libit, 2001). Both looniness and incorrectness—by-products of rushing to produce tests aligned with states' standards in order to comply with NCLB regulations—become less disdainfully funny, more outrageous, when they determine the future of a child and a school.

Claims.   In the previous period, when the aura of scientific objectivity surrounding standardized tests appeared laughable to critics, the public was not laughing; it believed the claim. In the current period, *scientific* has achieved even more cachet; it has become a key symbolic term in the political spectacle.[8] It is mentioned frequently in NCLB and is used by corporatists to control curriculum, instruction, and even research. *Scientific,* as used in the political spectacle, means only narrow experimental research; by implication, entire scholarly fields that engage in descriptive research must be defined as unscientific. The corporatists do not, however, hold their own educational policies to the same experimental-evidence-based standards. There is in fact no scientific research on the safety and efficacy of high-stakes testing, no evidence that annual testing and punitive consequences produce positive change for either students or schools (Strauss, 2002).[9] (Evidence on the negative effects of testing appears below.)

Scores.   Critics in the previous period argued that test scores were neither precise nor objective. A single score does not account for the "wobble" (the error of measurement) that would be revealed if someone took the same test several times. Testing companies are supposed to report the standard error of measurement for their products. But current policy mandates ignore that statistic—at great injustice to those who are prevented from graduating on the basis of only one score. Moreover, that one score may suffer not only from statistical error of measurement but also from outright errors in scoring. The massive increase in testing has created an overload for test processing. Temporary workers with a few hours of training, working at an assembly-line pace, spend an average of only 21 sec scoring a non-multiple-choice math question and a mere 2½ minutes scoring an essay (Houtz, 2001). Because of a scoring error, National Computer Systems, Inc. told 8,000 students that they had failed the math portion of Minnesota's high-stakes test when they had actually passed (Miner, 2004–2005). An error by CTB/McGraw-Hill mistakenly sent 9,000 New York City students to summer school (Steinberg & Henriques, 2001).

---

[8]The "science" that is so sacred in the Bush administration that it is used to justify anything from its failure to sign the Kyoto agreement to its mandates regarding phonics instruction has been termed "junk science" (Kennedy, 2004).

[9]There is evidence, though, that a relative absence of testing and a complete absence of high-stakes tests are related to high achievement. Finnish students are tested only every few years to get a composite national picture, not to evaluate individual students or teachers. Yet on international tests, Finnish students outperform all others (Bracey, 2005c).

More people are becoming aware of what was noted earlier—that is, that cut scores are political determinations; if too many of the "wrong" students pass or fail, the passing score is changed. Moreover, cut scores are often arrived at through arithmetical (not even statistical) sleight of hand. For example, Michigan reduced its number of "failing" schools from 1,500 to 216 in a single year by lowering its passing score from 75% to 42% (Gryphon, 2005).[10] Arizona's Task Force determined its 75% passing score on the Arizona Instrument to Measure Standards metaphorically. It translated rubric scores (from 1 to 4) into percentages. "Since 3 out of 4 was close to 75 percent, and since the public would judge any mastery level less than 75 percent as too lenient, therefore, a 3 would be the cutoff between mastery and non-mastery, between graduation and non-graduation" (M. L. Smith, 2004, p. 55).

Earlier critics pointed out that a score does not necessarily reflect a level of skill or achievement. If it did, high-scoring students should show considerable skill in the classroom and also on other tests purportedly of the same skill. But Texas teachers are not seeing "new and improved" students, even though scores on the Texas Assessment of Academic Skills have risen dramatically. And Texas' verbal SAT scores are among the lowest in the nation (Kazmin, 2000). It works the other way too; Minnesota's math scores on an international test (Trends in International Math and Science Studies) would put it near the top ("if Minnesota were a country"), but on its own state benchmark test its students made a poor showing (Perlstein, 2005).

Current policies have not only promoted scoring errors and discrepancies; they have encouraged lying and manipulating—"shenanigans" that prove Campbell's (1975) point, cited by Madaus (1988): "The more any quantitative social indicator is used for social decision making, the more likely it will be to distort and corrupt the social process it is intended to monitor" (p. 89). Thus, under the pressure of high stakes, districts have used underhanded means of improving their testing image. One is to prevent probable low-scoring students from taking the test and making their school or district look bad. For example, in 22 districts in the San Francisco Bay Area, scores rose, but the number of students taking the test dropped (Krashen, 2001c). Students have been retained in Texas (Kazmin, 2001), New York (Allington, 2000), and Boston (Allington, 2003) so they do not lower their school's scores at a key grade level and so that when they finally take the test a year later (if they do not drop out before that), they have had another year of growth and test preparation under their belts. According to

---

[10]Gryphon's critical piece written for the "pro-free market" Cato Institute may seem to contradict the claim that NCLB fits a neoliberal and corporatist agenda. The Cato Institute, however, is libertarian; as such, it opposes government intervention in education as well as other arenas.

Walt Haney (Kazmin, 2001) and Richard Allington (2003), low-scoring students across the United States have been put into special classes exempt from testing. Over 500 low-scoring students were "administratively withdrawn" in Alabama before the SAT9 was given (Ohanian, 2001).

Another tactic is to engage in shifty accounting and reporting practices. The Massachusetts commissioner of education bragged that 94% of the graduating class of 2004 had passed the Massachusetts Comprehensive Assessment System, but he neglected to account for those in the class of 2004 who had dropped out (Bracey, 2005c). Various states are negotiating their compliance agreements with NCLB in order gain favorable "cell sizes" (the number in a subgroup that requires the state to include those students' scores in AYP figures). Maryland, for example, proposed a cell size that would allow it not to count the scores of special education students or English language learners (FairTest, 2004a).

If "shenanigans" cannot be arranged and low scores become public, another manipulative tactic is for proponents of testing policies to make an about-face and proclaim the inadequacy of test scores. When charter school NAEP scores came in lower than regular public school scores, the president of the right-wing Center for Education Reform said "NAEP provides only one data point ... it is necessary to combine that information with more comprehensive data to accurately assess school performance" (Schemo, 2004b).[11] After Detroit Public Schools was taken over by corporate executives appointed by the state, the new CEO dismissed low scores by saying "test scores don't matter that much" (Pratt, Walsh-Sarnecki, & Turk, 2004). When scores were mixed from Ohio schools that had been awarded grants for using systematic, intensive phonics instruction (17 schools' scores improved, 17 got worse, and 4 were equivocal), advocates of phonics test-like curricula argued that test results should not be the final word on the success of phonics (Farenga, 1999).

If all else fails, test promoters try either arm-twisting or brazenly pretending to be above the fray. For instance, the College Board tried to force FairTest to remove from its Web site data that show the correlation between SAT scores and family income (Schmidt, 2004). And Secretary of Education Rod Paige, Superintendent of Houston Public Schools at the time of the Enron-style accounting that proclaimed a "Texas miracle," simply declined to address pointed questions about the irregularities coming to light—a spokesperson said "he stands by his record of accomplishment in Texas" (Schemo, 2003).

---

[11]In a draft of a letter to the editor of the *Washington Post,* test critic Susan Harman said, "I couldn't have said it better myself" (personal communication, August 24, 2004).

Negative Effects.   It is nothing new to note that teaching becomes "test prep" when major decisions rest on a single score. In many schools, however, the testing epidemic fomented by NCLB has driven out other instruction altogether. In some schools, recess is eliminated and lunch periods are shortened to allow more time for test-focused instruction. Anxious administrators allocate resources for increasing test scores and, in the process, deplete resources for art, music, and advanced placement courses. Subjects such as social studies that are not emphasized on the high-stakes tests are pushed out of the instructional day in elementary schools. In order to align its postbaccalaureate teacher certification program with state standards and its accompanying high-stakes test, Colorado decreased prospective elementary teachers' options for undergraduate majors from 55 to 11, eliminating foreign languages, psychology, sociology, fine arts, and dozens of other fields not reflected on the high-stakes test (Wirsing, 2000). The net effect is "academic atrophy" (Bracey, 2004, p. 166).

High-stakes tests create ethical binds for teachers no matter which way they turn. For example, in opposition to typical ideals of teaching, high-stakes tests sway teachers to act as free-market capitalists, "investing" more in those students who will earn the greatest profit. When a school's future is linked to disaggregated test scores, teachers are pressured to spend their time with students who are almost at the required cutoff score. That means, they must spend less time with—or even ignore—students whose scores are so low that there is little chance they will make the cut (Apple, 2004). A different dilemma for teachers is created by attempts to lessen the burden on students. In May 2005, the Arizona legislature began talking about softening the blow of a failing score on the state's graduation test (the Arizona Instrument to Measure Standards) by giving various percentages of credit for A, B, or C grades. Such a remedy would either make teachers vulnerable to coercion by students and parents or it would push sympathetic teachers to inflate grades across the board. In either case, given the commodification of education (wherein grades and scores—tickets to opportunities for future identities—are all that count), teachers' professional obligation to assess students' work is severely compromised.

Learning and thinking fare no better. Secrecy in the name of test security prevents teachers from providing posttest feedback. Two studies by Audrey Amrein and David Berliner (2002a, 2002b) showed that academic achievement in states with high-stakes testing appeared to decline in comparison to states that did not have high-stakes tests (the studies were conducted prior to the full implementation of NCLB). Moreover, high-stakes tests were associated with a number of "unintended consequences," from increased rates of student retention to increased flight from public schools by teachers who feel professionally compromised. A recent study (Nichols & Berliner, 2005) added cheating by administrators, teachers, and students to the list.

An excessive number of all-important, one-right-answer tests encourage binary thinking (*right* or *wrong*), rendering irrelevant the ability to historicize, contextualize, and critically analyze. At the societal level, this kind of thinking fits a mentality of *us* versus *them, good* versus *evil,* and *American* versus *un-American* (Lipman, 2005). At the individual level, it bears out Hoffman's (1962) complaint about the encouragement of superficial thinking. A study cited by Kohn (2001) that defined a superficial approach to tests as copying down answers, guessing a lot, and skipping the hard parts showed that such superficiality earned higher scores. Superficial trickiness was encouraged in Houston as teachers distributed "likely answers" (e.g., if the question is about the American Revolution, the answer is likely to be George Washington; Bracey, 2004). High-stakes tests, in other words, are pushing students to become superficial gamers.

With the surge in high-stakes testing, dropout rates have increased with an ensuing decrease in life options for adolescents (Amrein & Berliner, 2002a), and anxiety-induced health problems have increased for young children (Strauss, 2002).

Massive high-stakes testing programs do more than damage schools and individuals; they also help to legitimize surveillance and punishment by the state as a normal state of affairs (Lipman, 2005). In a nutshell, high-stakes testing is showing itself to be even more of a disaster than was predicted by critics in the previous period.

The Remedy: Organized Resistance

This period began with a few who saw that reasoned arguments are not going to change the current situation. Their number is rapidly growing as it becomes more clear that what is driving the educational context does not derive from policymakers' neutral rationality but from their alignment with the dominant corporatist agenda. Those who are changing their minds are not the policymakers in this time of policy as political spectacle but members of the audience. And what they are doing is using their new understandings as the impetus for political action.

Resistance. The first organized resistance to high-stakes testing appeared in the 1990s, when the then-new standards movement demanded a dramatic increase in testing. It was parents in both the poorest and the richest school districts who saw these tests as an assault on their children's education (FairTest, 1998–1999). What these parents did in California, Michigan, Massachusetts, Virginia, Washington, Illinois, Arizona, New York, Nevada, Florida, and elsewhere—soon joined by students and a few teachers—was to hold public rallies; take busloads of citizens to lobby state legislators; design and sell t-shirts ("high stakes are for tomatoes") and bumper stickers ("my child is more than a test score"); and, importantly, boycott the tests. But with the signing into law of NCLB, which established high stakes for schools and which also required schools to report 95% of scores for each student subgroup for calculating the school's AYP, boycotting the tests became an unlikely tactic; it would punish the local school (an undesirable consequence for a public which, by and large, still approves of and appreciates its local neighborhood school; Rose & Gallup, 2004). Resistance, therefore, is taking other forms.

Some of the resistance invokes satire (e.g., the Emperor's Clothes Award, given by Chicago's Commission to Recognize Courage in Education; media challenges to state legislators to take the state high-stakes test and post their scores; Ohanian, 2001). Some of it is educational (the Web site maintained by Susan Ohanian [susanohanian.org], the Web site and publications of FairTest, testing house parties in Ohio, the test resistance Web site (www.calcare.org) created by the California Coalition for Authentic Reform in Education and its organized teach-ins around the state). Some is formal (e.g., official statements by professional organizations such as American Educational Research Association, American Psychological Association, National Research Council, National Council on Measurement in Education as to the error of using a single score as a basis for decisions). But all of it is intended to bring public pressure to bear on policymakers—in other words, to be political. The media as well as some state policymakers are starting to take notice; the seemingly golden glow of NCLB seems to be tarnishing. *Ed Week* reported the results of a study by the bipartisan National Conference of State Legislatures that found considerable flaws in NCLB (Hoff, 2005). And the New York Times has presented news of various challenges to the law (e.g., lawsuits and state legislative actions; Dillon, 2005).

A Movement for Education Rights. Each such instance of political resistance is important, but more is needed—not only more instances of resistance but an umbrella movement to link them to each other. High-stakes testing is tied so tightly to narrow, mandated state standards, and both are such integral tools in the corporatist agenda to control education, that the entire agenda-plus-tools is what should be opposed. An Education Rights Movement is needed to wrest control of education from corporatists, to make the purposes of public education fit the interests of a democracy, not of neoliberal, global corporate competition. It might be helpful here to consider the example of the Civil Rights Movement of the 1960s. Activists in the 1960s saw themselves as struggling for broad fundamental rights, not merely the right to sit at the local lunch counter. With the growing public perception that open housing marches and bus boycotts were connected actions for something as broad as racial justice in civil life, the movement gained even more power and efficacy. Once it became "The Civil Rights

Movement," previously seemingly separate demands gained strength (in moral appeal, in analysis, in weight of numbers; Edelsky, 2002).

Like any large political movement, a movement for education rights requires an adequate analysis. This is how the critiques of testing presented in this chapter should be used—to relate immediately obvious oppressions (high-stakes testing and NCLB) to the corporatist agenda to control education and then to relate that agenda to other neoliberal attempts to take over public spheres. Especially helpful in developing an analysis for an Education Rights Movement (in addition to critiques of testing) will be analyses of educational policy as political spectacle (see, e.g., M. L. Smith, 2004, especially the chapter titled "Education Policy, Inc."; Wright, 2005a, 2005b) and analyses of corporate/government agendas in education (e.g., Altwerger, 2005c, 2005d, 2005e; Altwerger & Strauss, 2002; Lipman, 2005; Strauss, 2005a, 2005b).

A movement for educational rights also requires a clear organizing issue and a short but comprehensive list of demands. High-stakes testing and NCLB are the lightning rod issues here; a key demand, therefore, must be to rescind the law and to stop high-stakes testing. But there are other demands, as itemized by Altwerger (2005a, p. 259). Each of them has connections with high-stakes testing. In fact, highlighting high-stakes testing opens discussions about these other demands:

- "Full and equitable allocation of public funds for every public school system, including resources for classroom, school, and neighborhood libraries
- Education free of mandated programs and high-stakes testing resulting in punitive consequences for students, teachers, and parents
- Curriculum decisions determined by and reflective of the unique goals and needs of local school communities
- Instructional decisions based upon individual needs of students as identified by classroom professionals through ongoing assessment
- Availability of the full range of instructional approaches and materials for selection and use by classroom professionals
- Fully funded professional development opportunities designed and selected by local school communities to improve and maintain quality of instruction
- Freedom from corporate intrusions or legislative politics that infringe upon the above rights of teachers, parents, and students."

Along with demands, a movement needs a vision. This one calls for images of education that highlight justice, opportunity, and civic responsibility, all rendered vividly. Those images and the overall vision prod and give hope to resisters and also shape new forms of resistance. The resistance itself should take many forms—from protecting students from oppressive school conditions;[12] to joining teacher-focused study groups that take charge of their own professional development; to wearing buttons and sporting bumper stickers; to writing op-ed pieces; to organizing through the Internet; to marching, demonstrating, and organizing teach-ins and speak-outs; and to engaging in civil disobedience, including mass boycotts (Kohn, 2001). The object is to reach out to various publics who do not already understand the Movement's analyses—with those buttons, leaflets, guerilla theater, Internet petitions, and so on—so that the dissent grows. And to make coalitions with groups whose interests do not necessarily center on education but whose own analyses are in harmony with main points in the Movement's analyses. Numbers matter; in the end, what results in movements having their demands met is the threat of even more widespread activism by even greater numbers (Albert, 2001).

In this period of resistance, standardized tests, especially with high stakes attached, have been exposed as the political tools they have always been. The "solution" to the problems they embody, those they create, and the host of other injustices in education to which they are related must also be political; that, in fact, is the main lesson from this period of resistance.

---

[12]Kohn (2001) gives many suggestions for protecting students from high-stakes tests; for example, doing whatever is necessary, but absolutely no more, to prepare them; being as creative as possible in test preparation; refraining from bragging about test scores, and so on.

References

Adams, M. (1990). *Beginning to read.* Cambridge, MA: MIT Press.

Adams, R. (1985). Sex and background factors: Effect on ASAT scores. *Australian Journal of Education, 29,* 221–2.

American Educational Research Association. (2000, June/July). What education research needs: An analysis of the influences on legislative staff perspectives, ER & P archives. Washington, DC: AERA. Retrieved December 20, 2005, from http://35.8.171.42/aera/gov/archive/n0600-04.htm

Albert, M. (2001). The trajectory of struggle. *Z Magazine, 14*(6), 15–19.

Al-Fahid, J. (2000). Goodman psycholinguistic model of English reading and its applicability to semitic languages. Unpublished doctoral dissertation, University of Arizona.

Allen, R. V. (1976). *Language experiences in communication.* Boston: Houghton Mifflin.

Allington, R. (2000, June 20). E-mail personal communication. *LiteracyForAll@ egroups.com*

Allington, R. (2001a, June 6). E-mail. *LiteracyForAll@egroups.com*

Allington, R. (2001b, November 5). E-mail. Comments to Duval County Board of Education. What do we know about the effects of direct instruction on student reading? *LiteracyForAll@egroups.com*

Allington, R. (2002). *Big brother and the national reading curriculum: How ideology trumped evidence.* Portsmouth, NH: Heinemann.

Allington, R. (2003, June 23). E-mail. *LiteracyForAll@egroups.com*

Allington, R., & Woodside-Jiron, H. (1999). The politics of literacy teaching: How "research" shaped educational policy. *Educational Researcher, 28*(8), 4–13.

Alterman, E. (2005). Bush's war on the press. *The Nation, 280*(18), 11–20.

Altwerger, B. (1993, June). Expanding "personal response" to literature. Workshop presentation, Illinois Teachers Applying Whole Language Conference, DeKalb.

Altwerger, B. (2005a). A call to action. In B. Altwerger (Ed.), *Reading for profit: How the bottom line leaves kids behind* (pp. 257–260). Portsmouth, NH: Heinemann.

Altwerger, B. (2005b, May 1). E-mail. Baltimore schools. *LiteracyForAll@egroups.com*

Altwerger, B. (2005c). The push of the pendulum. In L. Poynor & P. Wolfe (Eds.), *Marketing fear in America's public schools* (pp. 31–50). Mahwah, NJ: Lawrence Erlbaum Associates.

Altwerger, B. (2005d). Reading for profit: A corporate coup in context. In B. Altwerger (Ed.), *Reading for profit: How the bottom line leaves kids behind* (pp. 1–10). Portsmouth, NH: Heinemann.

Altwerger, B. (Ed.). (2005e). *Reading for profit: How the bottom line leaves kids behind.* Portsmouth, NH: Heinemann.

Altwerger, B., & Resta, V. (1986, May). *Comparing standardized test scores and miscues.* Paper presented at the annual convention of the International Reading Association, Philadelphia.

Altwerger, B., & Saavedra, E. (1999). Foreword. In C. Edelsky (Ed.), *Making justice our project* (pp. vii–xii). Urbana, IL: National Council of Teachers of English.

Altwerger, B., & Strauss, S. (2002). The business behind testing. *Language Arts, 7,* 256–262.

American Psychological Association. (1954). *Technical recommendations for psychological tests and diagnostic techniques.* Washington, DC: American Psychological Association.

Amrein, A., & Berliner, D. (2002a). *An analysis of some unintended and negative consequences of high-stakes testing.* Retrieved December 3, 2004, from http://www. asu.edu/educ/epsl/EPRU/epru2002_Research_Writing.htm

Amrein, A., & Berliner, D. (2002b). *The impact of high stakes tests on student academic performance.* Retrieved December 3, 2004, from http://www.asu.edu/educ/ epsl/EPRU/epru2002_Research_Writing.htm

Anderson, R., Hiebert, E., Scott, J., & Wilkinson, I. (1985). *Becoming a nation of readers: The report of the Commission on Reading.* Champaign: Center for the Study of Reading, University of Illinois.

Apple, M. (1983). Work, gender, and teaching. *Teachers College Record, 84,* 611–628.

Apple, M. (1989). The political economy of text publishing. In S. DeCastell, A. Luke, & C. Luke. (Eds.), *Language, authority and criticism* (pp.155–169). East Sussex, England: Falmer.

Apple, M. (2004). Creating difference: Neo-liberalism, neo-conservatism and the politics of education reform. *Educational Policy, 18*(1), 12–44.

Archbald, D., & Newmann, F. (1988). *Beyond standardized testing.* Reston, VA: National Association of Secondary School Principals.

Aronowitz, S., & Giroux, H. (1985). *Education under siege: The conservative, liberal, and radical debate over schooling.* South Hadley, MA: Bergin & Garvey.

Ashton-Warner, S. (1963). *Teacher.* New York: Bantam.

Atwell, N. (1987). *In the middle.*Upper Montclair, NJ: Boynton/Cook.

Auerbach, E. (1989). Towards a socio-contextual approach to family literacy. *Harvard Educational Review, 59,* 165–181.

August, D., & Hakuta, K. (Eds.). (1997). *Improving schooling for language-minority children: A research agenda.* Washington, DC: National Academy Press.

Bacon, D. (2000, March 21). E-mail. The money in testing. *Los Angeles Times. LiteracyForAll@egroups.com*

Baker, C., & Freebody, P. (1989). *Children's first school books: Introductions to the culture of literacy.* Cambridge, MA: Basil Blackwell.

Baker, C., & Luke, A. (1991). Discourses and practices: A postscript. In C. Baker, C. Luke, & A. Luke (Eds.), *Toward a critical sociology of reading pedagogy: Papers of the XII World Congress on Reading* (pp. 257–68). Amsterdam: John Benjamins.

Barone, T. (1990, April). *On the demise of subjectivity in educational inquiry.* Paper presented at the annual convention of the American Educational Research Association, Boston.

Barron, M. (1990). *I learn to read and write the way I learn to talk.* Katonah, NY: Richard C. Owen.

Barth, N. (2005, February 24). E-mail personal communication. *LiteracyForAll@e groups.com*

Bates, E., Thal, D., & Marchman, V. (1991). Symbols and syntax: A Darwinian approach to language development. In N. Krasnegor, D. Rumbaugh, R. Schiefelbusch, & M. Studdert-Kennedy (Eds.), *Biological and behavioral determinants of language development* (pp. 29–66). Hillsdale, NJ: Lawrence Erlbaum Associates.

Bateson, G. (1972). *Steps to an ecology of mind.* New York: Ballantine.

Becker, A. (1988). Language in particular: A lecture. In D. Tannen (Ed.), *Linguistics in context: Connecting observation and understanding* (pp. 17–36). Norwood, NJ: Ablex.

Berends, M., Lucas, S., Sullivan, T., & Briggs, R. (2005). *Examining gaps in mathematics achievement among racial-ethnic groups, 1972–1992.* Retrieved May 26, 2005, from http://www.rand.org/publications/MG/MG255/

Bergeron, B. (1990). What does the term whole language mean? Constructing a definition from the literature. *Journal of Reading Behavior, 22,* 301–329.

Berkowitz, B. (2002). Bush & Bennett. *Z Magazine, 15*(6), 17–19.

Berliner, D., & Biddle, B. (1995). *Manufactured crisis.* Reading, MA: Addison-Wesley.

Berman, M. (1989). Why modernism still matters. *Tikkun, 4*(1), 11–14, 81–86.

Bigelow, B., Christensen, L., Karp, S., Miner, B., & Peterson, B. (Eds.). (1994). *Rethinking our classrooms.* Milwaukee, WI: Rethinking Schools.

Bigelow, B., Harvey, B., Karp, S., & Miller, L. (2001). *Rethinking our classrooms* (Vol. 2). Milwaukee, WI: Rethinking Schools.

Bigelow, B., & Peterson, B. (2002). *Rethinking globalization.* Milwaukee, WI: Rethinking Schools.

Bigelow, G. (2005). Let there be markets. *Harpers Magazine, 310* (1860), 33–40.

Birkerts, S. (1989). The nostalgia disease. *Tikkun, 4*(2), 20–22, 117–118.

Black, J., & Martin, R. (1982, November). *Children's concepts about writing at home and at school.* Paper presented at the annual convention of the National Council of Teachers of English, Washington, DC.

Bloom, A. (1987). *The closing of the American mind.* New York: Simon & Schuster.

Bloome, D. (1987). Reading as a social process in a middle school classroom. In D. Bloome (Ed.), *Literacy and Schooling* (pp. 123–149). Norwood, NJ: Ablex.

Bloome, D., & Bailey, F. (1990, February). *From linguistics and education, a direction for the study of language and literacy: Events, particularity, intertextuality, history, material, and dialectics.* Paper presented at National Conference on Research in English, Chicago.

Blumer, H. (1969). *Symbolic interactionism: Perspective and method.* Englewood Cliffs, NJ: Prentice Hall.

Bogdan, R., & Biklen, S. (1982). *Qualitative research for education.* Boston: Allyn & Bacon.

Bordo, S. (1994). Feminism, postmodernism, and gender skepticism. In A. Herrmann & A. Stewart (Eds.), *Theorizing feminism: Parallel trends in the humanities and social sciences* (pp. 458–481). Boulder, CO: Westview.

Borenstein, S. (2004, February 19). Bush accused of biased science. *St. Paul Pioneer Press,* p. A4.

Bowles, S., & Gintis, H. (1977). *Schooling in capitalist America: Educational reform and the contradictions of economic life.* New York: Basic Books.

Bowles, S., & Gintis, H. (1986). *Democracy and capitalism.* New York: Basic Books.

Bracey, G. (2002). International comparisons: An excuse to avoid meaningful educational reform. *Education Week, 21*(19), 30, 32.

Bracey, G. (2004). The 14th Bracey report on the condition of public education. *Phi Delta Kappan, 86*(2), 149–167.

Bracey, G. (2005a, January 16). E-mail. *LiteracyForAll@egroups.com*

Bracey, G. (2005b, February 17). E-mail. *LiteracyForAll@egroups.com* 2/17/05.

Bracey, G. (2005c, February 24). E-mail. Subject thread: "See. I knew someone out there would make it clear. Thanks." *LiteracyForAll@egroups.com*

Bracey, G. (2005d). *No child left behind: Where does the money go?* Retrieved August 10, 2005, from http://edpolicylab.org

Brandon, K. (2001, February 19). Test-prep pressure hits grade school. *Chicago Tribune,* p. 1.

Brandt, D. (1989). The message is the massage: Orality and literacy once more. *Written Communication, 6,* 31–44.

Brandt, D. (2005). Losing literacy. *Research in the Teaching of English, 39,* 305–310.

Breslin, J. (1987). *Table money.* New York: Penguin.

Bridges, L. (1995). *Assessment: Continuous learning.* York, ME: Stenhouse.

Britton, J. (1970). *Language and learning.* Hammondsworth, England: Penguin.

Brodkey, L. (1987). *Academic writing as social practice.* Philadelphia: Temple University Press.

Brophy, J., & Evertson, C. (1976). *Learning from teaching: A developmental perspective.* Boston: Allyn & Bacon.

Brown, C. (1987). Appendix: Literacy in 30 hours: Paulo Freire's process in northeast Brazil. In I. Shor (Ed.), *Freire for the classroom* (pp. 215–231). Portsmouth, NH: Boynton/Cook/Heinemann.

Brown, J., Goodman, K., & Marek, A. (1996). *Studies in miscue analysis: An annotated bibliography.* Newark, DE: International Reading Association.

Brown, R. (1987). Literacy and accountability. *Journal of State Government, 60,* 68–72.

Burke, C. (1980). The Reading Interview 1977. In B. Farr & D. Strickler (Eds.), *Reading comprehension: Resource guide.* Bloomington: School of Education, Indiana University.

Buros, O. (Ed.). (1961). *Tests in print: A comprehensive bibliography of tests for use in education, psychology, and industry.* Highland Park, NH: Gryphon.

Bussis, A., & Chittendon, T. (1972). Toward clarifying the teacher's role. In E. Nyquist & G. Hawes (Eds.), *Open Education* (pp. 117–136). New York: Bantam.

Calkins, L. (1983). *Lessons from a child.* Exeter, NH: Heinemann.

Calkins, L. (1986). *The art of teaching writing.* Portsmouth, NH: Heinemann.

Calkins, L. (1994). *The art of teaching writing* (2nd ed.). Portsmouth, NH: Heinemann.

Camilli, G., Vargas, S., & Yurecko, M. (2003). *Teaching children to read: The fragile link between science and federal education policy.* Retrieved July 19, 2004, from http://epaa.asu.edu/epaav11n15/

Campbell, D. (1975). Assessing the impact of planned social change. In *Social research and public policies: The Dartmouth/OEED Conference.* Hanover, NH: Public Affairs Center, Dartmouth College.

Canagarajah, A. S. (1999). *Resisting linguistic imperialism in English teaching.* Oxford, England: Oxford University Press.

Carini, P. (1982). *The school lives of seven children: A five year study.* Grand Forks: North Dakota Study Group on Evaluation.

Cazden, C. (1972). *Child language and education.* New York: Holt, Rinehart & Winston.

Cazden, C. (1979). Peekaboo as an instructional model: Discourse development at home and at school. In *Papers and Reports on Child Language Development* (Vol. 17). Stanford, CA: Department of Linguistics, Stanford University.

Cazden, C., John, V., & Hymes, D. (Eds.). (1972). *Functions of language in the classroom.* New York: Teachers College Press.

Center for Language in Social Life (1987). Critical language awareness. *CLSL Working Paper Series, No. 1.* Lancaster, England: Department of Linguistics and Modern English Language, University of Lancaster.

Chall, J. (1967). *Learning to read: The great debate.* New York: McGraw-Hill.

Chopin, K. (1972). *The awakening.* New York: Avon. (Original work published 1895)

Christensen, L. (2000). *Reading, writing, and rising up.* Milwaukee, WI: Rethinking Schools.

Christian, B., & Bloome, D. (2004). Learning to read is who you are. *Reading and Writing Quarterly, 20,* 365–384.

Christine, C. (1987). *Centering teaching and learning.* Proposal to the Comprehensive Program Fund for the Improvement of Postsecondary Education, Center for Establishing Dialogue, Tempe, AZ.

Church, S., Portelli, J., Macinnis, C., Vibert, A., & Kelly, U. (1994/1995). Reconsidering whole language: Five perspectives. *English Quarterly, 27,* 5–14.

Clandinin, D., & Connelly, F. (1987). Teachers' personal knowledge: What counts as "personal" in studies of the personal. *Journal of Curriculum Studies, 19,* 487–500.

Clarke, M. (1987). Don't blame the system: Constraints on "whole language" reform. *Language Arts, 64,* 384–396.

Clarke, M. (1990). Some cautionary observations on liberation education. *Language Arts, 67,* 388–398.

Clay, M. (1975). *What did I write?* Auckland, New Zealand, Heinemann.

Cole, A. (2001). E-mail. Who's writing teachers' essays. *LiteracyForAll@egroups.com* 11/11/01.

Cole, D. (2001). National security state. *The Nation, 273*(20), 4–5.

Coles, G. (1998). *Reading lessons.* New York: Hill and Wang.

Coles, G. (2000). *Misreading reading: The bad science that hurts children.* Portsmouth, NH: Heinemann.

Coles, G. (2001). Learning to read "scientifically." *Rethinking Schools, 15*(4), 3, 25.

Coles, G. (2003a). *The Bush attack on Head Start: "What this initiative is attempting to do."* Retrieved June 8, 2005, from http://www.pipeline.com/˜rgibson/rouge_forum/bushattacksHS.htm

Coles, G. (2003b). *Reading the naked truth: Literacy, legislation, and lies.* Portsmouth, NH: Heinemann.

Coles, G. (2004). Letter to the editor. *Ed Week.* (circulated on e-mail listserve, 2/4/04).

College Board (2005). *College-bound seniors 2004: A profile of SAT program test takers.* Retrieved January 1, 2006 from http://www.fairtest.org

Collins, J., & Michaels, S. (1986). Speaking and writing: Discourse strategies and the acquisition of literacy. In J. Cook-Gumperz (Ed.), *The Social construction of literacy* (pp. 207–222). New York: Cambridge University Press.

Comber, B. (2001). Critical literacy: Power and pleasure with language in the early years. *Australian Journal of Language and Literacy, 24*(3), 168–181.

Comber, B., & Nixon, H. (1999). Literacy education as a site for social justice: What do our practices do? In C. Edelsky (Ed.), *Making justice our project* (pp. 316–351). Urbana, IL: National Council of Teachers of English.

Comber, B., & O'Brien, J. (1993). Critical literacy: Classroom explorations. *Critical Pedagogy Networker, 6*(½), 1–11.

Comber, B., & Simpson, A. (Eds.). (2001). *Negotiating critical literacies in classrooms.* Mahwah, NJ: Lawrence Erlbaum Associates.

Cook, A., & Meier, D. (n.d.). *Reading tests: What does that score mean?* Grand Forks: North Dakota Study Group on Evaluation.

Cook-Gumperz, J. (1986). Literacy and schooling: An unchanging equation? In J. Cook-Gumperz (ed.), *The social construction of literacy* (pp. 16–44). New York: Cambridge University Press.

Coulmas, F. (1999). *Blackwell encyclopedia of writing systems.* Oxford, England: Blackwell.

Crafton, L. (1991). Whole language: Getting started ... moving forward. Katonah, NY: Owen.

Crawford, J. (1987, April 1). Bilingual education. Language, learning and politics. *Education Week,* 21–50.

Crawford, J. (2000a). *At war with diversity.* Clevedon, England: Multilingual Matters.

Crawford, J. (2000b). Proposition 227: A new phase of the English only movement. In R. Gonzales with I. Melis (Eds.), *Language ideologies* (Vol. 1, pp. 28–61). Urbana, IL, and Mahwah, NJ: National Council of Teachers of English and Lawrence Erlbaum Associates.

Cummins, J. (1976). The influence of bilingualism on cognitive growth: A synthesis of research findings and an explanatory hypothesis. *Working Papers on Bilingualism, 9,* 1–43.

Cummins, J. (1978). Educational implications of mother tongue maintenance in minority-language groups. *Canadian Modern Language Review, 34,* 395–416.

Cummins, J. (1979). Linguistic interdependence and the educational development of bilingual children. *Review of Educational Research, 49,* 222–251.

Cummins, J. (1981). The role of primary language development in promoting educational success for language minority students. In California State Department of Education, *Schooling and language minority students: A theoretical framework.* Los Angeles: Evaluation, Assessment and Dissemination Center.

Cummins, J. (1984). Wanted: A theoretical framework for relating language proficiency to academic achievement among bilingual students. In C. Rivera (Ed.), *Language Proficiency and Academic Achievement* (pp. 2–19). Clevedon, England: Multilingual Matters.

Cummins, J. (1986). Empowering minority students: A framework for intervention. *Harvard Educational Review, 56,* 18–36.

Cummins, J. (1994). Semilingualism. In *Encyclopedia of language and linguistics* (2nd ed., pp. 3812–3814). Oxford, England: Elsevier Science.

Cummins, J. (2000). *Language, power, and pedagogy: Bilingual children in the crossfire.* Clevedon, England: Multilingual Matters.

Cummins, J. (2003). BICS and CALP: Origins and rationale for the distinction. In C. B. Paulston & G. R. Tucker (Eds.), *Sociolinguistics: Essential readings* (pp. 322–328). Malden, MA: Blackwell.

Darling-Hammond, L. (1991). The implications of testing policy for quality and equality. *Phi Delta Kappan, 73*, 220–225.

Davis, M. (2002, September 18). No URL left behind? Web scrub raises concerns. Retrieved June 8, 2005, from http://www.edweek.org/ew/articles/2002/09/18/03web.h22.html

Davis, M. (2005, February 9). Utah is unlikely fly in Bush's school ointment. Retrieved June 8, 2005, from http://www.edweek.org/ew/articles/2005/02/09/22utah.h24.html

Deacon, T. (1997). *The symbolic species: The co-evolution of language and brain.* New York: Norton.

deCastell, S., & Luke, A. (1986). Models of literacy in North American schools: Social and historical conditions and consequences. In S. DeCastell, A. Luke, & K. Egan (Eds.), *Literacy, society and schooling* (pp. 87–109). Cambridge, England: Cambridge University Press.

DeFord, D. (1981). Literacy: Reading, writing, and other essentials. *Language Arts, 58*, 652–658.

DeFord, D. (1985) Validating the construct of theoretical orientation in reading instruction. *Reading Research Quarterly, 15*, 351–367.

DeFord, D., & Harste, J. (1982). Child language research and curriculum. *Language Arts, 58*, 590–600.

Denham, C., & Lieberman, A. (1980). *Time to learn.* Washington, DC: National Institute of Education and California Commission for Teacher Preparation and Licensing.

Deyle, D. (1986). Success and failure: A micro-ethnographic comparison of Navajo and Anglo students' perceptions of testing. *Curriculum Inquiry, 16*, 365–389.

Dillon, S. (2005, February 24). Report faults Bush initiative on education. *New York Times.* Retrieved February 25, 2005, from http://www.nytimes.com/2005/02/24/national/24child.html

Dombey, H. (2004). Revolutionary reading. *Journal of Curriculum Studies, 36*(6), 1–13.

Dowd, M., (2005, February 18). Bush gang's creepiness is starting to out-creep Nixon. *Arizona Republic,* p. V5.

Dressman, M. (2004). Dewey and Bakhtin in dialogue. In A. Ball & S. Freedman (Eds.), *Bakhtinian perspectives on language, literacy, and learning* (pp. 34–52). Cambridge, England: Cambridge University Press.

Dyson, A. (1987). *The social construction of written communication* (Tech. Rpt. No. 2). Berkeley: Center for the Study of Writing, University of California.

Dyson, A. (1989). *The multiple worlds of child writers: A study of friends learning to write.* New York: Teachers College Press.

Dyson, A. (1993a, November). *The Ninjas, the X-men, and the ladies: Playing with power and identity in an urban primary school.* Paper presented at the annual meeting of National Council of Teachers of English, Pittsburgh, PA.

Dyson, A. (1993b). *Social worlds of children learning to write.* New York: Teachers College Press.

Eagleton, T. (1983). *Literacy theory*. Minneapolis: University of Minnesota Press.

Eaton, S. (2005). Wrong for civil rights. *The Nation, 280*(2), 5–6.

Edelman, M. (1985). *The symbolic uses of politics*. Urbana: University of Illinois Press.

Edelman, M. (1988). *Constructing the political spectacle*. Chicago: University of Chicago Press.

Edelsky, C. (1978). "Teaching" oral language. *Language Arts, 55*, 291–296.

Edelsky, C. (with Hudelson, S., Altwerger, B., Flores, B., Barkin, F., & Jilbert, K.). (1983). Semilingualism and language deficit. *Applied Linguistics, 4*, 1–22.

Edelsky, C. (1986). *Writing in a bilingual program: Había una vez*. Norwood, NJ: Ablex.

Edelsky, C. (1987). *Buzz words*. Paper presented at the annual convention of the International Reading Association, Anaheim, CA.

Edelsky, C. (1988). Living in the author's world; analyzing the author's craft. *The California Reader, 21*, 14–17.

Edelsky, C. (1990). Whose agenda is this anyway?: A response to McKenna, Robinson, and Miller. *Educational Researcher, 19*(8), 7–11.

Edelsky, C. (1991). *With literacy and justice for all*. London: Falmer.

Edelsky, C. (1994a). Exercise isn't always healthy. In P. Shannon & K. Goodman (Eds.), *Basal readers: A second look* (pp. 19–33). Katonah, NY: Owen.

Edelsky, C. (1994b, November). *On justice, equity, and petards*. Keynote address delivered at the annual convention of the National Council of Teachers of English, Orlando, FL.

Edelsky. C. (1996). *With literacy and justice for all* (2nd ed.). London: Taylor & Francis.

Edelsky, C. (Ed.). (1999). *Making justice our project*. Urbana, IL: National Council of Teachers of English.

Edelsky, C. (2002). We need an education rights movement. *Talking Points, 13*(2). Retrieved July 16, 2004, from http://www.ncte.org/pub/journals/tp/contents/106717.htm

Edelsky, C. (2005). Relatively speaking: McCarthyism and teacher resisters. In L. Poynor & P. Wolfe (Eds.), *Marketing fear in America's public schools* (pp. 11–28). Mahwah, NJ: Lawrence Erlbaum Associates.

Edelsky, C., Altwerger, B., & Flores, B. (1991). *Whole language: What's the difference?* Portsmouth, NH: Heinemann.

Edelsky, C., & Cherland, M. (in press). A critical issue in critical literacy: The popularity effect. In K. Cooper & R. White (Eds.), *The practical critical educator*. Dordrecht, The Netherlands: Kluwer Academic.

Edelsky, C., & Draper, K. (1989). Reading/"reading;" writing/"writing;" text/"text." *Reading-Canada-Lecture, 7*, 201–216.

Edelsky, C., Draper, K. & Smith, K. (1983). Hookin' 'em in at the start of school in a "whole language" classroom. *Anthropology and Education Quarterly, 14*, 257–281.

Edelsky, C., & Harman, S. (1988). One more critique of testing—with two differences. *English Education, 20*(3), 157–171.

Edelsky, C., & Hudelson, S. (1980). Acquiring a second language when you're not the underdog. In S. Krashen & R. Scarcella (Eds.), *Research in second language acquisition* (pp. 36–42). Rowley, MA: Newbury House.

Edelsky, C., & Hudelson, S. (1989). Contextual complexities: written language policies for bilingual programs. Occasional Paper #10. Center for the study of writing, University of California, Berkerly, CA. (Reprinted in S. Benesch)

(ed.) *ESL in America: Myths and probabilities*, pp. 75–92. Portsmouth, NH: Boynton/Cook-Heinemann.

Edelsky, C. (with S. Hudelson, B. Flores, F. Barkin, B. Altweqer, & K. Jilbert). (1983). Semilingualism and language deficit. *Applied Linguistics, 4*, 1–22.

Edelsky, C., & Jilbert, K. (1985). Bilingual children and writing: Lessons for all of us. *Volta Review, 87*, 57–72.

Edelsky, C., & Johnson, K. (2004). Critical whole language practice in time and place. *Critical Inquiry in Language Studies, 1*, 121–141.

Edelsky, C., & Rosegrant, T. (1981). Language development for mainstreamed severely handicapped non-verbal children. *Language Arts, 58*, 68–76.

Edelsky, C., & Smith, K. (1984). Is that writing—or are those marks just a figment of your curriculum? *Language Arts, 61*, 24–32.

Edelsky, C., & Smith, K. (in press). Through the looking glass: Understanding academic work. In K. Rolstad (Ed.), *Rethinking classroom language*. Mahwah, NJ: Lawrence Erlbaum Associates.

Edelsky, C., Smith, K., & Wolfe, P. (2002). A discourse on academic discourse. *Linguistics and Education, 13*(1), 1–38.

Emmer, E., Evertson, C., & Anderson, L. (1980). Effective classroom management at the beginning of the school year. *Elementary School Journal, 80*, 5–10.

Engel, M. (2000). *The struggle for control of public education: Market ideology vs. democratic values*. Philadelphia: Temple University Press.

Enright, S. (1986). Use everything you have to teach English: Providing useful input to young language learners. In P. Rigg & S. Enright (Eds.), *Children and ESL: Integrating perspectives* (pp. 113–162). Washington, DC: Teachers of English to Speakers of Other Languages.

Erickson, F. (1979). Mere ethnography: Some problems in its use in educational practice. *Anthropology and Education Quarterly, 10*, 182–188.

Erickson. F. (1984). School literacy, reasoning, and civility: An anthropologist's perspective. *Review of Educational Research, 54*, 525–546.

Erickson, F. (1986). Tasks in times: Objects of study in a natural history of teaching. In K. Zumwalt (Ed.), *Improving teaching: ASCD yearbook* (pp. 131–147). Alexandria, VA: Association for Supervision and Curriculum Development.

Ervin-Tripp, S. (1970). Structure and process in language acquisition. In J. Alatis (Ed.), *Bilingualism and language contact: Anthropological, linguistic, psychological and social aspects* Georgetown University Roundtable(No. 23, pp. 313–353). Washington, DC: Georgetown University Press.

Evertson, C., & Emmer, E. (1982). Effective management at the beginning of the school year in junior high classes. *Journal of Educational Psychology, 74*, 485–498.

Fairclough, N. (1989). *Language and power*. Essex, England: Longman.

Fairclough, N. (1992a). The appropriacy of "appropriateness." In N. Fairclough (Ed.), *Critical language awareness* (pp. 33–56). Essex, England: Longman.

Fairclough, N. (1992b). *Critical language awareness*. Essex, England: Longman.

Fairness and Accuracy In Reporting. (2002a, April 3). PBS's "commanding" conflict of interest. E-mail. *LiteracyForAll@egroups.com*

Fairness and Accuracy in Reporting Action Alert. (2002b, June 17). A changed present—Or a new repression? E-mail. *LiteracyForAll@egroups.com*

FairTest. (1990). *Standardized tests and our children: A guide to testing reform*. Cambridge, MA: Author.

FairTest. (1998–1999). Michigan test boycott continues. *FairTest Examiner, 13*(1), 1, 12.

FairTest. (2004a). Feds tinker with NCLB regulations to relieve pressure. *FairTest Examiner, 18*(1–2), 18–19.

FairTest. (2004b). *Press release. College Board seeks to suppress SAT equity charts: Lawyers' letter claims copyright control over data on test's racial, gender, and income bias.* Retrievd January 9, 2004 from http://www.fairtest.org/univ/Suppression_PR.html

Faltis, C., & Hudelson, S. (1998). *Bilingual education in elementary and secondary school communities: Toward understanding and caring.* Boston: Allyn & Bacon.

Farenga, A. (1999). E-mail. Phour phonics plans humbug! *NRCEMAIL@ASU.EDU* (12/13/99)

Featherstone, J. (1995). Democratic vistas. *The Nation, 260*(24), 890–893.

Ferreiro, E., & Teberosky, A. (1982). *Literacy before schooling.* Exeter, NH: Heinemann.

Fillmore, L. W. (1976). *The second time around: Cognitive and social strategies in second language acquisition.* Unpublished doctoral dissertation, Stanford University.

Fillmore, L. W. (1978, October). *Directionality in second language acquisition.* Paper presented at Los Angeles Second Language Acquisition Research Forum, University of Southern California.

Fine, E. S. (with Slater, K.). (2003). Out there with the kids: Why bother? *Language Arts, 81*(1), 34–42.

Fine, M. (2005). Not in our name: Reclaiming the democratic vision of small school reform. *Rethinking Schools, 19*(4), 11–14.

Fingeret, A. (1987, February 13). Talk given at Literacy Assistance Center, New York.

Finn, C. (2003, March 27). The law people love to hate—And pretend to love. *Education Gadfly, 3*(11). Retrieved April 14, 2003, from http://www.edexcellence.net/foundation/gadfly/issue.cfm?id=16

Fiore, K., & Elsasser, N. (1982). "Strangers no more:" A liberatory literacy curriculum. *College English, 44,* 115–128.

Fishman, J. (1976). *Bilingual education: An international sociological perspective.* Rowley, MA: Newbury House.

Fiske, J., & Hartley, J. (1979). *Reading television.* London: Methuen.

Fleck, T. (2001). Days of Paige: Did Bush pick a master educator—Or an overpaid front man? Retrieved January 16, 2001, from http://www.houstonpress.com/issues/2001-01-11/insider.html

Flores, B., Cousin, P., & Díaz, E. (1991). Transforming deficit myths about learning, language, and culture. *Language Arts, 68,* 369–379.

Florio, S. (1980). *Very special natives: The evolving role of teachers as informants in educational ethnography.* Paper presented at 5th annual College of Education Symposium, University of Delaware, Newark.

Florio, S., & Clark, C. (1982). The functions of writing in an elementary classroom. *Research in the Teaching of English, 16,* 115–130.

Flurkey, A., Paulson, E., & Goodman, K. (in press). *Scientific realism in studies of reading.* Mahwah, NJ: Lawrence Erlbaum Associates.

Foorman, B., Francis, D., Fletcher, J., & Schatschneider, C. (1998). The role of instruction in learning to read: Preventing reading failure in at-risk children. *Journal of Educational Psychology, 92,* 37–55.

Fox, J. (1999). *Grilling our young.* Retrieved January 6, 2005, from http://www.salon.com/mwt/feature/1999/11/08/testing

Freeman, R. (2005). Is public education working? How would we know? Retrieved January 7, 2005, from http://www.commondreams.org/views05/0103–22.htm

Freeman, Y., Freeman, D., & Fennacy, J. (1997). California's reading revolution: What happened? *The New Advocate, 10*(1), 31–48.

Friends Committee on National Legislation. (2004). INFOLINE: Government surveillance hits home. Retrieved March 18, 2004, from https://dnbweb1.blackbaud.com/OPXREPHIL/Link.asp?link=15476

Freire, P. (1970). *Pedagogy of the oppressed.* New York: Seabury.

Froebel, F. (1826). *The education of man* (W. Hailmann, Trans.). New York: Appleton.

Fromkin, V., & Rodman, R. (1983). *An introduction to language.* New York: Holt, Rinehart & Winston.

Fusco, C. (2005). Questioning the frame: Thoughts about maps and spatial logic in the global present. *In These Times, 29*(3), 30–32.

Garan, E. (2001). Beyond the smoke and mirrors: A critique of the National Reading Panel Report on phonics. *Phi Delta Kappan, 82,* 500–507.

Garan, E. (2002). *Resisting reading mandates: How to triumph with the truth.* Portsmouth, NH: Heinemann.

Garan, E. (2005). Scientific flimflam: A who's who of entrepreneurial research. In B. Altwerger (Ed.), *Reading for profit* (pp. 21–32). Portsmouth, NH: Heinemann.

Garcia, E., & Curry-Rodriguez, J. (2000). The education of limited English proficient students in California schools: An assessment of the influence of Proposition 227 in selected districts and schools. *Bilingual Research Journal, 24*(1–2). Retrieved July 26, 2004, from http://brj.asu.edu

Gee, J. (1987). What is literacy? *Teaching and Learning, The Journal of Natural Inquiry, 2,* 3–11.

Gee, J. (1989a). Literacy, discourse, and linguistics: Introduction. *Journal of Education, 171,* 5–17

Gee, J. (1989b). What do English teachers teach? (or why isn't the Pope a bachelor?) *Journal of Education, 171,* 135–147.

Gee, J. (1989c). What is literacy? *Journal of Education, 171,* 18–25.

Gee, J. (1990). *Social linguistics and literacies.* London: Falmer.

Gee, J. (1992a). Reading. *Journal of Urban and Cultural Studies, 2*(2), 65–77.

Gee, J. (1992b). *The social mind.* New York: Bergin & Garvey.

Gee, J. (1994). First language acquisition as a guide for theories of learning and pedagogy. *Linguistics and Education, 6,* 331–354.

Gee, J. (1999). *An introduction to discourse analysis.* London: Routledge.

Gee, J. (2004a). New times and new literacies. In A. Ball & S. Freedman (Eds.), *Bakhtinian perspectives on language, literacy, and learning* (pp. 279–306). Cambridge, England: Cambridge University Press.

Gee, J. (2004b). *Situated language and learning.* New York: Routledge.

Geertz, C. (1973). *The interpretations of cultures.* New York: Basic Books.

General Accounting Office. (1987). *Bilingual education: A new look at the research evidence.* Washington, DC: U.S. Government Printing Office.

Giaccobbe, M. (1989). Workshop presented at the Center for Establishing Dialogue between Teaching and Learning, Tempe, AZ.

Gibson, R. (1986). *Critical theory and education.* London: Hodder and Stoughton.

Gilbert, P. (1989). Personally (and passively) yours: Girls, literacy and education. *Oxford Review of Education, 15,* 257–265.

Gilbert, P. (1991). Writing pedagogy: Personal voices, truth telling and "real" texts. In C. Baker & A. Luke (Eds.), *Towards a critical sociology of reading pedagogy* (pp. 27–47). Amsterdam: John Benjamins.

Gillespie, N. (2005). Connecticut to challenge No Child Left Behind education law. E-mail. *LiteracyForAll@egroups.com*

Gillis, C., Bixby, M., Crowley, P., Crenshaw, S., Henrichs, M., Reynolds, F., & Pyle, D. (Eds.). (1988). *Whole language strategies for secondary students.* Katonah, NY: Owen.

Gilman, C. (1973). *The yellow wallpaper.* Old Westbury, NY: Feminist Press. (Original work published 1892)

Giroux, H. (1984). Rethinking the language of schooling. *Language Arts, 61,* 33–40.

Giroux, H. (1987). Critical literacy and student experience: Donald Graves' approach to literacy. *Language Arts, 64,* 175–181.

Gitlin, A. (1980). *Understanding the work of teachers.* Unpublished doctoral dissertation, University of Wisconsin–Madison.

Gladwin, H. (1985). In conclusion: Abstraction versus "how it is." *Anthropology and Education Quarterly, 16,* 207–213.

Glaser, B. (1978). *Theoretical sensitivity.* Mill Valley, CA: Sociology Press.

Glass, G. (2003). Standards and redux. Retrieved May 10, 2005, from http://glass. ed.asu.edu/gene/papers/standards/

Goldberg, M. (2003, November 6). Osama university? *Salon.* Retrieved June 8, 2005, from http://archive.salon.com/news/feature/2003/11/06/middle_east/index_np.html

Gollasch, F. (1982). *Language and literacy: The selected writings of Kenneth S. Goodman* (Vols. 1 and 2). London: Routledge & Kegan Paul.

Gonzales, R. (with Melis, I.). (Eds.). (2000). *Language ideologies* (Vols. 1 and 2). Urbana, IL, and Mahwah, NJ: NCTE and Lawrence Erlbaum Associates.

Goodman, K. (1969). Analysis of oral reading miscues: Applied psycholinguistics. *Reading Research Quarterly, 5,* 9–30.

Goodman, K. (1984). Unity in reading. In A. Purves & O. Niles (Eds.), *Becoming readers in a complex society: 83rd yearbook of the National Society for the Study of Education* (pp. 79–114). Chicago: National Society for the Study of Education.

Goodman, K. (1986). *What's whole in whole language?* Portsmouth, NH: Heinemann.

Goodman, K. (1992, October). Response to Ray McDermott. Department of Reading, Language, and Culture Lecture Series, University of Arizona, Tucson.

Goodman, K. (1993). *Phonics phacts.* Portsmouth, NH: Heinemann.

Goodman, K. (2002, February 1). Absurdity of the month. *LiteracyForAll@egroups.com*

Goodman, K. (2005). Making sense of written language: A lifelong journey. *Journal of Literacy Research, 37*(1), 1–24.

Goodman, K., & Goodman, Y. (1978). *Reading of American children whose language is a stable rural dialect of English or a language other than English* (Final Report, Project NIE G00-3-0087). Washington, DC: National Institutes of Education.

Goodman, K., & Goodman, Y. (1981). *A whole-language comprehension centered view of reading development.* Occasional Paper No. 1, Program in Language and Literacy, University of Arizona, Tucson.

Goodman, K., Goodman, Y., & Flores, B. (1979). *Reading in the bilingual classroom: Literacy and biliteracy.* Rosslyn, VA: National Clearinghouse for Bilingual Education.

Goodman, K., Goodman, Y., Shannon, P., & Rapoport, R. (2004). *Saving our schools: The case for public education.* Oakland, CA: RDR.

Goodman, K., Shannon, P., Freeman, Y., & Murphy, S. (1988). *Report card on basal readers.* Katonah, NH: Owen.

Goodman, Y. (1978). Kid watching: An alternative to testing. *National Elementary Principal, 57,* 41–45.

Goodman, Y. (1985). "Kidwatching:" Observing children in the classroom. In A. Jaggar & T. Smith-Burke (Eds.), *Observing the language learner* (pp. 9–19). Newark, DE: International Reading Association.

Goodman, Y. (2003). *Valuing language study.* Urbana, IL: National Council of Teachers of English.

Goodman, Y., & Burke, C. (with Sherman, B.). (1980). *Reading strategies: Focus on comprehension.* New York: Owen.

Goodman, Y., Watson, D., & Burke, C. (1987). *Reading Miscue Inventory.* New York: Owen.

Goodman, Y., Watson, D., & Burke, C. (1996). *Reading strategies: Focus on comprehension* (2nd ed.). Katonah, NH: Owen.

Gore, J. (1993). *The struggle for pedagogies.* New York: Routledge.

Gould, S. J. (1981). *The mismeasure of man.* New York: Norton.

Graff, H. (1986). The legacies of literacy: Continuities and contradictions in Western society and culture. In S. DeCastell, A. Luke, & K. Egan (Eds.), *Literacy, society and schooling* (pp. 61–86). Cambridge, England: Cambridge University Press.

Graff, H. (1987). *The legacies of literacy.* Bloomington: Indiana University Press.

Graves, D. (1978). We won't let them write. *Language Arts, 55,* 635–640.

Graves, D. (1979). Colloquium, University of Arizona, Tucson.

Graves, D. (1983). *Writing: Teachers and children at work.* Exeter, NH: Heinemann.

Green, B. (1991). Reading "readings:" Towards a postmodernist reading pedagogy. In C. Baker & A. Luke (Eds.), *Towards a critical sociology of reading pedagogy* (pp. 211–238). Amsterdam: Benjamins.

Green, J., & Wallat, C. (1981). Mapping instructional conversation—A sociolinguistic ethnography. In J. Green & C. Wallat (Eds.), *Ethnography and language in educational settings* (pp. 161–205). Norwood, NJ: Ablex.

Greene, J., & Woods, J. (2000). *Language readers: Level 1, Book A, Units 1–6.* Longmont, CO: Sopris West.

Grosjean, F. (1982). *Life with two languages: An introduction to bilingualism.* Cambridge, MA: Harvard University Press.

Gross, R., & Gross, B. (1969). *Radical school reform.* New York: Simon & Schuster.

Grossen, B. (1997). *30 years of research: what we now know about how children learn to read.* Santa Cruz, CA: Center for the Future of Teaching and Learning.

Gryphon, M. (2005, February 28). Education law encourages fuzzy math. Retrieved April 25, 2005, from http://www.cato.org/ub_display.php?pub_id=3694

Gullingsrud, M. (2005). Email. *LiteracyForAll@egruoups.com*

Hakuta, K. (1986). *Mirror of language: The debate on bilingualism.* New York: Basic Books.

Hale, R., & Potok, A. (1981). Sexual bias in the Slosson Intelligence Test. *Diagnostique, 6,* 3–7.

Hall, S. (1966). *The hidden dimension.* New York: Doubleday.

Halliday, M. A. K. (1977). *Learning how to mean.* New York: Elsevier North Holland.

Halliday, M. A. K. (1978). *Language as social semiotic: The social interpretation of language and meaning.* Baltimore: University Park Press.

Halliday, M. A. K. (1985). *An introduction to functional grammar.* Baltimore: Arnold.

Halliday, M. A. K. (1990). *Linguistic perspectives on literacy: A systemic functional approach.* Paper presented at the Inaugural Australian Systemics Network Conference, Deakin University, Geelong, Victoria, Australia.

Halliday, M. (1993). Towards a language-based theory of learning. *Linguistics and Education, 5,* 93–116.

Haney, W. (1984). Testing reasoning and reasoning about testing. *Review of Educational Research, 54,* 597–654.

Haney, W. (2001). The myth of the Texas miracle in education. *Educational Policy Analysis Archives.* Retrieved April 13, 2004, from http://epaa/asu.edu/epaa/v8n41/

Haney, W., & Madaus, G. (1991). Searching for alternatives to standardized tests: Whys, whats, and whithers. *Phi Delta Kappan 70,* 683–687.

Hansen, J. (1987). *When writers read.* Portsmouth, NH: Heinemann.

Harman, S. (1990). The tests: Trivial or toxic? *Teachers Networking 9*(1), 1, 12.

Harman, S., & Edelsky, C. (1989). Risks of whole language literacy: Alienation and connection. *Language Arts, 66,* 392–406.

Harris, R. (1986). *Origin of writing.* London: Duckworth.

Harste, J. (n.d.). *A profession at risk.* Unpublished manuscript, Indiana University.

Harste, J. (1980). Examining instructional assumptions: The child as informant. *Theory Into Practice, 19,* 170–178.

Harste, J. (1989). The basalization of American reading instruction: One researcher responds. *Theory Into Practice, 28,* 265–273.

Harste, J. (2004, May). *Literature, literacy, and visual images.* Presentation given at the Critical Discourse Analysis Conference, Indiana University, Bloomington.

Harste, J., & Burke, C. (1977). A new hypothesis for reading teacher research: Both teaching and learning of reading are theoretically based. In P. D. Pearson (Ed.), *Reading: Theory, research, and practice: 26th Yearbook of the National Reading Conference* (pp. 32–40). St. Paul, MN: Mason.

Harste, J., Burke, C., & Woodward, V. (1982). *Children's language and world: Initial encounters with print* (Final Report, Project NIE G-79-0132). Washington, DC: National Institutes of Education.

Harste, J., Burke, C., & Woodward, V. (1983). *The young child as writer–reader and informant* (Final Report, Project NIE G-80-0121). Washington, DC: National Institutes of Education.

Harste, J., Short, K. (with Burke, C.). (1988). *Creating classrooms for authors.* Portsmouth, NH: Heinemann.

Harste, J., Woodward, V., & Burke, C. (1984). *Language stories and literacy lessons.* Exeter, NH: Heinemann.

Hart, P., & Hollar, J. (2005). *Fear & favor 2004—FAIR's fifth annual report.* Retrieved May 2, 2005, from. http://www.fair.org

Hatch, E. (1978). Discourse analysis and second language acquisition. In E. Hatch (Ed.), *Second language acquisition* (pp. 401–435). Rowley, MA: Newbury House.

Hawkins, M. (2004). Researching English language and literacy development in schools. *Educational Researcher, 33*(3), pp. 14–25.

Hearn, J. (1982). Notes on patriarchy: Professionalization and the semiprofessions. *Sociology, 16,* 184–202.

Heath, S. B. (1982). What no bedtime story means: Narrative skills at home and school. *Language in Society, 11,* 49–78.

Heath, S. B. (1983). *Ways with words: Language, life, and work in communities and Classrooms.* Cambridge, England: Cambridge University Press.

Heffernan, L., & Lewison, M. (2003). Social narrative writing: (Re)constructing kid culture in the writer's workshop. *Language Arts, 80,* 435–443.

Henkin, R. (1998). *Who's invited to share?* Portsmouth, NH: Heinemann.

Herman, E. (2005). "They kill reporters, don't they?" *Z Magazine, 18*(1), 42–46.

Hill, J. (2000). The racializing function of language panics. In R. Gonzales (with I. Melis) (Eds.), *Language ideologies* (Vol. 2, pp. 245–267). Urbana, IL and Mahwah, NJ: National Council of Teachers of English and Lawrence Erlbaum Associates.

Himley, M. (with Carini, P.). (2000). *From another angle.* New York: Teachers College Press.

Hirsch, E. (1987). *Cultural literacy: What every American needs to know.* New York: Houghton Mifflin.

Hobbs, N., and the Committee on Ethical Standards for Psychology. (1953). *Ethical Standards for Psychology.* Washington, DC: American Psychological Association.

Hoff, D. (2005). NCLB law needs work, legislators assert. *Ed Week, 24*(25), pp. 1, 20.

Hoffman, B. (1962). *The tyranny of testing.* New York: Crowell-Collier.

Holland, D., & Lave, J. (2001). History in person: An introduction. In D. Holland & J. Lave (Eds.), *History in person* (pp. 3–33). Santa Fe, NM: School of American Research Press.

Horton, M. (1990). *The long haul.* New York: Doubleday.

Houtz, J. (2001). Temps spend just minutes to score state education test. E-mail. *LiteracyForAll@egroups.com,* 1/2/01

Hudelson, S. (1981–1982). An investigation of children's invented spelling in Spanish. *NABE Journal, 9,* 53–68.

Hudelson, S. (1984). Kan yu ret an rayt en ingles: Children become literate in English as a second language. *TESOL Quarterly, 18,* 221–238.

Hudelson, S. (1985). *Janice: Becoming a writer of English.* (ERIC Document Reproduction Service No. ED249760).

Hudelson, S. (1986). ESL children's writing: What we've learned, what we're learning. In P. Rigg & S. Enright (Eds.), *Children and ESL: Integrating perspectives* (pp. 23–54). Washington, DC: Teachers of English to Speakers of Other Languages.

Hudelson, S. (1987). The role of native language literacy in the education of language minority children. *Language Arts, 64,* 827–841.

Hudelson, S., & Edelsky, C. (1980). Language acquisition and a marked language. *NABE Journal, 5*(1), 1.15.

Hudson, S. (1988). Children's perceptions of classroom writing: Ownership within a continuum of control. In B. Rafoth & D. Rubin (Eds.), *The social construction of written communication* (pp. 37–69). Norwood, NJ: Ablex.

Hurston, Z. N. (1979). *I love myself when I am laughing.* Old Westbury, NY: Feminist Press.

Hymes, D. (1970). The ethnography of speaking. In J. Fishman (Ed.), *Readings in the sociology of language* (pp. 99–138). The Hague, The Netherlands: Mouton.

Hymes, D. (1972a). Introduction. In C. Cazden, D. Hymes, & V. John (Eds.), *Functions of language in the classroom* (pp. xi–lvli). New York: Teachers College Press.

Hymes, D. (1972b). The scope of sociolinguistics. In R. Shuy (Ed.), *Sociolinguistics, Georgetown University Roundtable* (No. 25, pp. 313–333). Washington, DC: Georgetown University Press.

Hymes, D. (1980a). Functions of speech: An evolutionary approach. In *Language and ethnography series, language in education: Ethnolinguistic essays* (pp. 1–18). Washington, DC: Center for Applied Linguistics.

Hymes, D. (1980b). Speech and language: On the origins and foundations of inequalities among speakers. In *Language and ethnography series, language in education: Ethnologuistic essays* (pp. 19–61). Washington, DC: Center for Applied Linguistics.

Illich, I. (1970). *Deschooling society.* New York: Harper & Row.

Informant fever. (2002, July 22). *New York Times,* p. A18.

Ingalls, J., & Kolhatkar, S. (2004). Elections in Afghanistan. *Z Magazine, 17*(11), 3–4.

Itoh, H., & Hatch, E. (1978). Second language acquisition: A case study. In E. Hatch (Ed.), *Second language acquisition* (pp. 76–88). Rowley, MA: Newbury House.

Ivins, M. (2003, February 2). Maximizing a minimal media. *Arizona Republic,* p. V5.

Ivins, M. (2005, March 17). Brainwashed at our own expense. *Arizona Republic,* p. B7.

Jackendoff, R. (2003). Precis of *Foundations of language. Behavioral and Brain Sciences, 26,* 651–707.

Janks, H., & Ivanič, R. (1992). CLA and emancipatory discourse. In N. Fairclough (Ed.), *Critical language awareness* (pp. 305–331). London: Longman.

Jennings, K., & Jennings, S. (1974). Tests and experiments with children. In A. Cicourel (Ed.), *Language use and school performance* (pp. 248–299). New York: Academic.

Johnston, P. (1985). Understanding reading disability: A case study approach. *Harvard Educational Review, 55,* 153–177.

Jordan, J. (1985). *On call: Political essays.* Boston: South End Press.

Kamler, B. (1980). One child, one teacher, one classroom: The story of one piece of writing. *Language Arts, 57,* 680–693.

Katz, A. (2005, May 15). Walkout has schools, city at the ready. *Oakland Tribune.* Retrieved May 15, 2005, from http:www.insidebayarea.com/oaklandtribune/localnews/ci_2736691

Kazmin, B. (2001, January 5). Texas gains made with smoke, mirrors. E-mail. *Columbus [Ohio] Dispatch.* 1/5/00. LiteracyForAll@egroups.com

Keller, B. (2005). *N.D., Utah dispute federal findings on teacher quality.* Retrieved January 12, 2005, from http://www.edweek.org/ew/artilces/2005/01/12/18qualified.h24html

Kennedy, R. (2004, March 8). The junk science of George W. Bush. *The Nation.* Retrieved June 19, 2005, from http://www.thenation.com/doc.mhtml

Kessler, G., & Fletcher, M. (2001, May 13). Tax bill gives benefits for education: Subsidy for private schooling among $30 billion in breaks. *Washington Post,* p. AO1.

Kimberley, K. (1989). Community publishing. In S. DeCastell, A. Luke, & C. Luke (Eds.), *Language, authority and criticism* (pp. 184–94). East Sussex, England: Falmer.

Kingston, M. H. (1976). *Woman warrior.* New York: Knopf.

Kirsch, I., Jungeblut, A., Jenkins, L., & Kolstad, A. (1993). *Adult literacy in America: A first look at the National Adult Literacy Survey.* National Center for Education Statistics, NCES 93275. Retrieved from http://nces.ed.gov/pubsearch/pubsinfo. asp?pubid=93275

Kliewer, C., Fitzgerald, L., Meyer-Mork, J., Hartman, P., English-Sand, P., & Raschke, D. (2004). Citizenship for all in the literate community: an ethnography of young children with significant disabilities in inclusive early childhood settings. *Harvard Educational Review, 74,* 373–403.

Kohn, A. (2001). Fighting the tests. *Phi Delta Kappan 82,* 348–357.

Kozol, J. (1991). *Savage inequalities.* New York: Crown.

Krashen, S. (1982). *Principles and practice in second language acquisition.* Hayward, CA: Alemany.

Krashen, S. (1988). Do we learn to read by reading? The relationship between free reading and reading ability. In D. Tannen (Ed.), *Linguistics in context: Connecting observation and understanding* (pp. 269–298). Norwood, NJ: Ablex.

Krashen, S. (2001a, February 14) E-mail, Access to books, not SES. *LiteracyForAll@ egroups.com*

Krashen, S. (2001b, April 20). E-mail, Comments on NAEP. *LiteracyForAll@ egroups.com*

Krashen, S. (2001c, October 10). E-mail, Cold fusion in LA. *LiteracyForAll@egroups.com*

Krashen, S. (2005, January 16). E-mail, Intensive phonics and English-only didn't help. *LiteracyForAll@egroups.com*

Kress, G., & Trew, T. (1978). Ideological transformations of discourse: Or, how the *Sunday Times* got its message across. *Sociological Review, 26,* 755–776.

Kress, G., & van Leeuwen, T. (1996). *Reading images.* London: Routledge.

Krugman, P. (2002. March 29). The smoke machine. *New York Times.* Retrieved December 17, 2005, from http://www.pkarchive.org/column/032902.html

Krugman, P. (2003). Channels of influence. *New York Times.* Retrieved January 15, 2005, from http://www.pkarchive.org/column/032503.html

Kurtz, H. (2005, January 8). Administration paid commentator. *Washington Post,* p. AO1. Retrieved December 18, 2005, from http://www.washingtonpost.com/ wp-dyn/articles/A56339-2005jan2.html

Laboratory for Comparative Human Cognition. (1982). A model system for the study of learning difficulties. *Quarterly Newsletter of the Laboratory of Comparative Human Cognition, 4,* 39–66.

Labov, W. (1970). The logic of non-standard English. In F. Williams (Ed.), *Language and poverty* (pp. 153–189). Chicago: Markham.

Labov, W. (1972). *Language in the inner city.* Philadelphia: University of Pennsylvania Press.

Lakoff, G. (2002). *Moral politics* (2nd ed.). Chicago, University of Chicago Press.

Lakoff, G. (2004). *Don't think of an elephant.* White River Junction, VT: Chelsea Green.

Lakoff, G., & Johnson, M. (1980). *Metaphors we live by.* Chicago: University of Chicago Press.

Lakoff, G., & Johnson, M. (1999). *Philosophy in the flesh.* New York: Basic Books.

Lambert, W., & Tucker, G. (1972). *Bilingual education of children: The St. Lambert experiment.* Rowley, MA: Newbury House.

Laminack, L., & Lawing, S. (1994). Building generative curriculum. *Primary Voices K–6, 2*(3), 8–18.

Lamoreaux, L., & Lee, D. (1943). *Learning to read through experience.* New York: Appleton-Century-Crofts.

Lappé, F., & Lappé, A. (2003). *Hope's edge.* New York: Tarcher/Putnam.

Lau et al. v. Nichols et al., 414 U.S. 563 (1974). Certiorari to the United States Court of Appeal for the Ninth Circuit. Argued on December 10, 1973, in the U.S. Supreme Court. Decided January 21, 1974.

Lave, J., & Wenger, E. (1991). *Situated learning.* New York: Cambridge University Press.

Leland, C., & Harste, J. (with Huber, K.). (2005). Out of the box: Critical literacy in a first-grade classroom. *Language Arts, 82,* 257–268.

Leland, C., Harste, J., Ociepka, A., Lewison, M., & Vasquez, V. (1999). Exploring critical literacy: You can hear a pin drop. *Language Arts, 77,* 70–77.

Lemke, J. (1990). *Talking science: Language, learning, and values.* Norwood, NJ: Ablex.

Lensmire, T. (1994). *When children write: Critical re-visions of the writing workshop.* New York: Teachers College Press.

Leont'ev, A. (1978). *Activity, consciousness, and personality.* Englewood Cliffs, NJ: Prentice Hall.

Libit, H. (2001, October 3). Proposal for more testing draws criticism. *Baltimore Sun.* Retrieved October 4, 2001, from http://www.sunspot.net/news/local/bal-md.mspap03oct03.story?coll=bal%Dlocal%2Dheadlines

Lieberman, T. (2000). *Slanting the story.* New York: New Press.

Lindfors, J. (1984). How children learn or how teachers teach? A profound confusion. *Language Arts, 61,* 607–617.

Lindfors, J. (1987). *Children's language and learning* (2nd ed.). Englewood Cliffs, NJ: Prentice Hall.

Lipman, P. (2005, February). *Educational ethnography and the politics of globalization, war, and resistance.* Keynote address delivered at the 26th annual Ethnography in Education Research Forum, University of Pennsylvania, Philadelphia.

Lippi-Green, R. (1997). *English with an accent.* London: Routledge.

Loughlin, C., & Suina, J. (1982). *The learning environment.* New York: Teachers College Press.

Lucas, C. (1976). Humanism and the schools: The open education movement. In C. Lucas (Ed.), *Challenge and choice in contemporary education* (pp. 169–191). New York: Macmillan.

Luke, A. (1991). Producing the literate: From psychology to linguistics; metanarrative and the politics of schooling. In F. Christie (Ed.), *Literacy in social processes* (pp. 83–96). Darwin, Australia: Northern Territory University Press.

Luke, A. (1995). When basic skills and information processing just aren't enough: Rethinking reading in new times. *Teachers College Record, 97,* 95–115.

Luke, A., & Freebody, P. (1997). Shaping the social practices of reading. In S. Muspratt, A. Luke, & P. Freebody (Eds.), *Constructing critical literacies* (pp. 185–225). Cresskill, NJ: Hampton.

Luke, A., Freebody, P., & Gilbert, P. (1991). What counts as reading in the secondary school classroom: The selective tradition of reading practices and positions. In F. Christie (Ed.), *Teaching English literacy* (Vol. 2, pp. 56–70). Darwin, Australia: Northern Territory University, Centre for Studies of Language in Education.

Luke, A., O'Brien, J., & Comber, B. (1994). Making community texts objects of study. *Australian Journal of Language and Literacy, 17,* 139–149.

Lyotard, J. (1984). *The postmodern condition: A report on knowledge.* Manchester, England: Manchester University Press.

MacSwan, J. (1999). *A minimalist approach to intrasentiential code switching.* New York: Garland.

MacSwan, J. (2000). The threshold hypothesis, semilingualism, and other contributions to a deficit view of linguistic minorities. *Hispanic Journal of Behavioral Sciences, 22,* 3–45.

MacSwan, J., & Rolstad, K. (2003). Linguistic diversity, schooling, and social class: Rethinking our conception of language proficiency in language minority education. In C. B. Paulston & G. R. Tucker (Eds.), *Sociolinguistics: Essential readings* (pp. 329–340). Malden, MA: Blackwell.

Madaus, G. (1988). The influence of testing on the curriculum. In L. Tanner (Ed.), *Critical issues in curriculum: 87th yearbook of the National Society for the Study of Education* (pp. 83–121). Chicago: University of Chicago Press.

Mahoney, K., Thompson, M., & MacSwan, J. (2004). *The condition of English language learners in Arizona: 2004.* Retrieved June 8, 2005, from http://www.asu.edu/educ/epsl/AEPI/EPSL-0405-106-AEPI.pdf.

Manzo, K. (2005, June 8). States report Reading First yielding gains; Some schools getting ousted for quitting. *Ed Week.* Retrieved June 10, 2005, from http://www.edweek.org/ew/articles/2005/06/08/39read.h24.html

Martinez-Roldan, C. (2003). Building worlds and identities. *Research in the Teaching of English, 37,* 491–526.

Matthews, J. (2001, July 17). Adult illiteracy, rewritten. *Washington Post,* p. A 09.

McCarthyism Watch. (2003). Cop makes midnight raid of teacher's classroom. *The Progressive.* Retrieved May 13, 2003, from http://www.progressive.org/mcwatch03/mc051003.html

McDermott, R. (1977). Social relations as contexts for learning in school. *Harvard Educational Review, 47,* 198–213:

McDermott, R. (1992, October). *A short history of writing systems, with implications for reading cultures.* Lecture Series, Department of Reading, Language and Culture, University of Arizona, Tucson.

McDermott, R. (1993, April). *An anthropologist reads from his work.* Paper presented at the annual meeting of the American Educational Research Association, Atlanta, GA.

McLaren, P., & Farahmandpur, R. (2002). Breaking signifying chains. In D. Hill, P. McLaren, M. Cole, & G. Rikowski (Eds.), *Marxism against postmodernism in educational theory* (pp. 35–66). Lanham, MD: Lexington Books.

Media Reform. (2004). *Media monopoly made simple.* Retrieved January 22, 2004, from http://www.mediareform.net/media/tenthings.php

Mehan, H. (1979). *Learning lessons.* Cambridge, MA. Harvard University Press.

Mehan, H., & Wood, H. (1975). *The reality of ethnomethodology.* New York: Wiley.

Meier, D. (1981). Why reading tests don't test reading. *Dissent, 28,* 457–466.

Meisels, S. (1989). High stakes testing in kindergarten. *Educational Leadership, 46*(7), 16–21.

Mellor, B., Patterson, A., & O'Neill, M. (1991). *Reading fictions.* Scarborough, Western Australia: Chalkface.

Metcalf, S. (2002). Reading between the lines. *The Nation, 274*(30), 18–22.

Meyer, R. (2004). Rod Paige, super star. In K. Goodman (Ed.), *Saving our schools: The case for public education, saying no to No Child Left Behind* (pp. 101–103). Oakland, CA: RDR.

Miller, M. C. (2002). What's wrong with this picture? *The Nation, 274*(1), 18–22.

Mills, H., O'Keefe, T., & Stephens, D. (1992). *Looking closely: Exploring the role of phonics in the whole language classroom.* Urbana, IL: National Council of Teachers of English.

Miner, B. (2004–2005).Testing companies mine for gold. *Rethinking Schools, 19*(2), 5–7.

Minick, N. (1985). *L. S. Vygotsky and Soviet activity theory.* Unpublished doctoral dissertation, Northwestern University.

Moll, L. (1981). *The microethnographic study of bilingual schooling.* Paper presented at the Ethnoperspectives Conference on Bilingual Education, Eastern Michigan University, Ypsilanti.

Moll, L. (2004, January). *Biliteracy development in children: The mediating role of language ideologies.* Paper presented at the Early Literacy Conference in honor of Yetta Goodman, University of Arizona, Tucson.

Moorman, G., Blanton, W., & McLaughlin, T. (1994). The rhetoric of whole language. *Reading Research Quarterly, 29,* 308–329.

Mora, J. K. (2001, April 8). Letter to the editor of the *San Diego Union Tribune.* E-mail. *LiteracyForAll@egroups.com*

Morgan, T. (1990). Reorientations. In B. Henricksen & T. Morgan (Eds.), *Reorientation: Critical theories and pedagogies* (pp. 3–27). Urbana: University of Illinois Press.

Moskowitz, G., & Hayman, J. (1976). Success strategies of inner city teachers: A year-long study. *Journal of Educational Research, 69,* 283–289.

Moss, R., & Stansell, J. (1983). Wof stew: A recipe for growth and enjoyment. *Language Arts, 60,* 346–350.

Mufwene, S. (1998). Native speaker, proficient speaker and norms. In R. Singh (Ed.), *The native speaker* (pp. 111–123). New Delhi, India: Sage.

Nafisi, A. (2003). *Reading* Lolita *in Tehran.* New York: Random House.

Nairn, A., & Nader, R. (1980). *The reign of ETS.* Washington, DC: Center for the Study of Responsive Law.

National Commission on Excellence in Education. (1983). *A nation at risk.* Washington, DC: USA Research.

Neill, A. S. (1960). *Summerhill: A radical approach to child-rearing.* New York: Hart.

Neill, M. (2003, September 9). ARN-state Email. 'New scheme from U.S. Ed Dept. President Bush announces partnership between the Broad Foundation and the U.S. Department of Education to improve our country's public education system.' *LiteracyForAll@egroups.com*

Neill, M., & Medina, N. (1991). Standardized testing: Harmful to educational health. *Phi Delta Kappan, 70,* 688–697.

Nespor, J. (1987). The role of beliefs in the practice of teaching. *Journal of Curriculum Studies, 19,* 317–328.

New London Group. (1996). A pedagogy of multiliteracies: Designing social futures. *Harvard Educational Review, 66,* 60–92.

Newman, J. (1985). *Whole language: Theory and practice.* Portsmouth, NH: Heinemann.

Nichols, S., & Berliner, D. (2005, March). *The inevitable corruption of indicators and educators through high-stakes testing.* Unpublished report, Arizona State University, Educational Policy Studies Laboratory, Educational Policy Research Unit.

Nieto, S. (2004). *Affirming diversity: The sociopolitical context of multicultural education* (4th ed.). Boston: Pearson/Allyn & Bacon.

Niio, G. (2000). Kanzi II [NHK video documentary]. NHK of Japan.

Norton, B. (1997). Language, identity, and the ownership of English. *TESOL Quarterly, 31,* 409–429.

Norton, B. (2000). *Identity and language learning: Gender, ethnicity and educational change.* Essex, England: Pearson Education.

Nyquist, E., & Hawes, G. (1972). *Open education: A sourcebook for parents and teachers.* New York: Bantam.

O'Brien, D., & Bauer, E. (2005). New literacies and the institution of old learning. *Reading Research Quarterly, 40,* 120–131.

Ogbu, J. (1987). Variability in minority school performance: A problem in search of an explanation. *Anthropology and Education Quarterly, 18,* 312–334.

Ohanian, S. (2001, January). News from the test resistance trail. *Phi Delta Kappan.* Retrieved March 6, 2004, from http://www.pdkintl.org/kappan/koha0101.htm

Ohanian, S. (2002). *What happened to recess and why are our children struggling in kindergarten.* New York: McGraw-Hill.

Orasanu, J., McDermott, R., Boykin, A., & The Laboratory for Comparative Human Cognition. (1977). A critique of test standardization. *Social Policy, 8,* 61–67.

Owen, D. (1985). *None of the above: Behind the myth of scholastic aptitude.* Boston: Houghton Mifflin.

Oxford English Dictionary. (1933). Oxford, England: Clarendon Press.

Pace, G. (1991). When teachers use literature for literacy instruction: Ways that constrain, ways that free. *Language Arts, 68,* 12–25.

Peal, E., & Lambert, W. (1962). The relation of bilingualism to intelligence. *Psychological Monographs, 76*(27), 1–23.

Peller, G. (1987). Reason and the mob: The politics of representation. *Tikkun, 2*(3), 28–31, 92–95.

Pennycook, A. (2004). Performativity and language studies. *Critical Inquiry in Language Studies, 1,* 1–20.

Perlstein, R. (2005). The eve of destruction. *Village Voice.* Retrieved August 26, 2005, from http://www.villagevoice.com/generic/show_print.php?id=60130& page=perlseint&issue=0503&printcde=MzMxODg1NjY4Mw==&refpage=L25ld3MvaW

Peterson, B. (1994). Teaching for social justice: One teacher's journey. In B. Bigelow, L. Christensen, S. Karp, B. Miner, & B. Peterson (Eds.), *Rethinking our classrooms, a special edition of* Rethinking Schools (pp. 30–33, 35–38. Milwaukee, WI: Rethinking Schools.

Peterson, R. (1981). Language experience: A methodic approach to teaching literacy. *Georgia Journal of Reading, 7,* 15–23.

Peterson, R., & Eeds, M. (1990). *Grand conversations: Literacy studies in action.* Richmond Hill, Ontario, Canada: Scholastic-Tab.

Petrovič, J., & Olmstead, S. (2001). Language, power, and pedagogy: Bilingual children in the crossfire (Review of J. Cummins, 2000). *Bilingual Research Journal, 25*(3). Retrieved April 10, 2004, from http:brj/asu/edu/v253/articles/ar8.html

Poynor, L., & Wolfe, P. (Eds.). (2005). *Marketing fear in America's public schools: The real war on literacy.* Mahwah, NJ: Lawrence Erlbaum Associates.

Pratt, C., Walsh-Sarnecki, P., & Turk, V. (2004). In state takeover, student scores lag. *Detroit Free Press,* 10/16/04. Retrieved October 16, 2004, from http://www.freep.com/news/education/dps16e_20041016.htm

Quindlen, A. (2002, June 17). The destruction of literature in the name of children. *Newsweek.* Retrieved June 12, 2002, from http://nl.newsbank.com/nl-search/we/Archives?p_product=NWEC&p_theme=nwec&p_action=search&p_maxdocs=200

Quindlen, A. (2005). Testing: One, two three. *Newsweek,* 6/5/05. Retrieved July 7, 2005, from http://msnbc.msn.com/id/8099819/site/newsweek

Raimes, A. (1983). Tradition and revolution. *TESOL Quarterly, 17,* 535–552.

Read, C. (1975). *Children's categorization of speech sounds.* Urbana, IL: National Council of Teachers of English.

Report of the National Reading Panel: Report of the Subgroups. (2000). Washington, DC: National Institute of Child Health and Development.

Rethinking Schools. (2005). No funding left? *Rethinking Schools, 19*(4), 9.

Rhodes, L., & Dudley-Marling, C. (1988). *Readers and writers with a difference: A holistic approach to teaching learning disabled and remedial students.* Portsmouth, NH: Heinemann.

Rich, F. (2005, June 12). Don't follow the money. *New York Times.* Retrieved June 15, 2005, from http://www.nytimes.com/2005/06/12/opinion/12rich.html

Rivera, C. (Ed.). (1984). *Language proficiency and academic achievement.* Clevedon, England: Multilingual Matters.

Robelen, E. (2005, February 9). Bush's high school agenda faces obstacles. *Ed Week.* Retrieved June 10, 2005, from http://www.edweek.org'ew/articles/2005/02/09/22bush.h24.html

Rodriguez, R. (1981). *Hunger of Memory: The education of Richard Rodriguez, an autobiography.* Boston: Godine.

Rosch, E., & Lloyd, B. (Eds.). (1978). *Cognition and categorization.* Hillsdale, NJ: Lawrence Erlbaum Associates.

Rose, L., & Gallup, A. (2004). The 36th annual Phi Delta Kappa/Gallup poll. *Phi Delta Kappan, 86,* 41–52.

Rosen, H. (1988). *And none of it was nonsense: The power of storytelling in school.* London: MGP.

Rosen, R. (2002, January 6). On the public's right to know: The day Ashcroft censored Freedom of Information. *San Francisco Chronicle.*

Rosenblatt, L. (1978). *The reader, the text, the poem.* Carbondale: Southern Illinois University Press.

Rosenblatt, L. (1985). Transaction versus interaction: A terminological rescue operation. *Research in the Teaching of English, 19,* 96–107.

Rosenshine, B. (1971). *Teaching behaviors and student achievement.* Windsor, England: National Foundation for Educational Research in England and Wales.

Rosier, P., & Holm, W. (1979). *The Rock Point experience: An experiment in bilingual education.* Washington, DC: Center for Applied Linguistics.

Rothstein, R. (2001, March 7). Lessons: Seeing achievement gains by an attack on poverty. *New York Times,* p. B9.

Routman, R. (1991). *Invitations: Changing as teachers and learners K–12.* Portsmouth, NH: Heinemann.

Rowe, D. (2005, May). *What have we learned since* Language Stories and Literacy Lessons? *The potential of reframing early literacy learning as social practice.* Keynote address delivered at Harste–Burke Retirement Conference, Bloomington, IN.

Ryan, J., & Sackery, C. (1984). *Strangers in paradise: Academics from the working class.* Boston: South End.

Sacks, P. (1999). *Standard minds: The high price of America's testing culture and what we can do to change it.* Cambridge, MA: Perseus.

Samuda, R. (1975). *Psychological testing of American minorities: Issues and consequences.* New York: Harper & Row.

Sanford, J., & Evertson, C. (1980). *Beginning the school year at a low SES junior high: Three case studies.* Austin: University of Texas Research and Development Center for Teacher Evaluation.

Savage-Rumbaugh, S., & Lewin, R. (1994). *Kanzi: The ape at the brink of the human mind.* New York: Wiley.

Saville-Troike, M. (1988). From context to communication: Paths to second language acquisition. In D. Tannen (Ed.), *Linguistics in context: Connecting observation and understanding* (pp. 249–268). Norwood, NJ: Ablex.

Schemo, D. (2002, November 27). New federal rule tightens demands on failing schools. Retrieved November 30, 2002, from http://www.nytimes.com/ 2002/11/27/education/27EDUC.html

Schemo, D. (2003, July 11). Questions on data cloud luster of Houston schools. *New York Times,* pp. A1, A12.

Schemo, D. (2004a, March 25). 14 states ask U.S. to revise some education law rules. *New York Times.* Retrieved March 25, 2004, from http://www.nytimes. com/ 2004/03/25/education/25CHIL.html

Schemo, D. (2004b, August 17). Nation's charter schools lagging behind, U.S. test scores reveal. *New York Times.* Retrieved August 22, 2004, from http://www. nytimes.com/2004/08/17/education/17charter.html

Schmidt, G. (2004). College board tries to suppress publication of test score data. *Substance, 30*(1–4), 19.

Schneider, K. (2002, March). The Patriot Act: Last refuge of a scoundrel. Internet column, *Magazine of the American Library Association.* http://lll.org

Schon, I. (1978). *Books in Spanish for children and young adults.* Metuchen, NJ: Scarecrow.

School Finance Overview. (2005). *EdSource online.* Retrieved June 15, 2005, from www.edsource.org/edu_fin.cfm

Schoolboys of Barbiana. (1970). *Letter to a teacher.* New York: Random House.

Schrecker, E. (1998). *Many are the crimes: McCarthyism in America.* Boston: Little, Brown.

Schutz, A. (1962). *Alfred Schutz: Collected papers* (M. Natanson, Ed.). The Hague, The Netherlands: Martinus Nijhoff.

Schutz, A. (2004). Rethinking domination and resistance: Challenging postmodernism. *Educational Researcher, 33,* 15–23.

Scialabba, G. (2005). Zippie world! *The Nation, 280*(23), 37–40.

Scollon, R., & Scollon, S. (1981). *Narrative, literacy and face in interethnic communication.* Norwood, NJ: Ablex.

Scribner, S., & Cole, M. (1978). Literacy without schooling: Testing for intellectual effects. *Harvard Educational Review, 48,* 448–461.

Scribner, S., & Cole, M. (1981). Unpackaging literacy. In M. Whiteman (Ed.), *Writing: The nature, development, and teaching of written communication: Vol. 1. Variation in writing* (pp. 71–88). Hillsdale, NJ: Lawrence Erlbaum Associates.

Shannon, P. (1985). Reading instruction and social class. *Language Arts, 62,* 604–613.

Shannon, P. (1989). *Broken promises: Reading instruction in twentieth century America.* Granaby, MA: Bergin & Garvey.

Shannon, P. (1990). *Struggle to continue: Progressive reading instruction in the United States.* Portsmouth, NH: Heinemann.

Shaywitz, S., Shaywitz, B., Pugh, K., Skudlarski, P., Fulbright, R., Constable, R., et al. (1996). The neurobiology of developmental dyslexia as viewed through the lens of functional magnetic resonance imaging technology. In G. R. Lyon & J. Rumsey (Eds.), *Neuroimaging: A window to the neurological foundations of learning and behavior in children* (pp. 79–94). Baltimore: Brookes.

Shor, I., & Freier, P. (1987). A pedagogy for liberation. South Hadley, MA: Bergin & Garvey.

Shuck, G. (2005). Ownership of texts, ownership of language: Two students' responses to a student-run conference on language. *The Reading Matrix, 4*(3), 24–39.

Shuy, R. (1981). What the teacher knows is more important than text or test. *Language Arts, 58,* 919–930.

Siefer, N. (1989). *"We make understanding:" Communicative strategies of native and non-native speakers of English in the workplace.* Unpublished dissertation, Arizona State University.

Silberman, C. (1970). *Crisis in the classroom: The remaking of American education.* New York: Vintage Books.

Singh, U. (1998). Introduction by the series editor. In R. Singh (Ed.), *The native speaker* (pp. 11–25). New Delhi, India: Sage.

Skutnabb-Kangas, T., & Toukomaa, P. (1976). *Teaching migrant children's mother tongue and learning the language of the host country in the context of the socio-cultural situation of the migrant family.* Helsinki: Finnish National Commission for UNESCO.

Smith, A. (2004). "What recovery?" *Z Magazine, 17*(7/8), 43–48.

Smith, F. (1973). Twelve easy ways to make learning to read difficult. In F. Smith (Ed.), *Psycholinguistics and reading* (pp. 183–96). New York: Holt, Rinehart & Winston.

Smith, F. (1981a). The choice between teachers and programs. *Language Arts, 58,* 634–642.

Smith, F. (1981b). Demonstrations, engagement, and sensitivity. *Language Arts, 58,* 103–112.

Smith, F. (1982a). *Understanding reading* (3rd ed.). New York: Holt, Rinehart & Winston.

Smith, F. (1982b). *Writing and the writer.* New York: Holt, Rinehart & Winston.

Smith, F. (1983). *Essays into literacy.* Exeter, NH: Heinemann.

Smith, F. (1985). *Reading without nonsense* (2nd ed.). New York: Teachers College press.

Smith, F. (1986). *Insult to intelligence: The bureaucratic invasion of our classrooms.* New York: Arbor House.

Smith, K. (1990). Entertaining a text: A reciprocal process. In K. Short & K. Pierce (Eds.), *Talking about books* (pp. 17–32). Portsmouth, NH: Heinemann.

Smith, M. L. (2004). *Political spectacle and the fate of American public schools.* New York: Routledge/Falmer.

Snow, C., Burns, M., & Griffin, P. (Eds.). (1998). *Preventing reading difficulties in young children.* Washington, DC: National Academy Press.

Solomon, N. (2001). Media war without end. *Z Magazine, 14*(12), 5–9.

Solomon, N. (2002). Freedom to be heard. *MoveOn Bulletin.* Retrieved November 26, 2002, from http://www.moveon.org/moveonbulletin

Soto, G. (1973). *Spiks.* New York: Monthly Review Press.

Spencer, M. (1986). Emergent literacies: A site of analysis. *Language Arts, 63,* 442–453.

Spivak, L. (2005). *The conservative marketing machine.* Retrieved September 2, 2000, from http://www.alternet.org/story/20946/

Spolsky, B., & Irvine, P. (1982). Sociolinguistic aspects of the acceptance of literacy in the vernacular. In F. Barkin, E. Brandt, & J. Ornstein-Galicia (Eds.), *Bilingualism and language contact: Spanish, English and Native American languages* (pp. 73–79). New York: Teachers College Press.

Stanley, L., & Wise, S. (1983). *Breaking out: Feminist consciousness and feminist research.* Boston: Routledge & Kegan Paul.

Steinberg, J., & Henriques, D. (2001, May 21). When a test fails the schools, careers and reputations suffer. *New York Times.* Retrieved August 17, 2004, from http://www.nytimes.com/2001/05/21/business/21EXAM.html

Stewart, Jr., T., & Vaillette, N. (Eds.). (2001). *Language files: Materials for an introduction to language and linguistics.* Columbus: Ohio State University Press.

Strauss, S. (2002). Politics and reading. *Pediatrics, 110,* 193–195.

Strauss, S. (2005a). Operation "No Child Left Behind." In B. Altwerger (Ed.), *Reading for profit* (pp. 33–49). Portsmouth, NH: Heinemann.

Strauss, S. (2005b). *The linguistics, neurology, and politics of phonics: Silent "e" speaks out.* Mahwah, NJ: Lawrence Erlbaum Associates.

Street, B. (1984). *Literacy in theory and practice.* Cambridge, England: Cambridge University Press.

Street, B. (1999). The meanings of literacy. In D. Wagner, R. Venesky, & B. Street (Eds.), *Literacy: An international handbook* (pp. 34–40). Boulder, CO: Westview.

Szwed, J. (1981). The ethnography of literacy. In M. Whiteman (Ed.), *Writing: The nature, development and teaching of written communication* (Vol. 1, pp. 13–24). Hillsdale, NJ: Lawrence Erlbaum Associates.

Taylor, D. (1983). *Family literacy*. Exeter, NH: Heinemann.

Taylor, D. (1989). Toward a unified theory of literacy learning and instructional practices. *Phi Delta Kappan, 71,* 184–193.

Taylor, D. (1997). *Many families, many literacies*. Portsmouth, NH: Heinemann.

Taylor, D. (1998). *Beginning to read and the spin doctors of science*. Urbana, IL: National Council of Teachers of English.

Taylor, D., Coughlin, D., & Marasco, J. (Eds.). (1997). *Teaching and advocacy*. New York, ME: Stenhouse.

Taylor, D., & Dorsey-Gaines, C. (1988). *Growing up literate*. Portsmouth, NH: Heinemann.

Teale, W. (1982). Toward a theory of how children learn to read and write naturally. *Language Arts, 59,* 555–570.

Tikunoff, W., Ward, B., & Dasho, S. (1978). *Volume A: Three case studies* (Report No. A78-7). San Francisco: Far West Laboratory for Educational Research and Development.

Tittle, C. (1973). Sex bias in tests. *Phi Delta Kappan, 55,* 118–119.

Toohey, K. (2000). *Learning English at school: Identity, social relations and classroom practice*. Clevedon, England: Multilingual Matters.

Toppo, G. (2005). Education Department paid commentator to promote law. *USA Today,* January 7, 2005. Retrieved June 16, 2005, from http://www.usatoday.com/news/washington/2005-01-06-williams-whitehouse_x.htm

Torbe, M. (1988, August). *Reading meanings: A discussion of the social definition of literacy in relation to school and its approaches to reading for meaning*. Paper presented at Post World Reading Congress Symposium, Brisbane, Australia.

Torres, M. (1988). Attitudes of bilingual education parents toward language learning and curriculum and instruction. *NABE Journal, 12,* 171–185.

Toukamaa, P., & Skutnabb-Kangas, T. (1977). *The intensive teaching of the mother tongue to migrant children of preschool age and children in the lower level of comprehensive school*. Helsinki: Finnish National Commission for UNESCO.

Trabasso, M. (1981). On the making of inferences during reading and their assessment. In J. Guthrie (Ed.), *Comprehension and teaching* (pp. 56–76). Newark, DE: International Reading Association.

Treanor, P. (2004). *Neoliberalism: Origins, theory, definition*. Retrieved April 18, 2005, from http://www.inter.nl.net/users/Paul.Treanor/neoliberalism.html

Trimbur, J. (1989). Consensus and difference in collaborative learning. *College English, 51,* 602–616.

Troike, R. (1981). Synthesis of research on bilingual education. *Educational Leadership, 14,* 498–504.

Truss, L. (2003). *Eats, shoots & leaves*. New York: Gotham.

UNESCO. (1953). *The use of vernacular languages in education*. Paris: Author.

U.S. Commission on Civil Rights. (1975). *A better chance to learn: Bilingual/bicultural education* (Publishing No. 51). Washington, DC: U.S. Commission on Civil Rights Clearinghouse.

Valencia, R. (1997). Introduction. In R. Valencia (Ed.), *The evolution of deficit thinking* (pp. 1–125). London: Falmer.

Valencia, S. (1990). Alternative assessment: separating the wheat from the chaff. *Reading Teacher 44*(1), 60–61.

Vasquez, V. (2004). *Negotiating critical literacies with young children.* Mahwah, NJ: Lawrence Erlbaum Associates.

Veatch, J., Sawicki, F., Elliott, G., Barnette, E., & Blakey, J. (1973). *Key words to reading: The language experience approach begins.* Columbus, OH: Charles Merrill.

Vermont Society for the Study of Education. (2002, December 27). *Open letter to Secretary of Education Rod Paige.*

Villanueva, V. (1988). A rhetorically critical literacy. *Information Update, 4*(3), 3–4. New York: Literacy Assistance Center.

Vygotsky, L. (1978). *Mind in society.* Cambridge, MA: Harvard University Press.

Wald, A. (1989). Hegemony and literary tradition in the United States. In S. DeCastell, A. Luke, & C. Luke (Eds.), *Language, authority and criticism* (pp. 3–16). East Sussex, England: Falmer.

Walker, A. (1982). *The color purple.* New York: Pocket Books.

Walkerdine, V. (1990). *Schoolgirl fictions.* London: Verso.

Wang, S. (2005, April 26). *A study of L2 Chinese readers' behavior while reading orally.* Arizona State University/University of Arizona Doctoral Student Exchange Speaker Series, No. 1.

War, terrorism, and America's classrooms: Teaching in the aftermath of the September 11th tragedy. (2001). *Rethinking Schools, 16*(3), 15.

Watson-Gegeo, K. (2004). Mind, language and epistemology: Toward a language socialization paradigm for SLA. *Modern Language Journal, 88,* 331–350.

Weaver, C. (1990). *Understanding whole language.* Portsmouth, NH: Heinemann.

Weaver, C. (Ed.). (1994). *Success at last: Helping students with attention deficit (hyperactivity) disorders achieve their potential.* Portsmouth, NH: Heinemann.

Weber, L. (1971). *The English infant school and informal education.* Englewood Cliffs, NJ: Prentice Hall.

Webster, R., McInnis, E., & Crover, L. (1986). Curriculum biasing effects in standardized and criterion-referenced reading achievement tests. *Psychology in the Schools, 23,* 205–213.

Webster's New Collegiate Dictionary. (1976). Springfield, MA: G. & C. Merriam.

Weinstein-Shr, B. (1993). Literacy and social process: A community in transition. In B. Street (Ed.), *Discourse, ideology and context: Essays in the anthropology of literacy* (pp. 272–293. Cambridge, England: Cambridge University Press.

Wells, A. (2004, December 28). *Charter schools: Lessons in limits.* Retrieved January 4, 2005, from http://www.washingtonpost.com/ac2wp-dyn/A32611-2004Dec28?language=printer

Wells, G. (1977). Language use and educational success: An empirical response to Joan Tough's *The development of meaning. Research in Education, 18,* 9–34.

Wells, G. (1979). Describing children's learning: Development at home and at school. *British Educational Research Journal, 5,* 75–89.

Wells, G. (1981). *Learning through interaction: The study of language development.* New York: Cambridge University Press.

Wells, G., & Raban, E. (n.d.). *Children learning to read* (Final Report: Grant HR 3797/1). Bristol, England: Social Science Research Council, Research Unit.

Wexler, P. (1987). *Social analysis of education: After the new sociology.* London: Routledge and Kegan Paul.

Wheelock, A. (2005, May 12). ACLU to defend MCAS critic in court. E-mail circulated on *LiteracyForAll@egroups.com*

Wilde, J. (1988). The written report: Old wine in new bottles. In T. Newkirk & N. Atwell (Eds.), *Understanding writing* (pp. 179–190). Portsmouth, NH: Heinemann.

Wilde, S. (1992). *You kan red this!* Portsmouth, NH: Heinemann.

Wiley, T. (1996). *Literacy and language diversity in the United States.* Washington, DC, and McHenry, IL: Center for Applied Linguistics and Delta Systems.

Wiley, T. (in press). The "great divide" and popular bilingual education theory. In K. Rolstad (Ed.), *Rethinking classroom language.* Mahwah, NJ: Lawrence Erlbaum Associates.

Will, G. (2005, January 13). Propaganda poor choice for hyping education. *Arizona Republic*, p. B7.

Willes, M. (1981). Learning to take part in classroom interaction. In P. French & M. Maclure (Eds.), *Adult–child conversation* (pp. 73–95). New York: St. Martin's Press.

Williams, R. (1983). *Key words* (rev. ed.). New York: Oxford University Press.

Williams, R. (1989). Hegemony and the selective tradition. In S. DeCastell, A. Luke, & C. Luke (Eds.), *Language, authority and criticism* (pp. 56–60). East Sussex, England: Falmer.

Willinsky, J. (2001). What is progressive about progressive education? In C. Dudley-Marling & C. Edelsky (Eds.), *The fate of progressive language policies and practices* (pp. 59–79). Urbana, IL: National Council of Teachers of English.

Wirsing, M. (2000, June 20). CCHE and the alignment agenda. Subject thread: Chilling vision of the future of teacher education. E-mail. *LiteracyForAll@ egroups.com*

Wolfe, P. & Poynor, L. (2001). Politics and the pendulum: An alternative understanding of the case of whole language as educational innovation. *Educational Researcher, 30*(1), 15–20.

Wright, W. (2005a). English learners left behind in Arizona: The nullification of accommodations for ELLs in the intersection of federal and state language and assessment policies. *Bilingual Research Journal, 29,* 1–30.

Wright, W. (2005b). The political spectacle of Proposition 203. *Educational Policy, 19*(5), 662–700.

Yatvin, J. (2002). Babes in the woods: The wanderings of the National Reading Panel. *Phi Delta Kappan, 82,* 364–369.

Zavetsky, J. (2004). Extremism in the defense of liberty. *Z Magazine, 17*(11), 59–60.

Zinn, H. (2004, September 2). The optimism of uncertainty. *The Nation.* Retrieved December 19, 2005, from http://www.thenation.com/doc/20040920/zinn

Zuhara, B. (2005, January 2). Literacy (R. Krishnan, Trans.). *The Hindu*, Literary Reviewer, pp. 1–2. Retrieved December 18, 2005, from http://www.hindu.com/lr/2005/01/02/strories/

Author Index

A

Adams, M., 7, 158
Adams, R., 251
Albert, M., 64
Al-Fahid, J., 223
Allen, R. V., 171
Allington, R., 7, 60, 159, 161,
    162, 264, 265
Alterman, E., 8, 9
Altwerger, B., 3, 61, 69, 100, 104, 125,
    134, 149, 156, 157, 158,
    159, 160, 170, 176, 177,
    180, 182, 201, 221, 223,
    228, 229, 230, 232, 233,
    234, 254, 255, 258, 261, 269
Amrein, A., 63, 132, 266, 267
Anderson, L., 193
Anderson, R., 111, 156, 158, 250
Apple, M., 74, 237, 238, 266
Archbald, D., 257
Aronowitz, S., 199, 210, 211, 240, 243
Ashton-Warner, S., 150, 171
Atwell, N., 43, 91, 109, 151, 174, 257
Auerbach, E., 153
August, D., 62, 63

B

Bacon, D., 262
Bailey, F., 126
Baker, C., 86, 170, 215
Barkin, F., 100
Barnette, E., 171

Barone, T., 124
Barron, M., 134, 228
Barth, N., 6
Bates, E., 137
Bateson, G., 57
Bauer, E., 107
Becker, A., 113, 124
Berends, M., 2
Bergeron, B., 227
Berkowitz, B., 13
Berliner, D., 2, 6, 63, 132, 259,
    260, 266, 267
Berman, M., 221
Biddle, B., 2, 6, 259, 260
Bigelow, B., 96, 210, 218
Bigelow, G., 4
Biklen, S., 80
Birkerts, S., 222
Bixby, M., 149
Black, J., 110
Blakey, J., 171
Blanton, W., 231
Bloom, A., 200
Bloome, D., 111, 126, 151
Blumer, H., 84
Bogdan, R., 80
Bordo, S., 224, 232
Borenstein, S., 6
Bowles, S., 63, 200
Boykin, A., 85, 252
Bracey, G., 5, 15, 162, 259, 263,
    265, 266, 267
Brandon, K., 262
Brandt, D., 5, 41

Breslin, J., 207
Bridges, L., 257
Briggs, R., 2
Britton, J., 140
Brodkey, L., 41
Brophy, J., 193
Brown, C., 128
Brown, J., 223
Brown, R., 69
Browne, C., 170
Burke, C., 71, 79, 82, 91, 113, 114, 134,
    149, 166, 168, 171, 181, 200,
    202, 223, 229, 240, 254, 257
Burns, M., 158
Buros, O., 249
Bussis, A., 173

C

Calkins, L., 42, 72, 91, 149, 174,
    175, 229, 233, 240
Camilli, G., 60
Campbell, D., 264
Canagarajah, A. S., 138, 154
Carini, P., 239, 244
Cazden, C., 97, 134, 183
Chall, J., 167, 223
Cherland, M., 156, 234
Chittendon, T., 173
Chopin, K., 212
Christensen, L., 96, 210, 218
Christian, B., 151
Christine, C., 240
Church, S., 215
Clandinin, D., 79
Clark, C., 110
Clarke, M., 230
Clay, M., 134
Cole, A., 261
Cole, D., 13
Cole, M., 100, 105, 111, 122, 200
Coles, G., 6, 7, 14, 60, 63, 136, 151,
    156, 159, 160, 161, 164, 260
Collins, J., 93
Comber, B., 42, 102, 132, 218, 221
Connelly, F., 79
Constable, R., 111
Cook, A., 252, 253

Cook-Gumperz, J., 94, 223
Coughlin, D., 153
Coulmas, F., 139, 140
Cousin, P., 223
Crafton, L., 221, 233
Crawford, J., 48, 61, 62,
    63, 64, 69, 159
Crenshaw, S., 149
Crover, L., 251
Crowley, P., 149
Cummins, J., 0, 80, 81, 82, 83, 84, 86,
    87, 88, 89, 90, 95, 96, 97, 98,
    99, 100, 101, 102
Curry-Rodriguez, J., 95

D

Darling-Hammond, L., 255
Dasho, S., 180
Davis, M., 14, 15
Deacon, T., 136, 137, 139, 141
deCastell, S., 41, 109, 111
DeFord, D., 76, 168, 181
Denham, C., 193
Deyle, D., 251
Díaz, E., 223
Dillon, S., 268
Dombey, H., 250
Dorsey-Gaines, C., 153
Dowd, M., 9
Draper, K., xiv, 110, 115, 222
Dressman, M., 10
Dudley-Marling, C., 222, 231
Dyson, A., 42, 86, 87, 91, 218

E

Eagleton, T., 221
Eaton, S., 164
Edelman, M., 10, 60, 63
Edelsky, C., xiv, 19, 42, 53, 59, 66, 72,
    75, 76, 96, 98, 100, 109, 110,
    115, 116, 125, 132, 134, 140,
    148, 149, 153, 156, 170, 171,
    175, 180, 182, 196, 197, 200,
    201, 214, 218, 220, 221, 222,
    228, 229, 230, 232, 233, 234,
    252, 254, 257, 258, 269

Eeds, M., 175
Elliott, G., 171
Elsasser, N., 207, 210
Emmer, E., 192, 193
Engel, M., 157, 261
English-Sand, P., 164
Enright, S., 88
Erickson, F., 110, 237
Ervin-Tripp, S., 88
Evertson, C., 180, 192, 193

F

Fairclough, N., 210, 216
Faltis, C., 153
Farahmandpur, R., 4, 6
Farenga, A., 265
Featherstone, J., 232
Fennacy, J., 9, 11
Ferreiro, E., 166
Fillmore, L. W., 24, 26, 29, 30
Fine, E. S., 212
Fine, M., 228
Fingeret, A., 201
Finn, C., 14
Fiore, K., 210
Fishman, J., 28, 67
Fiske, J., 105, 106
Fitzgerald, L., 164
Fleck, T., 5
Fletcher, J., 158, 160
Fletcher, M., 5
Flores, B., 73, 100, 125, 134,
    149, 170, 180, 182, 201,
    221, 223, 228, 229, 230,
    232, 233, 234, 258
Florio, S., 110, 183
Flurkey, A., 223
Foorman, B., 158, 160
Fox, J., 2
Francis, D., 158, 160
Freebody, P., 86, 102, 132, 215, 217
Freeman, D., 9, 11
Freeman, R., 5
Freeman, Y., 9, 11, 74, 200
Freire, P., 110, 241
Froebel, F., 150
Fromkin, V., 117

Fulbright, R., 111
Fusco, C., 225

G

Gallup, A., 268
Garan, E., 7, 60, 161, 162, 163, 260
Garcia, E., 95
Gee, J., 75, 88, 97, 98, 99, 103, 106,
    107, 109, 112, 113, 134, 135,
    142, 143, 145, 149, 153, 165,
    193, 197, 202, 210, 215, 219,
    222, 224, 228, 233, 252
Geertz, C., 143
Gelb, S., 117
Giaccobbe, M., 43
Gibson, R., 172
Gilbert, P., 123, 132, 215, 227
Gillespie, N., 15
Gillis, C., 149
Gilman, C., 212
Gintis, H., 63, 200
Giroux, H., 199, 210, 211, 228, 240, 243
Gitlin, A., 237
Gladwin, H., 109
Glaser, B., 44
Glass, G., 157
Goldberg, M., 14
Gollasch, F., 167
Gonzales, R., 63
Goodman, K., 45, 60, 73, 74, 90, 91,
    104, 109, 113, 114, 134, 135,
    163, 171, 200, 201, 202, 222,
    223, 228, 233, 240, 250
Goodman, Y., 45, 60, 73, 91, 104,
    134, 149, 150, 166, 174, 202,
    210, 232, 233, 257
Gore, J., 225, 226, 227, 231
Gould, S. J., 251
Graff, H., 30, 85, 99, 111, 112, 138,
    198, 200, 222
Graves, D., 42, 72, 109, 174, 181, 228
Green, B., 215
Green, J., 185
Greene, J., 2
Griffin, P., 158
Grosjean, F., 68
Gross, B., 172

Gross, R., 172
Grossen, B., 158
Gryphon, M., 264
Gullingsrud, M., 15

H

Hakuta, K., 62, 63, 66
Hale, R., 251
Hall, S., 105
Halliday, M., 134, 139
Halliday, M. A. K., 97, 106, 113, 202
Haney, W., 101, 247, 249, 250,
    251, 254, 256
Hansen, J., 174
Harman, S., 222, 252, 254, 255, 256,
    257, 258, 265
Harris, R., 139, 140
Harste, J., 71, 76, 79, 82, 91, 113,
    114, 134, 168, 171, 175, 181,
    200, 202, 221, 223, 229, 230,
    234, 240, 252, 254
Hart, P., 8
Hartley, J., 105, 106
Hartman, P., 164
Harvey, B, 218
Hatch, E., 27, 29
Hawes, G., 172
Hawkins, M., 144, 150
Hayman, J., 180
Hearn, J., 238
Heath, S. B., 80, 86, 105, 112,
    131, 183, 209, 223
Heffernan, L., 234
Henkin, R., 215
Henrichs, M., 149
Henriques, D., 263
Herman, E., 8
Hiebert, E., 111, 156, 158, 250
Hill, J., 61
Himley, M., 244
Hirsch, E. D., Jr., 200
Hobbs, N., 247
Hoff, D., 268
Hoffman, B., 251, 255, 267
Hollar, J., 8
Holm, W., 66
Holland, D., 146

Horton, M., 213
Houtz, J., 263
Huber, K., 221, 234
Hudelson, S., 19, 59, 66, 72, 75,
    76, 100, 153, 171
Hudson, S., 110, 124
Hurston, Z. N., 212
Hymes, D., 18, 72, 77, 85, 97, 113

I

Illich, I., 200
Ingalls, J., 204
Irvine, P., 73
Itoh, H., 29
Ivanic, R., 151
Ivins, M., 8, 9

J

Jackendoff, R., 136
Janks, H., 151
Jenkins, L., 150
Jennings, K., 86
Jennings, S., 86
Jilbert, K., 42, 44, 100
John, V., 97
Johnson, K., 196, 221, 234
Johnson, M., 135, 138, 254
Johnston, P., 207
Jordan, J., 210
Jungeblut, A., 150

K

Kamler, B., 91
Karp, S., 96, 218
Katz, A., 16
Kazmin, B., 264, 265
Keller, B., 3
Kelly, U., 215
Kennedy, R., 6, 263
Kessler, G., 5
Kimberley, K., 74
Kingston, M. H., 201
Kirsch, I., 150
Kliewer, C., 164
Kohn, A., 267, 270

Kolhatkar, S., 204
Kolstad, A., 150
Kozol, J., 2
Krashen, S., 109, 135, 142, 159,
　　160, 199, 264
Kress, G., 106, 107, 222
Krugman, P., 13
Kurtz, H., 163

L

Labov, W., 85, 146, 201
Lakoff, G., 64, 135, 138, 254
Lambert, W., 80
Laminack, L., 232
Lamoreaux, L., 171
Lappé, A., 38
Lappé, F., 38
Lave, J., 75, 143, 146, 152, 165, 215
Lawing, S., 232
Lee, D., 171
Leland, C., 221, 234
Lemke, J., 97
Lensmire, T., 215
Leont'ev, A., 125
Lewin, R., 137
Lewison, M., 234
Libit, H., 262
Lieberman, A., 193
Lieberman, T., 159
Lindfors, J., 134, 166,
　　200, 222, 232
Lipman, P., 4, 16, 258, 261, 267, 269
Lippi-Green, R., 141
Lloyd, B., 132
Loughlin, C., 173
Lucas, C., 172
Lucas, S., 2
Luke, A., 41, 70, 102, 109, 110,
　　111, 132, 154, 170, 215,
　　217, 218, 227
Lyotard, J., 221

M

Macinnis, C., 215
MacSwan, J., 62, 63, 94, 95, 96,
　　98, 99, 112, 135

Madaus, G., 255, 256, 258, 264
Mahoney, K., 62, 63
Manzo, K., 16
Marasco, J., 153
Marchman, V., 137
Marek, A., 223
Martin, R., 110
Martinez-Roldan, C., 153
Matthews, J., 150
McDermott, R., 40, 85, 93, 122,
　　152, 183, 217, 222, 252
McInnis, E., 251
McLaren, P., 4, 6
McLaughlin, T., 231
Medina, N., 256, 258
Mehan, H., 84, 188, 252
Meier, D., 251, 252, 253, 255, 257, 258
Meisels, S., 255, 256
Melis, I., 63
Mellor, B., 217
Metcalf, S., 163, 262
Meyer, R., 14, 62
Meyer-Mork, J., 164
Michaels, S., 93
Miller, L., 218
Miller, M. C., 8, 159
Mills, H., 233
Miner, B., 96, 262, 263
Minick, N., 57, 125, 126
Moll, L., 79, 86
Moorman, G., 231
Mora, J. K., 2
Morgan, T., 222
Moskowitz, G., 180
Moss, R., 110
Mufwene, S., 138
Murphy, S., 74, 200

N

Nader, R., 251
Nafisi, A., 204
Nairn, A., 251
Neill, A. S., 172, 173
Neill, M., 256, 258, 261
Nespor, J., 79
Newman, J., 150, 171, 201
Newmann, F., 257

Nichols, S., 266
Nieto, S., 153
Niio, G., 137
Nixon, H., 132
Norton, B., 148, 150, 151, 154
Nyquist, E., 172

O

O'Brien, D., 107
O'Brien, J., 102, 218
Ociepka, A., 234
Ogbu, J., 201
Ohanian, S., 4, 262, 265, 268
O'Keefe, T., 233
Olmstead, S., 99
O'Neill, M., 217
Orasanu, J., 85, 252
Owen, D., 251, 253

P

Pace, G., 230
Patterson, A., 217
Paulson, E., 223
Peal, E., 80
Peller, G., 221
Pennycook, A., 150, 151, 154
Perlstein, R., 264
Peterson, B., 96, 210, 218
Peterson, R., 171, 175
Petrovic, J., 99
Portelli, J., 215
Potok, A., 251
Poynor, L., 158, 234
Pratt, C., 265
Pugh, K., 111
Pyle, D., 149

Q

Quindlen, A., 16

R

Raban, E., 86
Raimes, A., 109

Rapoport, R., 60, 104
Raschke, D., 164
Read, C., 175
Resta, V., 254, 255
Reynolds, F., 149
Rhodes, L., 222
Rich, F., 9
Rivera, C., 86
Robelen, E., 16
Rodman, R., 117
Rodriguez, R., 201
Rolstad, K., 94, 95,
            96, 99, 135
Rosch, E., 132
Rose, L., 268
Rosegrant, T., 140
Rosen, H., 240
Rosen, R., 12
Rosenblatt, L., 118, 182, 254
Rosenshine, B., 183
Rosier, P., 66
Rothstein, R., 260
Routman, R., 221
Rowe, D., 216, 217, 224
Ryan, J., 201

S

Saavedra, E., 176, 177
Sackery, C., 201
Sacks, P., 247
Samuda, R., 85
Sanford, J., 180
Savage-Rumbaugh, S., 137
Saville-Troike, M., 29
Sawicki, F., 171
Schatschneider, C., 158, 160
Schemo, D., 16, 261, 265
Schmidt, G., 265
Schneider, K., 12
Schon, I., 73
Schrecker, E., 10, 11, 13
Schutz, A., 126, 225
Scialabba, G., 4
Scollon, R., 105, 131
Scollon, S., 105, 131
Scott, J., 111, 156, 158, 250

Scribner, S., 100, 105,
111, 122, 200
Shannon, P., 60, 74, 104, 154,
200, 226, 240
Shaywitz, B., 111
Shaywitz, S., 111
Sherman, B., 166
Shor, I., 241
Short, K., 229
Shuck, G., 110
Shuy, R., 183
Siefer, N., 145
Silberman, C., 172
Simpson, A., 42
Singh, U., 138, 154
Skudlarski, P., 111
Skutnabb-Kangas, T., 80, 87
Slater, K., 212
Smith, A., 104
Smith, F., 46, 71, 72, 86, 87, 109,
110, 113, 114, 118, 134, 147,
151, 152, 171, 174, 206, 228,
229, 233, 241
Smith, K., xiv, 98, 109, 110, 115, 116,
125, 132, 148, 222
Smith, M. L., 4, 6, 60, 63, 111, 157,
159, 161, 162, 220, 249, 260,
261, 264, 269
Snow, C., 158
Solomon, N., 8, 12
Soto, G., 212
Spencer, M., 106, 107
Spivak, L., 260
Spolsky, B., 73
Stanley, L., 242
Stansell, J., 110
Steinberg, J., 263
Stephens, D., 233
Stewart, T., Jr., 138, 139
Strauss, S., 5, 7, 61, 69, 84, 104, 111,
136, 157, 159, 163, 164, 197,
199, 234, 260, 267, 269
Street, B., 41, 99, 100, 104, 106, 111,
112, 198, 215, 222, 223
Suina, J., 173
Sullivan, T., 2
Szwed, J., 111, 112, 222

T

Taylor, D., 58, 153, 159, 160
Teale, W., 202
Teberosky, A., 166
Thal, D., 137
Thompson, M., 62, 63
Tikunoff, W., 180
Tittle, C., 251
Toohey, K., 150
Toppo, G., 163, 244, 260
Torbe, M., 110
Torres, M., 29
Toukomaa, P., 80, 87
Trabasso, M., 167
Treanor, P., 4, 258
Trew, T., 106
Trimbur, J., 217
Troike, R., 66
Truss, L., 131
Tucker, G., 80
Turk, V., 265

V

Vaillette, N., 138, 139
Valencia, R., 96
Valencia, S., 257
van Leeuwen, T., 106, 107, 222
Vargas, S., 60
Vasquez, V., 42, 102, 218, 234
Veatch, J., 171
Vibert, A., 215
Villanueva, V., 199
Vygotsky, L., 44

W

Wald, A., 74
Walker, A., 212
Walkerdine, V., 215
Wallat, C., 185
Walsh-Sarnecki, P., 265
Wang, S., 223
Ward, B., 180
Watson, D., 149, 257
Watson-Gegeo, K., 137, 149, 153

Weaver, C., 222, 233
Weber, L., 150
Webster, R., 251
Weinstein-Shr, B., 77, 153
Wells, A., 5
Wells, B., 72
Wells, G., 85, 86, 97
Wenger, E., 75, 143, 152, 165, 215
Wexler, P., 70
Wheelock, A., 15
Wilde, J., 110
Wilde , S., 233
Wiley, T., 94, 95, 99, 100, 104
Wilkinson, I., 111, 156, 158, 250
Will, G., 1
Willes, M., 185
Williams, R., 70, 78, 107
Willinsky, J., 70
Wirsing, M., 266
Wise, S., 242

Wolfe, J., 207
Wolfe, P., 125, 148, 158, 234
Wood, H., 84, 252
Woods, J., 2
Woodside-Jiron, H., 161, 162
Woodward, V., 71, 91, 113,
        114, 134, 171, 200, 202,
        223, 229, 240, 254
Wright, W., 61, 62, 269

Y

Yatvin, J., 60, 161
Yurecko, M., 60

Z

Zavetsky, J., 10
Zinn, H., 249
Zuhara, B., 207

Subject Index

A

Ability, test claims about, 251–252
Achievement, second language
    proficiency and, theory
    on, 79–104
Achievement test score gap, 2
Acquisition
    versus learning, 142–143
    term, 135
Activity theories, 125
Adequate yearly progress
    (AYP), 260–261
Administration, changes in, and
    children's writing, 55–56
Advocacy, explicit, 100
American Civil Liberties Union, 15
Assignments
    and children's writing, 49, 52
    distinctions regarding, 108–109
Autonomous orientation, 99–100
AYP. *see* Adequate yearly progress

B

Basal readers, whole language
    and, 169–171
Basic interpersonal communicative
    skill (BICS), 81
    critique of, 85–86
Bernacki, Cynthia, 37
Bilingual education programs, 32–40
    contexts of, 59

political grounds for, 46–48
rhetoric versus reality of, 45–46
writing in, 41–58
    contexts of, 45–46
    study of, 43–45
written language policies
    for, 59–78
    considerations for, 69–71
    local, issues in, 71–78
Bilingualism
    teachers and, 67–68
    valuing, 33–35
Biliteracy, teachers and, 67–68
Bonobos, and language use, 137
British Infant School model, versus
    whole language, 172–174
BRT. *see* National Business
    Roundtable
Bush, Laura, 14

C

California
    education laws in, 11–12
    whole language versus
        phonics in, 160
California Coalition for Authentic
    Reform in Education,
    178, 268
CALP. *see* Cognitive academic
    language proficiency
Carnine, Douglas, 158–159
Cato Institute, 264

Center for Establishing Dialogue in
    Teaching and Learning,
    Inc. (CED), 240–242
Center for Language in Social
    Life (CLSL), 210–211
Chimpanzees, and language use, 137
Chomskyan linguistics, 89, 98–99, 135
CLSL. *see* Center for Language
    in Social Life
Coercion
    study of, 183–187
    term, 183
Cognitive academic language
    proficiency (CALP), 81
    critique of, 85–86
Cognitively demanding to cognitively
    undemanding language
    tasks, 82
    critique of, 87–88
Common underlying proficiency
    (CUP), 81, 86
Community
    and bilingual education, 46–48
    language use in, and policy, 68
    and learners, 212–213
    and literacy, 204–207
Competence, versus performance, 89
Conflict resolution, in bilingual
    education program, 37–38
Conscientization, 128
Consultant/Coach role, 188–189
Context
    of bilingual education
        programs, 59
    and policy, 66–69
    larger, and policy, 68–69
    skills instruction in, 168–169
    as thickest imaginable, as lens for
        literacy pedagogy, 153
Context embedded to context reduced
    communication, 81–82
    critique of, 87–88
Contextual theories, 125
Corporatist agenda, 4–5
    and deprofessionalization, 236–238
    for education, 156–164
    and media, 8
    and testing, 260–262

Covert propaganda, 163
Critical, term, 70
Critical literacy, 196–213
    current state of, 208–213
    principles of, 201–208
    problem of, 200–201
Critical stance, Cummins and, 103–104
Critics of whole language, 214–234
    definition of, 215
    misunderstandings and, 226–227
Cues, in whole language
    classroom, 190–192
Culture
    acquisition and, 143
    as lens for literacy
        pedagogy, 152–153
CUP. *see* Common underlying
    proficiency
Curriculum
    in bilingual education
        program, 38–39
    high-stakes tests and, 266–267
    manifest, and children's writing, 51
    and resistance, 243

D

Decoding orientation, 82
    and classroom practice, 181
Demarcation problem, 7
Democracy, whole language
    and, 204–205
Deprofessionalizing forces
    context of, 236–238
    resistance to, 235–246
Descriptive methodologies, 7
Deskilling, 237
Developmental interdependence
    hypothesis, 81
Discipline, critics on, 225
Discourse
    critique of, acting on, 210–211
    stretching, 212
Doodling, 120
Douglass, Frederick, 198
Dowd, Maureen, 9
Dropout rates, high-stakes testing
    and, 267

E

Education
 corporate/government
  agenda on, 156–164
  connections among, 162–164
  and deprofessionalization, 236–238
  pillars of, 157
  research on, 159–162
  and testing, 260–262
 Cummins on, shifts in, 97
Educational reform, need
 for, 259–260
Education rights movement,
 recommendations
 for, 268–270
Elementary and Secondary
 Education Act, 250
Eliot, George, 198
English, functions of use of, 21–22
English-language learners.
 see Bilingual education
 programs
Essentializing pedagogy, whole
 language and, 221–225
Exercises
 versus nonexercises,
  109–112, 126–127
 sample, 108–109
 special conditions for, 126–127
Experimental methodologies, 7
Expertise, political use
 of, 161–162
Explicit advocacy, 100

F

FairTest, 258, 267
Family, literacy and, 204–207
Federal government
 and education, 156–164
 and language education, 1–3
 resistance to, 15–17, 164, 178, 197
Form, attention to, in immersion
 experience, 145–146
Frames, 64
Function, Cummins on, 97
Fuzzy examples, 123f, 127–129

G

Gannon, Jeff, 9
Gedlaman, Gabie, 178
Gender
 and deprofessionalization, 238
 and resistance, 242
General ability, test claims about, 251–252
Genre, and children's writing, 50–51
Globalism, crisis of, 16–17
Goodman, Ken, 178
Government. *see* Federal government
Grassroots teachers' movement,
 235, 238–243
Graves, Donald, 90
Great Debate, 167
Great Divide, 94, 106, 112

H

Haitian Creole literacy, 72
Hard-wiring argument, 135–138
Harman, Susan, 178
High-stakes tests, 1–2, 63, 247–270.
 see also Standardized tests;
 Testing
 Cummins on, 101
 negative effects of, 264–267
 resistance to, 178, 258–270
Home environment, literacy
 and, 204–207
Horne, Tom, 62
Human functioning, theories on, 125

I

Identity
 and language acquisition,
  143, 147–149
 as lens for literacy pedagogy, 151
 nature of, 146
 testing and, 108
Ideological orientation, 99–100
Immersion experiences, and literacy
 learning as case of second
 language acquisition, 142–143
Immersion pedagogies, 228
Immersion programs, 29, 33

Individualism, whole language
and, 215–217
Inequality, reproduction of, language
acquisition and, 28–32
Information Dispenser role, 188–189
Integrated day, versus whole
language, 172–174
Interactivity, and literacy
proposals, 118–119
Introspective methodologies, 7
IQ tests, critiques of, 248
Isolating theories, 125

K

Knowledge, as political, as lens for
literacy pedagogy, 153–154
Kohn, Alfie, 15
Krashen, Stephen, 178

L

Language
beliefs about, 165–166
written language as, 135–140
Language education
current context of, 1–17
federal government and, 1–3
hope for, 15–17
Language experience approach, versus
whole language, 171–172
Language learning, beliefs
about, 165–166
Language proficiency
confusion regarding, 97–98
shifts with, 96–97
theory on, 79–104
Language resources, nature of, 72–75
Language socialization (LS) paradigm,
149–150
Language universals, 136
Language use
in community, and policy, 68
nature of, 113
Learner-as-whole-person
lens, 150–151
testing and, 266

Learner role
adoption of, 24–26
resistance to, 26
Learning
versus acquisition, 142–143
as political, as lens for literacy
pedagogy, 153–154
term, 135
Lenses, of literacy pedagogy, 150–154
Lesson Leader role, 188
Limited bilingualism, 81, 95
Lincoln, Abraham, 198
Lippmann, Walter, 248
Literacy
ceiling on, 199
consensus on, 70–71
content of, 63
definition of, 115
distinctions regarding,
105–133, 122f–123f
as liberation, 197–200
orientations toward, 82, 99–100
and classroom practice, 181
power, 91–93
recommendations for
assumptions in, 112–114
background for, 109–112
current state of, 130–133
Eighties proposal on, 114–116
Nineties proposal on,
116–122, 122f, 129–130
risky, 196–213
current state of, 208–213
term, 106–107, 112
Literacy event, meaning/purpose
of, 125–127
Literacy instruction, traditional,
effects of, 198–199
Literacy learning
as case of second language
acquisition, 140–154
pedagogical value of, 146–154
tactical value of, 141–146
reconsideration of, 134–154
Local policies
development of, issues in, 71–78
versus general, 69–70

LS. *see* Language socialization
    paradigm
Lyon, Reid, 12, 14

M

Marked language, 28–29
    learning, 39–40
Material environment, and
    children's writing,
    49–50, 52–53
McCarthy, Joseph, 10–11
McCarthyism, new, 10–14
McClellan, Scott, 9
Meaning
    definition of, 143
    of immersion experience,
        143–144
    of literacy event, 125–127
Media, 7–10
    and corporate/government agenda
        for education, 158–159
    and McCarthyism, 11
    templates in, 61, 159
Medium, definition of, 146–147
Meeder, Hans, 159
Metalinguistic awareness, 24
Modernism
    characteristics of, 221
    postmodern critique of, 225
    whole language and, 221–225
Multiple literacies, 106

N

National Assessment of Educational
    Progress, 159–160
National Business Roundtable
    (BRT), 157
National Center for Fair and
    Open Testing, 258, 267
National Institute of Child Health and
    Human Development
    (NICHD), 157, 160–161
National Research Council, 160–161
Native language, term, 89–90
Native language literacy, 72–73

Native language texts,
    availability of, 72
Native speaker, term, 138
Navajo literacy, 73–75
NCLB. *see* No Child Left
    Behind Act
Neo-conservatism, 3
Neo-liberalism, 3–6, 264
    resistance to, 16–17
    and standardized tests, 258–259
Neutral Recorder role, 188–189
New McCarthyism, 10–14
NICHD. *see* National Institute of
    Child Health and Human
    Development
No Child Left Behind (NCLB)
    Act, 1, 60, 260–261
    challenges to, 15–17
    effects of, 197
    research and, 162
Nonexercises
    versus exercises,
        109–112, 126–127
    term, 110
NOT-reading, term, 120

O

Ohanian, Susan, 178
Open classroom, versus whole
    language, 172–174

P

Paige, Rod, 62, 265
Patriot Act, 12
Pedagogy
    Cummins on, 100–103
        shifts in, 97
    literacy, lenses of, 150–154
    and literacy learning as case of
        second language
        acquisition, 146–154
    modernist, whole language
        and, 221–225
    and standardized tests, 249–250
Performance, versus competence, 89

Phonics
  direct versus embedded
      code, 160
  federal government and,
      12, 156–157
  research and reports on,
      60, 159–162
Political spectacle, 6–7, 60,
      62–63, 161–162, 262
Politics
  knowledge and learning and,
      as lens for literacy
      pedagogy, 153–154
  of literacy, 197–200
  of second language acquisition,
      18–40
  testing resistance movement
      and, 268–270
  and test scoring, 264
  whole language movement
      and, 176–178, 234
Postmodernism, 221, 225
Power literacy, 91–93
  accounting for group differences
      in, 92–93
  data collection on, 91–92
  hypotheses on, 92
Preacher role, 188–189
Predictive power, test claims
      about, 253–254
Prescriptivism, 99
Priming, and performance, 93
Print environment, and children's
      writing, 54–55
Print literacy, focus on, rationale
      for, 105–108
Print use, distinctions within, 123f
Privatization of schools, 5
  testing and, 261
Professional, term, 237–238
Professional development, 36
Professionalism, defense
      of, 235–246
Progressive, term, 70
Proletarianization, 237
Propaganda, covert, 163
Proposition 203, 34–35, 47

Psychometric imperialism, 255
Public Broadcasting Service,
      corporatist agenda and, 8

R

Reading
  definition of, 115
  nature of, test claims
      about, 254–255
  versus writing, 63
Reading Excellence Act, 158
Real thing. see Nonexercises
Reframing, 64
Register, Cummins on, 97–98
Reporters without Borders, 9
Researchers, "theories" of, 79–80
Resistance, 235–246
  acts of, 243
  current state of, 243–246
  to federal government,
      15–17, 164, 178, 197
  to neo-liberalism, 16–17
  recommendations for, 267–270
  to testing, 178, 258–270
Reskilling, 237
Responsibility, conflict resolution
      and, 37–38
Risky literacy, 196–213
  current state of, 208–213
Romanticism, traditional, and
      standardized reading
      tests, 107–108
Rules, in whole language
      classroom, 187–188

S

Science, Bush administration
      and, 6–7, 263
Scores, test claims about, 252–253
  critique of, 263–265
Scout Leader role, 188–189
Scribbling, 120
Secondary discourse, Cummins
      on, 97–98
Second language, nature of, 138

Second language acquisition (SLA)
context of, 21–24
reconsideration of, 28–32
current state of, 32–40
effects of, 24–28
literacy learning as case
of, 140–154
pedagogical value of, 146–154
tactical value of, 141–146
politics of, 18–40
reconsideration of, 134–154
Second language instruction,
children's perceptions of, 23
Second language instructional
competence (SLIC), 94
Second language proficiency, theory
on, 79–104
Self-criticism, 214–234
Semilingualism, 81
critique of, 86–87, 94
term, 89, 95
Separate underlying proficiency
(SUP), 81
September 11, 2001, 12
Shaw, George Bernard, 208
Situated learning, 152
Skills
literacy immersion and, 149
teaching in context, 168–169
Skills orientation, 82
and classroom practice, 181–182
and context, 203
Cummins and, 82–83
SLA. *see* Second language acquisition
SLIC. *see* Second language
instructional competence
Small-schools movement, 228
s.m.i.l.e., 240–241
Social languages, 98
Social relations
definition of, 124
and literacy, 122–125
Sociopsycholinguistic orientation, 82
Spanish
acquisition as second language
politics of, 18–40
study of, 19–21

functions of use of, 21–22
performance, changes in, 27–28
production of, 27
texts in, availability of, 73
valuing, 33–35
Standardized tests, 247–270. *see also*
High-stakes tests; Testing
critique of, proprietary/
professional fixes, 248–258
history of, 247
and literacy, 107–108
negative effects of,
255–256, 266–267
recommendations for, 256–258
resistance to, 258–270
Standardness, test claims
about, 252
Standards-driven education
corporate/government agenda
and, 157
critique of, 255–256
Cummins on, 102
Status quo, whole language
and, 217–221
Students
as colearners, 36–37
and communities, 212–213
SUP. *see* Separate underlying
proficiency
Superficiality, testing and, 267
Support, immersion experience
and, 145
Support and Maintenance for
Implementing Language
Expression (s.m.i.l.e.), 240–241

T

Tacit "theory," 100
Teacher(s)
as colearners, 36–37
control of children's writing, 53
education of
corporatist agenda and, 261
federal government and, 2–3
and high-stakes tests, 266
influence on policy, 64

language profiles of, and
 policy, 67–68
and literacy development, 74
preferences of, and children's
 writing, 51–52
professionalism of, 235–246
as professionals, 38
in whole language
 classroom, 179–195
 goals of, 185–186
 observation of, 183–184
Teachers Applying Whole
 Language, 176, 178
Teacher-scholars, as activists, 64
Technology, writing as, 139–140
Terrorism, term, 12
Testing, 247–270. *see also* High-stakes
 tests; Standardized tests
 critique of, proprietary/
 professional fixes, 248–258
 Cummins on, 101–102
 history of, 247
 and identity, 108
 recommendations for, 256–258
 resistance to, 258–270
 and written language
 policy, 68–69
Test items, critique of, 251, 262–263
Texts, native language, availability of, 72
THEORY, 79–104
 of Cummins
 changes to, 94–96
 confusions in, 89–91, 97–104
 critique of, 82–85, 94
 data in, disputed, 84–85
 elements of, 81–82
 shifts in, 88–89, 96–97
 definition of, 79
Theory, and resistance, 242–243
"Theory," 79–104
 of Cummins, critique of, 82–85
 definition of, 79
Threshold hypothesis, 81
 critique of, 94
Time, and immersion
 experience, 145
Title I, 250

Traditional romanticism, and
 standardized reading
 tests, 107–108
Trust, and performance, 93
Truth, conflict resolution and, 37–38

U

Universal Grammar, 98–99, 136
Unmarked language, 28–29
Unz, Ron, 61

V

Values, in whole language
 classroom, 187
Vision, in bilingual education
 program, 35–36

W

Wann, John, 32–34, 39
Western bias, on written language
 acquisition, 138–140
Whole language
 confusion regarding, 155
 criticism of, 214–234
 current state of, 155–178
 defense of, 164
 dual potential of, 213
 lack of respect for, 227–230
 versus language experience
 approach, 171–172
 as method/program/
 slant, 169–171
 misunderstandings
 about, 167–178
 and critics, 226–227
 as movement versus
 perspective, 230–231
 nature of, restatement of, 165–166
 new McCarthyism and, 10–14
 versus open classroom, 172–174
 oversimplification in, 231–232
 as political movement,
 176–178, 234
 principles of, 201–208

proponents of, faults of,
        230–234
recommendations for, 177–178
versus teaching skills in
        context, 168–169
versus whole word
        approach, 167–168
and writing process, 174–176
Whole language classroom
    cues in, 190–192
    goals for, 185–186
    roles in, 188–189
    rules in, 187–188
    start of school year in, 179–195
    values in, 187
Whole language literacy,
        as risky, 196–213
Whole language orientation
    and classroom practice, 181
    to literacy, 82
Whole word approach, versus
        whole language, 167–168
Widmeyer Communications, 161, 163
Wilson, Charles E., 157
Writing
    in bilingual program, 41–58
        contexts of, 45–46
        study of, 43–45
    and contexts, 48–49

development of,
        reconsideration of, 56–58
historians of, biases of, 139
influences on
    direct, 49–52
    indirect, 52–56
versus reading, 63
as social practice, 41
Writing ability
    consequences of, 77–78
    value of, 77–78, 90
Writing Centers, 49–50
Writing process, and whole
        language, 174–176
Written language, as
        language, 135–140
Written language acquisition
    assumptions on, 112–113
    nature of, and local policy, 71–72
    reconsideration of, 134–154
Written language policies
    background of, 65–66
    for bilingual programs, 59–78
        local, issues in, 71–78
    considerations for, 69–71
Written products
    status of, 141
    treatment of, and local
        policy, 75–76